María Blume and Barbara C. Lust
Research Methods in Language Acquisition

Language and the Human Lifespan Series

Bilingualism Across the Lifespan
Factors Moderating Language Proficiency
Edited by Elena Nicoladis and Simona Montanari

Innovative Investigations of Language in Autism Spectrum Disorder
Edited by Letitia R. Naigles

Research Methods in Language Acquisition
Principles, Procedures, and Practices
María Blume and Barbara C. Lust
With Yuchin Chien, Cristina D. Dye, Claire A. Foley,
and Yarden Kedar

Research Methods in Language Acquisition

―

Principles, Procedures, and Practices

María Blume and Barbara C. Lust
With Yuchin Chien, Cristina D. Dye, Claire A. Foley, and Yarden Kedar

Cornell Language Acquisition Lab and Virtual Center for
Language Acquisition Virtual Linguistic Laboratory

DE GRUYTER
MOUTON

American Psychological Association • Washington, DC

Copyright © 2017 by the American Psychological Association and Walter de Gruyter GmbH. All rights reserved. Except as permitted under the United States Copyright Act of 1976, no part of this publication may be reproduced or distributed in any form or by any means, including, but not limited to, the process of scanning and digitization, or stored in a database or retrieval system, without the prior written permission of the publishers.

Published by
American Psychological Association
750 First Street, NE
Washington, DC 20002-4242
www.apa.org

Walter de Gruyter GmbH
Genthiner Straße 13
10785 Berlin / Germany
www.degruyter.com

To order in the United States and Canada:
APA Order Department
P.O. Box 92984
Washington, DC 20090-2984
Tel: (800) 374-2721; Direct: (202) 336-5510
Fax: (202) 336-5502; TDD/TTY: (202) 336-6123
Online: www.apa.org/pubs/books/
E-mail: order@apa.org

To order in Europe:
HGV Hanseatische Gesellschaft für Verlagsservice mbH
Holzwiesenstr. 2
72127 Kusterdingen / Germany
Tel.: +49 (0)7071 9353 – 55
Fax.: +49 (0)7071 9353 – 93
Online: www.degruyter.com
E-mail: orders@degruyter.com

Other customers, including those in the United Kingdom, may order from either publisher.

Typeset in DG Meta Serif Science by Circle Graphics, Inc., Columbia, MD
Printer (U.S. & Canada): United Book Press, Baltimore, MD
Printer (Europe): CPI books GmbH, Leck, Germany
Cover Designer: Walter de Gruyter GmbH, Berlin, Germany

The opinions and statements published are the responsibility of the authors, and such opinions and statements do not necessarily represent the policies of the American Psychological Association or Walter de Gruyter GmbH.

Library of Congress Cataloging-in-Publication Data
Names: Blume, María, author. | Lust, Barbara, 1941- author.
Title: Research methods in language acquisition : principles, procedures, and practices / Maria Blume and Barbara C. Lust.
Description: First Edition. | Washington, DC ; Boston : American Psychological Association ; Walter de Gruyter, [2017] | Series: Language and the human lifespan series | Includes bibliographical references and index.
Identifiers: LCCN 2016030001 | ISBN 9783110415223 | ISBN 3110415224
Subjects: LCSH: Language acquisition—Research—Methodology. | Language acquisition—Research—Data processing. | Language acquisition—Psychological aspects—Research. | Language and languages—Age differences. | Children—Language—Psychological aspects. | Speech acts (Linguistics)—Research. | Psycholinguistics.
Classification: LCC P118.15 .B58 2017 | DDC 401/.930721—dc23
LC record available at https://lccn.loc.gov/2016030001

British Library Cataloguing-in-Publication Data
A CIP record is available from the British Library.

Bibliographic information published by the Deutsche Nationalbibliothek
The Deutsche Nationalbibliothek lists this publication in the Deutsche Nationalbibliografie; detailed bibliographic data are available in the internet at http://dnb.dnb.de

Printed in the United States of America and Germany
First Edition

http://dx.doi.org/10.1037/15968-000

Contents

Preface —— vii

Acknowledgments —— ix

Introduction —— 3

I Fundamentals of Language Acquisition Research

1   The Challenge of Studying Language —— 11

2   Preparing to Work With Children, Schools, and Families —— 29

3   Creating the Data I: Working in Teams, Basic Data Collection, Data Sharing, and Data Management —— 49

II Experimental and Observational Methods in Language Acquisition Research

4   Studying Language Acquisition Through Collecting Speech —— 71

5   Introduction to Experimental Methods: Design and Analysis —— 93

6   Experimental Tasks for Generating Language Production Data —— 119

7   Experimental Tasks for Generating Language Comprehension Data —— 137

8   The Grammaticality Judgment Task —— 155

III Managing and Interpreting Speech Data

9   Creating the Data II: Begin Data Processing —— 167

10   Creating the Data III: Preparing for Data Analysis —— 187

11   Interpreting the Data: Scientific Inference —— 211

IV Special Considerations in Language Acquisition Research

12 Assessing Multilingual Acquisition —— 229

13 Introduction to Infant Testing Methods in Language Acquisition Research —— 247

14 Conclusions and Proceeding to the Future —— 259

Appendix A Transcription Symbols —— 271

Appendix B The International Phonetic Alphabet —— 273

Appendix C Outline for Preparation of Schematic Research Proposal —— 275

Suggested Readings —— 277

References —— 283

Index —— 303

About the Authors —— 313

Preface

This manual has grown out of years of research conducted at Cornell University in the Cornell Language Acquisition Lab (CLAL) and research conducted by former CLAL students subsequently in various labs across the world. Generations of students worked to develop the lab principles and procedures described here to support and sustain research in the area of language acquisition. The practical "hands-on tips" are the result of many years of expertise from members of the CLAL and others in training new students and promoting peer-to-peer teaching among students, and from our experience in building a new lab where we realized that the vast amounts of practical knowledge had to be transferred to future generations of students. This manual is an attempt to collect such knowledge for guiding student work in a lab and helping the researchers who are training students to do so. This manual may be used in conjunction with any overview of the field of language acquisition (e.g., *Child Language: Acquisition and Growth* [Lust, 2006] or *The Development of Language* [Gleason & Ratner, 2012]). *The Articulate Mammal* (Aitchison, 2011) provides a conceptual overview.

Acknowledgments

First and foremost we want to acknowledge our contributors, Yuchin Chien, Cristina D. Dye, Claire A. Foley, and Yarden Kedar, who graciously accepted our invitation to contribute independent chapters and without whose expertise the manual would be incomplete.

Creation of this manual was propelled by Tina Ogden Woetzel, whose commitment to the scientific method and to advancing the study of language acquisition to reach its highest possible scientific rigor forced first versions of the manual to begin to take form years ago.

We are particularly indebted to the founding members of the Virtual Center for Language Acquisition (VCLA), especially Suzanne Flynn at MIT, Claire Foley at Boston College, Qi Wang at Cornell University, Liliana Sánchez at Rutgers University at New Brunswick, Jennifer Austin at Rutgers University at Newark, and Usha Lakshmanan at Southern Illinois University at Carbondale. We are also grateful for the collaboration of scholars who are VCLA affiliates, including Gita Martohardjono and Isabelle Barrière (City University of New York) and Sujin Yang (Ewha Womans University, South Korea). Their concepts and devotion to development of the science of language acquisition underlie this manual and its development.

Catherine Ging Reyes critically helped us shepherd the manual to completion. Natalia Buitrago helped to compile years of previous materials. Martha Rayas and Marina Kalashnikova helped extensively on some of the chapters. Many colleagues and students contributed to the Multilingualism Questionnaire (included in the online materials at http://pubs.apa.org/books/supp/blume/).

Finally, we are deeply and fundamentally indebted to James Gair, whose inspiration and insight has led us all through the years.

Two anonymous reviewers and especially our development editor, David Becker, provided excellent advances to our manuscript.

Work on this manual was supported by several funding sources: "Transforming the Primary Research Process Through Cybertool Dissemination: An Implementation of a Virtual Center for the Study of Language Acquisition," National Science Foundation grant to María Blume and Barbara Lust, 2008, NSF OCI-0753415; "Planning Grant: A Virtual Center for Child Language Acquisition Research," National Science Foundation grant to Barbara Lust, 2003, NSF BCS-0126546; "Planning Information Infrastructure Through a New Library–Research Partnership," National Science Foundation Small Grant for Exploratory Research to Janet McCue and Barbara Lust, 2004–2006; American Institute for Sri Lankan Studies, Cornell University Einaudi Center; Cornell University Faculty Innovation in Teaching Awards, Cornell Institute for Social and Economic Research; New York State Hatch Grant; and Grant Number T32 DC00038 from the National Institute on Deafness and Other Communication Disorders.

María Blume and Barbara C. Lust
Research Methods in Language Acquisition

Introduction

The purpose of this manual is to introduce the concepts, principles, and procedures of a unique field of linguistic study, that of language acquisition. Our objective is to provide an overview of scientific methods for the study of language acquisition and to present a systematic, scientifically sound approach to this study. We hope to lead the reader to a greater understanding of the subject matter while providing him or her with the foundations to build a new body of knowledge through the scientific generation and analysis of new data.

Specifically, we intend to provide the background for one to be able to answer the following questions:

- How can one study language and language acquisition scientifically?
- What empirical methods are used in the scientific study of language acquisition? We concentrate on the simplest of methods—those that do not require complex equipment (other than recording equipment) and those on which other more complex methods are built, those which are useful with very young children but also potentially useful with a full developmental range. In particular, we favor those that can be used crosslinguistically. The principles of the scientific method we introduce for simple tasks carry over to more specialized tasks.
- How is the concept of *data* defined in the study of language?
- How does one generate such data?
- How does one prepare language data so one can process and analyze it once it has been collected?
- What methods and processes ensure that one's inductions or inferences are best grounded scientifically when designing or participating in language studies?
- How can principles of data management and insurance of data replicability best be developed?

Our emphasis herein is on methods for directly assessing a learner's language and on primary research designed to test specific hypotheses regarding this language knowledge. Thus, we do not provide a review of various standardized tests in the field or of various caretaker assessment tools. We deal with the most fundamental methods for primary language assessment to introduce basic principles and procedures. We do not attempt to provide a comprehensive review of the more specialized methods for language assessment currently available (e.g., "on-line" processing methods) or of numerous variations on tests of language comprehension and production. Nor do we attempt to provide what a "statistics" manual would provide. Rather, we aim to articulate the basic principles that underlie various statistical models for the conversion of complex collected raw data to the quantitative analyses of those data. We introduce the reader to principles of the "data pipeline" that must underlie successful and scientifically sound research in this area (e.g., Leek & Peng, 2015). Armed with these basic principles, the user of this manual can be prepared to pursue the numerous variations in statistical modeling that are available to the field.

We begin by providing general principles of research in the area of the language sciences and scientific methods. We introduce basic methods and principles for data collection. We then move on to provide examples of specific approaches to data capture, such as elicitation of language production or language comprehension, and we present basic data analyses. This manual concludes by providing general approaches to data management and collaborative data sharing.

Although most of the tasks and procedures we introduce are aimed at children who have begun to produce and comprehend speech, we include a chapter that briefly reviews methodology for the study of infants, often prior to the production or comprehension of speech. We do this because of the many important results being obtained today through the study of early infant discrimination of language and because we believe these forms of infant studies, requiring specialized methods, can provide critical developmental continuity in the study of language development.

This manual differs from previously published ones in several ways. First, it aims to explicate fundamental principles and practices of applying the scientific method to study of linguistic data. Although the research methods presented here apply to many areas in language acquisition, the examples come mainly from studies of the acquisition of syntax and morphology and mainly from first language acquisition. However, we use these examples to explicate more general principles of the scientific method applied to linguistic data. The principles and methods we introduce have been easily extended to the study of second- (or more) language acquisition in children and adults and to other areas of language knowledge.

Second, this volume is aimed at new researchers. This may include students or teachers of students in this area or advanced scholars who are new to primary research in language acquisition. It does not assume any knowledge of what constitutes research data or proper experimental methodology and explains in detail the basic principles underlying scientific research. It does not assume more than a general familiarity with linguistics and linguistic terms, although for anyone who wants to become truly involved in the study of language acquisition, a basic course in linguistics, at minimum, is advisable. An attempt has been made here to provide introductory definitions of critical linguistic concepts. Similarly, we recommend to anyone wishing to apply experimental methods at least an introductory course in statistics.

Third, this volume explicitly presents practical aspects of lab work and data management. These practical aspects are usually absent from research manuals, but they constitute fundamental, basic knowledge for anyone intending to work in this field.

Last but not least, the importance of collaborative research in our field is stressed. The study of language acquisition must reach beyond the study of English alone, and it must include comparative cross-linguistic studies. For this, collaboration among researchers across languages is critical. In addition, the study of language acquisition is inherently interdisciplinary; researchers from across fields (e.g., psychology, linguistics, neuroscience) must develop an infrastructure for shared research designs, shared data, and shared collaborative data analyses. Linguists are usually not trained in experimental methods, and scholars trained in experimental methods are often not trained in linguistics. Thus, interdisciplinary team cooperation is essential, and an infrastructure allowing this collaborative sharing of the research endeavor is essential to facilitate this.

Overview of the Book's Contents

A brief chapter-by-chapter outline is presented next, highlighting the main concepts we wish to convey.

Part I describes some fundamental concepts in language acquisition research. Chapter 1 outlines the goals of the manual, describes the scientific method, contrasts experimental and observational methods, and explains what constitutes linguistic data. Because this manual is aimed at the new researcher, Chapter 2 provides a brief introduction to research with human subjects, reviewing the specific requirements for working with children. In it, we discuss the researcher's preparation for working with participants and schools. In Chapter 3, we introduce the concept of *metadata*—mainly with respect to subject and session metadata—and explain its importance in research. We also explain general principles for using recording equipment and present common lab practices before and after a recording session to allow for effective collaboration and data management.

Part II builds on the foundations outlined in Part I by describing various observational and experimental methods for gathering speech data. In Chapter 4, we discuss the issue of using speech to provide primary data in the study of language acquisition. This chapter addresses the "natural speech" data collection method as one approach to gathering such primary data, along with its advantages and disadvantages when contrasted with experimental methods. Chapter 5 covers basic concepts of experimental research design at a beginner level: What is a good research question? What is a hypothesis? What is good experimental design? Basic principles of statistical analysis and recommendations for more advance readings are introduced. In Chapter 6, we discuss tasks used in conjunction with experimental methods for gathering language production data, focusing mainly on elicited imitation and elicited production. In Chapter 7, we discuss experimental tasks for gathering language comprehension data. We focus mainly on the act-out task and the truth–value judgment task. In Chapter 8, we review the relationship of grammaticality judgment data to competence and performance. Its advantages and disadvantages and the challenges of using it for testing children are discussed as well.

The tasks described in Part II result in a large collection of data, so Part III explores how to work with those data in more detail. In Chapter 9, we discuss how to create scientifically valid data from language, and we detail the complex process of data creation for both natural speech and experimental research. In this chapter, we explain basics for transcription and reliability checking and introduce some of the complexities of cross-linguistic research. In Chapter 10, we explain principles of preparation of data for analysis, whether using natural speech or experimental data. We introduce principles for basic linguistic analysis in a way that can help train new students with little linguistic background, laying the foundation for researchers to develop more precise data analyses directed to their specific research question. In Chapter 11, principles for interpreting results from different types of research tasks and methods are discussed. We help students become aware of complexities of interpretation of results at the end of a data pipeline.

Part IV concludes the book with some considerations about working with different populations, as well as some final thoughts about the volume as a whole. In Chapter 12, María Blume presents special challenges inherent in assessing multilingual acquisition and surveys developments in methods for multilingual research. Chapter 13 provides a brief introductory review of the principles underlying research on infant language. It overviews some of the main methodologies while referring students to more specialized bibliographical sources. Finally, in Chapter 14, we draw conclusions regarding what we hope to have conveyed in this manual, and we sketch directions for the future of the field of language acquisition to strengthen its scientific foundations. We also introduce the vision for a new resource available to students and researchers working in the field. We describe an example of a web-based portal (Virtual Linguistics Lab) of materials for learning and practicing methods introduced in previous chapters. The portal provides an overview of a cybertool: the Data Transcription and Analysis Tool, which allows web-based shared data management, data transcription, and data analyses supporting collaborative research.

We also provide a number of supporting materials in our chapter and end-of-book appendices and online at http://pubs.apa.org/books/supp/blume/. These include, for example, sample scoring criteria, scoring sheets for specific experiments using specific tasks, explanations of some transcription symbols (Appendix A), the International Phonetic Alphabet commonly used in speech transcription (Appendix B), and a template for writing a research proposal (Appendix C).

Although the principles and procedures we introduce in this manual have been developed over more than 30 years in the Cornell University Language Acquisition Lab as well as in several related labs, we hope that the principles that underlie them will be helpful to many labs approaching the scientific study of language acquisition. We hope they help to advance the scientific foundations of our field.

The Virtual Linguistic Laboratory: An Introduction

Before continuing, it is relevant for all educators, students, and researchers to understand the manual's context and the complementary materials that are available to be used in conjunction with it.

The Cornell Language Acquisition Laboratory has created an Internet portal, the Virtual Linguistic Laboratory (VLL), introduced in Chapter 14, where the user of this manual can find a multitude of resources to complement his or her learning experience. These resources include pedagogical materials for setting up and teaching a class on methods for studying language acquisition, learning modules with actual child data in audio and video formats, a discussion board for collaborating with other students and institutions, and a Data Transcription and Analysis Tool for storing and processing acquisition data.

The VLL portal can be found at http://www.clal.cornell.edu/vll. Full access to all its materials is made available to participating members.[1] Membership is offered to educational institutions seeking to offer a class on language acquisition research methodology using the VLL materials or to researchers interested in using the tools developed at the Cornell Language Acquisition Laboratory and the Virtual Center for Language Acquisition. The VLL is offered as an example of the type of Internet-based portal that could be designed and established at any institution with the resources to support server access and dissemination.

---

[1] For membership details contact the authors: Barbara C. Lust (bcl4@cornell.edu) and María Blume (mblume@pucp.pe).

I Fundamentals of Language Acquisition Research

1 The Challenge of Studying Language

Studying language is challenging because of the nature of the object of inquiry. For instance, you cannot see language knowledge because it is in the mind of the person who knows that particular language. It is in the mind of the sender (the person originating the message) and in that of the receiver (the person receiving the message). We can observe manifestations of language, such as someone saying something, understanding it, writing it down, or reading it, but even with these manifestations, language is complex to study. The object of inquiry is the generative grammar in the mind that constitutes knowledge of language. This language knowledge is manifest when we speak or hear language (or use sign language in a visual modality), but only indirectly. The generative system in the mind involves a set of principles and rules that allow the production and/or comprehension of an infinite set of sentences, including any single utterance we observe. Thus, language is difficult to study scientifically.

Scientific research in this field, as in others, must involve a combination of theoretical and empirical methods. To understand how language is generated, one tries to build a theory of what the generative system in the mind may look like. Thus, one can form hypotheses for testing. However, this theoretical model must also be scientifically validated. In scientific practice, the creation of a "true theory" must be complemented by "evidence." There must be predictability that can be evaluated so that false hypotheses can be disconfirmed. What constitutes the evidence (the data) in the case of language knowledge? Here, one has to clearly understand the answer to this question to pursue linguistic studies. As in all scientific inquiry, the data must be analyzable in terms of discrete units. We must ask then, What are the discrete units of language knowledge?

In language studies, the data are complex and often multivariate in nature. Data can involve behavior, such as speech, the understanding of speech, or thinking about speech. The behavioral variable, however, is continuous, not discrete. No particular behavior will ever reflect the entire cognitive system directly. Speech data, whether resulting from speech production or speech comprehension, provide only a basis for the scientist's inference regarding the grammatical system and its discrete units.

The focus of our work, and thus the content of this manual, is an exploration of how we can obtain empirical evidence, which is scientifically well-grounded. To do so, we must study language through the window of language behaviors (e.g., speaking, understanding, judging language) to attain evidence and data. Thus, given the nature of the object of inquiry, applying scientific methods to language studies becomes a challenge. But it is essential.

This chapter includes contributions by Liliana Sánchez and Claire Foley.

This challenge is even greater when one considers that all languages and all grammars are complex. No one language is more or less complex than another, although each may be so in different ways. Language data from any language will always reveal an extremely intricate system with interactions among the elements. At the same time, by hypothesis, it will reveal commonalities that underlie all possible natural languages and that are biologically programmed through the brain. We must seek to discover evidence for these underlying commonalities, as well as their manifestations, in specific behaviors in a specific language.

The science of linguistics must combine with behavioral science to pursue a definition of language data and language data measurement to apply the scientific method. Only in this manner can systematic evidence be collected to provide insight into the study of language acquisition. For instance, it has long been recognized that "the linguist is in a relatively fortunate position as compared with other social scientists in being able to analyze his raw data—the sound materials that constitute spoken messages—into discrete units" (Osgood & Sebeok, 1965, p. 50). In addition, Joos (1950, as quoted in Joos, 1966) even earlier proposed that

> Of all the sciences and near sciences which deal with human behavior, linguistics is the only one which is in a fair way to becoming completely mathematical, and the other social scientists are already beginning to imitate the strict methods of the linguists. (Joos, 1966, p. 350)

The modern science of linguistics thus has moved away from Darwin's approach: "Language is an art, like brewing or baking" (Darwin, 1859/1874, p. 121).

The study of language is now recognized as a cognitive science, integrating the interdisciplinary study of linguistics, philosophy, psychology, and computer science. We assume that strengthened grounds for induction from empirical data (i.e., enhanced scientific method) will lead to and from stronger links between theoretical and analytical approaches to the nature of language knowledge. At the same time, we recognize that when studying language acquisition, we are always dealing with special human subjects. Collecting empirical language data from children, for example, will involve numerous complexities linked to behavioral variability. However, these empirical data are crucial to the possible development of a linguistic or cognitive theory regarding language acquisition. When working with young children, we must assume that both the subjects and the environment cannot be controlled in the same way that they can be with an adult. We cannot assume the ability or willingness of children to communicate their knowledge as we can with adults. In this manual, we attempt to make this process of empirical data collection and analysis more tractable to strengthen foundations for scientifically sound research in this area.

1.1 Scientific Research

Given the unique complexities in the current state of the study of language acquisition, we believe that it will significantly benefit the reader or the researcher to review the foundations and the basic axioms of the scientific method. With a solid foundation of the meth-

Tab. 1.1: Analytic and Empirical Methods of Scientific Inquiry

Analytic method	Empirical method
• Theoretical constructs • Numerical models • Predictions	• Based on observation • Typically a laboratory or fieldwork environment • Tests hypotheses • Tests theories of incorrect prediction

ods, processes, and assumptions inherent in scientific research, the individual studying language acquisition has the tools to better design experiments and interpret results.

1.1.1 Methods of Scientific Inquiry

Scientific inquiry must begin with a leading question (or with leading questions). The researcher begins with a search for knowledge. Research typically involves a combination of analytical and empirical efforts.[1] *Analytical* efforts use theoretical constructs with numerical models, or only just numerical models, to make predictions about a subject area.[2] *Theories of grammar* refer to linguistic categories, principles, and constraints.[3] These are posited to formalize the mental competence and computation involved when we know a language, and they allow us to formalize what we will test for. Some quantitative or mathematical models that attempt to model how we process language data also exist.[4] *Empirical* methods lead us to investigate data as they bear on our theories.

A comprehensive and full program of research needs two forms of empirical methods: experimental and observational. These provide two types of data, and both are necessary. A systematic approach, which includes hypothesis testing, allows us to build a scientific framework regarding our theory. With a framework in place, we can recognize patterns in the systematically collected data, or we can recognize exceptions in the data. Including observational as well as experimental methods helps us to identify special cases we might not find through the single application of either the experimental method or observational method alone. The objective of our manual is to focus specifically on scientific inquiry for the study of language acquisition, including the introduction of an experimental component. With a focus on experimental work, the nature of our research will include methods of scientific inquiry (see Table 1.1).

---

[1] For useful introductions to these foundations of scientific research, see Edward Wilson (2013) and Santiago Ramón y Cajal (1916, 1999).
[2] For examples of analytic approaches to linguistic and language processing theory, see Sportiche, Koopman, and Stabler (2014) and Hale (2014).
[3] The term *grammar* is ambiguous. It can refer to a theory of language structure, and in the manner we use it here, it refers to a model of the computational system in the mind, which is involved when we know a language (a model of our language competence).
[4] In language "processing," we map from one form of language representation to another (we hear or read a sentence and map this to its linguistic structure or its meaning). Issues regarding how language "knowledge" and language "processing" interact remain actively debated in the field today.

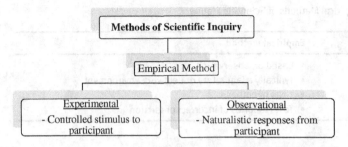

Fig. 1.1: Empirical method distinctions: experimental and observational.

1.1.2 Experimental Versus Observational Methods

Within the field of language acquisition, two primary types of empirical methods are used in research. Figure 1.1 provides a conceptual overview. The first method is referred to as *experimental*. In our field, *experimental method* refers to an empirical research method in which designed and calculated sets of stimuli are presented to the subject to elicit a response using some type of elicitation technique (i.e., task). The response one is looking for is typically speech production, comprehension, or judgment from the subject. All these types of responses can give evidence of what an individual knows about language. The results from the experimental session are coded and analyzed. If a researcher has a specific question related to a particular construction or principle of language knowledge, the researcher designs test sentences that vary properties of this construction or principle. These designed sentences are then presented to the research subject.[5] One example of this is a researcher who questions how a child acquires the ability to form questions in English. Sentences may be then designed that vary forms of questions. The child is tested on them to assess the child's knowledge in the area of question formation.

The second method is *observational*. When using the observational method, the researcher does not apply a specifically designed stimulus for the participant. Instead, the subject may have no stimulus, or the stimulus may be random (no designed sentences, no predetermined patterns of interaction). Both language production and language comprehension behaviors are interwoven as they are in the normal situation between speaker and hearer. For example, a researcher may simply observe a young child in his or her home or other "natural" contexts and observe the child's use of language. This situation is called *naturalistic*.[6] In the following sections, we provide an outline of the processes involved in these two approaches.

---

5 In psychology, the term *research subject* may also appear as *research participant*. The term refers to the human subjects who will provide the language data being studied in the research project.
6 Some researchers have developed naturalistic and observational methods to include certain explicit forms of "triggering" of natural speech (Berk, 1996; Labov & Labov, 1978).

For the researcher in the field of language acquisition, the selected empirical method of study determines many facets of how the data are generated and processed. The following components should all be determined before a study is conducted:

- how the data will be generated,
- how it will be collected,
- how it will be analyzed, and
- how it will be interpreted.

Thus, your first step as a researcher in the cognitive science of language studies, after choosing the leading research questions, begins with choosing the type of empirical method for generating data: experimental or observational (see Figure 1.1). Each method is discussed in more detail next.

Both experimental and observational methods are necessary to the study of language and language acquisition. Without observational methods, we do not have foundations for generating well-founded hypotheses to test, and we do not have a rich understanding of the type of language we are studying. Without experimental methods, we cannot subject specific hypotheses to rigorous scientific testing. Although much existing research in the field of language acquisition is currently based on naturalistic observations of "natural speech" by children, we introduce here the experimental methods that can advance this research approach.

1.1.2.1 Experimental Methods

Empirical methods may include *experimental methods*, which are conducted in laboratories or other fieldwork environment, where the subject matter may be studied under controlled conditions. Experimental methods are conducted to test a hypothesis, disconfirm an alternative hypothesis, test whether a prediction is incorrect, or contribute to reforming a theory on the basis of evidence. When selected, the experimental method of researching language acquisition will produce data through explicit elicitation techniques designed to test specific preformed hypotheses. The process involves eight steps: form the hypothesis, develop the experimental design, construct the elicitation technique, select the population, test the hypothesis, collect raw data, analyze (process) the data, interpret the data. These steps are briefly sketched next (see Chapter 5, this volume).[7]

---

[7] For an introduction to this area, see also the web presentation by Yuchin Chien (2009): "An Overview of Experimental Research Methodology for Language Acquisition," available from http://clal.cornell.edu/vll/ (Virtual Linguistics Lab—VLL portal), which was first presented in a course at Stanford University, Linguistic Society of America Summer Institute, 2007.

A. Form a Hypothesis

The first step of experimental research design is to form a research question. Such a question can be formed as a result of natural observations, from the results of previous research that was inconclusive, or from a preexisting theory. Always, creative insight is critical in determining a question that is significant and deeply interesting (Ramón y Cajal, 1999; Wilson, 2013). To test a research question, the researcher forms a hypothesis about language knowledge (e.g., a hypothesis regarding a grammatical principle, grammatical constraint, or type of meaning allowed by the language studied). Some decisions the researcher must make when formulating a hypothesis are to select the field of linguistics to be studied (e.g., theoretical linguistics, sociolinguistics) and the component of language to be investigated (phonology, morphology, syntax, semantics, pragmatics) and whether the hypothesis looks at aspects of language development or whether the goal is to test the effectiveness of a teaching method or a research method.

Also, it is necessary to assess the relevance of the phenomena under examination according to a theory and decide whether the aim is to support or reject an existing theoretical standpoint or postulate a new theory. Results could address an unresolved issue embedded in the theoretical framework itself, contribute to either side of a debate, or look at a yet unexplored question. The hypothesis can also be framed as descriptive (narrating the processes involved in a phenomenon), explanatory (attempting to give a reason for the phenomenon), or predictive (giving an informed guess of what the outcome of an experiment or study will be).

B. Develop an Experimental Design

Once the hypotheses are formed, an experimental design can be developed. In this design, the researcher will decide which factors to vary to test his or her hypothesis. The experimental factors selected by the researcher define the variables to be manipulated in the experimental design. An example of a variable for possible focus in the study of language acquisition might be knowledge of "word order,"[8] a critical variable in the computational system necessary to language. Independent and dependent variables have to be defined, as will be explained in Chapter 5.

Say, for example, a researcher is interested in studying whether a child knows where word order can be changed or not (i.e., whether movement of constituents

---

[8] *Word order* is the order in which words belonging to different syntactic categories appear in a sentence or phrase; for example, whereas English uses an article–adjective–noun order, as in *the blue ball*, Spanish uses an article–noun–adjective order, as in *la pelota azul* 'the blue ball', where *la* is the article, *pelota* is the noun, and *azul* is the adjective.

can occur). The researcher interested in the learner's knowledge of word order may design several variations in word order to compare these. For example, *Bunny kisses Big Bird* cannot be changed to *Big Bird kisses Bunny* without changing the meaning of the sentence, but *I love ice cream* can be changed to *Ice cream I love* without changing the basic meaning (with the right intonation). Yes/no questions[9] can be asked with or without inversion[10] (e.g., *You can eat the soup?* vs. *Can you eat the soup?*). Other word order variations are simply grammatically impossible; for example, English speakers could not reorder the words from *Big Bird likes to dance* to form **likes Big Bird dance to*, so the researcher may want to test whether the child knows **likes Big Bird dance to* is ungrammatical.[11]

Experimental research design involves a determination of requisite controls and systematic administrative procedures. As explained in Chapter 5, this aspect of experimental design is necessary to ensure that the research can be replicated. It helps ensure that other factors do not interact with the specific factors under investigation and, thus, supports valid interpretation of the data resulting from the experiment (Christensen, 2006; Trochim, 2001).

C. Construct an Elicitation Method

With the experimental design in place, the next step is to choose an elicitation technique, or elicitation task. Linguistic stimuli[12] can then be prepared for presentation to the subject using this elicitation technique. An *elicitation technique* is a method for presenting to the subject a stimulus or stimuli designed by the researcher to elicit some specific form of linguistic behavior. An elicitation technique may be used to provoke production of language or comprehension of language. Several such tasks are available for eliciting each of these types of behavior with language, and several are exemplified in subsequent chapters.

---

9 *Yes/no questions* are questions that can be answered with a *yes* or *no*—for example, *Do you like apples?* or *Is Rebecca sick?* Other questions (usually called *wh-questions*) require an answer that provides new information, usually in the form of a phrase or sentence; for example, to answer *Where does John live?* you have to say *(John lives) on King Street*, and to answer *What's that?* you have to say *(It's) a strange animal* (parentheses indicate optional parts in the answer).
10 *Inversion* here refers to the order in which the subject *you* and the modal *can* appear. *You can* is considered noninverted because the subject and the modal appear in the same order in which they would appear in a declarative sentence (e.g., *You can eat the soup*). The order *can you* in the question *Can you eat the soup?* is therefore considered inverted.
11 Here as elsewhere throughout this volume we use the symbol * to designate sentences that are grammatically impossible in a language because they violate syntactic rules of the language.
12 A *linguistic stimulus* is the particular form of language (e.g., a word, a question, a sentence) the researcher uses in his or her experiment to trigger child production (speech), child comprehension, or child judgment.

Language production (speech by the research subject) may be elicited by asking the child to repeat an utterance (elicited imitation) or to create an utterance (elicited production).[13] Data revealing *language comprehension*, however, may be elicited by requesting different behaviors that demonstrate an interpretation of a stimulus sentence. In this case, the child hears language and is asked to indicate in some way how he or she interprets this language. For instance, children may be asked to show the researcher the meaning of a sentence by using dolls and props (toy-moving or act-out task), or they may be asked to make a judgment about a sentence (by asking the subject to say whether they think it is a true sentence or not in a certain context). The linguistic stimuli used to elicit linguistic behaviors in any of these techniques are based directly on the researcher's experimental design. They provide a set of specific linguistic expressions focused narrowly on testing the hypothesis. For example, a child may be asked to judge whether a certain type of sentence with certain forms of complex structures is correct in his or her language.

Choice of an elicitation technique must be determined to some degree by the age of the child being studied.[14] Very young infants, for example, cannot be assessed for language production, and testing for language comprehension is difficult. Infants can be tested for their language "discrimination," however. A number of techniques for assessing infant language knowledge and processing have now been developed and are briefly surveyed in Chapter 13. These techniques provide a supplement to the production and comprehension methods we focus on in this manual.

D. Select a Population

A population to be tested is selected by the researcher. This means that sets of subjects or participants are chosen in accordance with the terms of the research design. For example, children at certain ages (or language development levels) may be chosen to test a particular hypothesis about language development at those specific ages. Alternatively, different groups of children at different ages (or language development levels) may be chosen for comparison, providing an experimental factor.

A common strategy in the study of language acquisition is to conduct *transversal* or *cross-sectional* studies, in which the performance of different children is compared at a given age or developmental period. This cross-sectional design can be contrasted with a *longitudinal* one, in which development is observed in the same

---

13 Throughout this volume, we focus on oral language. However, the issues and methods we raise here carry over to research on language in the manual mode (sign language).
14 For an overview of elicitation techniques for the study of children's acquisition of syntax, see McDaniel, McKee, and Smith Cairns (1996). For an overview of methods for assessing language production, see Menn and Ratner (2000). A more general overview is provided by Hoff (2012).

subject(s) over time. Besides requiring a much greater time commitment than a cross-sectional study (extending months or years), a longitudinal study does not lend itself easily to the careful controls of experimental methods and more often may be suited to an observational technique, often including case study approaches (Lust et al., 2014).

Researchers must also consider the source, and amount, of subjects to be tested. Although observational methods can often involve one or a few participants, resulting in case studies or small group-studies, experimental methods often draw their strength from larger sample sizes. Subjects for experimental tasks in language acquisition are most likely drawn from day care centers or schools, where age and relevant demographic factors are easy to determine and narrow down before recruiting volunteers.

For even larger sample sizes, it has become increasingly common to rely on large compilations of child language material collected by many researchers for multiple studies and made available to the other researchers in printed, recorded, or electronic format.[15] These samples are often based on observational studies of child or adult "natural speech." Such a database is called a *corpus*, and such research is referred to as *secondary*. The disadvantage of secondary research is, of course, that a researcher cannot apply his or her own tasks and controls to the selection of subjects or to the study design. The type and size of the sample strongly depend on the factors of design and on the research question established by the researchers that created each corpus. Results will be generalizable to the degree that a population is randomly sampled. They will be interpretable to the degree that related metadata[16] are available.

E. Test the Hypothesis

With the foundations for experimental research in place, one can execute or complete the designed research. The researcher follows an established procedure, testing pre-designed experimental factors through the presentation of specific linguistic stimuli under controlled procedures of administration. The results of these processes yield raw data. Study design and hypothesis testing are covered in Chapter 5.

F. Collect Raw Data

The captured behavior produced by the subject constitutes the *raw data*. The linguistic raw data result from a set process: (a) a stimulus is presented to the subject (e.g., a model sentence or a question); (b) the behaviors, or *responses*, given by the subject

---

[15] The Child Language Data Exchange System (CHILDES) corpus is the best-known and probably the largest collection of this type. It is available at http://childes.psy.cmu.edu
[16] *Metadata* are data about the data; for example, if we have a recording of an Inuktitut-speaking child, the metadata give us the information about the subject (e.g., the child's age, level of education, dialect), research (e.g., hypotheses, stimuli), and recording session (e.g., when and where was the child recorded, by whom, for how long).

to the stimulus provide the raw data (the subject's language production, language comprehension behaviors, judgments or truths of language grammaticality). This material in its entirety is the raw data, which must be stored, accessed, transcribed, and coded prior to scoring, analysis, and interpretation.[17] *Coding*, as we describe in subsequent chapters, involves a researcher's first transformation of the raw data to a form that can be analyzed to test a hypothesis.

The specific processes related to obtaining and storing the data must also be recorded. This step is critical if one wants the experiment to build on the preexisting body of knowledge. The information about the process, so recorded, becomes part of the *data creation process* (i.e., date and time of experiment, researcher, subject name, age, and other defining factors). These provide the metadata. *Metadata* are essentially data about your data. They allow the researcher to store and access the raw data for analyses. In addition, if one applies a standardized metadata format, it will allow insight or access to the research results by other researchers. It will also empower a single researcher who conducts programmatic research with numerous related experiments over time and must relate these experiments to each other. It will allow one to link one's data to other data.

G. Analyze the Raw Data

The raw data are systematically coded, scored, and cataloged, ensuring that the research can be replicated and verified by independent means. The data analysis process can begin when the raw data are fully documented:

- Depending on the type of method and elicitation techniques chosen, the responses of the subjects or participants (their speech or other responses during the experiment) must be transcribed in a specific way.
- Units of analysis of these transcribed data must be determined and applied.
- The data must be first coded and scored to prepare it for analysis.
- Analyses are then performed on the results of this scoring.

We review these processes in subsequent chapters.

Analyses may be quantitative (statistical), qualitative, or both. *Qualitative* research is often used as a means of discovering new phenomena, although these are often subjective. Also, because observation is a phenomenon that cannot be replicated, it is harder to generalize findings arrived at in this way. *Quantitative* research, however, yields data

---

[17] Coding the data involves annotating metadata surrounding it and annotating its properties that are of interest to the researcher. Scoring the data involves established scoring criteria for determining the type of response the child produced: Did he or she change the structure? What errors or mismatches did the child produce? What constitutes an error? Scoring makes quantitative analysis of patterns in the data possible. These aspects are described in this book in subsequent chapters.

Tab. 1.2: Differences Between Quantitative and Qualitative Research

Quantitative research	Qualitative research
• Not natural, involving controlled measurement • Objective and controlled measurement of specific data • Verification oriented, confirmatory • Outcome oriented • Reliable, involving "hard" and replicable data • Generalizable • Assumes a stable reality	• Subjective • Discovery oriented • Process oriented • Generates "soft data" • Ungeneralizable, single case studies • Assumes a dynamic reality • Close to the data

fitting in a small range of possibilities (presence vs. absence of a feature) and is, thus, readily quantifiable. Quantitative analyses of research results go hand in hand with experimental methods. This makes results replicable and more reliable for purposes of generalization. Quantitative research starts with an experimental design in which a hypothesis is followed by the quantification of data. In addition, some sort of numerical analysis is carried out on the data using one statistical model or another. Alternatively, qualitative studies are not set up as experiments; the data cannot be easily quantified, and the analysis is interpretive rather than statistical (Altarriba & Heredia, 2008).

It is important to keep in mind that both types of research have unique advantages and disadvantages, and the best results are obtained by using them complementarily. Some researchers are pursuing integration methods linking, for example, qualitative research in case studies to quantitative methods (Scholz & Tietje, 2002). Table 1.2 shows the differences between qualitative and quantitative analysis.

H. Interpret the Data

On the basis of the quantitative and qualitative analyses of data, researchers can interpret an experiment's results with regard to a given hypothesis. Researchers can relate their specific hypotheses to their general theory. Valid interpretation of research results depends critically on the strength of the experimental research design and on the controls for factors other than the ones the design was intended to test. See Chapter 5 for a "strong" research design and Chapter 11 for a discussion of the complexity of deriving a strong interpretation of one's research results and suggestions for increasing the "strength" of these interpretations.

I. Experimental Method of Inquiry: Summary

As in all areas of science, in the study of language acquisition, the experimental method of scientific inquiry allows the researcher to test specific hypotheses. However, because the entire method is a process that involves many stages, including data collection, documentation, and analysis, the data collected and analyzed by experimental method must now be rendered comparable between different sessions of the same subject, across different subjects, or even across languages. To enable this power, researchers must share standards of each stage of scientific research.

The foundations of scientific research allow an experiment—properly designed, conducted, and documented—to be replicated. For this, properly documented and clearly defined experimental design and methods for the study of language acquisition must be comparable across different data collectors and researchers. Data collected in this systematic manner can contribute to a larger comparable body of data that can be utilized for other purposes. New data can be systematically collected, analyzed, and compared with previous data at any time in the future using the methods have documented in the study. Collaboration between researchers (e.g., working in different languages) can be calibrated.

For an example of a cybertool that structures the management, storage, and dissemination of these basic properties of an experiment in an "experiment bank" and its methods see the Data Transcription and Analysis Tool available through the Virtual Linguistic Lab web portal (http://www.clal.cornell.edu/vll) and Chapter 14.

1.1.2.2 Observational Method

The application of the *observational method* involves some differences in the scientific process. This method collects data from participants without specifically designed and controlled stimuli. The researcher usually generates observations regarding these data post hoc. Once the recording equipment is in place, the data provided by the subject (speech) is expected to flow "naturally" from the participant or with minimal "triggers" to elicit "natural" speech. This produces *naturalistic data*.

Naturalistic data result in a data set of one. By definition, potential interacting factors cannot be eliminated or controlled in the production of these data. Several of these data sets of one can be culled to provide further insight into language acquisition, and they can suggest new hypotheses for future testing. However, these data are not able to sum directly into a larger knowledge base due to the unique and independent set of noncomparable factors that contributed to production and collection of each set of data. Thus, without further study, data from natural speech cannot be assumed to be generalizable.

Researchers sometimes generate and consult corpora of naturalistic language data that can be preserved and studied repeatedly in conjunction with different questions over time (e.g., CHILDES [http://childes.psy.cmu.edu/], The Language Archive [https://tla.mpi.nl/], Talkbank [http://talkbank.org/]). Current approaches attempt to develop mechanisms for achieving "Linked Open Data in Linguistics" to support collaborative interdisciplinary research because the databases allowing wide dissemination of data cannot be merged due to various challenges, such as lack of

Tab. 1.3: Similarities and Differences Between the Experimental and Observational Methods in Empirical Data

Data generation step	Empirical method	
	Experimental	Observational ("naturalistic")
1. Form hypothesis	Yes	Optional
2. Develop research design	Yes	No
3. Construct elicitation method	Yes	No
4. Select population	Yes	Yes
5. Test hypothesis	Yes	Optional
6. Collect raw data	Yes	Yes
7. Analyze data	Yes	Yes
8. Interpret data	Yes	Yes

interoperability, the need to interface different vocabularies, and data ownership and confidentiality issues.[18]

Systematic procedures for data collection, transcription, and analysis can assist the researcher in transforming naturalistic data so that it is more amenable to scientific analysis, thus allowing comparability and increasing its scientific value. These systematic procedures for transcribing and analyzing natural language data through which we capture and analyze language utterances in a natural situation in a reliable and a replicable manner are included in the methods we use when language production data has been elicited through experimental methods. Thus, there is some overlap in scientific methods used in the analysis of experimental and observational studies of natural language data.

1.1.2.3 Empirical Methods: Summary

Table 1.3 highlights the similarities and differences between the empirical methods discussed earlier.

1.1.3 Sound Scientific Methodology

In recent years, there has been increasing concern about empirical methods using sound methodology. It is often the case that researchers, especially in social sciences,

---

[18] A recent National Science Foundation funded workshop at the Linguistic Society of America Linguistic Summer Institute 2015 brought together scholars from different areas to discuss these challenges and begin to plan the vision that would allow us to achieve open data in linguistics in the area of language acquisition. Abstracts and presentations are available at http://quijote.fdi.ucm.es:8084/LLOD-LSASummerWorkshop2015/Home.html

collect nonrepresentative or biased data either because human subjects are not readily available (sometimes even resulting in samples sizes of one) or because they are not properly selected, and confounding variables result (refer to Chapter 5 for elaboration on this point).

In addition to sampling concerns, researchers have to consider carefully the data-collection methods they use. For example, when eliciting grammaticality judgments from speakers, the data are not easily quantifiable or easy to standardize (see Chapter 8). Researchers have to ensure as much as possible that their data elicitation and collection methods are in fact eliciting the desired data and controlling for undesired effects. The appropriate statistical analysis is also crucial, and researchers in the natural or social sciences would be well advised to consult expert statisticians when designing their experiments.

Linguists are showing a growing concern about sound methodology in their field. Sprouse, Wagers, and Phillips (2012), for example, reconsidered the validity of two long-standing, competing linguistic theories in light of experimental and statistical techniques. The two contending theories attempt to explain the nature of the linguistic constraints behind the phenomenon of *islands*, which are, broadly speaking, syntactic environments from which content cannot be removed. Consider the following (b) sentences:

1. (a) *Adam wore a shirt [with a stain].*
   (b) **What did Adam wear a shirt [with ____]?*
2. (a) *Sally wonders [whether Mark bought pickles].*
   (b) **What does Sally wonder [whether Mark bought ____]?*

Whereas one contending view, a *grammatical* theory, hypothesizes that these extractions are not allowed because of grammatical rules, another view, a *reductionist* theory, hypothesizes that such constructions are not allowed because of constraints in speakers' memory load. Sprouse et al. (2012) set out to test these views by hypothesizing that, on the second view, acceptability of the (b) sentences should correlate with an individual's memory capacity. They conducted a large-scale study (more than 150 subjects per experiment) as well as multiple statistical analyses and argued that they found no empirical support for the reductionist theory.

1.2 What Are Linguistic Data?

Researchers who have studied even an introductory course in linguistics have a good foundation for the analysis of language data. In this section, we introduce basic concepts of linguistic data for the new researcher.

When someone speaks to us, how do we know what he or she has said?[19] Speech is conveyed through the air in a continuous speech stream. The continuous speech stream must be converted to discrete units so that we can analyze it and convert it to language. We do this unconsciously when we produce or comprehend speech. The human mind somehow makes this conversion from a continuous speech stream to the units, which are the basis for the knowledge of language. But how do we get "inside the mind?" The researcher studying language acquisition must make this process overt. The science of linguistics provides the basic methods for this and provides concepts of linguistic components, which provide the building blocks of linguistic data. They form the basis for analyzing any linguistic data.

1.2.1 Finding the Units in Analyzing Language Data

There are two types of units: behavioral and linguistic. *Behavioral* units describe the language behavior that has occurred. *Linguistic* units characterize the form of the linguistic expression conveyed by the behavior. We discuss these in later sections of our manual. Their characteristics are introduced briefly next.

1.2.1.1 Behavioral Units

As we suggested, all language data must be based on some form of behavior with language (speaking, comprehending, making a judgment about a meaning or a form). These behaviors must first be characterized so that they can be collected, analyzed, and built on in further research.

A. The Utterance
The *utterance* is the most basic unit of behavior with language. Speech samples researchers analyze are usually described in terms of the utterances the sample includes. An utterance is any speech produced by a speaker (e.g., a single syllable, a word, a phrase, a sentence, or even an incomplete structure). However, characterizing what constitutes an utterance is not always easy (we discuss the difficulties in Section 9.2.1.4). Once identified, each utterance can be characterized in several ways. For example, it can be characterized in terms of its speech act or in terms of its style.

B. The Speech Act
Speech acts refer to the purpose of the utterance, and they may be of different types (i.e., is the person making a declaration, exhorting, questioning).

---

[19] C. F. Hockett (1997) articulated this problem in "Approaches to Syntax."

C. The Style of Speaking

The style of speaking may vary for each utterance (i.e., is the utterance spontaneous, repetitive, responsive to a question).

1.2.1.2 Linguistic Units

Whereas an utterance is a unit of behavior, a sentence is a *linguistic unit*. An utterance may or may not include a sentence. For example, an utterance such as *Hello there* does not because sentences minimally require a verb. The sentence is the most basic linguistic unit, and it consists of at least a noun or pronoun[20] and a verb, as in *Juan corre*, 'Juan runs' or *Él corre*, 'He runs.' All linguistic operations apply to the sentence (movements of elements or ellipsis of elements). Sentences may be combined recursively, as in *He thinks John can run very fast*, where the sentence *John can run very fast* is embedded in the larger sentence *He thinks John can run very fast*, reflecting a complex computational system.

Sets of linguistic units, which linguists have discovered, allow us to characterize the sentence an utterance may convey. The units form the building blocks of more complex units in language data and their analysis. These units include minimally the following: the sentence; the constituents of the sentence, including clauses and phrases; the words that make up the constituents; the morphemes that make up the words; and the phonemes that characterize the sounds and phones that make up the morphemes. A list of basic linguistic units is briefly sketched next. Weisler and Milekic (2000) provided an introduction to these basic linguistic concepts, as do numerous introductory texts in the field of linguistics (e.g., Fromkin, 2000).

A. Sentence

A *sentence* is the basic linguistic unit. It involves a subject and a predicate and, thus, conveys an idea. Sentences may be simple, or simple sentences may be combined to become complex or compound (to use traditional terms).

B. Clause

A *clause* is a unit of a sentence that may be smaller than a sentence but larger than a phrase, word, or morpheme (e.g., *John can run fast*). Traditional terminology refers to main and subordinate clauses. In the sentence *He thinks John can run fast*,

---

[20] In some languages, such as Spanish, the noun may not be overtly pronounced but is nevertheless understood as part of the sentence; for example, *corre*, literally 'runs,' is understood to mean 'he, she, or it runs' because of the verb ending.

the *main clause* is [*He thinks*], and the *subordinate clause* is *John can run fast*. Main clauses are sometimes referred to as *root clauses*. Subordinate clauses (of various types) are dependent on the main or root clause. A clause is formed minimally by a verb phrase and its argument noun phrases, although in discourse some of these elements may be elided. Different verbs need different numbers of noun phrases to complete their meaning. These noun phrases are referred to as their *arguments*; for example, the verb *to sleep* typically needs just one noun phrase referring to the person who sleeps, so a sentence such as *John sleeps* is well formed. The verb *to buy* needs two noun phrases referring to the buyer and what is bought, so a sentence such as *John buys apples* is grammatically well formed, but sentences such as *John buys* or *Buys apples* are not because they are missing one of their obligatory noun phrases. Simple sentences contain only one clause (e.g., *John likes milk*). Complex or compound sentences involve more than one clause (e.g., *The fact that John likes milk will speed his recovery*).

C. Phrase

Noun phrases and verb phrases form the constituents of each clause. A sentence such as *The man bought three apples* can be divided into a *noun phrase* or *determiner phrase*, *The man*, and a verb phrase, *bought three apples*, which contains another noun phrase, *three apples*.

D. Words

The *words* of language build phrases and clauses.

E. Morphemes

Morphemes are smaller units of meaning that build words. For example, the word *cats* contains two morphemes, *cat* and *-s*, which is the plural morpheme; the word *danced* contains two morphemes, *dance* and *-ed*, which is the past morpheme.

F. Phonemes

Morphemes are composed of smaller units of sound called *phonemes*. The word *cats* thus has four morphemes: /k/, /a/, /t/, and /s/.[21] Units exist at every level of language representation (sounds, words, phrases, clauses, sentences). This digital property

---

[21] The letters between the slashes indicate that this is not regular spelling but phonetic spelling using the International Phonetic Alphabet (see Chapter 9 and Appendix B).

of language underlies its discrete infinity.[22] Because we have different units at different levels, we can combine them in different ways to produce new utterances; for example, the sound units /p/, /a/, /t/, and /s/ can be combined to form the words *pot* /pat/, *top* /tap/, *pots* /pats/, *tops* /taps/, *spot* /spat/. Although linguists do not totally agree on the exact definition of each of these types of units (some argue whether some forms of units can be replaced by others) and specific theories of language hypothesize additional units, some form of these units provides the means by which language data can be analyzed. We assume that all linguists and psycholinguists operate on this assumption.

1.3 Summary

Together, behavioral units and linguistic units provide researchers elemental components for analysis when they begin to analyze language data. On the basis of these units, researchers can begin not only to collect language data but also to study language and draw insights from observations of language as data. They can begin to draw inferences about the generative system in the mind that constitutes language knowledge and that created the language data. Data must be created to allow these analyses.

Across different languages, these units take different forms; some units are more central than others, and unit combinations vary (M. Baker, 2001). But in all cases, researchers must find and characterize them. Across different developmental levels of language acquisition, we must ask whether the child has the same units as the adult. We must ask this same question with regard to pathological and normal populations of language users. Computational modes of analyses of language data (Hale, 2014; Lawler & Dry, 1998), as well as psychological or linguistic models, require reference to these units. Both experimental and observational methods are necessary for the scientific study of language acquisition.

---

22 *Discrete infinity* is one of the basic properties of language. It refers to the fact that language is built on a few sounds, and with those sounds you can build thousands of words and with words you can build an infinite number of phrases and sentences. Thus, the fact that language has discreet units and a combinatorial system makes it infinite.

2 Preparing to Work With Children, Schools, and Families

With the background of the discussion of linguistic data from the prior chapter, this section discusses how a researcher prepares to have a successful data collection session with human participants.

Before a researcher can generate raw data in the form of human language, regulatory requirements must be met, and extensive documentation has to be put in place regarding human subjects.[1] The regulatory requirements originate from federal, state, and other agencies regarding research work with humans as subjects.[2] In addition, when working with children, and especially with young children, researchers must be trained in methods for dealing with such a population, and parental or caretaker permissions must be attained. Finally, a researcher needs techniques for effectively and consistently dealing with human subjects to encourage them to participate gladly and safely in the intended research. When working with children, an entire area of best practice has evolved over decades of experimental work.

2.1 Regulatory Requirements: Working With Human Subjects

In language acquisition studies, we work with human subjects. There are ethical and legal issues surrounding such research to protect the human subjects as well as the integrity of the research.[3] Regulations have been put in place because, in the past, human participants in research have been misinformed or even lied to. The training programs we refer to later provide extensive information on the cases of unethical research that prompted the regulations and the history of the development of our

---

[1] The term *human subject* refers to any human being participating as a subject or participant in a research study.

[2] In first language acquisition, the term *subject* is frequently used to refer to people participating as subjects of study in research. In second language acquisition, the term *participant* is more common, and in other areas of linguistics, the term *collaborator* is preferred.

[3] See Standard 8, particularly Standard 8.03, Informed Consent for Recording Voices and Images in Research, of the American Psychological Association's *Ethical Principles of Psychologists and Code of Conduct*, 2010, for guidelines for conducting this type of research.

current guidelines. (For a short but good introduction, see Wikipedia's article, "Human Subject Research.") When working with human subjects, their permissions to participate in the research and their release to have their data be part of future research papers must be secured. If data are to be archived, permission for this must be explicitly sought.

Each institution in the United States works with federal human subjects regulatory procedures, and institutions in other countries have to comply with similar regulatory procedures. Each research center, university, and level of government (local, county, state, country) has its own set of specific requirements that must be met before commencing such work. Because these requirements change frequently due to the changing body of laws, insurance requirements, and documentation, and because each institution may interpret federal guidelines differently, it is fundamental that before any work with human subjects commences, researchers check with their institutional procedure office to find out how to meet the requirements. For example, at Cornell University, the Cornell University Institutional Review Board guides researchers in their work with human subjects. They maintain a website with information that is kept up to date at http://www.irb.cornell.edu/.

Highlights of this regulatory information are

- *completion of a training and certification course.* Researchers must complete a mandatory training and certification course explaining the origin and reasons for the regulations with human subjects, the responsibility of researchers to subjects, and the rights of subjects. Frequently used training programs are the Collaborative Institutional Training Initiative online course "Human Subjects Research" (https://www.citiprogram.org/index.cfm?pageID=88) and the National Institutes of Health's "Protecting Human Research Participants" course (https://phrp.nihtraining.com/users/login.php).[4]
- *submission of forms describing research details, intended uses, and so forth.* Follow the required compliance procedures set forth by your institution. At Cornell University, this must be completed according to compliance set forth by the IRB for human participants as described on the web page noted previously.
- *proof that one has completed consent forms for all subjects before the research commences.*
- *human subjects committee approval for each new research study,* which must be renewed annually, according to human subjects committee procedures.

A sample adult permission letter is shown in Figure 2.1. We have highlighted some key points of what the letter should contain. A consent form should accompany the letter to the parent, legal guardian, or adult participant. There should be two copies

---

[4] Many institutions provide a direct link to the courses you should use. Check with your institution.

A letter of information must state the following:

Date

Dear Participant:

Our research group is currently involved in a study that examines language in [Spanish-speaking/bilingual, etc.] adults. At this time, we are interested in [state a topic here, such as "how adult speakers of English understand certain grammatical structures"].

Your participation is interesting to us because [state a reason, such as "you are a monolingual speaker of English"]. With your permission, we would like to have the opportunity to observe and interview you.

Our interviews take place at the [name place of study/institution]. An interviewer may record your natural speech, interacting with either the interviewer or other participants or researchers. In other cases, we will ask you to produce certain sentences, or you will be asked about how you interpret them. Sometimes, you will be shown pictures and asked to judge whether the pictures show actions that match the sentences or words.

We record these sessions on audio and/or video tape so that we can focus our full attention on you during the

> What the research is about (in general terms).

> That you are requesting the participant's permission to interview him or her.

> Where the session will take place.

> What the interaction between researcher and participant will consist of. What the participant is expected to do. In each case, it is necessary to describe only the activities that will actually take place.

> How the sessions are being recorded (computer, audio, video, etc.).

Fig. 2.1: Sample adult participant letter of information.

(continues)

interview and review the data later in our laboratory. Our recordings of participants are preserved and studied carefully over time. We do not destroy records and recordings because language data continue to be valuable to researchers long after it was recorded. The audio and videotape recordings are maintained in our research labs and can be accessed only by authorized researchers. During the recordings, the researcher will address you by your first name but your last name will never be used. Records are confidential, and participant's names are removed when any data are reported publicly or in a publication. A subject number replaces the participant's name when records are accessed.[a] Please inform us if at any point you decide you do not want us to use your data in research publications, academic conferences, databases, or in teaching. Otherwise, we will assume that we have your permission to use them.

There is no possibility of physical or psychological harm involved in these recording sessions. The research possesses no more risk than that associated with daily activities.

You can stop your participation in our research at any time. There are no "right" or "wrong" answers in our studies. We are attempting to discover what is most natural for adult speakers.

[a] Because video recordings usually include the participant's image, someone who knew the participant (at the time of recording) may be able to recognize the participant without our revealing his or her identity.

That the participant's identity is going to be kept confidential and how this is going to be accomplished.

That during the recording sessions the researcher will address the participant frequently by his or her first name, but will not use the last name.

That once consent is given to record the participant and use the recordings in the terms stated here, the researcher will assume that he or she continues to have permission to use the recordings as described above unless otherwise informed by the participant.

How long the recordings will be kept and how they will be used (in research, teaching, etc.).

Who will have access to the recordings and data.

It is important to stress that the participant is allowed to stop the recording session at any time and that his or her answers will not be considered right or wrong because this is not a test.

Fig. 2.1: (Continued)

> A typical interview is expected to take approximately [specify length] at any one time, depending on your natural pace. Ideally, we would like to interview you over the course of [specify duration, such as "3 weeks"] involving different tasks.
>
> We would very much like to have you participate in our study. If you are willing to give us your consent, <u>please complete and sign the permission slip enclosed and return it to us</u>.
>
> If you have any questions, or would like to discuss this study in any way further, please feel free to contact [primary researcher(s) name(s) and phone numbers] at [primary research institution, or affiliation of study and phone numbers]. Thank you—we very much appreciate your participation.
>
> Sincerely,
>
> [Name of researchers and affiliations]

[Annotation: How long the recording session is expected to last and how many recording sessions you will have with the participant.]

Fig. 2.1: (Continued)

of the permission slip: one for the researcher and one to be kept by the parent, legal guardian, or participant. A sample consent form for both adults and children is shown in Figure 2.2.

2.2 Special Requirements: Working With Child Subjects

In addition to the requirements for working with human subjects, when one works with children, another layer of regulations and permissions is required. At the Cornell Language Acquisition Lab and other research labs, each child's parent or guardian receives a parent permission letter describing the intended research study

Consent for Participation in Language Study

Child/adult participant's name _____

Participant's age _____ Date of birth _____

Is English your child's/your first language? Yes _____ No _____

If no, what is your child's/your first language? _____

Are any languages other than English spoken in the home? Yes ____ No ____

If so, what other language(s)? _____

Participation in this study is voluntary. No risk is involved more than that associated with daily activities.

I (your name), _____ consent to participate/to my child's participation in the language acquisition studies as have been described to me in the letter accompanying this consent form. I understand the nature of this project.

You are making a decision whether to take part/to allow your child to take part in this study. Your signature indicates that you have read the information provided and have decided to participate/to permit your child to participate. **You may discontinue participation in this study at any time, without penalty, regardless of having signed this form. All information associated with you/with you and your child will remain confidential.** We have also provided a copy of this consent form for you to keep.

_____   _____
(Your signature)   (Today's date)

Note: The video and/or audio samples we collect will be archived, maintaining the anonymity of the participant's family name, and may be studied over time by researchers on language who are authorized by the [name of lab or institution].

Would you have any objections to the sharing of these audio and/or video recordings? If so, we will remove your data from the archive.

Yes ___ No ___ Your signature: _____ Date _____

Would you like to receive a copy of reported results of this study? Yes ___ No ___ If so, where would you like us to send these results?

Fig. 2.2: Sample consent form for children and adults.

In the following section we ask for additional permissions for the use of your/your child's data resulting from this research project. This is independent of your participation in this research project. Please, check all the actions you are giving us permission for and sign at the end to show you have authorized us for these actions.

We ask for your authorization for the researchers to . . .	Check if you agree
Present transcribed material from the audio or video recordings at academic meetings and in academic journals.	☐
Present transcribed material from the audio or video recordings in their teaching.	☐
Present the audio or video recordings at academic meetings and in academic journals.	☐
Present the audio or video recordings in their teaching	☐

Please, sign here if you allow us to share your/your child's data in the ways described previously that you have checked.

Your signature: _____

[principal investigator's name, principal investigator's phone number, primary laboratory of research phone number]

If you have any questions or concerns about your child's rights as a research participant, you may contact the [your university's review board for human participants] by telephone at [review board phone number], e-mail at [review board e-mail address], or visit their website at [review board website]. The institutional review board (IRB) office is located at [IRB physical address]. Consent form approved by the IRB on [date] _____.

Fig. 2.2: (Continued)

and a consent form for the parent or guardian to sign for that study. A copy of this signed consent form is placed in each child's file before initiating research. A sample parent permission letter is shown in Figure 2.3. The purpose of this particular letter is to tell parents of the potential subjects what the study is about and what it entails, so that they can make an informed decision about whether to let their child participate in the study. In the letter, we have highlighted some special issues relevant to writing letters for children's participation.

In addition to the letter, parents of potential subjects or adult participants receive a consent form they must sign stating that they are willing to participate (or let their child participate) in the research study. A sample consent form is shown in Figure 2.2. If an institution such as a day care center is involved, that center, along with the child's caregiver, must also have permissions on file before research commences.

2.3 Contacting Families and Schools

The researcher must establish which schools or centers (or other sources) have children of the age and type needed for the study. He or she has to attain permission from such schools or centers and get their class or group lists. The researcher has to meet with the school or center director to explain the study and methods and needs. Before data collection can begin, one of the senior members of the research team (e.g., graduate students, experienced undergraduates) will have contacted the director at the school or center about permissions and met with him or her to establish a relationship with the school or center. At the interview, the research team member should have (or send in advance) a set of documents explaining the research and general material about the lab. Usually, the researcher gives the director a letter describing the project, the time needed with each child, and permission letters and consent forms so that he or she may distribute them to the parents or caretakers. A sample letter for schools and centers is shown in Figure 2.4.

During the visit, the director will give a general description of the organization of the center (some day care centers are organized into classrooms, others into one large group) and their policies regarding working with their children. At the interview, the researcher should obtain class lists of names and ages of children. The researcher should arrange a time with the school for when he or she arrives and departs. The procedure for this varies from school to school; some schools prefer the times to be arranged directly with the teachers, some with the director. Negotiations must be completed with the institution so that the research can be conducted there without severe inconvenience to the school classrooms and teachers. Researchers should note the procedures that each school would like followed and follow them exactly. Also, they should make sure that the school is expecting them and that they know when they are going to arrive. When working in the home setting, researchers should contact the child's family, ask for an interview, and give the parents the same materials and explanations provided for the school.

Date

Dear Parent or Legal Guardian,

Our research group is currently involved in a study that examines early language development in children. At this time, we are interested in [state a topic here, such as "how it is possible for a child to learn more than one language at a time"]. Although we know children do this naturally, no one yet understands how they do so.

Your child's language acquisition is particularly interesting to us because [state a reason, such as "your child is monolingual or bilingual speaker who speaks Spanish"]. With your permission, we would like to have the opportunity to observe and interview your child and to talk with you about your child's language acquisition.

For our interviews with children, which take place at the [name place of study or institution], our research team will take your child to Room [X] or Office [Y] to be able to work without distractions. An interviewer may record your child's natural speech, interacting with either the interviewer or another child. In other cases, an experimenter reads sentences ("stories") to a child. The child then is asked either to repeat the sentence in his or her own way or to act out the sentence using toys provided. Sometimes, the child will be shown pictures and asked to judge whether the pictures show actions that match the sentences or words. In other cases, the child may be asked to watch a TV screen and point or look at certain events. Finally, we may ask your child to play a game with an adult who will teach your child a novel word for an object or an action.

A permission letter must state the following:

That you are requesting the parent's permission to interview the child.

That we record the child in an isolated room.

What the interaction between researcher and child will consist of and what the child is expected to do. Here we have included a variety of tasks because we like to get a range of data from each child, but it can be made more specific depending on the research study.

Fig. 2.3: Sample parent permission letter.

(continues)

We record these sessions on audio and/or video tape so that we can focus our full attention on the child during the interview and review the data later in our laboratory. Our recordings of children are preserved and studied carefully over time. We do not destroy records and recordings because language data continue to be valuable to researchers long after they are recorded. The audio and video tape recordings are maintained in our research labs and can be accessed only by authorized researchers. Records are confidential, and children's family names are removed when any data are reported publicly or in a publication. A subject number replaces the child's name when records are accessed.[a] Please inform us if at any point you or your child decide you do not want us to use his or her data in research publications, academic conferences, or in teaching. Otherwise, we will assume that we have your permission to use them.

> That once consent is given to record the child and use the recordings in the terms stated above, the researcher will assume that he or she continues to have permission to use the recordings as described previously unless otherwise informed by the parent, legal guardian, or the child (once he or she becomes an adult).

There is no possibility of physical or psychological harm involved in these recording sessions. The research involves no more risk than that associated with daily activities. Parents who wish to do so may watch the recording sessions of their child through a two-way mirror or may request to watch the video or listen to the audio recording at any time.

> That parents can request to attend the recording session or watch the resulting recordings.

We use these methods of conducting research in the form of games so that the child enjoys the experience. There is no risk involved. Our interviewers will spend time with each child prior to the actual administration of our interview

---

[a] Because video recordings usually include the child's image, someone who knew the child (at the time of recording) may be able to recognize the child without our revealing his or her identity.

Fig. 2.3: (Continued)

in the school setting so that the child is familiar with the persons conducting the interview.

> Ways in which the research team will ensure the child has a good experience. It is important to stress that the child is allowed to stop the recording session at any time and that his or her answers will not be considered right or wrong because this is not a test.

If the child does not enjoy a game or experiences any frustration or discomfort at any point, the interview is discontinued. The child is allowed to stop the game at any time. There are no "right" or "wrong" answers in the games; no child can do either poorly or well. We are attempting to discover what is most natural for the child.

A typical interview is expected to take approximately [specify length] at any one time, depending on a child's natural pace. Ideally, we would like to interview your child over the course of [specify duration, such as "3 weeks"] using different games or tasks.

We would very much like to have your child participate in our study. If you are willing to give us your consent, <u>please complete and sign the permission slip enclosed and return it to the school director</u> [or other supervisor, researcher, etc.]. If you were not contacted through a school or day care center a researcher can meet with you before the session starts to take the consent form. We will then contact you to consult with you on your child's [reason why the child was included in the study, such as "multilingualism"] and to discuss the study further with you.

> That in the home setting, one can meet with the parent or legal guardian some time before the actual session to take the consent form.

If you have any questions or would like to discuss this study further in any way, please feel free to contact [primary researcher(s) name(s) and phone numbers] at [primary research institution or affiliation of study and phone numbers]. Thank you—we very much appreciate the participation of you and your child.

Sincerely,

[Name of researchers and affiliations]

Fig. 2.3: (Continued)

> Date
>
> Dear Director:
>
> Thank you for taking the time to discuss the possibility of involving your center in our language development research project. We are writing this letter as a follow-up to our recent conversation.
>
> As was related to you, our research group at [institution name] is currently involved in a study that examines the early language development of children. For purposes of comparison, we have been studying children acquiring various languages such as English, German, Swedish, Spanish, Arabic, Chinese, Hindi, Sinhalese, and Japanese. At this time, we are interested in how children naturally develop the ability for complex sentences (sentences with more than one clause), as well as the normal changes in development over time, specifically for children whose first language is English. We are currently targeting children from ages __ to __ years old [fill in correct ages].
>
> Naturally, one of your concerns would be how this would affect your center, specifically your classrooms, staff, and program. Hopefully, we have addressed these concerns in the design of the project. Our relationship with you and your center staff is vital to the success of this study. We are willing to address your staff's concerns individually or in a group meeting. Our initial approach to the classroom is to become familiar with the staff and program within the individual rooms. It is during this time that we are willing to receive input as to the best way to obtain parental permission. After parental consent has been received and when the staff feels it is convenient, we will schedule a time (or times) when the actual interviewers can informally visit with the children to get to know them and also to become familiar with the classroom. Only after this point will children actually be formally interviewed for the study.
>
> We intend our games to be something the children can enjoy. We interview children using a game to find out how children naturally use language. If the child experiences any frustration or lack of interest during the interview, the interview is discontinued. The child is never told he or she has made a mistake. In fact, there are no "right" or "wrong" answers. The child has the right to stop the interview at any time. The total interview time for each child is approximately [number of minutes] over [number of sessions] sessions, depending on the child's

Fig. 2.4: Sample letter for teachers and schools.

> age, development, and classroom and individual circumstances. If a teacher feels that the timing of a particular visit or interview is not appropriate or convenient, the visit can be rescheduled.
>
> Our current study involves a set of several different "games" for the children. The first is [description of task in nontechnical terms—e.g., an imitation game in which children repeat sentences they hear, an act-out game in which children act out sentences using puppets and toys, a picture-choice game in which children are asked to judge whether a sentence matches a scene depicted by cartoon characters]. The second is [description of task in nontechnical terms]. The third is [description of task in nontechnical terms]. Children's responses will be audio and/or video recorded. Each child participates in one or two of these games.
>
> As discussed, our only need is a quiet space to avoid distractions and record clearly what the child and interviewer are saying. This can be done in two ways: in a separate room or during time inside when the other children are outside. This decision is left to you and your staff and can be changed on a per-visit basis if necessary.
>
> We appreciate your willingness to consider having your center participate in this research project. If you have any questions at any time, please feel free to contact [primary researcher(s) name(s) and phone numbers]. We will contact you within the next week to determine your decision. Thank you very much for your consideration.
>
> Sincerely,
>
> [primary researcher(s) name(s) and affiliations]

Fig. 2.4: (Continued)

When working at schools, recent guidelines may require anyone working alone with a child to obtain clearance, meaning at minimal obtaining a document saying the research has no record of child abuse. Regulations vary from state to state in the United States and may also vary from country to country. For example, the Pennsylvania Department of Human Services requires anyone working in direct contact with children to obtain clearance, which includes

- a report of criminal history from the Pennsylvania State Police,
- a Child Abuse History Certification from the Department of Human Services (Child Abuse), and
- a fingerprint-based federal criminal history submitted through the Pennsylvania State Police or its authorized agent (FBI).

Check with institution, state, and local regulatory agencies similar to Cornell University's Office of Sponsored Projects information website and with the school or institution you are working in with regard to these regulations. When a researcher has completed the steps regarding regulatory requirements and permissions for working with human subjects and children, she or he can proceed to the next steps concerning metadata and general research methods.

2.4 General Principles for Working With Children, Families, and Schools or Day Care Centers

Keep in mind that children, their families, and their teachers are doing you a favor by participating in the research; therefore, you must find a way of conducting the research with the least disturbance to their work and life as possible.

2.5 Visiting Schools, Day Care Centers, or Homes

In the field, the researcher is a representative of his or her university and lab. We cannot stress enough the importance of establishing a respectful relationship with the staff of the center in which you are working and with each child. Be sure to consult the teachers or families regarding how you might conduct the research with the least inconvenience to them and how to take the best care of the child and establish the best relationship with the child. For example, because the best language sample in many cases requires that you work individually with each child in a separate room so you can hear and study his or her language, this may interfere with planned school activity. Be sure to come at a time when this is not the case. Also, be aware that many nursery classrooms are made up of children from different ethnic and socioeconomic groups. Be sensitive to these differences. The researcher should always become familiar with a child by visiting the classroom or home and playing with the child, preferably several days before the interview. Remember that the child will be in your care.

The first time you visit a school, day care center, or home, be sure that you give a brief description of the experimental procedure (e.g., elicited imitation, where the child is asked to repeat a sentence, or act-out task, where the child is asked to manipulate puppets) so the teacher or family will know what is being done with each child. Also explain that only one child at a time can be tested (unless the experimental design specifies otherwise). This is because recordings with multiple children's language on them can be difficult to discern and analyze. Interaction between a child and a researcher should take place on an individual basis, one on one. In nursery schools, there is usually a quiet room or area to the side where the child can come to play individually with the experimenter. Talk with teachers to find an appropriate area. If possible, teachers and other children should be asked not to attend. Ask for a somewhat isolated spot to conduct the session because the child's speech (or actions) must be recorded. Sometimes younger children will not want to leave the group, and the experiment must be set up in the classroom.

If in the home, the caretaker may want to be present, but as the researcher, you should speak to the caretaker first about his or her involvement. It is best for the caretaker to be present, but not speaking or interacting during the data collection session. It is best not to have more than one or two adults in the testing situation because having many adults may affect the child's spontaneity with his or her language. If two adults are present, as required in many testing situations, one adult should conduct the major interaction with the child; it is usually best that the other should remain in the background as much as possible.

When the team arrives at the day care center or nursery school at the prearranged time, find the director or contact person. On the first visit, introduce all members of the research group to this person. If the day care center is split into smaller classrooms, introduce the team to each teacher. Ask the director about the consent forms. The team's contact person should collect written permission from each family for each child who might participate. Be sure that the group gets the original copy or photocopy of the written permission the family gave. This will become part of the child's permanent file. You may not work with any child whose family's consent form has not been returned and is not in your possession, even if the teacher says that you may do so because the parents said verbally it was OK. Equipment should be first set up so that it is as little as possible of a distraction to the child.

2.6 Getting to Know the Participants

In any research involving human subjects, the research team has to get to know the participant a little so that he or she feels comfortable during the research session and feels confident enough to express his or her needs. This is especially important when working with children. You have to spend some time getting to know the children and having the children get to know you, the researcher. Make a particular effort to play with the children that you have permission to interview. This is an extremely important time for both you and the children. The purposes of this time are (a) for you to get to know the children so you can select those most suited to your research and (b) for the children to get to know you as a person who is trustworthy and interested in them so they will want to spend time with you.

Some basic rules are as follows:

- Ask where you should leave your coat, pack, or other belongings.
- When you enter the classroom, make yourself a name tag and let the teacher know you are there.
- Sit down with or near a child or group of children. Stay at eye level as much as possible.
- You can just observe for a while; do not feel you should be doing or saying something all the time.
- Introduce yourself to the children. Call the children by their names.
- Children often will spontaneously include you in play or conversation. If not, you can begin a conversation about what they are doing, expressing interest in their work or inviting them to tell you about it. It is easier to be included in activities when children are doing art, puzzles, playing with sand, or playing with building blocks than when they are engaged in group dramatic play or larger motor activities, indoors or out.
- After you feel you have made a solid beginning of a relationship and you have an initial impression of the child's personality and the child has made a positive, open response to you, you might want to move on to get acquainted with other children. Let the child know that you enjoyed the contact and will be back to play another day.
- Allow yourself plenty of time for this phase of your work. The quality of the relationships you establish now will affect the way the children respond to you.
- Let the teacher know which children you are interested in working with. He or she can advise you if there are any reasons your choices might not work.
- If you decide at this session which children you would like to work with, tell them that you will be back tomorrow (or another day) with a game they might like to play.
- Try to do your research as soon after your get-acquainted visit(s) as possible so the children will be more likely to remember you and the good time they had with you.

Once you feel participants are at ease with you and may be willing to do the research session with you, ask them whether they do want to participate and go with them to the recording area. With children, you have to make sure their teacher is aware you are removing them from the classroom.

2.7 Taking the Children to the Recording Session

Some more rules are as follows:

- Spend a little "warm-up time" in the classroom.
- Follow teachers' instructions for how to approach children. In some places, teachers may want to do this themselves; others will want you to. If the teacher approves, approach a child who is between activities or playing alone, if possible

because that child will be more likely to agree to go with you than would one who is actively playing in a group. You might say, "Remember yesterday I played with you?" If you just ask, "Would you like to come play with me?" young children often say no. Because you must always obey the child's wishes, you do not want to get a no for an answer. Reminding the child that you played together before might increase the child's willingness to say yes.

- When the child is ready to play the game, tell the teacher where the child will be, how long the game will take, and where you will bring the child when the game is over. While the research group is with the child, the group is responsible for the child's safety. Always make sure the teachers know that you are working with a child. Before you leave the room with a child, let the teacher know you are going. You might say, "Let's tell your teacher we're going to the library."
- If the school or classroom does not have a sign-in/sign-out sheet for research, you may make one yourself to provide a record for the teachers and for yourself.
- The teacher must have the child potentially in sight at all times, so if there is not a wide window looking into the classroom you will be using for the interview, be sure to leave the door open.

Your primary objective at this point is for a child to go with you, have a good time, and return to the group full of enthusiasm for your activity. Your early successes will help you in obtaining children's cooperation with subsequent invitations. If necessary, take two playmates to try your research, even if the data are not useful; you are trying to establish your credibility at this point. However, you must always actually test one child at a time (unless the research design determines otherwise). Be flexible. Have several alternative children in mind; your first choice may be busy, refuse to come with you, or be absent. Respect a child's right to say no. Do not take it personally, and try to handle the refusal with confident acceptance. You might make a second attempt by playing. If the child still refuses, you can say, "Well, maybe you'd like to try it later [or tomorrow]," and often he or she will. You may have to spend more time winning this child's trust before you offer a second invitation.

2.8 Child Safety and Care

The child's safety is paramount. The child is in your care when you are working with him or her. Your priority must be the protection of the child from all harm. You are responsible for anything that might happen to the child when in your care. You are responsible for the child's safety at every moment, so be sure to observe the following rules:

- Never take your eyes off the child. Children move quickly, often in unanticipated ways—the more so the younger they are. You must never allow the child out of your sight while you are working with him or her.
- Make sure all toys are safe (i.e., recommended for children under age 3 if you are with a young child).

- Remember, even 3- and 4-year-olds may put things in their mouths.
- Avoid toys with small parts. Make sure you take all toys when you leave.
- Be wary of plug points. If the outlets in the room have safety devices, remember to replace them when you leave.
- Accidents often happen when the child is not ready to settle down and participate. If the child cannot settle down, say firmly, "It looks like you are not ready to play the game now. Let's go back to the classroom and try another time." This will often make it clear to the child that it is time to get down to business. If he or she agrees, quickly go back to the classroom, and be sure to let him or her know he or she will have another turn to participate later.
- Never allow a child to be distressed. Never "force" a child to participate. The child should always be comfortable with you and the data collection procedure. You must be sure that the child wants to work with you before continuing to work with the child. This may be difficult to assess. Many children will initially be uncomfortable with unfamiliar adults. The initial time you spend with the child before your research work is necessary to overcome this as much as possible. However, some children, because of their personality, may never want to participate in the type of research tasks you bring, and you must determine this so you do not persist in working with this child.
- You must be sensitive at every moment to the child's reactions to you and the situation. If the child becomes distressed or bored, your priority must be to alleviate this, even if it means discontinuing the research session.
- If a child is not consolable at any time during the "game," return him or her immediately to the teacher or parent. If the child becomes uncomfortable at any time during the testing, allow the child to do what he or she wants for a while. This may entail playing a game of the child's choosing or allowing the child to return to the areas where other children are playing.
- If you are in the child's home, it is a good idea to have the parent nearby with an open door. This makes the child feel more comfortable. Remember that most children will enjoy being with you if you are interacting well with them. It is important that the child not feel that he or she is being tested. Sessions should be fun. They may be introduced as a "game."
- Realize that the child may be afraid at first. Do not be forceful; get a feel for the child's apprehensiveness or confidence and use appropriate levels of persuasion.
- Make the child feel comfortable and help to maintain her or his self-esteem. No child who does not wish to participate should be forced to do so.

Children of different ethnic backgrounds possibly will reflect different cultural assumptions (e.g., about quietness, when to speak, how and whether to speak to adults). Familiarize yourself with these backgrounds so that you can be sensitive to them during your work with the child.

Children at different developmental levels and age levels will be different to work with (e.g., a 2-year-old vs. a 4-year-old vs. an 8-year-old). Familiarize yourself with the developmental psychology of the age you are working with, and any special requirements.

Children with disabilities will also require special modes of interaction. You will be expected to familiarize yourself not only with the general principles of work with children but also with the disability you are dealing with before initiating research with these populations.

2.9 Researcher–Child Interaction

It is a good idea to watch example videos demonstrating model experimenter–child interaction to prepare yourself for interactions with children before going out into the field (many are available at the Virtual Linguistics Lab portal). The researcher's goal is to obtain the most productive child utterances while restricting his or her speech as much as possible. The researcher should stay in the background, centering on the child, giving time for the child's response, and never interfering. Always guide the child toward demonstrating his or her competence. Interactions with the child in your role as researcher differ from your interactions with the child only on a personal level. Your primary task is to elicit the data you need for your particular study. You will only be successful if you can make the child your partner and your teacher in this endeavor.

Bring yourself to the level of the child so you are interacting with him or her well. Minimize your language, and maximize the child's. Speak as little as possible yourself—only enough to inspire the child's speech. Your job is to discover what the child knows and thinks. Thus, you must be careful always to let the child and the child's responses dominate the situation as much as possible. Your role is to draw these out, not dominate the child by imposing your behaviors and your language on the situation.

The child must realize that you take seriously everything he or she says or does; thus, do not display any behaviors that would cause the child to question him- or herself (e.g., laughing or repeating an answer in a surprised tone when the child has unexpected behavior or gives a strange answer). In general, every answer a child gives is perfectly fine (it constitutes data), and the child should be encouraged. Positive reinforcement must be general and across the board. Some recommendations are as follows:

- Always tell the child that he or she is doing a good job.
- Do not demean the child by saying things such as, "You are so cute."
- Always treat the child with respect.
- Work with the child's natural abilities.

At all times, the researcher should be aware of the age of the child and appropriate levels of functioning. Age-appropriate tasks are important because tasks that are too difficult may cause the child to feel bad about poor performance, whereas tasks that are too simple may cause boredom. In addition, the materials used during the interaction should reflect the child's age.

Sometimes it may help children's comfort level and/or motivate them if you allow them to "push the buttons" or even hear themselves speak on tape. If this is the case, make sure it happens before starting the "game" and/or after the game is over, not during the game. During the interaction, it may be useful for the experimenter to make notes concerning the context of the session. This is helpful at the transcription stage.

Remember that in a research experiment with the child, your goal is to collect the necessary data under standardized conditions (experimental) by keeping the child's attention on task while assuring the child enjoys the game. If not specified, the goal is to elicit the most production of spontaneous speech possible in any way.

Allow yourself plenty of time—more than you think you will need. Research with young children often takes longer than planned. Knowing this in advance may help you relax and enjoy the experience rather than feeling rushed and frustrated.

2.10 After Your Research Session

It is important to give some closure to your experience with the child:

- Thank the child for playing your game. The children's willingness to participate in your research is essential to you, so show genuine appreciation of their help.
- When you have finished interviewing the child, return with him or her to the classroom or playground. Inform the teacher that you have returned the child. After you take the child back to the room, spend a little time helping him or her become involved again in play or with friends.
- Do not forget to "check out"—tell the teacher you are leaving and when you will be back. Thank the teachers for their cooperation.

2.11 Summary

In this chapter, we have introduced the concepts related to the protection of the humans participating in research, and we have presented the general guidelines for complying with human subject committees requirements, which should be complemented with the researcher's institution recommendations and procedures. Finally, we provided advice on how to proceed when interacting with schools, parents, and the subjects themselves.

3 Creating the Data I: Working in Teams, Basic Data Collection, Data Sharing, and Data Management

Each research study may involve the collection of a large amount of data. These data must be collected in a manner that allows organization, summarizing, and comparing. Scientific research must also involve replicability. Replicability requires complete accountability for how the research was accomplished. Finally, researchers must be able to collaborate on collecting and/or analyzing and interpreting shared data. For these reasons, one must provide documentation that goes with the raw data.[1] This information is called *metadata*. Such information infrastructure allows a researcher to process his or her data and allows others to use the same data for research. The documentation helps other researchers to understand the basis of comparison, thus allowing replication of another researcher's results. The metadata put the collected raw data information into a scientific context.

Creating research data is a complex endeavor. In doing so, your management of the data you collect will be crucial. You have to be able to compare your results from a task you do with one subject today with those from a subject you work with tomorrow, the week after, and even another year later. Even more so, you have to be able to compare your results from a single subject with another set of results from that same subject at another time. You have to be able to compare your results with those of other researchers and teachers. You have to share your results so different analyses can be done on those data by others and by yourself at another time. You have to be able to access your data so that you can publish valid, reliable, scientifically sound results, and you have to be able to verify all of your human subjects' documents through the life of your research data. For all these reasons, you always have to be able to find each piece of data and calibrate it with other data in the present and the future. This necessity for data preservation, access, retrievability, and comparability provides an immense "data management" challenge for every researcher.

Language studies are frequently conducted by teams of researchers, and if every piece of data is not properly labeled and stored, other team members will not be able to understand what each researcher did and how much has been accomplished. If you and others on your scientific team cannot locate and identify your data, you will not be able to use it. Your research program cannot proceed, and you will not be

---

[1] *Raw data* refers to data that has been collected in video or audio format but not yet transcribed, analyzed, or processed in any other way.

able to verify your results because your results will be unreliable. The more data that are collected, the more serious the problem of poorly managed data becomes. For interdisciplinary and collaborative projects, data management planning is especially challenging.

Thus, your responsibility as a researcher is not just to collect data but also to manage it so that it is preserved and accessible for future analyses, so that it is reliable and verifiable. Today, federal funding agencies such as the National Science Foundation[2] and the National Institutes of Health in the United States require that you describe your data management plans when you apply for grant funding for your research. These data management plans must address how you will disseminate and share your research results. Universities and institutions have established groups to assist in the articulation of data management plans. For example, Cornell University has established a Research Data Management Group (http://data.research.cornell.edu/content/data-management-planning). Researchers should consult their institutions for similar groups.

In summary, to manage your data, you have to create metadata—information about your data and the details and information related to the research that "surrounds" the actual raw data recorded during the subject's recording session. When we speak about data management, we mean managing your data and its related metadata so that both you and others can access them and understand your data. In this chapter, we briefly overview fundamental concepts for establishing best practices in this area. We also discuss best practices for data collection and offer general guidelines for generating raw linguistic data.

3.1 Preliminary Assumptions

Before you participate in any research study, you should create an experimental folder for your study. Usually, a lab has all the materials for a particular research study organized on a server or other storage website or hard drive. We assume that such a file exists in which you keep your data identified by the name of the study on which you are working. This file is ready to receive copies of all records involved in your study or experiment. It should be created and accessed after you have gone

---

[2] Beginning January 18, 2011, proposals submitted to the National Science Foundation (NSF) must include a supplementary document of no more than two pages labeled "Data Management Plan" (DMP), accessible from http://www.nsf.gov/bfa/dias/policy/dmp.jsp. This supplementary document should describe how the proposal would conform to NSF policy on the dissemination and sharing of research results. Proposals that do not include a DMP cannot be submitted. For more information about this new requirement, see the NSF "Grant Proposal Guide," Chapter II.C.2.j at http://www.nsf.gov/pubs/policydocs/pappguide/nsf13001/gpg_2.jsp#dmp and the "Data Management and Sharing Frequently Asked Questions" at http://www.nsf.gov/bfa/dias/policy/dmpfaqs.jsp.

through all the necessary preliminary steps before conducting the experiment (i.e., completed the human subjects training and other requirements before proceeding, been given appropriate training in the audiovisual equipment you will need[3] after an experiment director has been identified on your research team).

A central database where you can record basic aspects of your experiment or research study can aid this process. Here, you can enter your experiment or study in an experiment bank. Through this central experiment bank entry, all aspects of your design and methods should be recorded. This is so that all components of the experiment or project can be accessed at any time and replicated and used by others on your team. One example of an infrastructure developed for this purpose is the Data Transcription Analysis (DTA) Tool, a cybertool that was developed in conjunction with the Virtual Linguistics Laboratory portal (http://www.clal.cornell.edu/vll). It provides a systematic structure for guiding the researcher in the entry of every step of metadata required for complete research documentation. The DTA Tool (https://webdta.clal.cornell.edu) provides a standardized web-based user interface using prompts through metadata collection, transcription, and analysis. Using screens that result in a standardized data entry, the DTA Tool uses a question and answer format that prompts researchers to enter information about their research and results. This process includes introductory screens that collect information on the research project metadata. Use of this tool results in a database providing the foundation for both active collaboration on research and an experiment bank of records allowing reproducibility of research (see Chapter 14, this volume).

All of the following guidelines may be completed in paper form (and may have to be in some types of field work), but digital files have gradually come to supplement, if not replace, hard copies in many cases. If so, all hard copy materials have a parallel digital form that must be filed, and that must include computer (or server) storage and organization. This organization of digital files is as important as that of the hard copy files.

3.1.1 Collecting Raw Data Successfully

The steps involved in the collection of raw data for language acquisition studies make the successful, precise collection and retrievability of such data valuable. Figure 3.1 illustrates the key steps involved in collecting raw linguistic data.

---

[3] We assume that your data will involve an audiovisual component, as language data do. However, similar principles would apply to other forms of data (e.g., questionnaires, paper and pencil tests). Also, data collection may still involve some form of tapes (e.g., in certain forms of field work), although with digital recording devices, data can be entered directly on the computer and then subjected to the same principles of data management.

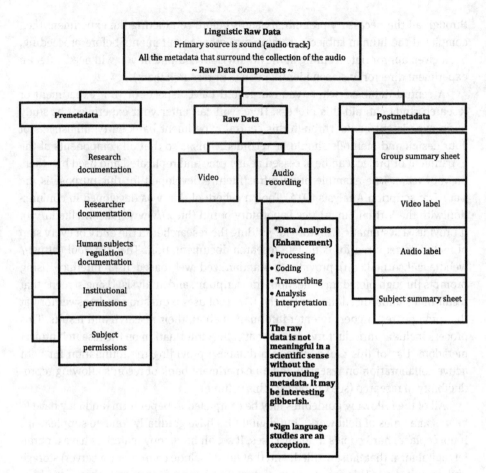

Fig. 3.1: Linguistic raw data—raw data component.

3.1.2 Metadata

There are two phases of metadata: pre-raw data collection and post-raw data collection. The "Premetadata" section expands into the following segments in Figure 3.2. The first five areas of premetadata—research documentation, researcher documentation, human subjects regulation documentation, institutional permissions, and subject permissions—must all be completed, collected, and documented before the collection of any linguistic data. The remaining areas of metadata (see "Postmetadata," Figure 3.1) are completed during and after the collection of the raw data.

Basic metadata regarding the research you are conducting must be recorded. There are general metadata formats developed by the community studying language. It is recommended that each research laboratory be familiar with this standard and collect metadata information in accordance with it. One can find detailed background

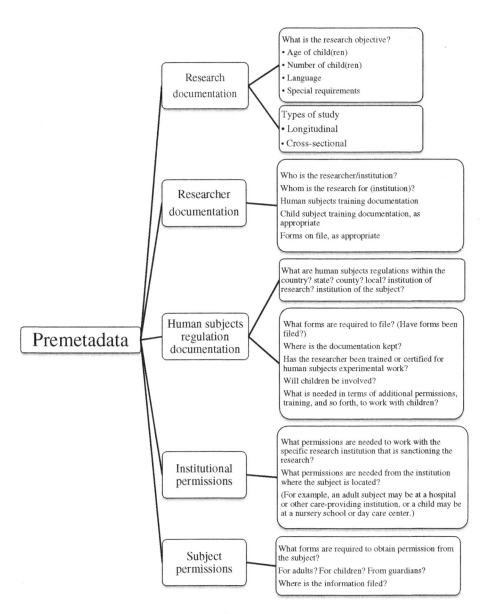

Fig. 3.2: Premetadata components from raw data.

Exhibit 3.1: Research Documentation and Researcher Documentation Examples

Examples of Research Design Documentation
- Research objective
- Age of subjects
- Number of subjects
- Language
- Special requirements
- Type of study
  - Longitudinal
  - Cross-sectional
- Funded by whom ... ?

Examples of Researcher Information Metadata
- Who is the researcher?
- What is their institution?
- Who funded the research?
- Human subjects training documentation
- Child subject training documentation, as appropriate
- Forms on file, as appropriate

information and descriptions of some of these standards at http://www.language-archives.org/OLAC/olacms.html. The content of this site includes elements from the metadata set used by the Open Language Archives Community[4] (OLAC) for the interchange of metadata within the framework of the Open Archives Initiative (OAI).[5] Exhibit 3.1 provides examples of research and researcher documentation, which expands on the concepts shown in Figure 3.2. With all the pre-study metadata in place, one can proceed to the experiment or observational study itself.

3.2 Preparation Before the School or Home Visit

3.2.1 Determining Your Subject Population

Begin by determining the characteristics of the subjects you need to work with and how many participants you hope to record. The age range, language, socioeconomic level,

---

[4] The OLAC is an international partnership of individuals and institutions that are working to create a worldwide virtual library of language resources by developing standards for metadata specialized to language resources and to create a network of interacting institutions housing such resources (Bird & Simons, 2001; Simons & Bird, 2000a, 2000b, 2001).

[5] The OAI is an initiative in which a metadata format is being developed for all forms of library resources, neither limited to language nor specialized for language. It is based on Dublin Core as a protocol for metadata harvesting. It forms the basis for the development of the OLAC "Schema for OAI implementation of Dublin Core metadata," available at http://www.openarchives.org/OAI/openarchivesprotocol.html (Van de Sompel & Lagoze, 2001).

level of bilingualism (if any; see Chapter 12), and other characteristics of the subjects and the length of study are determined according to the purpose of the study. If the study does not involve looking only at subjects of a specific gender, it is important to have gender balance and an equal number of subjects in each group. Unless otherwise specified, subjects should have no cognitive deficits and no history of ear infections.

3.2.2 Setting up the Research Team

When going to nursery schools or day care centers, researchers often work in teams of two. To make things run smoothly, there will be a designated experimenter and a designated manager/transcriber. The experimenter will be responsible for communicating with the teachers and administering the batteries to the subjects. The transcriber will be in charge of the logistics of the session (e.g., equipment set up, keeping track of subject information, the order in which the batteries should be administered). Everyone has to get to know the subjects, and everyone has to interact with the teachers. Everyone should also try to keep track of the number and type of subjects still needed and the batteries to be administered.

3.2.3 Setting up a Research Folder

For each new subject (i.e., each new child or adult you interview), verify that the parent/caretaker permission form or participant letter has been administered and the consent form signed. Set up a folder labeled with the subject's ID. It should contain a subject sheet for the participant and a copy of the consent form. This allows you to keep a running record of every time you see this subject and what you have done. Establish a secure place for storage of these subject folders. Human subjects regulations require that a subject's name be kept confidential in all public or shared use of the subject's data.

After obtaining the child's family's permission or the adult participant's consent and school permission, the researcher must fill out a Subject Summary Sheet for each subject. The subject sheet should be established for each subject before working with him or her. This establishes essential background information on each participant and the nature and date of each interview and initiates a file for a new participant whose data will become part of your research data. The sample subject summary sheet presented in Figure 3.3 is used for every subject involved in a language acquisition study. With this document, start a file on each subject. This form must be completed at the start of any work with a subject, and it must constantly be updated to list every task administered to the subject. Even if subjects do not complete any task, this sheet must record that event. A separate file called "Attrition" should show all the information plus your notes on the cause of termination of the interview. Fill out

```
Date: _____
Participant's name (print last name, first name, and middle initials):
_____

Birth date (MM/DD/YYYY): _____

Subject ID: _____

Audio tape/file number: _____

Video tape/file number: _____

Other number(s) (specify type, e.g., DAT tape, CD, DVD, Digital Audio/Video file):

Interview location: Home: _____ School: _____ Other: _____
(specify) _____

Sex: Male _____ Female _____

Age (YYYY;MM,DD): _____

School name (if applicable): _____

Parent's name (for child subjects only): _____

Address: _____

Phone: _____

Parents present at interview session (for child subjects only)? Yes _____ No _____

        Is the subject monolingual?   Yes _____ No _____

        If not, other language(s) _____

Interviewer/researcher: _____
```

the child's name on the group summary sheet in whatever age group or condition he or she will be in. Documents containing the subject's information, such as name and birth date, are only for the internal use of the research team. Data containing identifying information such as these should never be made public.

3.2.4 Using Recording Devices

In the past, studies of language acquisition were conducted with researchers taking notes of a subject speaking (e.g., diary studies). Notes, however precise, cannot provide the full picture of a subject's language. Notes on language behaviors or speech may be missing information such as intonation, precise pronunciation, or context, or they may not be able to show us clearly the frequency of production of many structures. They cannot be made fast enough to record a veridical speech transcript in most cases. Often, it is difficult to hear what a speaker has said, especially with natural variations in voice amplitude, pitch, and speech. Notes alone can never allow replicability; the "same data" can never be reanalyzed by an independent researcher. As we discuss in Chapter 9, it is true that no two hearers, especially on first pass, will transcribe an audio sample in the same way. Fortunately, modern recording devices allow us to collect raw data in a form that can be preserved and reanalyzed at any time in the future, a form against which transcriptions can be checked for reliability.

The type of research and particular research study will determine the precise equipment needs and requirements for its use. The nature of the context (e.g., in the field or a lab setting, in a country or cultural situation where the Internet is or is not available) will determine the possibilities. Digital recorders greatly increase the acoustic quality of sound recordings, thus increasing reliability of their analysis. External handheld microphones, wireless broadcast microphones, or preinstalled omnidirectional microphones located at the recording site (or in the child's clothing) may be used. Wind screens may be necessary if recording outdoors.

In general, the primary data of a speech sample will be high-quality audio data, but video-recorded data allow the researcher to capture properties of the context in which the speech sample is occurring. They also often allow the researcher to understand better the intentions of the speaker and may disambiguate the meanings of the subject in ways audio samples alone cannot. Video recording equipment does not include highest audio quality, so it is advisable that video recording is supplemented by powerful audio recording equipment as well. Some forms of video recording equipment may be intrusive, requiring another adult in the environment.[6]

All language acquisition studies require recording equipment that has to be readied before each research session. Skilled in equipment use, the researcher can create

---

[6] For technical guidance on high-quality recording equipment and procedures, it may be useful to consult the Cornell Laboratory of Ornithology's (http://birds.cornell.edu) Macaulay Library website (http://macaulaylibrary.org/).

an accurate record of the subject's language production or linguistic raw data by capturing the sounds of speech on a digital audio file (previously, audiotapes and CDs were also common). With digital video recording, the researcher can also create a record of the subject, including raw audio data as the sound track of a simultaneous video file or tape. The sound track of the video can be a backup for an independent audio file whereas the video track can provide insights into language behaviors and interpretation of the overall research session. These devices allow a researcher to go back and review the research session with the subject. The materials can be replayed to clarify interpretation of sounds and gestures. In addition, recording equipment facilitates having independent researchers provide an opinion or interpretation of the same subject.

The researcher must become familiar with the complete set of equipment and its use before entering the field. This is a critical success factor in language acquisition research. The researcher who is practiced and skilled in the use of equipment does not have to figure out technical operations during the research, which could easily distract the subject. Also, if a researcher is not familiar with the equipment, he or she risks losing critical data, which he or she believes is properly recording and later finds out was not.

3.2.4.1 Recording Equipment Needed

Appropriate recording equipment (either audio or video or both) is required, including a good quality microphone. Although audio and video can be recorded directly into a computer, the sound quality is better when appropriate recording equipment is used.[7] Batteries of portable equipment often need to be charged for several hours before use.

3.2.4.2 Ancillary Recording Equipment

Ancillary equipment related to the recording equipment may be needed to complete a recording session. Examples of this include additional memory cards and charged batteries, USB cables, equipment carrying cases, and additional batteries as necessary or electrical or extension cords.

---

7 For good recommendations on recording equipment, researchers are advised to consult with the language acquisition research community by e-mailing the Child Language Data Exchange System mailing list (http://talkbank.org/share/email.html) or by posting a query to the Linguist List (http://linguistlist.org/LL/posttolinguist.cfm).

3.2.4.3 Preparing the Recording Situation

Analysis of speech data collected depends on high-quality audio data. The researcher has to identify clearly the participant's voice and each of his or her utterances. Therefore, the following caveats are essential in preparing the recording situation.

- A quiet background. Most sounds will sound louder in the recording than they sound in the recording session, so background noise, such as radios, should be eliminated as much as possible.
- Avoidance of multiple voices on the recording. You will be recording one subject at a time unless there are research questions that involve participants interacting with others. The latter situation, which can be productive for natural speech, will impose particular challenges for data transcription (identifying which voice belongs to which subject). Video recordings are critical in this case.
- Ideal microphone placement is as close as possible to the child to maximize audio quality without distracting the child.
- Discrete placement of recording equipment. The child's attention should not be drawn to the equipment.

3.2.5 Research Materials

3.2.5.1 Documents

The team should have two folders (both hard copy and electronic if possible). One folder should contain the researcher's instructions and must be available during the research session. Researchers' instructions for a particular study lay out the precise procedures to be followed with each subject and outline the number of subjects desired in each group. If the research is experimental, stimulus materials (e.g., list of sentences to be repeated by the child, set of pictures to be recognized by a subject) must be prepared (placed in a plastic cover for repeated use, if working with hard copies). The lists of stimulus sentences are frequently called *batteries*. This folder contains copies of the test batteries and blank transcription sheets.

The second folder is for each of the schools you will be visiting. This folder should contain

- permission slips,
- subject lists,
- group summary sheets, and
- blank subject sheets and subject sheets from uncompleted sessions.

The team should make sure that there are blank copies of all of the forms or computer-available templates and refill these pages before leaving, if necessary.

3.2.5.2 Materials and Props

Depending on the type of research, and as specified in the research design, different materials and/or props may be included (e.g., toy dolls, picture books). Above all else, be sure that any prop brought for use with a child is safe. Small objects must be avoided because they can be swallowed by a child. Because children put objects in their mouths, nothing that could be dangerous in any way may be included as a prop. Be sure there are no loose edges; sharp points; metal, plastic, or glass pieces; and so forth. Confirm that the product you are using is approved for the age group of the child. Noisy objects that may interfere with recording quality must be eliminated.

3.2.5.3 Equipment

Recording devices should be tested before going out into the field. Usually, a video camera and an audio recorder are used. Whenever possible, digital recorders should be used. Remember to take

- cassette tapes or videotapes and labels (if needed);
- any device allowing for audio and/or video recording;
- extra batteries, memory cards, chargers, extension cords;
- toys, books, and so forth, to elicit conversation; and
- whatever toys and props are specific to your study.

3.2.5.4 Research Kit

Typically, the researcher or research team assembles a research kit that includes all the material mentioned earlier, in an ordered binder, either digitally or in hard copy, depending on the research situation. This kit includes a description of all the material needed to administer the particular research task. If the task is an experiment, it will also include the stimuli that have been designed for it (e.g., sentences, pictures). A list of the children who may be available for the study during that session should be added to this kit, with documentation of their consent forms and basic information on their age and birth date (usually provided by the school or center where the researcher is working).

3.2.6 Research Team Preparation for Each Recording Day

The team should also make a list for the day with the names and rooms of the participants needed for the study. They should note which participants have completed part of the batteries and should try to interview these participants first. Furthermore, they should check the age group summary sheet to see which age groups are lacking in subjects. For example, if many 4-year-olds and almost no 2-year-olds have been interviewed, they should concentrate on interviewing some 2-year-olds that day.

3.3 The School or Home Visit Session With the Participant

It is a good idea to watch example videos demonstrating model experimenter–child interactions to prepare yourself for interactions with children before going out into the field (several are available at the Virtual Linguistics Lab portal). The researcher must be mindful that recording equipment does not create a distraction to the subject. Placing such devices near a subject may have the unintentional result of drawing the subject's attention to the equipment rather than the planned research. A practiced researcher develops techniques for microphone placement that limit distraction to the subject. When the research session is completed, additional metadata information must be developed and included in the research file (postmetadata). This total package of metadata (both pre- and post-) provides the documentation for the supporting materials of the research session: audio and video files, tapes or disks, and summary sheets.

3.4 After the School or Home Visit

3.4.1 Back at the Lab

- Make sure you return all the equipment to the lab.
- Complete the required information on the running subject sheets.
- Check to see that materials are ready for your next session.
- Note on your log sheet what you did. This is the only way for other people in the lab to keep track of your work.
- If you have time, transcribe the recordings of the children interviewed that day.
- File all the forms you completed that day. Each child's subject sheet and transcription sheets should be filed in a folder with his or her name and number on it in the master file with your study's name on it.
- In the "Progress" file, find the list of subjects, and write down the subject's name and number and whether that child's data has been transcribed, reliability checked, and coded.

3.4.2 Data Creation Overview

Capturing language so that it can become reliable scientific data requires a multistep process. The Virtual Center for Language Acquisition has created an infrastructure by which the multistep process of data creation can be orchestrated and integrated. Although the creation steps follow a sequential order, many stages can and will be performed simultaneously. The full process involving these steps, which we summarize here, is designed to provide reliable data for collaborative and interactive research through the Virtual Center for Language Acquisition.

1. An audio (and/or video) recording is made of language behaviors. The behavior of the participant (e.g., his or her speech or images or him or her moving toys) so recorded provides the foundation for the following steps of data creation.
2. Basic metadata surrounding the item is entered in inventory screens. The metadata provides the basis for labeling in further data creation steps. These first screens enter metadata regarding the subject and regarding the session(s) of recording.
3. A copy is made of the original audio (and/or video) recording.
4. Ideally, the original data are collected in digital form. This file must be labeled and stored in a secure repository. If original data collection is not in digital form, a Stage I digitization should be made from the original audio or videotape and saved in a specified format (e.g., .aiff, .wave). *Stage I files* are simply the files from which the data came (possibly involving more than one subject or session per tape).
5. A backup copy is made of this Stage I file and stored on a separate storage device.
6. A Stage II file must then be created for each subject and saved on a server and in another place (e.g., a hard drive). This provides the authoritative digital audio record that will become the basis for research. This second stage digitization involves separating data that may have been combined on the original audio file, such as separate subjects and separate tasks for a single subject (e.g., natural speech as well as experimentally derived language). A Stage II file should contain all sessions for a single subject, regardless of type of data elicitation (experimental or naturalistic). Each Stage II file contains audio data for only one subject. Links to inventory metadata are made.
7. A backup copy is made of this Stage II digital file.
8. A Stage III digital file is then created from each Stage II record. Here, it is edited and formatted to assure the highest audio quality possible. Precise links to metadata for each task and each subject are made.
9. Several types of backup copies are made of this Stage III digital file (e.g., storage on server, backup hard drive, CD or DVD in duplicate).
10. An initial transcription is made of the recorded speech (audio). It should be labeled in a way that indicates clearly that this is the first transcript.[8] Ideally,

---

[8] Chapters 4 and 9 provide guidelines and methods for speech transcription. If the initial transcription has not been done following the guidelines shown there, subsequent retranscriptions will be able to add this value in final reliability checking.

transcription is done on the basis of a digitized form of the audio data, preferably a Stage III form.
11. A second independent transcription is made of the recorded speech. It should be labeled in a way that indicates clearly that this is the second transcript.
12. A reliability check is conducted by comparing and contrasting these previous transcriptions, noting discrepancies and resolving these to provide an accepted "working transcript."[9] This reliability check includes listening to the whole recording. Reliability checking is discussed in detail in Chapter 9.
13. A phonetic edit is added to the accepted working transcript. These phonetic edits are also conducted in accord with the digital audio file. Both the audio and written data are precisely integrated. Editing especially includes cases in which speech has been in some way deformed, (e.g., where the speaker has made an error in pronunciation, where he or she uses a nonstandard dialect). Here, the standard spelling system may not be accurate enough. The phonetic edit provides a final reliability check on the data.[10]
14. The accepted working transcript is then entered into the database tool you are working with, and a sequence of structured analyses and annotations can begin then.[11]
15. If the speech data involve a language other than English, literal and general glosses are entered into the database accordingly.
16. At each stage in this process, the data involve an ID or signature, indicating the full set of steps that have been completed to date and allowing the researcher to indicate which stage of data he or she is using. Individual researchers who participate in various stages of data creation at various times are recorded in the database accordingly. Human subjects criteria for anonymity of records are maintained throughout.

The full process of data creation is not a linear one. In fact, each time the created data are used and reused by researchers, further value is added to the data; transcriptions are newly amended and/or added to.

---

[9] A *working transcript* is the transcript on which further analyses will be based. It is called *working transcript* rather than *final transcript* because it is possible that other researchers with whom one shares the data may create different transcripts for the same recording.

[10] Phonetic edits may be *partial* (emphasizing the child's deformed forms only) or *full* (in which a transcription is made completely in a phonetic alphabet). The latter is required for a study concerned with the phonology of the data; partial edits may suffice when the research questions concern the syntax of semantics of the language. Standard data creation in the Cornell Language Acquisition Lab/ Virtual Linguistics Laboratory assumes partial phonetic edits unless specified otherwise.

[11] In the case where both a video and an audio recording exist, transcriptions of these have to be calibrated and comments on "context" entered accordingly into the database.

3.4.3 Entering Subject and Session Metadata

When you return from your initial interview with the subject, record what you did in the interview on the subject sheet, and file that in the subject's folder. Also, in the subject screen of your central database, enter the subject's information and the information about what you did with the subject on that date in the session or segment field of your database. This provides you with an electronic database version of what you have initiated.

A standardized system for converting participants' personal names to a code maintaining confidentiality of your subject must be a part of this process. For example, at Cornell, initials and birthdays are used for identification for researchers with permission to access the data; therefore, GA080771 refers to a subject whose first name starts with G, whose last name starts with A, and who was born on August 7, 1971 (using the MM/DD/YY format). When showing information for the subject to the general public, this ID is replaced by an identifier with no personal information (e.g., *Subject 1* in the research study or other code).

Enter your subject's information on the "master database" for your study. The database should be in electronic form, allow access to all researchers, and be backed up regularly. This master database keeps track of your research study (i.e., which subjects have participated in the research you have designed, how many, and what was completed so far). Given the design of your study, the master database determines what still needs to be done and how far you are from completion. It also prevents the same subject being tested twice in the same way by two different people on the research team who did not know what the other did. Each week (if not more often), a trained team member for your study should review this master database.

3.4.4 Backing Up and Making All Data Accessible

Always back up your data. Backup copy files are essential. This is especially true because digital files are ephemeral and software for data representation and storage changes continually. When working in a team on a research project, always make sure all your data and your related work are stored on a central repository or server so others on your team can calibrate with you. Never store your work simply on your own computer.

3.4.5 Labeling the Data

Labeling the digital files, audiotapes, or videotapes from the research session is one of the most critical factors in the research process. The audio (and or video) data are not meaningful if the information about the subject and the research is not tied to the files or tapes. The researcher must accurately document all the files and/or tapes involved in the research with a consistent labeling procedure. As you are collecting data, make sure your digital file is immediately labeled. This label will be the critical link for locating your audio and visual data, linking it to the master database and all further analyses. As you are collecting data and after you return to the lab, ensure that the labeling of the recordings and files has proceeded according to specification. Even if you intend to add more data to your recording at another time, the labeling must begin with records of what you have already on that file. Store the digital recordings in an orderly manner in the secure repository that has been established for your study. Always follow a systematic labeling system for your data and your work. Do not adopt an informal label, such as "new file" or "new data"—what is new today is old tomorrow. Data must last over time and be available for shared use and reuse by others. Remember that data creation is a long and extensive stepwise process. The scientific validity and significance of your data depend on every step of this process. Each level of data collected must be systematically labeled.

3.4.5.1 Labeling Procedures: The Initial Stage

Data recordings should be saved in the following three forms:

- the original file (audio or visual) on which original data are brought in (the authenticating archival data)—for example, a digital file collected on computer, a data card used with a recorder, an individual tape;
- the backups of these data (e.g., CD or DVD or separate digital file, stored elsewhere); and
- the digital files stored on the repository (e.g., computer, hard drive, and/or server). All of these forms of the data must be labeled in a coherent way. The backup copies must be identically labeled, and specified as "copy."

A. Original Recordings

If original data are collected digitally, this labeling information should be linked to the original audiovisual file. If data are collected initially in a physical format, this information should be entered both on the physical record directly (e.g., the sticky label on a tape if tapes are used) and the tape case and should be used for both sides of the tape, in the case of analog or digital tapes. The information for this template should be stored electronically. The electronic entry becomes part of the central database of audio and/or video files. Table 3.1 shows an example template for label recordings.

This information regarding the audio and video file is followed by specific information on the subjects appearing in the file. Table 3.2 shows an example template for organizing the subject information.

Tab. 3.1: Template for Label Recordings

Category	Examples
Lab name	CLAL for Cornell Language Acquisition Lab (should include name of institution—Cornell, MIT, Rutgers, etc.)
Language	SPA for Spanish
Record number[a]	###
Record format	• DIG—digital • AC—analog cassette • DAT—digital audio tape • VHS—VHS video tape • HI 8—digital HI 8 video tapes • DD—data disc
Side	A or B
Project name[b]	• SI ID—Sloppy Identity Study or Blume Diss—particular dissertation (include last name)
Place of recording	Lima, Peru

Note: [a]Corresponds to tape number if original data has been collected on tape. [b]Project names should be established, standardized, and held constant across all aspects of a research project.

Tab. 3.2: Template for Organizing Specific Subject Information

Subject ID number	Initials plus birth date (e.g., LC01022002), then transferred to a further identified form—initials plus year of birth or lab specific numbering system.[a]
Date of recording	MM/DD/YYYY
Session #	1, 2, or more if the subject has been recorded several times. (If a recording runs over to more than one file, then list this as "session # cont'd" (e.g., "1 cont'd," "2 cont'd.")
Tasks recorded (in order recorded)	Abbreviated: • NS = natural speech • EI = elicited imitation • EP = elicited production • AO = act out • TVJ = truth–value judgment • GJ = grammaticality judgment • etc.[b]

Note: [a]Birthdates are considered identifying information, so these should be simplified when data are processed. [b]Task names should be standardized.

In this first example, only one subject's speech was recorded on a single audio file, but this subject has natural speech, elicited production, and elicited imitation data.

LC01022002-10/12/2005-1-NS, EP, EI

If several subjects are recorded on a file, the same format should be applied to all of them.

In the following example, multiple children are recorded on a single recording.

CLAL:Spa-0013-AC
Núñez del Prado Pro drop
San Juan, Puerto Rico
MR03251989-8/12/1993-1-EI
ER05181987-8/12/1993-1-EI
TF02121990-8/12/1993-1-EI
MR11071989-8/12/1993-1-EI
MA10301990-8/12/1993-1-EI

If not all information is available when a file is initially being stored and/or digitized, fill out whatever information is available and leave blank the other fields. Subsequent analyses of the file can fill these in at a later time.

Identical information in the identical structure should be entered (linked) to both physical and electronic copies of recordings. The electronic archive that results from this labeling system should be linked to your central database. For audio data, digital tracks have to be consistently labeled for access and analysis. For the Virtual Center for the Study of Language Acquisition, for example, for Stage I files, *CLAL-NS-Eng-Berk-#01GA070771* refers to a track that was collected at the Cornell Language Acquisition Lab (CLAL) in a session where the task was natural speech (NS) and the language of the session was English; it was collected by Berk and is the first session (01) for subject G. A., whose birthday is on 07/07/1971.

B. Labeling Stage II Records

Following Stage I, which essentially archives the original data collected, further analyses require subdividing each original piece of data. When data analysis begins, original data are broken down into various stages of analyses (e.g., individual subjects and/or tasks may have to be separated out for your records—further states of labeling would be required). Here you begin to structure your data. These subdivisions of data are called *segments*. Minimally, each separated segment must be (a) linked to the Stage I file and (b) given a unique label. This unique label must specify (a) session, (b) subject ID, and (c) task. These details provide the unique information necessary for integrating with the database, where further information can be located. Labels allow you to begin to organize your data so you can go on to the stage of research analyses in which you will be looking at all subjects in a certain group or all data elicited with a similar task (e.g., elicited imitation).

Example Template for Stage II
[Session number][ID][Task]   01MK040896NS
For Stage II files:
1) NS-#01GA070771
2) NS-#02GA070771
3) EI-#03GA070771

These refer to Track 1 being part of the natural speech session #01 of G. A., whose birthday is on 07/07/1971; Track 2 being the continuation of the natural speech session #1 of G. A.; and Track 3 being the elicited imitation session #3 of G. A.

3.4.5.2 Labeling Specific Utterances to be Cited in Papers or Presentations

Specific utterances from a corpus should be referred to by utterance number consistent with a database format (e.g., "me up" [1GA070771NS; age 3;02;01, utterance #125]).[12]

3.5 Summary

From the previous sections, we understand that to conduct research in language acquisition, there is an enormous investment of time and resources involved in a given project before the researcher even collects an audio sample of the raw linguistic data from the subject and subsequently during the process of data management. Also, working with human subjects during the actual research recording session can be unpredictable. As a result of this "high cost" of doing linguistic research with human subjects, the CLAL in conjunction with the Cornell University VLL developed the previous guidelines, which apply whether one is conducting naturalistic/observational research or experimental research. The purpose of these guidelines is to provide a set of established steps that, if followed, typically produce a meaningful result for the purposes of collecting raw linguistic data after the lengthy preparatory effort.

---

12 In language acquisition research, this format (or similar ones) is used to indicate children's ages: 3;02;01 means the child is 3 years, 2 months, and 1 day old.

II Experimental and Observational Methods in Language Acquisition Research

4 Studying Language Acquisition Through Collecting Speech

Generative linguists are interested in discovering the grammar (the generative linguistic system) in the mind. They typically ask an adult informant whether they consider a sentence grammatical or not. Through this, the linguist attempts to test a theory-derived hypothesis about the system generating language, its principles, and/or constraints (see Chapter 8 on grammaticality judgment). The judgments provide the linguist's critical data. Other linguists emphasize the data appearing in the form of preexisting collections of actually occurring natural speech. As we suggested in Chapter 1, this has led to what has come to be called *corpus linguistics*, whereby researchers have recorded and transcribed naturally occurring speech across a wide variety of situations.[1] Nowadays, aided by computers, large bodies of such data (in American English, British English, and in other languages) can be, and are being, accumulated and analyzed for various patterns of usage. *Computer corpora* involve wide sets of machine-readable texts, which are used in the development of machine translation, speech recognition, or natural language processing software involved in *computational linguistics.*[2] Generative and corpus-based linguistics are often viewed as in opposition, with the generative approach viewed as theory based, and the latter as data based. However, these approaches are not mutually exclusive. Both approaches must access and study natural speech. These data types must both be reliable.

In studying the young child acquiring language, particularly at the earliest periods, the child's natural speech has historically provided the data of choice (if not necessity). This has been largely because grammaticality judgments, which treat the child as an informant, are not accessible to very young children.[3] The young child at earliest periods of speech production is often not interested in systematic, standardized experimental procedures and situations. Thus, language data must often be captured in the "natural situation" as observed in the child's spontaneous use. As we discuss in Chapter 13, methodologies developed over the last decades

---

[1] See Rosenthal (2002) and Biber, Conrad, and Repen (1998) for introductions to this theory, as well as Clear (1993), Quirk (1992), and Barlow (1996).

[2] The Penn Treebank Project, for instance, annotates large sets of naturally occurring text for subsequent natural language processing analyses—see Marcus, Santorini, and Marcinkiewicz (n.d.; https://catalog.ldc.upenn.edu/docs/LDC95T7/cl93.html).

[3] This is primarily due to the "metalinguistic" analyses the child is required to access (for more information, see Chapter 8).

have now provided new ways to develop experimental studies of infants' language discrimination and/or comprehension even before their language production. However, we are especially interested in evaluating the child's first overt production and comprehension of language and in the developmental course of children's language knowledge over time as revealed through their language production and comprehension.

Thus, although, as we saw in Chapter 1, hypotheses cannot be scientifically tested through observational methods in the way that they are through experimental methods, observations of "natural speech" are critical data for the child language researcher. By strengthening principles and procedures for systematic collection, transcription, and analyses of natural speech, this "observational" method can be strengthened, thus providing a rich basis for future hypotheses testing. As we discuss in this chapter, the first step, collecting reliable natural speech data, requires a sound methodology on the part of the researcher. Natural speech is also collected from adult participants, but it is less frequently used than with children in language acquisition because adults can be studied through more controlled methodologies.

4.1 What Is Natural Speech Data?

Natural speech data consist of speech productions by a subject which have been captured by the researcher in a naturalistic situation. The primary authentic and archival form of these data lies in audio recordings of the sampled speech, possibly supplemented by video recordings. Subsequent transcriptions of the data provide texts that represent and are linked to the audio and video data. Although the audio and/or video files are the authoritative sources of the natural speech data, the speech transcriptions are derivative because they represent a first stage of processing of natural speech data. Natural speech must be so processed to create a corpus that is amenable to reliable research study (Chapters 9 and 10 cover data processing and preparation for analysis in more detail).

As in all research, however, we must follow a systematic and standardized set of procedures to ensure that the observational data obtained will aid us in reliably answering our research questions, leading to the formulation of effective new hypotheses for future testing. A "good" speech sample is one that will provide a significant amount of rich data that can inform these hypotheses and our interpretations. We have developed best practices for collecting good samples of natural speech, which we sketch in the following sections.

The precise methods of natural speech data collection and the purposes for which it is used may vary depending on whether the researcher is working with monolingual or multilingual adults, health- (and/or language-, speech-) impaired subjects, or children during normal language acquisition. We first concentrate on data collection procedures for the purpose of studying normal monolingual language acquisition in children. Most of the procedures we adopt may generalize to other populations and other research purposes related to these (i.e., the assessment of bilingualism in children or adults or the assessment of language or speech pathology in children or adults).

4.2 Creating a Corpus

A *corpus* is created when language has been systematically collected, transcribed, analyzed to some degree, and then annotated. Transcripts, validated by their metadata, can then become available for secondary research. In *primary research*, a researcher generates, collects, transcribes, and analyzes new data. In *secondary research*, a researcher reuses previously collected data, which is often collected by another person for another purpose. The research may be based solely on a previous transcript or transcripts collected by other researchers.

Currently, researchers attempt to collect, store, and disseminate previously collected transcripts of child language, providing Web resources for users around the world. The main such provider for child language acquisition is the Child Language Data Exchange system (http://childes.psy.cmu.edu), as we mentioned in Chapter 2.[4] The Max Planck Institute for Psycholinguistics has developed The Language Archive (https://tla.mpi.nl/), collecting and disseminating various language data and resources, supplemented by data analysis tools such as ELAN (http://www.mpi.nl/corpus/manuals/manual-elan.pdf). Specialized software programs are being developed for the automatic analysis of speech corpora (e.g., http://www.lena foundation.org/lena-pro).

Our emphasis in this manual is on primary research. Our assumption is that the value of any corpus dissemination system will be increased by the quality of the original authoritative data collected through primary research. In this section, we concentrate on methods for generating and collecting new and rich natural speech data.

4.3 Background Information

Early research on language acquisition in the child was founded on studies of children's natural speech. The study of natural speech (also called *spontaneous speech*) began as diary studies, in which a researcher (usually the parent) took notes on his or her

---

[4] See also http://childes.psy.cmu.edu/manuals/Clin-CLAN.pdf.

observations of a child's language. The acceleration of child language studies, which began with Roger Brown's (1973) work at Harvard, was based on systematic and comprehensive longitudinal studies of natural speech samples, initiated with those of three now famous children, "Adam," "Eve," and "Sarah," during early periods of their language acquisition. Today, many studies of language acquisition are based on analyses of children's natural speech samples such as these.

4.4 Why Choose the Natural Speech Task

You may choose to use a natural speech task when you are working with a very young child who has begun some forms of verbal production but whose language production or comprehension cannot be tested easily through experimental methods. Alternatively, you may choose this method when you want to provide converging evidence with experimental methods and tasks (see Chapters 5–8). Some researchers consider natural speech as more indicative of "real language competence" than experimentally elicited speech.

4.4.1 Advantages

Natural speech collection allows us to begin evaluation of the language of very young children at the earliest stages of language production. Natural speech collection captures language from the child that is not determined or "contaminated" by adult language and/or grammar. For both adult and children subjects, natural speech can reveal different language possibilities about which the researcher would not have any preconceptions or would not have thought to test because they do not resemble exactly standard adult productions. It is not influenced by the contrived situations often necessary for controlled experimental methods and is not dependent on specialized performance modes such as the motoric actions necessary for toy-moving or act-out tests of language comprehension. Once collected and converted to data, natural speech can be used and reused in the study of various and differing phenomena and in answering questions about language acquisition and use over time. Like observational data, natural speech data allow the researcher to develop questions, hypotheses, or theories that can subsequently be tested experimentally.

4.4.2 Disadvantages and Limitations

Natural speech is by definition "natural." That is, it is assumed to be occurring spontaneously, without external manipulation of any form or predetermined context.

In fact, each natural speech situation involves specific conditions of the context in which it occurs. Both what is happening around the subject, as well as within the subject, will necessarily affect each condition of language use. Because of its naturalness, any specific natural speech sample includes a specific context which is not replicable. That is, the participant is in a particular place, at a particular time, thinking and talking about particular issues, with particular people, and so forth. It is difficult to generalize beyond a single participant in a specific environment.

Although natural speech samples help us investigate the language a subject produces, it does not help us know what the subject cannot produce or what else the subject can produce and did not produce during the recording session.[5] Thus, it does not directly reveal the grammatical system behind a subject's language knowledge. The absence of a particular linguistic structure in a participant's speech can be explained by many reasons: lack of linguistic competence, lack of exposure to the construction, lack of appropriate discourse or pragmatic motivating contexts in the sample, or simple lack of occurrence in the finite amount of time of the speech sample collected. In a classic example attributed to Karl Popper (1934; see Chapter 11, this volume), we cannot conclude that "platypuses do not lay eggs" because "we have watched platypuses and they did not lay eggs."

Interpreting what a child intends to say is often difficult. Methods such as *rich interpretation* have been developed, wherein the context of natural speech must be carefully considered to determine what a child's utterance may mean and what its structure then must be (Bloom, 1970). Such rich interpretation includes individual decisions by the researcher present at the time of the interview. Bloom (1970) showed that different structures may be assigned to an utterance such as *Mommy sock*, for example, depending on what the child apparently intended at the time (i.e., it can be interpreted as 'This is Mommy's sock' or 'Mommy, put my sock on,' for example).

4.5 What Is Your Purpose? The Role of the Researcher

Your purpose is to capture (on recorded media) instances of the most free, productive, elaborate language that the subject is capable of producing and do so in a manner that can be later studied scientifically. Ideally, in the speech sample, the

---

5 For adult monolingual native speakers of a language who speak a standard dialect, it is possible to assume that they have the linguistic competence to produce and comprehend sentences in their dialect, even if a particular construction has not been found in their natural speech. That assumption cannot be made with other types of speakers (e.g., children, bilingual speakers, second language learners, impaired populations).

child should be trying his or her best to say or capture complex meanings with the best grammatical knowledge at his or her disposal. The child should ideally be "stretching" his or her grammar to say what he or she wants to say. On the basis of such data, the researcher can attain evidence from which to infer the child's grammar.

When collecting natural speech data, the role of the researcher is to trigger, induce, inspire, and allow free productive speech from the subject. The role of the researcher is not to produce a lot of language him- or herself, but to remain in the background until it becomes necessary to encourage or facilitate the production of language by the subject.

Some researchers prefer to act as observers and let the child interact with a parent or other person familiar to the child. However, one has to be careful with this approach. The parent or caretaker is not familiar with good practices for eliciting the best natural speech samples. For example, caregivers that know that the child's language is being studied may try to show the researcher how much the child knows by having him or her say all the animal names he or she knows or having the child sing all the songs learned at school, and so forth. Unless specifically interested in the acquisition of naming, singing, poem recitation, or counting, these samples are of little interest to the researcher who is studying a child's grammatical knowledge. Of course, there are situations in which the main research agenda involves the study of the interaction between adult and child speech, such as those looking at the influence of parental input in early child speech production.

In studying child language, the researcher is interested in the various, perhaps different, ways that children may speak. Apparent deformations of the adult language are the grist for the mill of the researcher because they inform us how the child may or may not differ from the adult. Children must never feel they are making errors because they are not—they are demonstrating their natural language and the grammar for this language. In the same way, studies with adult subjects usually look at the ways in which their speech differs from the adult standard norms, without considering their production a reflection of poor or wrong language.

4.5.1 How to Collect Natural Speech Data

Learning how to elicit a good natural speech sample requires practice. Natural speech may at first appear to be the easiest method of collecting research data with children, but in many ways, it may be the most difficult one. It does not have a clear structure, and it is up to the researcher's imagination to engage the child in conversation or to work with another interlocutor who can ensure rich data. In the following sections, we first review procedures for natural speech sample data collection. We then describe and exemplify properties of "good" and "bad" natural speech samples. We then review a variety of techniques that may help the researcher to generate a good quality natural speech sample and some techniques to avoid. We include insights that individual researchers have developed in learning how to conduct the natural speech method.

4.5.2 Where to Collect Natural Speech Data

The environment has an impact on speech samples. This is especially important for a child, who may feel especially insecure in unfamiliar circumstances. The child should be in an environment that is most conducive to the child talking freely and spontaneously. Lab settings can be intimidating. This may mean that the child is in his or her home and you are with him or her, watching for opportunities where productive natural speech from the child occurs naturally. Alternatively, a researcher may set up an informal "play" or "conversation" setting with a child in a day care center or school. In both cases, the exact place of recording may vary (children may move from inside to outdoors to play).

4.5.3 When to Collect Natural Speech Data

It is recommended that natural speech samples be captured when the best opportunity arises. That is, it is best to follow the child's lead and capture the speech samples at times when the child is most productively speaking. This will happen when children are at a point at which they want to express something to the people they are with. The researcher cannot predetermine when this will happen. Sometimes it will be when a child is taking a bath, going to sleep at night, or climbing a scary staircase; it can be at any time during the day or night, during any activity. Researchers who are collecting a natural speech sample in the home may simply follow the child during the day, starting the recorder whenever the child is productively engaged in speech. This may mean turning the recorder on and off at different moments. Be free to move around. If the researcher is collecting a natural speech sample in a day care center or school as part of a larger research project, the speech sample can be collected at any time during the research session when you judge the child to be most comfortable. Some researchers simply collect all natural speech before, during, and after an experimental interaction and add extra time either before or after the experiment for natural conversation with the child.

4.6 Procedures of the Natural Speech Task: How Does One Capture Natural Speech Data?

4.6.1 Types of Natural Speech Sample Collection

In some cases, a single speech sample will be collected, and a researcher will attempt to derive hypotheses about a particular child's grammar or language knowledge from that sample. In other cases, numerous natural speech samples will be collected, either from a single child or a group of children so that they can be compared. Natural speech samples can be compared in two ways: longitudinally or cross-sectionally (see Chapter 1).

4.6.2 Length and Frequency of Natural Speech Samples

More is always better. It has been estimated that a minimal child speech sample for analysis would contain at least 100 utterances (R. Brown, 1973).[6] Although a sample totaling less than 100 utterances is not recommended, evaluation of the quality of a speech sample depends on the quality of the utterances collected. One hundred utterances that are yes/no responses to questions or naming responses to *What is that?* are not highly valuable (unless one is researching the acquisition of nouns). One can assume that the more natural speech one can collect during a session, the better these data are. There is no ideal length of time to capture a speech sample; the researcher may plan for a minimum of 30 to 60 minutes of recording time.

How frequently one has to collect data will depend on the phenomenon being studied. If one is looking for a particular structure (e.g., wh-questions, relative clauses), the frequency of occurrence of such structure should be taken into account when deciding how much and how frequently to record the subjects to ensure that samples are representative and can capture the desired structures. Tomasello and Stahl (2004) discussed in detail through statistical analyses how likely one is to capture a desired structure depending on sample frequency and structure frequency, thus advocating for determining an appropriate sample characteristic before collecting the data. Ambridge and Rowland (2013) discussed ways in which sampling can underestimate or overestimate production and suggested ways to evaluate the validity of a sample after it has been collected, such as by using the adult interlocutor's data as a control or calculating how particular combinations of items are likely to occur.

---

6 R. Brown (1973) also began the speech sample analysis after an initial set of utterances had been discounted, presumably because the child would need time to acclimate to the researcher. In cases in which the researcher has already established good rapport with the child, such a step in natural speech sample analysis is not necessary.

Exhibit 4.1: Properties of a "Good" Natural Speech Sample Collected From Children

- Provides the researcher with examples of a wide range of sentence structures and types of language use
- Numerous multiword utterances (unless the child is naturally using only single words)
- Lots of talking by the child
- The child attempts to convey many different ideas in different ways
- The child repetitively attempts different sentence structures and word forms
- Little adult domination in the sample
- Questions by adults lead to full sentence explanations by the child
- Good audio quality
- Examples of the child saying things "in their own way" (e.g., *feets*, without adult corrections)

4.7 Characteristics of "Good" and "Poor" Natural Speech Samples

Exhibits 4.1 and 4.2 provide some key properties of "good" and "poor" natural speech samples.

4.7.1 "Good" and "Poor" Natural Speech Examples

Transcribed examples of samples of "good" and "poor" natural speech research sessions are provided in Exhibits 4.3 and 4.4. The samples have been transcribed "free form." Before such samples become actual data, they require phonetic editing (i.e., the phonetic alphabet should be used, especially in cases in which the child has deformed the adult model) so a researcher can tell exactly how the child (and/or adult) pronounced these deformations. See Chapters 3 and 9, which include systematic metadata systems of identifying speech, and Appendix A for an explanation of symbols and abbreviations used in the transcripts.

Exhibit 4.2: Properties of a "Poor" Natural Speech Sample Collected From Children

- Minimal production by the child
- Lots of one-word utterances, few multiword productions
- Poor audio quality
- Lots of naming in answers to adult questions (e.g., *What's that?*)
- Lots of monosyllabic child utterance (e.g., yes/no answers)
- Adult interference in the child's speech or utterances
- Requests for rote responses (e.g., *Thank you*)
- Many unintelligible utterances
- The researcher may not realize that the child's pace may differ from the adult's. The adult may think that the child has finished talking just because the child is silent for a while. In fact, the child may actually be just pausing between sentences. One must learn to wait.

Exhibit 4.3: Example of a "Good" Natural Speech Sample

Child (Initials, 2;05,08)—produced Multi-Word Utterances

S1:	whatcha find there? *(watcha = what did you)*
S:	anove doggie. *(anove = another)*
S1:	another one?
S1:	does he move his legs?
S1:	he does.
S:	dis is a bwown doggie. *(dis = this, bwown = brown)*
S1:	you're right.
S1:	it is a brown one.
S:	I dwoppeduh. (can't tell what *dwoppeduh* is, it may be *dropped*)
S1:	there e is. *(e = he)*
R:	do you have a dog at home, Emma?
S:	no.
R:	no.
R:	do you like dogs?
S:	yu. *(yu = yes)*
R:	{what}
S:	{bu}I'm scared of dum. *(bu = but, dum = them)*
R:	you are?
R:	how come?
S	be . . . because de bak ame. *(de = they, bak = bark, ame = at me)*
R:	oh, they do.
R:	I know sometimes dogs bark loud, huh?
S:	yea.
R:	oh, what kind of animals do you like?
R:	oop.
S:	uh oh.
R:	uh oh.
R:	what happened?
S:	I puwd dis out [åvls] ho. *(puwd = pulled, dis = this, [åvls] = of this/his, ho = hole)*
S:	pud it back in hea. *(pud = put, hea = here)*
R:	can you do it?
S:	e can. *(e = I, can = can't)*
R:	oh that's hard.
R:	it's a small hole, isn't it?
S:	pus! *(pus = push)*
S:	can you do it?
R:	sure, I can try.
R:	oop, let's see.
R:	you wanna watch me do it? *(wanna = want to)*
R:	you wanna help me?

Exhibit 4.3: Example of a "Good" Natural Speech Sample (Continued)

S:	why?
R:	lemme see. (*lemme = let me*)
R:	push!
R:	www
R:	there ya go, all fixed. (*ya = you*)
R:	so what kind of animals do you like, Emma?
S:	he have a teeny little tail. (referring to a toy animal they are looking at)
R:	he does, doesn't he?
R:	oh he's cute.
R:	I wonder where his other leg is.
S:	whea? (*whea = where*)
R:	I don't know.
S:	can dis stand up? (*dis = this*)
S:	no.
R:	no?
S:	I must bwoke et too. (*bwoke = broke, et = it*)
R:	I don't know if you broke it.
	www
R:	see?
R:	you didn't break it.
R:	it's ok.
S:	I can do it. (*can = can't*)
R:	I can try.
R:	let's see.
R:	so, which one is your favorite animal, Emma?
R:	can you show me and tell me what it is?
R:	why is that one your favorite?
S:	because i's my fave. (*i's = it's/he's, fave = favorite*)
S:	an dis one is my favri. (*an = and, dis = this, favri = favorite*)
R:	yea.
R:	how come?
R:	tell me!
R:	why?
R:	{what do you^}
S:	{becus>...}becus i's my favorite. (*becus = because, i's = it's/he's*)
R:	what do you like about it?
R:	do you like his{face?}
S:	{an} de cat. (*an = and, de = the*)
R:	and the cat?
S:	and I like de cas. (*de = the, cas = cats*)

Exhibit 4.4: Example of a "Poor" Natural Speech Sample

Child (Initials, 2;00;02)

R: okay, let's see what we have here.
M: say *thank you*!
S: thank you.
R: do you have a teddy bear like that?
S: yeah.
R: you do?
M: it's not true.
R: do you have a teddy bear like that?
M: where's the *thank you*?
S: thank you.
R: X how about ...
M: that's even littler.
M: it's the tiniest teddy-bear.
M: where's the *thank you* for that one?
S: anch you. (*anch* = *thank*)
M: well, we get lots of *thank you*'s anyhow.
R: X
R: how about....
M: another one.
M: how many?
M: do you have one teddy bear?
S: yes.
M: do you have two teddy bears?
M: do you have two?
S: yeah.
M: how old are you?
S: [æmwa]. ([æmwa] = *I'm one*)
M: are you two?
S: yeah.
M: when were you two?
S: one
R: one.
R: you were one first and then you were two?
R: is that right?
S: yes.
M: yes.
M: how many teddy bears do you have?
M: you have two over here.
M: do you have another teddy bear?
M: how about that teddy bear?
M: where did you get your teddy bear?
M: ...where did it come from?
S: um, de [baejg]. (*de* = *the*, [baejg] = *bag*)
M: the bag.
R: in bag, right.

Exhibit 4.4: Example of a "Poor" Natural Speech Sample (Continued)

M:	did Grandpa have teddy bears?
S:	yes.
M:	in the country?
M:	how did you get to the country?
S:	[ej] tray, ee. (may be *by train*)
M:	how?
S:	[ejii]. (can't tell what child is saying)
M:	X that's a little dull.
R:	did you fall down?
R:	you know I think he sits down … does he sit down?
S:	no.
R:	no?
R:	do his legs move?
S:	… is ands. (*is = his, ands = hands*)
R:	his hands move?
M:	does he have ears?
R:	uh.
M:	are those his ears?
S:	yeah.
M:	do you have ears?
M:	where're my ears? (*where're = where are*)
M:	it's more like show and tell, right?
S:	here.

4.7.2 Going From "Poor" to "Good"

One researcher, as an undergraduate student in the Cornell Language Acquisition Lab, recounted the gradual development of her application of the natural speech method:

> Throughout the semester, I improved my technique to minimize … negative outcomes. For instance, when I look back at my first natural speech sample with [one of the children I interviewed], there is a lot more interruption of the child on my part than there is nearer to the end of the semester (during which there was hardly any). This was not because I meant to interrupt her, but because I wanted to seem like I was listening to her story, rather than having her feel like she was talking to a wall. She could have talked and talked and talked without any interruption from me, but I felt necessary to interject so that she knew I was listening to her. I was using the "empathy" approach I learned when counseling, and responding with *uhhuh* and *mmhm* and *wow* to the different parts of her story. But I learned that is not necessary when working with all children. It is better not to interrupt and to let the child continue, if the child is speaking.
>
> Some children do need responses, but if they do, then they will stop talking, in which case then I can respond. But other children are content to talk on and on without any verbal feedback. My other reason for interrupting was because sometimes I thought the children were done speaking, but it would turn out that they weren't. I disliked awkward pauses, so I would talk to fill the silence if they paused for too long. But I started learning (and am still learning) to allow more time for silence, to see if the child has anything else to say. … I learned that "naming" is sometimes

necessary, but is only really useful when it is used as a springboard. One does not want to ask the child questions to which they will reply *yes/no* or one-word answers or names. But we have to start somewhere. So, often, I would start out asking the child the name of his/her stuffed animal, and then progress to more in-depth questions, such as how he got the stuffed animal, or why he named it that, or who gave it to him/her. (Moskowitz, 2000, pp. 5–6)[7]

No single technique for generating rich natural speech samples can be predetermined. Every natural speech situation is dependent on the individual personality of the child and the researcher or interlocutor and their relation at the moment the sample is collected. No collection experience will be perfect. Several issues can be considered, however.

4.8 Topic Selection

When trying to induce children's natural speech, topic selection (i.e., what will be the topic being discussed?) by the researcher may not be necessary. Because the task is to follow the child's lead, it is always the child who should determine the topic of conversation, if possible (e.g., the bubbles in the bath water, the dripping stripes on an ice cream cone). However, if a researcher is working with a limited amount of time and in a restricted situation, as is often the case, the researcher must be able to elicit conversation from the child. An inspired researcher, in this case, will have to be able to relate to the child, finding a topic about which the child can become enthused. Choosing a topic in this way can be key to getting the child engaged to participate in the research. When preparing to work with a child, it is beneficial if the researcher can identify topics that are salient and intriguing to children or to the specific child who is the research participant. Student researcher **Lauren Moskowitz** suggested some possible topics 2- to 5-year-olds love to talk about

- their stuffed animals;
- real animals;
- their brothers or sisters;
- times that they were sick or got hurt:

    Every child seems to enjoy telling their war stories and showing their battle wounds and provoking your sympathy and awe at what brave children they are (e.g., *see my bruise here?* . . . *And here's the cut I got when I falled off it* . . . *My doctor put stitches in-in-in-in my ear.*) (Moskowitz, 2000, pp. 8–9);

---

7 Lauren Moskowitz, now Dr. Moskowitz, teaches at St. John's University. The quotations from her unpublished manuscript are reprinted with her permission.

- famous characters, either from popular children's movies or TV shows or books or theme parks (e.g., Disneyland); and
- birthdays and holidays and the presents that they receive.

4.9 Questioning

Questioning can trigger productive natural speech. However, such questioning must be open ended. Yes/no questions will most probably lead to monosyllabic answers (yes or no). Open-ended questions require that the response is in the form of a sentence (see Chapter 2). Questions about actions, events, behaviors, or causal relations are often more effective than questions about objects or individuals. One strategy in getting children to talk is to ask them questions that have to do with who, why, or how, rather than what or when questions, which can be answered more simply and without elaboration. For instance, Moskowitz (2000) observed:

> When I showed Maya one of the "job cards" (of a firefighter) and asked her what the person in the picture was doing, she replied *getting the fire out*. The most important thing I've found, when a child answers any question, is to try to take that answer to the next level by asking the child *how* or *why*. So I asked Maya, *Getting the fire out? How do you do that?* to which she replied, *You get water and fired it on.* I marveled at her novel usage of language. (p. 10)

4.10 Requests for Repetition

Children's speech is often not as clear as that of adults. Many times, even the parent does not understand what the child is saying. One can ask for repetitions and clarification from time to time, although most children will get frustrated if one does this too often. Lauren Moskowitz again shared her insight:

> Sometimes, you just have to pretend you understood what the child said (since you don't want to make them feel like they aren't making sense). It is also useful to repeat what the child just said to make sure you heard him or her correctly. This helps when collecting the data, since you can clarify what it is the child is saying; and it also helps in transcribing the data later. (Moskowitz, 2000, p. 6)

4.11 Use of Books

Conversation with a child can be elicited in the presence of a storybook. Often, this situation can lead to productive speech by the child and serve to initiate a topic of discourse between child and interlocutor. However, children are often used to having books read to them, so they may not be inclined to offer much spontaneous productive speech in the context of a book. Individual children will differ in this context, as in others. Be aware of the possibility that the child is simply copying or imitating stories that she or he has heard, rather than creating his or her own—in this case, the speech sample will be not as natural as it would be during other forms of researcher–child dialogue. Books can be useful props, but in using them, the researcher must avoid the child being drawn into listening to the book rather than producing creative, productive speech.

4.12 Storytelling and Pretend Play

By asking children to make up a story or to play make-believe with dolls, we can get a sample of their most complex productions, which happen as they try to "create" stories and situations. Their utterances will be less hindered by adult interference during the monologue of a child's story versus a dialogue between the child and researcher. Sometimes, children are not used to telling stories (they are usually used to hearing stories told by adults), so one can usually not simply ask these children to "tell me a story" and have them do it. One approach is to use a doll or stuffed animal and to pretend to be that animal while talking to them. Some researchers have found that children interact more easily with stuffed animals than with the researcher.

A technique that may work is telling the child that the stuffed animal is going to take a nap. This eases the children and gives them an explanation of why they are away from the classroom. The researcher then asks the child whether he or she could make up a story to tell to the animal to help him fall asleep. This makes sense to most children because most of their parents tell them or read them stories at night when they go to sleep. In the best-case scenario, the child then creates his or her own tale, and we see how complex a preschooler's use of language can be. Moskowitz (2000) again offered her insights:

> In this way, we can see the wonderful things a child's mind can create, such as [this story from one of the child subjects about a sharptooth] *suddenly a big monster came in that was a sharptooth and the sharptooth were gonna eat them.* I know she's never encountered a sharptooth, but we see how a child can think of things that she's never experienced. (pp. 13–14)

By asking the child to tell a bedtime story to a stuffed animal, the child can be convinced of the value of what he or she is about to say because children know how valuable a bedtime story is. We may see repetitions of attempts at different sentence structures because the child is making the sentences up on the spur of the moment and is constantly revising her or his sentences as she or he speaks to get it out as wanted. In some cases, the child repeats the same utterance over and over, saying it the same way or changing it. In other cases, the child changes his or her sentence before actually finishing it. These are the types of deformations, changes, and self-corrections that we are interested in because we interpret these as possible evidence regarding the child's grammar.

Sometimes the researcher can tell a story first. Storytelling helps build rapport with children and inspires them to tell their own tales and talk about their feelings. Although the researcher is supposed to remain in the background, it helps build the children's trust if the researcher reveals his or her emotions and the self-disclosure in turn makes children reveal thoughts or feelings to the researcher. As Moskowitz (2000) articulated:

> I think that children's most complex linguistic interactions occur when they are speaking to other children in the context of playing together. So, in my interactions with the children, I try to replicate that scenario . . . because the children recognize that I am not one of them, yet they don't see me on the same level as other adults. As [one child participant] once told me, *you're just like my mommy . . . except she growed up more.* (p. 15)

4.13 Use of Props and Cautions to Consider

The use of props and context set-up can be a powerful tool for the researcher to cultivate children's natural speech. However, these are situation dependent. For example, the personality of one child may lead him or her to respond better when the researcher uses a prop than when the researcher applies some of the discussion techniques described earlier, or the child may respond better to one prop than another. However, props have to be the right kind because the child can end up quietly playing with the toy and not speaking.

4.14 Eliciting Specific Linguistic Phenomena

As we have seen, if one is interested in a specific phenomenon or issue in language acquisition, a particular speech sample may not reveal evidence regarding what you most want to study. Sometimes it may; however, at other times, the researcher may want to take steps to adapt a natural speech methodology.

Depending on the question in which the researcher is interested, natural speech samples may be more or less useful. For example, overgeneralization may occur in natural speech samples without any trigger. *Overgeneralization* is the process by which a child applies a general rule to inappropriate cases—for example, when the child applies a regular verb rule to an irregular verb producing *broked* or *breaked*. Overgeneralizations are an example of an important phenomenon that the researcher may want to study because they may show the child's creativity and his or her acquisition of a grammatical system. Here the child is using forms that he or she cannot have heard from an adult speaker.

Moskowitz (2000) developed ways of favoring the occurrence of overgeneralization:

> I learned that one way to try to inspire that is to ask the child a question pertaining to what he just said or did while using the past tense. For instance, children most often speak in the present tense when you ask them about what they're doing. One strategy I often employed was to ask them to repeat what they just said, but asking my question using *what did you do?* versus *what are you doing?* For instance, when I ask [one of the child participants] *What is Franklin doing?* she replied, *He jumping too!* (which, in itself, was interesting because she left out the word *is*). I had heard her say the word *flied* before in conversation that was not on tape, so I asked her (using *did* and not *doing*), *Did he fly over there or did he jump?* She then replied, *He flied*. I wanted to get her to say the past tense of *fly* again, to see if she would correct herself or repeat it incorrectly, so I asked her, *Did the rock fly over that too?* She answered me with, *I flied over it too!* I found this interesting because she repeated the incorrect version twice in a row, whereas other times I've heard her say something incorrectly, and two minutes later say the same thing in a grammatically correct way. This showed me the variance not only between different children, but the variance within the same child. (p. 8)

4.15 Triggered Natural Speech

Triggered natural speech (TNS) is a speech elicitation technique that involves natural speech collection but that adds a more structured role for the researcher who has specific research questions in mind. The TNS task was used at the Cornell Language Acquisition Laboratory by a former student, Stephanie Berk, in an attempt to make natural speech sessions more productive in terms of specific language productions—namely, questions by the child (Berk, 1996). An earlier version of this method was developed by Labov and Labov in 1978. In Berk's (1996) study, it was found that nontriggered natural speech samples often produced a great amount of fragment utterances, such as shown in the following example from Berk (p. 39):

> Subject 1, age 2;8
>
> R: can we make them play with each other?
>
> R: let's see if they can play.
>
> S: uh.
>
> S: [dej] um camel. (*[dej]* may be *there*, *um* may be a mark of hesitation or the determiner *a*).
>
> S: and there's [wʌn] rhinoceros. (can't tell what *[wʌn]* is)
>
> R: there are two of them.

R: www (Researcher talking for a while.)

R: they look

S: dat hippo! (*dat = that*).

The problem with such fragmentary utterances is that they rarely contain any complex constructions that a child may have the competence for but seldom the opportunity to produce in everyday situations. Through repeated experience collecting natural speech, Berk discovered that longer and more complex sentences could be elicited by asking a child to flesh out his or her questions and comments by claiming to not understand them.

TNS collection, like natural speech collection, consists of allowing a child to produce his or her utterances with no or few experimental constraints (maybe using pictures or toys as stimuli). Through the intervention of the researcher, the child is requested to produce more complete sentences. Although Berk (1996) was interested in children's acquisition of questions, in the natural speech samples she was collecting, there were few occurrences of questions to study. Children would often ask *Why?* but here the researcher does not discover evidence regarding the child's knowledge of the syntax or semantics of question formation. In TNS, Berk developed a "trigger," by responding, *Why what?* This often led the child to describe the question in a more complete form, including a fully formed sentence with a question.

4.15.1 Example of the Triggered Natural Speech Task: Question Formation

As part of her broader study investigating subject–verb inversion in questions from child speech (Santelmann, Berk, Austin, Somashekar, & Lust, 2002), Berk (1996) developed and used the TNS method to collect samples of wh-questions in children's language development. The purpose was to inquire about children's knowledge of inversion in this context. The study used 16 subjects aged 1;06 to 3;07 and divided them into five age groups. The researcher chose passages from popular storybooks (*101 Dalmatians, Bambi, Peter Pan*, and *The Little Mermaid*), accompanied by drawings of the actions described, as stimuli to elicit speech. Each subject was read 24 to 28 of these passages and shown the accompanying picture. He or she was instructed to say *flip it* when he or she wanted to move on to the next picture. During the time a picture was being shown and a passage being read, the child was free to ask questions, make comments, or be silent. Some relevant pieces of the story were missing so the child would have to ask clarification questions.

The novel element introduced by TNS came whenever a child produced a question consisting of a single wh-word. This is when the researcher would ask for elaboration by adding *what*, as in *Why what?* As seen in the partial transcript that follows, this tended to yield a complete wh-question, which of course increased the proportion of the latter in the overall sample.

> R: they're sitting in the water.
>
> S: why?
>
> R: why what?
>
> S: why dey sidding in de water? (*dey* = they, sidding = sitting) (Berk, 1996, p. 48)

The final speech sample consisted of 19.44% questions, with more wh-questions than yes/no questions. This was opposite to findings from studies of nonguided natural speech, which have produced fewer questions as a whole and fewer yes/no than wh-questions.

4.15.2 Advantages of Triggered Natural Speech

- More utterances and more utterances of a more complex nature are elicited than in usual natural speech sessions.
- The speech sample produced, although not completely predictable, can be directed to cover certain constructions of interest (e.g., wh-questions) through handling of the stimuli.
- This task can be useful to researchers who wish to study a certain area of child language and who have a research question in mind.
- TNS data contain a greater variety and amount of speech acts, including complete declaratives, fragments, interjections, questions, and explicatives (Berk, 1996), compared with nontriggered natural speech.
- These data reflect a child's competence and preference for certain structures because children are free to produce speech in whatever way and quantity they choose with no direct restrictions from the researcher.
- This method has been successfully used with children as young as 2;04 years of age.

4.15.3 Disadvantages of Triggered Natural Speech

- Even when using specific stimuli such as toys or children's books, it is not guaranteed that certain structures of interest will be produced or that they will be produced in great enough amounts for systematic study by a researcher.
- Like all natural speech collection methods, TNS is less suitable for studies that ask specific questions about language acquisition.

4.15.4 Summary

The TNS task has its origins as a strategy for making natural speech collection sessions more productive and allowing researchers to elicit more speech from children who may not "naturally" say much relevant to the researcher's question. TNS combines the benefits of naturalistic observation and experimental methods. You would choose this method if you are looking for data about a particular area of a child's language, yet you are open to collecting a variety of utterances and to making new discoveries.

4.16 Preparation of Natural Speech Data for Transcription and Analyses

Natural speech, by definition, is characterized by an immense amount of variation that cannot be controlled. Thus, natural speech does not become research data until the audio recording has been transcribed, metadata recorded and linked to the speech sample, transcription reliability checked and edited, and the audio recording and final transcript archived. Until these steps have been taken, natural speech is simply equivalent to whatever we continually hear each other say in passing every day. We describe these procedures in Chapters 3 and 9.

4.17 Summary

Natural speech samples vary greatly in quality, depending largely on the skill, inspiration, and training of the researcher or interlocutor who is collecting the sample. In some sense, such samples are never completely natural because they depend on the skill of the researcher to elicit rich productive speech by the subject. The richness of a particular speech sample will depend on the amount and quality of elicited speech the researcher has been able to induce. The scientific worth of a particular speech sample (its potential for providing reliable data that can be compared across speech samples and with data from experimental methods of language elicitation) will rest on the adoption of best practices for metadata archiving and data processing (e.g., transcription and analyses; see Chapters 9 and 10).

5 Introduction to Experimental Methods: Design and Analysis

Because language knowledge represented in a child's mind cannot be directly observed but only inferred from the child's language behavior, we must adopt a well-grounded scientific method to elicit reliable language data from children. Only then can we use this language data to validate theoretically guided predictions about children's language competence.

Children's language data can be obtained in two different ways: (a) they can be observed naturally, giving us "natural speech data" or (b) they can be elicited experimentally through a prompted task. Though natural speech data produced spontaneously by children in natural settings are considered to reflect language competence, these data are highly "uncontrolled." Any given utterance in a particular speech setting can be affected by a number of factors operating independently or in combination; thus, it is sometimes difficult to interpret. For example, if a child does not produce a particular sentence within a given speech sample collected by a researcher, it could be argued that the child does not have the competence to produce that particular sentence. However, this instead may simply mean that the child had no motivation or no opportunity to produce that sentence. Thus, to clearly assess a child's grammatical competence, we need language data elicited experimentally under controlled conditions using different tasks. Language data elicited experimentally are considered to be more relevant for testing hypotheses. The experimental method begins with asking a research question and formulating a research hypothesis. Then a series of well-planned procedures are formed that allow a researcher to test directly a theory-driven hypothesis by manipulating variables and observing the outcome of the manipulation under strictly controlled conditions. Major activities in experimental research include

- asking research questions and formulating research hypotheses,
- designing the experiment,
- choosing an appropriate language-eliciting task and preparing the testing materials,
- identifying the participant population and selecting a sample,
- following the predetermined procedure and conducting the experiment,
- using appropriate statistics for analyzing the data and testing the hypothesis, and
- documenting the research results and sharing the research findings.

This chapter is contributed by Yuchin Chien, PhD, Department of Psychology, California State University, San Bernardino, and is based on her presentation at the Linguistic Society of America at Stanford University, titled "An Overview of Experimental Research Methodology for Language Acquisition."

5.1 Asking Research Questions and Formulating Research Hypotheses

The starting point of any scientific research involves asking a "good" research question. In science, a "good research question" must be researchable and specific. Moreover, it must be a question that does not already have a robust answer. *Researchable* means "testable," and *specific* means "not ambiguous" or "not vague." If a question can be refined to a degree that it is not ambiguous and can be empirically tested, then the question is a "good" research question. Consider Example (1).

Example (1): "Which comes first, the chicken or the egg?"

Example (1) is not a good research question because it is not researchable, or testable. On the one hand, you need a chicken to lay an egg, but on the other, you need an egg to hatch a chicken. No chickens, so no eggs, and no eggs, so no chickens. There is no way we can conduct research to find out the answer. How about example (2)?

Example (2): "Will babies who listen to music produce more cooing sounds than babies who do not listen to music?"

This question is a good research question because it is testable and it is specific (not vague, not ambiguous). To find the answer, you can create a situation under which a group of babies will listen to music and a situation under which a group of babies will not listen to music. You can then measure the babies' production of cooing sounds to see whether the babies who listen to music actually produce more cooing sounds than the babies who do not. Now consider example (3), a language acquisition question raised in Flynn and Lust (1980).

Example (3): "Are headless or free relative clauses developmental precursors of lexically headed relative clauses?"

In other words, will children find sentences like *Cookie Monster hits **what pushes Big Bird*** easier to produce than sentences such as *Big Bird pushes **the balloon** which bumps Ernie*, in which the relative clause is headed by a full noun phrase (the balloon) instead of a pronoun (what)? Example 3 is a good research question because it is testable and not ambiguous.

Once a research question has been stated in researchable and specific terms, a corresponding research hypothesis can then be generated. A *research hypothesis* is a statement closely related to the research question that can be viewed as the tentative "yes" answer to the research question and states the predicted relationship between the variables in which we are interested. For example, a tentative "yes" answer to the "baby-cooing" question in Example 2 can be "Babies who listen to music will produce more cooing sounds than babies who do not listen to music." This is the research hypothesis. Here, a clear prediction is made between two variables that interest us: one has to do with the situation concerning "music presentation" (i.e., music or no music) and the other one has to do with "the amount of cooing sounds produced by the babies" (i.e., more or less). This hypothesis can be tested and verified (confirmed or disconfirmed).

In Example 3, the corresponding research hypothesis to the language acquisition question might be "Headless relative clauses are developmental precursors of lexically headed relative clauses." In other words, children will find sentences such as *Cookie Monster hits what pushes Big Bird* easier to produce than sentences such as *Big Bird pushes the balloon which bumps Ernie.*

To generate a research hypothesis corresponding to your research question, follow the theory you assume and convert your research question into an affirmative statement.

5.2 Designing the Experiment

Designing the experiment is a crucial activity. A well-thought-out experimental design ensures the capability of collecting reliable and valid experimental data. Designing an experiment involves the following steps:

- making certain the proposed hypothesis can be tested,
- specifying the major variables (independent and dependent),
- identifying potential extraneous or confounding variables that may obscure our results, and
- finding an appropriate way to control for possible extraneous or confounding variables.

5.2.1 Ensuring That the Hypothesis Can Be Tested

In designing an experiment, first make certain that the experimental design allows testing of the proposed hypothesis. In our baby-cooing example, the hypothesis is "Babies who listen to music will produce more cooing sounds than babies who do not listen to music." To make certain this hypothesis can be tested, we have to include two conditions: (a) a condition under which a group of babies will listen to music and (b) a condition under which a group of babies will not listen to music. If we include only one condition, the "music" condition, but not the "no-music" condition, we are not testing the proposed hypothesis because there is no basis for making a comparison. The same is true with regard to the relative clause example. To test the hypothesis "Headless relatives are developmental precursors of lexically headed relatives," we make sure we consider all relevant sentence structures required to test it, at least the headless relative clauses and the lexically headed relative clauses.

5.2.2 The Independent and Dependent Variables

In most experimental studies dealing with determining potential cause-and-effect relationships, the *independent variable* is the variable we manipulate—the presumed cause. The *dependent variable* is the variable we observe or measure—the presumed effect. When we say, "if X then Y," we have the conditional conjunction between an independent variable *X* and a dependent variable *Y*. The "if" part is the *antecedent* (the presumed cause), and the "then" part is the *consequent* (the presumed effect).

It is important that we do not confuse an independent variable with a dependent variable. An easy way to find out which variable is the independent variable and which is the dependent variable in our study is to plug the two variables into the "if...then" statement. If the "if...then" statement is logical, the variable that goes with the "if" part is the independent variable, and the variable that goes with the "then" part is the dependent variable. Here, the two possibilities are (a) "If the babies listen/not listen to music, then they will produce more/less cooing sounds," and (b) "If the babies produce more/less cooing sounds, then they will listen/not listen to music." Only the first one makes sense. Therefore, listening or not listening to music is the independent variable and amount of cooing sounds (more or less) is the dependent variable.

Consider the relative clause example. "Sentence type" (including headless relative clauses and lexically headed relative clauses) is the independent variable, and children's responses (i.e., number of correct imitations) is the dependent variable. This is because, presumably, sentences with different types of relative clauses will have differential effects on the child's responses (i.e., number of correct imitations). We would say: "If headless relatives are developmental precursors of lexically headed relatives, then children's correct imitations of the sentences with headless relatives will be greater than those with lexically headed relatives." The antecedent associated with the "if" part is "sentence type"—the independent variable. The consequent associated with the "then" part is "number of correct imitations"—the dependent variable.

In most language acquisition studies, age or language development (language proficiency) level is often the independent variable. However, it is important to note that age must be treated as what is known as a *quasi-independent variable*. In an experiment, a true independent variable can be manipulated, and, if desired, one could randomly assign different participants to different conditions of the independent variable. A quasi-independent variable, however, is an independent variable that cannot be manipulated. It is a variable on which groups of participants naturally differ. Thus, it is not possible for us to randomly assign different children to different age groups. When we are interpreting our results, it is important to keep in mind that a potential cause-and-effect relationship can only be inferred between a true independent variable and a dependent variable. It is not possible to infer a cause-and-effect relationship between a quasi-independent variable and a dependent variable.

Furthermore, an independent variable can be classified as either a between-subjects variable or a within-subjects variable. This distinction has to do with how a subject will be tested when different conditions of a particular independent variable are considered. An independent variable should include at least two conditions. If a subject is tested just one time under one particular treatment condition of an independent variable, we say that the independent variable is a *between-subjects variable*. If each subject is repeatedly tested one at a time under all treatment conditions of an independent variable, we say that the independent variable is a *within-subjects variable*.

Suppose we are interested in finding out whether different types of music (piano, violin, guitar) have differential effects on babies' production of cooing sounds. If we test 12 babies in each condition, and each baby is tested just one time under one condition, we need three different groups of 12 babies each for a total of 36 babies. Here, the independent variable "type of music" is considered to be a between-subjects variable. Each baby can be tested only one time under one condition; if a baby is randomly assigned to the piano condition, he or she will listen only to piano music, not violin or guitar music. Therefore, the independent variable is a between-subjects variable. A between-subjects variable can also be called a *nonrepeated measures variable* (see Figure 5.1).

If we are interested in finding out whether three types of music have differential effects on the babies' production of cooing sounds, we could test 12 babies in each condition, but this time, instead of testing each baby just one time under one condition, each of the 12 babies would first be tested under one of the three music conditions (the piano). After a reasonable time (say after 1 day), the same 12 babies would be tested under another music condition (the violin). Then after another day, they would be tested under the third (guitar) condition. In this situation, we only need one group of 12 babies. Here, the independent variable "type of music" is considered to be a within-subjects variable.

	Type of music	
Piano	Violin	Guitar
G1 ($n = 12$)	G2 ($n = 12$)	G3 ($n = 12$)

Fig. 5.1: An example of a between-subjects (nonrepeated-measures) variable. G = group; n = number of subjects. Each baby is randomly assigned into one of the three groups (G1, G2, or G3), with 12 babies in each group. The babies in G1 listen to the piano music; G2 listen to the violin, and G3 listen to the guitar.

	Type of music	
Piano	Violin	Guitar
Day 1	Day 2	Day 3
G1 ($n = 12$)	→	→

Fig. 5.2: An example of a within-subjects (repeated-measures) variable. G = group; n = number of subjects. We only need one group of 12 babies (G1), and every baby in the group listens to piano, violin, and guitar one at a time (e.g., Day 1, Piano; Day 2, Violin; and Day 3, Guitar). With six possible presentation orders, it is recommended that two babies be tested with each order. In the table, we only illustrate one of the six presentation orders (i.e., piano → violin → guitar).

The order for presenting the three different types of music to subjects does not always have to be the same for every subject;[1] different subjects can be tested with different orders. However, it is better if we test the same number of subjects with each order. This has to do with an important concept called *counterbalancing*, which we briefly discuss later. Imagine that you are one of the baby subjects; because you will repeatedly be tested under different conditions, you will listen to piano music one day, violin music another day, and guitar music the third day, completing the three different conditions of the independent variable "type of music" within each subject. Therefore, the independent variable is a within-subjects variable. A within-subjects variable can also be called a *repeated measures variable* (see Figure 5.2).

In language acquisition studies, grammatical factors (e.g., "sentence type") are often manipulated as within-subjects (or repeated measures) variables. In the relative clause study, three different types of sentences were included (each with a different type of relative clause): Type I sentences—lexically headed relative clauses with determinate heads such as *balloon* (*Big Bird pushes **the balloon** which bumps Ernie*); Type II sentences—lexically headed relative clauses with indeterminate heads such as *thing* (*Ernie pushes **the thing** which touches Big Bird*); and Type III sentences—free relatives with nonovert heads indicated by Ø (*Cookie Monster hits Ø what pushes Big Bird*). Each child was asked to imitate all sentence types and, thus, was repeatedly tested or measured using all sentence types. This means within each subject the different conditions of the independent variable were completed. Thus, sentence type was a within-subjects variable.

Here, there was also a second grammatical independent variable, "function of relative clause." This variable included two conditions (OS vs. OO), and it was also manipulated as a within-subjects (repeated measures) variable. OS—object in main clause and subject in relative clause (*Ernie pushes **the thing** which ø touches Big Bird*);

---

[1] Considering piano (*P*), violin (*V*), and guitar (*G*), there are six possible presentation orders (PVG, PGV, VPG, VGP, GPV, GVP).

Tab. 5.1: Twelve Test Items of the Relative Clause Study Organized by Independent Variables: Sentence Type (Type I, Type II, and Type III) and Function of Relative Clause (OS and OO)

		Type I	Type II	Type III
OS	1	Big Bird pushes the balloon which bumps Ernie. (A3)	Ernie pushes the thing which touches Big Bird. (A1)	Cookie Monster hits what pushes Big Bird. (A4)
	2	Kermit the Frog bumps the block which touches Ernie. (B2)	Scooter hits the thing which touches Kermit the Frog. (B1)	Kermit the Frog pushes what touches Scooter. (B5)
OO	1	Ernie touches the balloon which Big Bird throws. (A5)	Cookie Monster eats the thing which Ernie kicks. (A2)	Cookie Monster pushes what Big Bird throws. (A6)
	2	Scooter grabs the candy which Fozzie Bear eats. (B4)	Fozzie Bear kisses the thing which Kermit the Frog hits. (B6)	Fozzie Bear hugs what Kermit the Frog kisses. (B3)

Note: The 12 items were organized into two test batteries or lists (A and B). Each battery contains six items (one from each of the six treatment combinations). The number associated with each list denotes the presentation order (A1–A6 and B1–B6). Some children were tested with List A before B and some were tested with List B before A.

OO—object in main clause and object in relative clause (*Cookie Monster eats **the thing** which Ernie kicks Ø*). Each child subject was asked to imitate both the OS and the OO sentences. Thus, "function of relative clause" was also a within-subjects (or repeated measures) variable.

The two variables ("sentence type" and "function of relative clause") together make up six treatment combinations: Type I-OS, Type I-OO, Type II-OS, Type II-OO, Type III-OS, and Type III-OO. There were two items for each treatment combination, yielding a total of 12 test items, as shown in Table 5.1.

5.2.3 The Link Between Variations of Variables and Experimental Designs

The concepts related to the independent variable can be used to determine the design of an experiment. If a design has only one independent variable, the design is called a *single-factor design*. If the independent variable in the experiment is a between-subjects variable, the design is a *single-factor between-subjects design*. If the independent variable is a within-subjects variable, the design is a *single-factor within-subjects design*. If a design has two or more independent variables, the design is a *factorial design*. A factorial design can be a *between-subjects factorial design* if all independent variables are between-subjects variables. A factorial design can be a *within-subjects factorial design* if all independent variables are within-subjects variables. There is

		Type I lexically headed semantically determinate		Type II lexically headed semantically indeterminate		Type III free relative/headless semantically indeterminate	
		OS	OO	OS	OO	OS	OO
Age group	G1						
	G2						
	G3						
	G4						
	G5						
	G6						
	G7						
	G8						

Fig. 5.3: Design of the relative clause study: A univariate 3 × 2 × 8 mixed factorial design.

also another kind of factorial design called the *mixed factorial design*. If a design has two or more independent variables and at least one of them is a between-subjects variable and at least one of them is a within-subjects variable, the design is a mixed factorial design.

A design can be further specified to include information regarding the number of levels or conditions of the independent variables involved and the number of dependent variables involved.[2] The design used in the actual relative clause study was a univariate 3 × 2 × 8 mixed factorial design, which is illustrated in Figure 5.3. The numbers (3, 2, and 8) in the specification 3 × 2 × 8 represent the number of variations of the independent variables. There are three independent variables. The first independent variable, "type of sentence" (a within-subjects variable), contains three levels (Type I, Type II, and Type III). The second independent variable, "function of relative clause" (a within-subjects variable), contains two conditions

---

2 If, in an experiment, only one dependent variable is included, the design is a *univariate design*. If two or more dependent variables are included, the design is a *multivariate design*.

(OS vs. OO). The third independent variable (a between-subjects quasi-independent variable) contains eight levels (children were divided into eight groups, G1–G8, according to age, with 6-month intervals). The dependent variable (not shown in Figure 5.3) is "number of correct imitations" (with a score range of 0–2 correct imitations).

As mentioned earlier, in language acquisition studies, grammatical factors (e.g., "sentence type") are often manipulated as within-subjects (or repeated measures) variables. This implies that if we do not consider the nongrammatical between-subjects quasi-independent variable (e.g., "age" or "language development/proficiency level"), the designs adopted in language acquisition studies are often within-subjects designs. There are at least two reasons why within-subjects designs are more favorable than between-subjects designs for language acquisition studies. First, a within-subjects design requires fewer participants. For example, children in the relative clause study were asked to imitate all six different kinds of sentences (Type I-OS, Type I-OO, Type II-OS, Type II-OO, Type III-OS, and Type III-OO). If a between-subjects design were adopted, the researchers in the relative clause study would have to recruit six times as many children as they did. Moreover, it does not seem cost-efficient to have a group of children tested with only a small number of items in regard to a particular sentence type (e.g., two items of Type I-OS) and have a different group of children tested with another small number of items in regard to another sentence type (e.g., two items of Type I-OO).

Another advantage of a within-subjects design is that it provides a more sensitive test of the effect of an independent variable on the dependent variable. In a within-subjects design, because fewer participants are needed and the participants in various treatment conditions of the experiment are "perfectly matched," the variability due to individual differences associated with participant characteristics observed in a within-subjects design is smaller than that observed in a between-subjects design. This is beneficial because if the variability associated with participant characteristics is too great, it may mask or conceal the potential effect of the independent variable on the dependent variable. In other words, compared with a between-subjects design, a within-subjects design is more powerful in terms of its capability in detecting the effect of an independent variable on the dependent variable—in language acquisition studies, the effect of various grammatical factors on children's language production or comprehension.

5.2.4 Additional Concepts Related to the Dependent Variable

A dependent variable or measure has to be sensitive, reliable, and valid. If an effect of an independent variable on a dependent variable exists, even if the effect is subtle, a *sensitive* measure should allow us to detect that effect. A *reliable* measure should provide us with similar, consistent, and stable data if we use it to measure the same subject under the same conditions on different occasions. A *valid* measure should allow us to test what we want to test.

In the relative clause study, the dependent variable is "number of correct imitations" produced by children for sentences with a particular type of clause. This dependent variable is sensitive, reliable, and valid. If it turns out that headless relative clauses are developmental precursors of lexically headed relative clauses, children should find sentences such as *Cookie Monster hits what pushes Big Bird* easier to produce than sentences such as *Big Bird pushes the balloon which bumps Ernie*. Different "numbers of correct imitations" should be observed (or produced by children) for sentences with different types of relative clauses. If we had a chance to test the same child with the same set of sentences within a reasonably short period (within which the "developmental effect" could be kept constant), the "number of correct imitations" given by the same child to the same set of sentences should be quite similar on these two occasions. Moreover, the measure—namely, "number of correct imitations" observed for different types of sentences used in the experiment—is valid as well because it allows the researchers to test what they want to test. It allows the researchers to infer children's differential abilities to produce these sentences with different types of relative clauses.

5.2.5 Identifying and Controlling Potential Extraneous or Confounding Variables

Potential extraneous or confounding variables may obscure our results and, thus, prevent us from reaching a clear conclusion for our experiment; furthermore, they are not variables we want in an experiment. A *confounding variable* is a specific *extraneous variable* that covaries systematically with the independent variable. Thus, because it systematically covaries with the independent variable, it obscures experimental results.

In the baby-cooing example, we hypothesized that babies listening to music would produce more cooing sounds than babies not listening to music. To test this, we included the "music" condition, under which a group of babies will listen to music (experimental condition), and the "no music" condition, under which a group of babies will not listen to any music (a control condition). But suppose each time music is presented, the baby's mother is also present, and when music is not presented, the baby's mother is not present. In this situation, the presence or absence of the baby's mother is a potential confounding variable. The presence or absence of the baby's mother covaries systematically with the independent variable (music, mother; no music, no mother); thus, the baby's mother obscures and confounds our results. If the babies in the experimental condition produced a large number of cooing sounds, and the babies in the control condition produced few cooing sounds, can we confidently conclude that the babies in the experimental group produced more cooing sounds than the babies in the control group because they were exposed to music and the babies in the control group were not? We cannot conclude this because it is possible that the babies did not care about music, but loved having their mother around. If the mother was there, the baby produced a lot of cooing sounds, and if the mother was not there, the baby produced few cooing sounds. Maybe music presentation alone makes no difference in babies' production of cooing sounds.

There are many ways to control for different types of extraneous or confounding variables, but they depend on the exact design and variables of each experiment, so we cannot present them all; we introduce only a couple here. For the baby-cooing experiment, one way to control for the confounding variable of mother's presence or absence is to keep this variable constant across the two conditions related to music presentation. Thus, if in the experimental condition (i.e., the music condition), there is no mother, then in the control condition (i.e., the no music condition), the mother should also not be there. Similarly, when the mother is present in the experimental condition, she should also be present in the control condition. If we keep the presence or absence of the baby's mother constant across the control and experimental conditions, if the babies in the experimental condition produce more cooing sounds than the babies in the control condition, we can clearly conclude that this outcome is due to the music but not the mother.

Consider the relative clause study with the hypothesis "Headless relatives are developmental precursors of lexically headed relatives." Suppose you used the sentences in Figure 5.4 to test the hypothesis and found that children produce sentences with headless relative clauses more easily than sentences with lexically headed relative clauses. Can you still confidently conclude that headless relatives are developmental precursors of lexically headed relatives? You cannot draw this conclusion because there are two potential confounding variables in the design.

If we look more closely in Figure 5.4 at each example's sentence length and difficulty of the lexical items used, we see that the sentence with a headless relative clause is much shorter than the one with a lexically headed relative clause (seven vs. 13 words), and we see that the lexical items used in the sentence with a headless

Type of sentence	
Headless relatives	Lexically headed relatives
Cookie Monster hits what pushes Big Bird.	Professor Barbara Lust pushes the heavy research manual, which bumps Professor Suzanne Flynn.

Fig. 5.4: Potential confounding variables in the relative clause study.

relative clause are much easier than those used in the sentence with lexically headed relative clauses. Very young children are more likely to be familiar with Cookie Monster and Big Bird than with Professors Barbara Lust and Professor Suzanne Flynn. The potential confounding variables (i.e., sentence length and difficulty of the lexical items) will have to be controlled (or kept constant).

One other potential confounding variable (or confounding effect) is the *sequencing effect* or the *order effect*, which is likely to occur in language acquisition studies because, as mentioned before, grammatical factors are often manipulated as within-subjects variables. When a within-subjects variable is involved in an experiment, each participant has to be repeatedly presented with, or tested under, all treatment conditions—one at a time, in a sequence—related to that variable. Sequencing effects can occur when the experience of participating in a condition presented earlier affects performance in a condition presented later. When grammatical form is treated as a within-subject factor, a child has to be repeatedly tested with different types of sentences (grammatical forms). To control for the potential sequencing effect, the presentation order of the different sentence types has to be "randomized" or "counterbalanced" across different child participants. In Appendix 5.1, we briefly describe the procedures for two counterbalancing techniques—the complete counterbalancing technique and the incomplete counterbalancing technique—which can be used to generate different sequences (or presentation orders) of the treatment conditions related to the within-subjects variable involved in an experimental design.

5.3 Choosing an Appropriate Task for the Participants

There are many tasks that can be used to elicit language data (see Chapters 6–8 for some examples). Keep in mind, there is no one task suitable for all experiments. The task deemed most appropriate will depend on the purpose of your study, the research question you are asking, and the research hypothesis you intend to test. For instance, if the purpose of your study is to validate children's knowledge of N. Chomsky's (1981) Binding Principles A, B, and C, then children's abilities to deal with referents of different types of noun phrases (NPs)—which include anaphors/reflexives (*himself* or *herself*), pronouns (*him* or *her*), and r-expressions (e.g., *Tom* and *Jerry*)—will have to be tested. A comprehension task such as the picture selection task may not be sufficient to reveal children's true knowledge of the binding principles. This is because if a child chooses one picture with one referent rather than another picture with a different referent, it may simply reflect the child's "preference" of the co-reference relation between the target NP and the referent in that chosen picture, instead of his or her rejection of the co-reference relation between the target NP and the unselected referent. Here, an appropriate task would be the truth–value judgment task, which would allow a child to indicate clearly acceptance or rejection of a co-reference relation between the target NP and the particular referent without a "preference" bias.

In the relative clause study, we may choose to use the elicited imitation task and the act-out task. This allows us to compare different data sets for convergent evidence, which can then be used to confirm or disconfirm the proposed hypothesis. After choosing an appropriate language-eliciting task, the next step is to prepare the corresponding testing materials (pretraining sentences, props, etc.; see more in Chapter 3). Experimentally, for each type of sentence tested, it is recommended that two or more items be generated. This allows us to use the right kinds of statistical procedures for analyzing the right kinds of dependent measures or data (e.g., binary vs. continuous), which are briefly discussed later.

5.4 Identifying the Population and Selecting the Sample

When conducting language acquisition research, we are not interested only in what is observed in the small samples of children participating in the study; rather, we are interested in using the sample outcome to make inferences about the corresponding population. In the relative clause study, 84 children (between ages: 3;6–7;6) were tested, and the researchers intended to show what, in general, children within the same age range can (or cannot) do if presented with similar kinds of relative clause sentences, not just what the 84 could do. Therefore, we have to identify the participant population from which to select an appropriate and representative sample.

To accurately infer population outcomes from sample outcomes, the selected representative sample has to be "large enough" to ensure a decent level of statistical power and an adequate effect size. A *representative sample* is an unbiased sample accurately representing the members of the participant population. The *statistical power* of the test is a probability index that tells us the test's capability to correctly detect an effect if an effect does exist. An *effect size* is a numerical index that informs us of the strength of the effect. What constitutes a "large enough" sample size depends on the experimental design (number of independent variables, number of levels of each independent variable to be varied). It also depends on the level of statistical power we are seeking and how large an effect size we want. It is always useful to consult a statistician or a statistics book (e.g., Cohen, 1988) before making a decision about the number of participants or subjects needed.

5.5 Following the Predetermined Procedure

To avoid introducing extraneous or confounding effects in our experiment and contaminating the data collected, procedures used must follow the experimental design for all participants. In some experiments, after data collection, debriefing or post-experimental interviews must be conducted with the participants to ensure that no negative or undesirable influence was caused for the participants by the experiment. If a child participant comes to participate in your experiment with a happy face, he or she should also leave your experiment with a happy face (discussed further in Chapters 2 and 3).

5.6 The Need for Statistics in Language Acquisition Studies

An experimental finding has little or no scientific value if the finding is restricted to the specific sample of participants being tested and/or the specific sample of test items being used in the experiment. In other words, experimental findings must be generalized across different samples of participants and different samples of test items to be considered scientifically significant. At the data analysis and hypothesis testing stage, we must ensure that appropriate statistical tests are used to analyze the kind of data we have collected and test the hypothesis we have proposed.

Like other behavioral data, language data involve variability. Two major types of variability should be accounted for: (a) variability from participants and (b) variability from items. *Variability from participants* includes individual differences and sampling errors related to the participants we have selected. It also includes some potential inconsistent responses given by our participants. *Variability from items* includes potential measurement or sampling errors related to the language materials (or test items) we selected or created for our experiment.

Consider the variability from participants. A researcher cannot assume that all children will respond identically to a given language task, even when they are the same age, in the same stage of language development, and/or at the same level of language proficiency. Just as adult participants may not perform 100% correctly or similarly under some circumstances, it is expected that variability (or individual differences) in children's language data will be observed. Variability in children's language data can also occur due to sampling error. When only a sample—a small subset of a population—is studied, it is likely that variability will occur due to sampling error. Variability from participants may also occur because of inconsistent responses given by the participants. Because of some unpredictable factors, the same participant may not always respond exactly the same way to two language stimuli sharing a similar structure.

Consider the variability from items. Language data have been generated by means of a variety of eliciting tasks, each using a different set of language stimuli. Certain eliciting tasks for measuring language behaviors may not always allow language researchers to measure what they want as accurately as they would like. Moreover, when we create test items for our language experiment, it is virtually impossible for the "item sample" to exhaust all the potential test items we could have selected. In other words, in an experiment, only a small subset of an "item population" will be studied. When only sample items are used, it is likely that variability from items chosen will occur due to sampling error.

Statistical analyses allow us to find out whether the observed treatment effect of an independent variable (e.g., sentence type) on a dependent variable (e.g., number of correct imitations) is simply due to chance (i.e., experimental errors: individual differences, sampling errors, and/or other errors related to the experiment). If the observed effect is significantly different from chance, we can conclude that our results are "real." This means that the expected relationship between the independent variable and the dependent variable stated in our research hypothesis can be confirmed.[3] For example, if children produce "significantly" more correct imitations when they are asked to imitate sentences with headless relative clauses than when they are asked to imitate sentences with lexically headed relative clauses, we can conclude that headless relative clauses are developmental precursors of lexically headed relative clauses.

5.7 Common Statistical Analyses for Analyzing Language Acquisition Data

Design and analysis go hand in hand. For each particular experimental design, there is always a corresponding statistical analysis that is most appropriate to use. Previously, we mentioned the following experimental designs commonly used in language acquisition studies: a single-factor within-subjects design, a factorial within-subjects design, and a mixed factorial design. The statistical test used with single-factor or factorial designs is the F-test (also known as the analysis of variance [ANOVA] test).

---

[3] In the online supporting material (http://pubs.apa.org/books/supp/blume), we briefly introduce the underlying logic of hypothesis testing and some related basic statistical concepts. This material can be helpful for beginning researchers who have limited statistical knowledge.

When an *F*-test is conducted, we compare the between-group/condition variability with the within-group/condition variability. Because participants under different treatment conditions of an independent variable are tested with different types of sentences and because individual differences are likely to exist between any two participants, the between-group/condition variability should reflect the potential treatment effect (TE) plus potential experimental errors (EE). The within-group/condition variability, however, reflects only the EE. The participants under the same treatment condition of an independent variable are treated alike (e.g., tested with the same type of sentences). Thus, if any variability does exist among the participants' responses, this variability can only be linked to individual differences, sampling errors, and/or other possible errors related to the experiment, rather than the potential TE.

In an *F*-test, an observed *F*-value (F_{obs}) is calculated by dividing the between-group/condition variability by the within-group/condition variability

$$\left(F_{obs} = \frac{TE + EE}{EE} \right).$$

If we could test every potential participant, and there is no treatment effect (TE = 0), the observed *F* value should equal 1

$$\left(F_{obs} = \frac{TE + EE}{EE} = \frac{0 + EE}{EE} = 1 \right).$$

If there is some treatment effect (TE ≠ 0), F_{obs} is > 1.

However, because we can only test a sample from a population, we would have to compare F_{obs} with an *F* critical value, established in accordance with several factors related to the experimental design we have adopted. The critical value indicates how large the between-group/condition variability must be relative to the within-group/condition variability before we can feel reasonably confident that the former involves an actual TE. The critical value depends heavily on two key concepts, degrees of freedom related to the between-group/condition variability (df_B) and the degrees of freedom related to the within-group/condition variability (df_W), where df_B considers the number of conditions we have for an independent variable and df_W considers the number of participants we have for each condition in the experiment. A significant F_{obs} value tells us that the observed differences between the treatment conditions of an independent variable are unlikely to be due merely to chance or EE, given the number of experimental conditions and the size of the sample. Thus, statistical significance means that there is a real TE and that this effect is replicable.

Before 1973, it was assumed that if traditional *F*-tests (or *F*1 tests, as termed by H. H. Clark, 1973) were significant, the findings were automatically generalizable beyond the specific sample of participants tested and beyond the specific set of language materials used for the experiment.[4] However, as pointed out by H. H. Clark (1973), a significant $F1$ test, at best, only tells us that the experimental finding can be replicated with (or generalized to) new samples of participants; it does not tell us that the finding can be replicated with new sets of test items. For example, a significant $F1$ test obtained from Participant Sample 1 (PS1) using Item Set 1 (IS1) tells us that the finding from this data set (PS1 + IS1) may be generalized to a new participant sample (PS2) if the same item set (IS1) is used; it does not tell us whether this finding can be generalized to a different item set (IS2), either with the same sample (PS1) or a different sample (PS2). That is, (PS1 + IS1) → (PS2 + IS1) is a reasonable generalization, whereas (PS1 + IS1) → (PS1 + IS2) and (PS1 + IS1) → (PS2 + IS2) are questionable.

To find out whether a finding can be replicated with new sets of test items, an $F2$ test (as termed by H. H. Clark, 1973) should be conducted. As with the constraints associated with the $F1$ test, a significant $F2$ test only tells us that an experimental finding can be replicated with new sets of test items if the same participant sample is tested; it does not tell us whether the finding can also be replicated if a new participant sample is tested. In other words, although (PS1 + IS1) → (PS1 + IS2) is a reasonable generalization, (PS1 + IS1) → (PS2 + IS1) and (PS1 + IS1) → (PS2 + IS2) are questionable. Moreover, even if $F1$ and $F2$ are both significant, (PS1 + IS1) → (PS2 + IS1) and (PS1 + IS1) → (PS1 + IS2) are each reasonable, we still cannot conclude that our experimental findings are generalizable to both new samples of participants and to new sets of test items at the same time—that is, (PS1 + IS1) → (PS2 + IS2) remains questionable. To solve this problem, H. H. Clark (1973) suggested that a $minF'$ test, which takes into account both the "variability from participants" and the "variability from items," should be conducted.

The $minF'$ value can be calculated using the observed values of $F1$ and $F2$ and their corresponding degrees of freedom—between (df_B) and within (df_W).[5] The procedures for calculating the $minF'$ suggested by H. H. Clark (1973) and an easy way for obtaining the p-value (suggested by Brysbaert, 2007) are summarized in Exhibit 5.1. For more discussion on the importance of considering all three parameters ($F1$, $F2$, and $minF'$) rather than focusing only on $F1$ and/or $F2$ when interpreting results from psycholinguistics studies, see Raaijmakers, Schrijnemakers, and Gremmen (1999) and Raaijmakers (2003).

In psycholinguistic studies (including language acquisition studies), the traditional repeated measures ANOVA has been widely adopted as one of the major tools for statistical analysis and inference. However, as pointed out by Maxwell and

---

[4] In 1973, Herbert H. Clark published: "The Language-as-Fixed-Effect Fallacy: A Critique of Language Statistics in Psychological Research," which discussed the issue of the meaning of the $F1$ test in language studies and suggested additional tests to use.

[5] The values $F1$ and $F2$ and their degrees of freedom can be found by running two separate SPSS analyses. The SPSS program for the $F1$ test is the "General Linear Model-Repeated measures," and for the $F2$ test, it is the "General Linear Model-Univariate."

Exhibit 5.1: Procedures for Calculating the MinF' Value

---

minF': An F value to generalize across participants and items at the same time

$$\min F'(i,j) = \frac{F1 \times F2}{F1 + F2}$$

$F1$: An F value to generalize across participants
$F2$: An F value to generalize across items

$$i = df1 \text{ of } F1 = df1 \text{ of } F2$$

$$j = \frac{(F1+F2)^2}{\frac{(F1)^2}{df2 \text{ of } F2} + \frac{(F2)^2}{df2 \text{ of } F1}}$$

The probability index (the p-value) that determines the significance of the minF' is obtainable through the Excel Function: FDIST (the value of minF', i, j)

An informal example:

$$\{F1(1,7) = 8.79; p = .021\} \quad , \quad \{F2(1,6) = 4.65; p = .074\}$$

$$i = df1 \text{ of } F1 = df1 \text{ of } F2 = 1$$

$$j = \frac{(F1+F2)^2}{\frac{(F1)^2}{df2 \text{ of } F2} + \frac{(F2)^2}{df2 \text{ of } F1}} = \frac{(8.79+4.65)^2}{\frac{(8.79)^2}{6} + \frac{(4.65)^2}{7}} = \frac{(13.44)^2}{\frac{77.26}{6} + \frac{21.62}{7}}$$

$$= \frac{180.63}{12.88+3.09} = \frac{180.63}{15.97} = 11.31 \cong 11$$

$$\min F'(i,j) = \frac{F1 \times F2}{F1+F2} = \frac{8.79 \times 4.65}{8.79+4.65} = \frac{40.87}{13.44} = 3.04$$

$$\min F'(1,11) = 3.04$$

In an Excel spreadsheet cell type the following:

=FDIST(3.04, 1, 11)

& the result (.109) is your p-value

Delaney (2004) and Quené and van den Bergh (2004, 2008), among others, there are at least three major problems concerning repeated measures ANOVAs that have to be carefully evaluated. The three major problems are (a) the violation of the "sphericity assumption," (b) limitations in managing the "design effect" related to "sampling hierarchy," and (c) inflexibility in handling missing data and incomplete designs.

Quené and van den Bergh (2004, 2008) postulated that to perform an ANOVA with repeated measures, there is a required condition: the sphericity assumption. For the assumption to hold, the variances of the differences between all possible pairs of treatment conditions of an independent variable must be approximately equal. However, in many studies, this required condition is often violated. The repeated measures ANOVA is also limited in its capacity for handling the "design effect" related to "sampling hierarchy." Although the repeated measures ANOVA is useful in handling data sets with a two-level structure (e.g., a level for participants and a level for measurements within participants), it is not suitable for handling data sets with a multilevel structure (e.g., languages, participants within languages, measurements within participants within languages). Finally, the repeated measures ANOVA is subject to criticism concerning its inflexibility with regard to missing data and incomplete designs. Put simply, incomplete designs and missing data are not permitted in repeated measures ANOVAs. If a piece of data (or observation) is missing from a participant, all the remaining data (or observations) from that participant should be excluded from the analysis.

To deal with these three problems, a highly functional statistical tool has been adopted as a favorable alternative to the repeated measures ANOVA for analyzing psycholinguistic data. This tool is *multilevel modeling* (also known as *mixed-effects modeling* or *hierarchical linear model*; see Maxwell & Delaney, 2004; Quené & van den Bergh, 2004, 2008). Instead of conducting two individual F-tests ($F1$ for participants and $F2$ for language items) and using $F1$ and $F2$ to derive an integrated minF' to find out whether findings from an experiment are generalizable to new samples of participants and new sets of language items, multilevel (or mixed-effects) modeling allows "simultaneous and joint generalizations" (Quené & van den Bergh, 2008, p. 417). Moreover, multilevel (or mixed-effects) modeling can be used safely even if the sphericity assumption is violated and the experimental design is incomplete and/or has missing data. As Maxwell and Delaney (2004) and Quené and van den Bergh (2008) stated, not only can multilevel (or mixed-effects) models handle designs with both fixed and random effects in the same analysis but they can also flexibly handle multiple random effects that are nested or crossed. In addition, they can be used to analyze continuous data (e.g., reaction time) as well as binary data (e.g., correct or incorrect response). Continuous data are typically analyzed with basic multilevel or mixed-effects models, whereas binary data should be analyzed with the mixed-effects models of logistic regression or generalized linear mixed models (see Guo & Zhao, 2000; Quené & van den Bergh, 2008). As suggested by Maxwell and Delaney (2004) and Quené and van den Bergh (2008), among others, computer programs for multilevel or mixed-effects models include the Statistical Package for the Social Sciences for mixed models and the function lmer (linear mixed effects regression) in program "R" developed by D. Bates (2005).

The R project for statistical computing can be downloaded from http://www.r-project.org. For more detailed discussion, useful tutorial guides, and examples about multilevel (or mixed-effects) modeling, see Baayen (2008); Baayen, Davidson, and Bates (2008); Guo and Zhao (2000); Maxwell and Delaney (2004, Chapter 15); and Quené and van den Bergh (2004, 2008).

5.8 Documenting the Research Results and Sharing the Findings

Making research methods and findings available to other people is of great importance. If we do not share our research methods and findings with others, they will have limited or no scientific value and, more important, the advancement of the discipline and science will not be possible. Thus, the final step involved in experimental research is documentation: stating the meaning of the findings and writing a research report describing the results for communication with others. In the research report, state how the research was conducted, what was found, and how you interpreted your results (see Chapters 10 and 11). The report must be clearly written in a way that allows other researchers to replicate the experiment (if they wanted to) without considerable confusion. You also may consider presenting your research results at a professional conference or submitting your research paper to a professional journal, or both.

5.9 Summary

In this chapter, we discussed the application of the scientific method to studies in child language acquisition. We introduced the foundations of the concepts and principles that underlie the scientific method. We provided a rationale for the need for experimental research in addition to naturalistic observation, outlining the core components that an experiment should include to be scientifically valid. We emphasized that every experiment must result from testable and unambiguous hypotheses related to specific research questions; that its design must specify variables, controls, and statistical methods; and that the right participant sample and item (or language) sample must carefully be selected. Finally, when the experiment is conducted and the hypothesis is tested, the results must be shared with fellow researchers to facilitate scientific advancement. If you are interested in more detailed descriptions and explanations regarding these concepts, principles, and/or procedures, consult the References section for additional material.

Last, it is highly recommended that researchers committed to conducting high-quality experimental research in language acquisition take at least one introductory level and one advanced level course related to experimental design and statistical data analysis. It is also highly recommended that researchers with different strengths in methods and statistics work cooperatively to complement each other and share expertise.

Appendix 5.1
Complete Counterbalancing Technique and Incomplete Counterbalancing Technique

To control for the potential sequencing effect when a within-subjects (or repeated-measures) variable is involved in an experimental design, the researcher has to create different sequences (or presentation orders) of the treatment conditions related to the within-subjects variable. The procedures for creating the counterbalancing sequences and the examples are summarized as follows.

If the *complete counterbalancing technique* is adopted,

- Generate every possible order of the treatment conditions and use every generated order an equal number of times.
- Let n = the number of conditions that have to be balanced in a within-subjects variable. The number of sequences needed = $n!$ and $n! = (n) \times (n-1) \times (n-2) \times \cdots \times 1$

To create the $n!$ sequences, build a "tree" structure according to the following logic: For the first ordinal position, there are n choices; for the second ordinal position, there are $(n-1)$ choices; and so forth until the last ordinal position, where there is one choice. To build the "tree" structure, first, list the n conditions, then, for each of the n conditions, draw the $(n-1)$ branches and list the corresponding $(n-1)$ conditions. For each of the $(n-1)$ conditions, draw the $(n-2)$ branches and list the corresponding $(n-2)$ conditions. Continue the procedures until there are no more branches to draw.

For example, Bob is running an experiment in which a within-subjects variable is included. Consider Bob's experiment and answer the following question: If the independent variable has three levels (P, V, and G) and the complete counterbalancing technique is adopted to control for the sequencing effect, then (a) how many sequences are required for Bob's experiment and (b) what are Bob's counterbalancing sequences?

Answers: (a) Because $n = 3$, $3!$ sequences are required; that is, six sequences are needed ($3! = 3 \times 2 \times 1 = 6$).

(b) The six sequences are P-V-G, P-G-V, V-P-G, V-G-P, G-P-V, and G-V-P.

Independent variable "type of music" is a within-subjects variable with three treatment conditions (piano, violin, and guitar)		
P	V	G

1st ordinal position (three choices)	2nd ordinal position (two choices)	3rd ordinal position (one choice)	
P	V	G	P-V-G
P	G	V	P-G-V
V	P	G	V-P-G
V	G	P	V-G-P
G	P	V	G-P-V
G	V	P	G-V-P

If the *incomplete counterbalancing technique* is adopted,

- Let n = the number of conditions that need to be balanced in a within-subjects variable. If n is even, generate n sequences; if n is odd, generate $2n$ sequences (or two sets of n sequences).
- For the generated n or $2n$ sequences, (a) each treatment condition must appear an equal number of times in each ordinal position, and (b) each treatment condition must occur before and after every other condition an equal number of times. Moreover, (c) every generated order must be used an equal number of times.
- There are two required steps: First, create a set of "number sequences," and second, translate the set of number sequences into "condition sequences."

The step-by-step procedures (if n is even):

1. If n is even, n sequences are required.
2. Generate the first "number sequence" by using the formula[1] 1, 2, n, 3, $(n-1)$, 4, $(n-2)$, 5, ...
3. Create the remaining "number sequences" by adding 1 to each number in the previous sequence. For the highest number, go back to 1.

---

[1] The formula and the basic principles are adopted from Christensen, Johnson, and Turner (2014).

4. Arbitrarily decide on the first "condition sequence" to go with the first "number sequence." Establish the one-to-one correspondence relationship between the first number sequence and the first condition sequence. Keep the established one-to-one correspondence relationship unchanged throughout the experiment.
5. Translate the remaining "number sequences" into "condition sequences" in accordance with the one-to-one correspondence relationship established earlier.

For example, Bob is running an experiment in which a within-subjects variable is included. Consider Bob's experiment and answer the following questions: If the independent variable has four treatment conditions (P, V, G, and D) and the incomplete counterbalancing technique is adopted to control for the sequencing effect, then (a) how many sequences are required for Bob's experiment, and (b) what are Bob's counterbalancing sequences?

Answers: (a) Because $n = 4$, 4 is even, n sequences are required; that is, four sequences are needed.

(b) The four sequences are P-D-G-V, D-V-P-G, V-G-D-P, and G-P-V-D.

Independent variable "type of music" is a within-subjects variable with four treatment conditions (piano, violin, guitar, and drum)			
P	V	G	D

Number sequences	Condition sequences
To create the first number sequence, follow the formula: 1, 2, n, 3, $(n-1)$, 4, $(n-2)$, 5 . . . (because $n = 4$, only the first four numbers from the formula are needed):	Arbitrarily decide on the first condition sequence (e.g., P-D-G-V) to go with the first number sequence (1-2-4-3), establish the one-to-one correspondence relationship between these two, and translate the number sequences into condition sequences:
1-2-n-3	
1-2-4-3	P-D-G-V (*P = 1, D = 2, G = 4, V = 3)
2-3-1-4	D-V-P-G
3-4-2-1	V-G-D-P
4-1-3-2	G-P-V-D

The step-by-step procedures (if n is odd):

1. If n is odd, $2n$ sequences (or two sets of n sequences) are required.
2. For the first set of n sequences, create the first "number sequence" by using the formula 1, 2, n, 3, $(n-1)$, 4, $(n-2)$, 5, and so forth. Create the remaining "number sequences" by adding 1 to each number in the previous sequence. For the highest number, go back to 1.
3. Arbitrarily decide on the first "condition sequence" to go with the first "number sequence," establish the one-to-one correspondence relationship between the first "number sequence" and the first "conditions sequence," and translate the remaining "number sequences" into "condition sequences" in accordance with the established one-to-one correspondence relationship.
4. The second set of n "condition sequences" are mirror images of the first set of "condition sequences."

For example, Bob is running an experiment in which a within-subjects variable is included. Consider Bob's experiment and answer the following questions: If the independent variable has five levels (P, V, G, D, and F) and the incomplete counterbalancing technique is adopted to control for the sequencing effect, then (a) how many sequences are required for Bob's experiment, and (b) what are Bob's counterbalancing sequences?

Answers: (a) Because $n = 5$, 5 is odd, $2n$ sequences (or 2 sets of n sequences) are required; that is, $2(5) = 10$ sequences are needed.

(b) The 10 sequences are V-P-G-F-D, P-F-V-D-G, F-D-P-G-V, D-G-F-V-P, G-V-D-P-F, D-F-G-P-V, G-D-V-F-P, V-G-P-D-F, P-V-F-G-D, and F-P-D-V-G.

Independent variable "type of music" is a within-subjects variable with five treatment conditions (piano, violin, guitar, drum, and flute)				
P	V	G	D	F

Number sequences (for the first set of 5)	Condition sequences	
To create the first number sequence for the first set of five, follow the formula: 1, 2, n, 3, ($n-1$), 4, ($n-2$), 5 ... (because $n = 5$, only the first five numbers from the formula is needed: 1, 2, n, 3, ($n-1$)	Arbitrarily decide on the first condition sequence (e.g., V-P-G-F-D) to go with the first number sequence (1-2-5-3-4), establish the one-to-one correspondence relationship between these two, and translate the number sequences into condition sequences:	Mirror images
1-2-5-3-4	V-P-G-F-D (*V = 1, P = 2, G = 5, F = 3, D = 4)	D-F-G-P-V
2-3-1-4-5	P-F-V-D-G	G-D-V-F-P
3-4-2-5-1	F-D-P-G-V	V-G-P-D-F
4-5-3-1-2	D-G-F-V-P	P-V-F-G-D
5-1-4-2-3	G-V-D-P-F	F-P-D-V-G

Both the complete counterbalancing technique and the incomplete counterbalancing technique allow us to adequately control the potential sequencing effect. However, when a large number of treatment conditions are to be balanced, it is recommended that the incomplete counterbalancing technique be adopted. This is due to the fact that the complete counterbalancing technique would require many more sequences to be generated and, thus, many more participants to be tested. For example, if there are five treatment conditions to be counterbalanced ($n = 5$) and the complete counterbalancing technique is adopted, we would need $n! = 5 \times 4 \times 3 \times 2 \times 1 = 120$ sequences. If we wanted 10 participants to be tested with each sequence, we would need 1,200 participants. However, if the incomplete counterbalancing technique is adopted, because $n = 5$, 5 is odd, we need only $2n = 2(5) = 10$ sequences. Again, if we wanted 10 participants to be tested with each sequence, we would only need 100 participants.

6 Experimental Tasks for Generating Language Production Data

In conjunction with experimental designs, one must decide how to elicit language for analysis. There are many ways to elicit speech production from subjects. For example, if one wants to elicit language production data to observe and analyze, the elicited imitation task and the elicited production task can provide language production data relevant to an experimental hypothesis. We use these tasks as examples of methodology development in this area. The principles for standardization developed here can be generalized and adapted to other means of eliciting language production.

6.1 The Elicited Imitation Task

Elicited imitation (EI) is widely used as a means of studying subjects' language knowledge through eliciting specific forms of their language production bearing on particular aspects of language competence.

6.1.1 What Is the Elicited Imitation Task?

6.1.1.1 Elicited Imitation Task Description

In an EI task, the experimenter says a particular sentence and asks the subject to say the sentence "just the way I said it." The main idea of the imitation task is to collect speech data through which one can investigate each subject's grammar or language knowledge. This is accomplished by having the participant attempt to produce the model (or *stimulus*) sentences (i.e., the sentences chosen for repetition). In this way, the experimenter investigates whether the subject has the grammatical competence for the construction of the model sentence. Stimulus sentences are especially designed to include various factors under investigation in a particular research study. The sentences are carefully subjected to standardized conditions to allow the researcher to test a hypothesis regarding a subject's knowledge of language. The crucial point of interest is to see whether a subject either repeats exactly the model sentence or changes the grammatical forms of the sentence to fit his or her language system. A research study can investigate how a subject ranges in ability to produce different sentence types that have been varied in the experimental design (i.e., altering, failing to produce some, failing to produce most types of sentences). Thus, we get insight into the grammatical system the subject normally uses in his or her mind. One can use this method to study language development in both children and adults. Participants at different ages and/or levels of language development in either their first or second language will imitate sentences differently, sometimes changing them in interesting ways.

6.1.1.2 Logical Structure of the Elicited Imitation Task

In the EI task, the subject must attend to, listen to, understand, analyze, and represent the stimulus sentence and then reconstruct it to produce his or her response. In some ways, the EI task is thus like other tasks, (i.e., the act-out task testing language comprehension, a picture judgment task). That is, memory and attention, as well as auditory competence, are involved in explaining the final behavior. The level of the sentence "reconstruction" from subjects' behavior in this task requires them to invoke and use their grammatical system. Through this grammatical system, the subject may be able to construct a well-formed sentence.

6.1.2 What Are Elicited Imitation Data?

EI data consist of the complete set of language produced by the subject when asked to imitate the stimulus sentences. EI data are specifically linguistic. They involve language that can be analyzed in comparison with the language of the stimulus sentences, with regard to the factors that have been designed in those sentences, and with regard to a linguistic theory that lies behind the design of the sentences. The researcher is interested in differences in sentences a subject may imitate without change versus those that he or she may have trouble with or imitate in an inexact way.[1] The researcher interprets patterns in subjects' matched or mismatched imitations (e.g., certain types of structure are correctly imitated whereas others are not) as possible evidence of their grammars. In addition, the researcher wants to analyze the particular types of inexact (or changed) imitations that subjects make in contrast to those they imitate without significant change.

6.1.3 Background Information: Elicited Imitation Task

The EI task has been widely used by the Cornell Language Acquisition Lab and elsewhere. It has been used for the study of first language acquisition in the child, second

---

[1] We are interested in the principles that underlie the construction of those sentences.

language acquisition in the adult (Flynn, 1986, 1987; Vinther, 2002), and bilingualism in the child (Lust et al., 2014). It has been used for the study of language acquisition in impaired populations (Garrett & Sherman, 1989; Pinhas & Lust, 1987; Riches, Loucas, Baird, Charman, & Simonoff, 2010), including aging populations with impairment (Holland, Boller, & Bourgeois, 1986). Anecdotal applications exist (Slobin & Welsh, 1968), as well as many experimental applications (Lust, Flynn, & Foley, 1996). Morpheme analysis in young children's speech (Gerken, Landau, & Remez, 1990), the role of prosody in subject versus object omission (Gerken, 1991), different theoretical approaches to child language omission (Valian, Hoeffner, & Aubry, 1996), and the functional role of closed-class vocabulary in children's language processing (Egido, 1983) have also been studied using this task.

Debates regarding this task concern the degree to which imitation can be "rote" or "passive copy" and not "reconstructive." Other debates focus on "how it works" cognitively (Vinther, 2002), as well as what the relation is between subjects' perception of a stimulus sentence and their reconstruction of it (Lasnik & Crain, 1985)—for example, "how children in an elicited imitation task can make seemingly intelligent conversions on the adult model" (Lust et al., 1996, p. 69).

Interestingly, N. Chomsky (1964) suggested what we now believe to be true: The child's ability to repeat sentences and non-sentences might provide some evidence as to the underlying system he or she is using.[2] Imitation data do not reflect a "rote" or passive copy of the model or stimulus sentence but a reconstruction of this stimulus (Lust et al., 1996). It appears that to perceive and process language, we must "generate" that language. Language perception and processing is never a passive process. Even in the young child

> it is not the case that anything can be imitated at any time in the child's development. Imitation of new, complex behavior appears to wait until the child mind has developed the "cognitive structure" required for generation of the behavior. For example, although newborns may initially imitate simple tongue protrusion of the type in their own behavioral repertoire, they would not be found to imitate a new sequence or combination of new tongue movements they did not already have the competence for (Piaget, 1968). Imitation is therefore not a passive copy, but a reconstruction of the stimulus. (Lust et al., 1996, pp. 55–56)

As evidence for the "reconstruction" a subject provides in EI, we see that the participants (even children) can reintroduce in a sentence elements that have been deleted

---

[2] In the Cornell Language Acquisition Lab, we do not administer "nonsentences" or "nongrammatical" sentences in the elicited imitation task. This is because we would expect it to change children's fundamental assumptions regarding the task—in other words, that the task is to construct real language, thus calling on their grammar. Some researchers, however, have used the method with ungrammatical model sentences. The problem with using ungrammatical sentences is that if the participants exactly imitate the ungrammatical sentence, it could be due either to subjects' belief that the sentence is grammatical or to their willingness to produce a sentence they know to be ungrammatical to comply with what they have been asked to do.

(these gaps are marked in the following examples by the symbol ø) or reduce redundancy in the sentence by eliminating the redundant elements and thus creating gaps.

Example 1. *Adult*: the red beads (ø) and brown beads are here.
Child: brown beads **here** an' a red beads ø here. (2;03;03)
Example 2. *Adult*: the owl eats candy and (ø) runs fast.
Child: ø owl eat candy ... ø owl eat **the** candy and ... **he** run fast. (2;04;03)

In Example 1, the child restores the redundant missing element *here* (at the same time eliminating the main verb *are* in both clauses), and in Example 2, the child restores the missing subject *he* in the second clause, provides the determiner *the* for the noun *candy* and at the same time eliminates the determiner *the* in the phrase *the owl* (Slobin & Welsh, 1968, p. 490). The subject goes beyond the surface properties of the model sentence. Further evidence for "reconstruction" in EI responses shows that a subject's responses are analytic. The subject may isolate syntactic or semantic factors, often losing one while maintaining the other, as in Example 3.

Example 3. *Adult*: Mozart got burned, and the big shoe is here.
Child: Mozart got burned an-duh ... big shoe **got burned**.

The child maintains the syntactic structure (coordinate sentence) but loses the meaning because he or she replaces *is here* with *got burned* (Slobin & Welsh, 1968, p. 492). In other cases, the subject will maintain the meaning of the sentence but change its syntactic structure (see Example 1). The subjects appear to comprehend the sentence to imitate it. This confirms that the data from this task are reconstructive (Chien & Lust, 1985).

6.1.4 Why Choose the Elicited Imitation Task?

As a researcher, you may choose this method if you have a specific aspect of language knowledge you would like to investigate and/or a specific hypothesis about the child's grammatical competence. Bear in mind that the purpose of the EI task is to allow the researcher to elicit language from a subject, relying precisely on a hypothesis or specific question about language knowledge.

6.1.4.1 Advantages

When using the EI task, elicited speech, unlike natural speech, can be targeted for the specific structures or phenomena in which the researcher is interested. For example, if a researcher is interested in the child's development of embedding (i.e., inserting a sentence inside another sentence or phrase) through relative clause structures,[3] it is possible that a natural speech sample could never demonstrate that the child can produce these structures, even if the subject has the grammatical competence for them. Also, unlike natural speech data, the language data collected reflects a particular underlying representation (i.e., a model that we know the subject or child is attempting to say). In natural speech, it is difficult to determine the true intent of any particular child utterance. Consider the phrase *Mommy sock*—the child could be attempting to produce *Mommy's sock* or *Mommy please put on my sock* (see Bloom, 1970, for a discussion of the need for "rich interpretation" to resolve such indeterminacies). EI thus helps to reveal the child's underlying representation for any particular utterance.[4]

In EI, nonlinguistic factors can also be controlled. In natural speech, this cannot be done because a child's attention and memory and the meaning he or she ascribes to sentences are by definition allowed to range infinitely. EI allows a researcher to control nonlinguistic cognitive competence factors; for instance, the child's attention is clearly determined, and factors of memory can be controlled by standardizing length of sentences as well as structure.

EI can be used to test children as young as 1 or 2 years of age. It can be used for developmental analyses when the hypotheses involve different age groups and possible developmental changes across these. Because some form of imitation is innate, it is not necessary to invest a large amount of time and effort in "teaching the rules of the game." The "idea" of imitation is naturally available. Therefore, data obtained from this method of language production, used in conjunction with experimental design, can be compared with data obtained from natural speech situations, strengthening argumentation from converging evidence.

Finally, because sentence design and experimental controls can be precisely standardized, it is also possible to test large sample sizes of children and/or adults under experimentally rigorous conditions. EI can be applied cross-culturally and cross-linguistically because sentence design and stimulus controls are precisely determined. This task can also be used with other experimental methods, (e.g., tests of comprehension), thus strengthening converging evidence on a subject's grammatical knowledge.

---

[3] For example, in the sentence *The cat that Susan likes is gray*, the relative clause *that Susan likes* is embedded inside the phrase *the cat that Susan likes*.

[4] This point is important because subjects' grammatical knowledge, particularly their syntactic knowledge, lies in their mapping of an underlying representation to a surface form. (We use the term *underlying* in a general sense here to connote "nonovert"). A child may "perceive" a particular sentence in a way different from the adult. One can never know the actual underlying representation. We can only say that this elicited imitation task comes closer to identifying this (see Lasnik & Crain, 1985; Lust et al., 1996).

6.1.4.2 Disadvantages

The following are disadvantages of the EI task.

- Sentences in an EI task are best designed by researchers with some linguistic and/or psycholinguistic background. The design of the stimulus sentences can be quite complex because it requires precise manipulation of the linguistic factors under study and precise control of other linguistic or nonlinguistic factors that may affect the results.
- Processing or general cognitive factors must be controlled to isolate effects due to the selected grammatical factors.
- Language responses produced through this task are typically better understood if the person doing the scoring and the analyses has some training in linguistics and/or psycholinguistics because the subject's answer may diverge from the model in subtle linguistic aspects.
- As with other methods, the EI method is appropriate for studying certain aspects of language knowledge (e.g., word order, pronoun directionality) and less appropriate for others (e.g., questions because child subjects tend to answer the questions instead of imitating them).
- As with all tests of language production, the cognitive and linguistic processing that underlies the subject's elicited behavior with language is complex.
- Finally, it is very important to have training and knowledge in experimental methods if this task is to be used in conjunction with the scientific method and hypothesis testing.

6.1.5 How Does One Capture Elicited Imitation Data?

6.1.5.1 What Is Your Task? The Role of the Researcher

The role of the researcher is twofold: (a) To have the subject elicit an attempted production of each of the sentences in the experimental batteries and (b) to obtain good quality recordings of data for subsequent analysis.

As the experimenter, explain to the subject that you are going to play a talking game in which you will read a "story" and that you would like her or him to say the story "just like I do" or to "say just what I say." Another researcher may be present to assist in keeping records and to control recording equipment; however, this researcher should not be central to the child's attention and should remain in the background as much as possible.

6.1.5.2 The Subject

As with all other tasks, it is essential that the subject feel comfortable with the experimenter before initiating an EI session.

6.1.5.3 Recording Devices

Good quality audio data are essential to this task. EI data are transcribed directly from audio files that are listened to after the recording session. The quality of the audio file determines the accuracy of the data. Double recording (using more than one audio recorder) may aid in the accuracy of the data and provide a backup against potential loss of critical data. The researcher's model utterance should also be heard clearly on the tape, although the emphasis is on the child's speech.

6.1.5.4 Recording Situations

Some researchers have had success with different approaches to EI administration. Some have made limited use of a doll as speaker. For example, Berk (1996) used stuffed animals or dolls of characters familiar to the children for eliciting the imitation. These children were told that the dolls were special because they could not hear a grown-up's voice, but they loved to hear little stories. Therefore, when the experimenter told the child a "story" or sentence, the child had to tell it to the doll as soon as he or she heard it and in exactly the same way. The experimenters made the stuffed toys talk to the children too, thereby allowing the child to have fun and feel more comfortable.

Blume (2002) used a similar procedure. She used a turtle puppet to ask the child whether he or she wanted to play the game of "the turtle and the parrot." She then introduced the turtle and said that this turtle wanted to know what her other animal friends were doing. The child was told that the experimenter knew what the animals were doing and that the experimenter would tell the turtle. But this turtle was really old and a little deaf, so she could not hear the experimenter's voice well. The child's task was then to play "parrot" for the experimenter and to repeat exactly what the experimenter had said in a loud voice so that the turtle could hear the answers.

6.1.5.5 Design of Elicited Imitation Sentences

A. Design of Experimental Sentences
Design of EI sentences is one of the most critical aspects of research using this task. The properties of each model sentence (e.g., length, semantic and grammatical complexity) interact to determine a subject's response. The age and language level of the subject also influence the results. In addition, sentences should be interesting for the subject. Stimulus sentences are varied precisely in terms of the grammatical factor under investigation. For example, in a study of children's development of coordinate sentence structures, coordinate sentences may be fully explicit (e.g., *Mickey Mouse eats an apple, and Donald Duck eats an apple too*) or characterized by ø (*Mickey Mouse eats an apple, and Donald Duck does ø too*). In the experimental design to test such

variables, all other properties of the stimulus sentence must be controlled and held constant; for example, sentence length (calculated in word and/or syllable length) and lexical complexity (e.g., all subject and object words should be two morphemes long) must be held constant across the model sentences.[5] In each experimental condition, if the design involves one replication (more are possible), each replication item must vary only in lexicon. In this case, subjects think they are hearing a "new story," although the underlying grammatical structure is the same.

Pilot data may help the researcher determine critical properties of the stimulus sentence (e.g., to identify which grammatical complexity is underdeveloped in the children studied or what their processing capacity is). The experimental design using the EI task must determine the right length and complexity for the subject's level. The model sentences must not be too easy, or there will be little or no analysis by the subject, but they cannot be so difficult that the subject will not even try. If a sentence is too long and complex, for example, a child may leave the scene. Different lengths and complexities of sentences will be necessary to accommodate the age and language level of the subject.

When sentences are precisely designed and the EI data shows significant variation in the subject's imitation of sentences, the researcher has found strong evidence that the chosen linguistic factors do affect the subject's behavior. If a particular factor is the only possible explanation for the significant variation in imitation success across two types of structures, the EI method has revealed a property of the subject's grammatical competence. If the experimental design is grounded in linguistic theory and particular syntactic analyses, the difference between structures being tested has relevance for the theory.

B. Correct and Incorrect Imitations

Imitation data involve either a subject repeating the model sentence without significant change (a correct imitation) or a subject repeating the model with some change (an incorrect imitation, or an "error"). Scoring as *correct* or *incorrect* depends on the scoring criteria for the particular research study. An incorrect imitation simply reflects the subject's theory about how language works and the results of a researcher's scoring criteria. Thus, it is not necessarily incorrect or an error in any real sense. The subject's structure may be grammatically correct but not a correct imitation of the sentence; for example, if the sentence is *Mickey Mouse danced* and the subject says, *Mickey Mouse dances*, the subject's answer is a correct grammatical sentence, but it is an incorrect imitation of the model sentence. For this reason, we prefer to characterize a subject's imitation data as *matched* or *mismatched* instead of *correct* or *incorrect*.

---

5 Alternatively, these other factors may be specifically designed into the study as another independent variable that can be tested.

C. Design of Pretraining Sentences

Pretraining sentences are precisely designed and controlled for factors that are relevant to the specific study. Sentence structure varies according to each specific study. Pretraining may start with short sentences (e.g., *Johnny jumps*) and increase sentence length until it approaches the length of the experimental sentences. This familiarizes the subject with the length that will be used in the experimental sentences. For example, coordinating structures can build sentence length, (e.g., *Ernie jumped, and Oscar jumped*) without other forms of structural complexity. Pretraining sentences are also often designed to establish the "rules of the game" for the particular research study. This was done, for example, in a study designed to test children's knowledge of ambiguity, in which children were asked to repeat sentences with various forms of interpretation (Foley, Núñez del Prado, Barbier, & Lust, 1997).[6] Thus, the child will be made aware that different meanings are possible for particular sentence structures and that this is acceptable.

Although each study may differ, suggested criteria for passing pretraining for an experiment on the acquisition of coordinate sentence structures might include the following:

- Subjects must attempt every structure. If they do not get all of the inflection correct (e.g., they say, *Mickey drink Donald's milk*), that is OK. This shows you the participant is willing to attempt the sentence in his or her own way and to approach the structure you are testing (i.e., verb phrase ellipsis).
- Errors in reference are OK (e.g., they say, *Oscar eats Oscar's apple, and Big Bird eats Big Bird's apple*, when the sentence was *Bert eats Bert's apple, and Oscar eats Oscar's apple*) if the subject still got the structure of the sentence correct.
- Subjects do not have to pronounce everything correctly. For instance, if they say *frows* for *throws*, it can be scored in this study for this purpose.
- On occasion, children do not seem to understand how to do the task, even when all the pretraining sentences have been administered. In such cases, researchers may administer a second batch of pretraining sentences, usually called *alternate sentences*, which have the same structure but different lexical items. Whether this is allowed depends on each particular study and the structures being analyzed. If the decision is made to allow for these additional set of pretraining sentences, they should be prepared in advance.

---

6 Subjects were asked to act out or to repeat (depending on whether they participated on a test of language comprehension or production) sentences in which the same subject (co-reference) or different subjects (non-co-reference) acted out the two clauses of the sentence (e.g., *Bernie runs fast, and Bernie jumps far too* [co-reference] or *Mommy cooks the soup, and Twinky-Winky eats the soup* [non-co-reference]). Thus, the subject knew that the "game" allowed either type of interpretation. These pretraining sentences followed others to build up the subject's ability to deal with the length and complexity of the experimental sentences (e.g., *Piglet bites Piglet's orange* and *Mickey Mouse bites Kermit's orange*).

6.1.6 Collection of Elicited Imitation Data: Specific Procedures

6.1.6.1 Suggested Instruction to the Subject

The instruction to the child might be, "In this game, I want to know whether you can say this little story just the way I say it" or "Can you say what I say, just the way I say it?" You can refer to the EI task as a "talking game."

6.1.6.2 Pretraining

During pretraining, the experimenter is allowed to provide encouragement, explanations, and as many repetitions as needed. With pretraining sentences, unlike experimental sentences, it is possible to interact with the child in a way that may affect his or her responses. The experimenter may coach children during pretraining, although he or she may not do so during the experiment itself. Pretraining sentences may be repeated many times whereas during the experiment only one repetition is allowed.

Administer the pretraining as quickly as possible. If you decide that the child understands the nature of the EI task (i.e., he or she knows what is expected of him or her during the "game" and has completed a representative set of the pretraining sentences), end the pretraining even if you have not finished administering all the pretraining sentences, and go on next to the experimental sentence batteries. You do not want the subject to be tired of the game before the experimental session has begun.

If the child does not understand the task after all the pretraining sentences have been administered, you may administer the alternate sentences until you feel the child is ready for the experimental battery. You do not necessarily have to administer the whole batch of the alternate sentences if the child shows understanding of the task before you have finished administering the alternates. If children cannot do the pretraining according to the criteria established for the study, the experimental sentences should not be administered, and you can try another planned task or engage children in conversation so that they do not feel they have failed. Children should not perceive a difference between the pretraining and experimental sentences. Subjects should not be aware of when the experimenter switches to the experimental sentences.

6.1.6.3 Administration of Experimental Elicited Imitation Sentences

The following points are provided to guide a researcher through the administration of EI sentences. Without such standardization, data collected will not be able to be compared with other data.

- Sentences should be administered once.
- Repetitions. One repetition is allowed if the child requests it or if the experimenter judges the subject to be inattentive on the first administration. The experimenter has to recognize when the child is not attending and not trying; the experimenter must,

therefore, try again at another time to get the child involved in the task. A total of two attentive readings are allowed to keep the repetitions to a minimum and for them to be standardized across all children and all conditions in the research study. In other words, you may read the stimulus once and repeat it once, but if the child is clearly not paying attention, you may repeat it an additional time. Any repetitions beyond these guidelines will not be scored in the experimental data.

- <u>Administer entire sentences at once.</u> Do not break the sentence into pieces to make it easier for the child. The child has to be able to repeat the whole sentence (or as much of it as he or she can), not just parts of it. If the child only imitated a part of the model sentence, ask, "Is there any more?" The data you want is the child's attempted reproduction of the syntax and semantics of the whole sentence. If the child cannot or will not add any more, repeat the sentence again and ask the child to give you the "whole story." If after this the child still repeats only part of the sentence, it constitutes the data. It may indicate the child's inability to represent the complete structure of the sentence. Move on to the next sentence.
- <u>Interruptions.</u> If the child interrupts the experimenter when he or she is presenting the sentence, start the sentence again.
- <u>Getting the child to repeat the whole sentence.</u> To get the child to repeat the whole sentence, you may have to stop every once in a while and use a sentence that has a different structure from the experimental sentences (e.g., if the experimental sentences are declarative sentences, you may ask the child to repeat a question or a command) to remind the child that the game requires the whole sentence to be repeated. There is no fixed number of reminder sentences you can use. In our labs, we have used a couple per battery at most. Nevertheless, some young children may only be able to produce part of the sentence, and this must then be accepted.
- <u>Challenges with last word repetition.</u> To prevent challenges with last word repetition, try to prevent a "recency effect" when administering pretraining sentences. That is, if a child gives only the last word, try to encourage him or her to do his or her best to give the "whole" story. Repeat one time if the child simply echoes the last part of the sentence. If after the repetition the child still gives a one-word response, as may occur with very young children, go on to the next sentence.
- <u>Child start and restart response.</u> If the child starts and restarts, this is fine; the first reaction should be silent encouragement.
- <u>No coaching</u> should be provided during battery administration. The experimenter should not speak at all after a sentence has been administered. If a child does not respond, wait until you are certain that the child will not or cannot give a response. This may take more time than you expect. After reading the stimulus sentence, say nothing. If the child does not respond after a while (give him or her a long time to respond—he or she may just be thinking), ask, "Can you tell me the story?" Then wait again. If the child asks for a repetition, encourage him or her to repeat what he or she remembers (e.g., "Tell me what you remember" or "Whatever you think"). Never give the child answers. If the child still insists on an answer, ask whether the child would like a repetition.

- Limit unplanned interaction. If a child asks about the meaning of a sentence, do not answer in a way that would determine or interfere with the child's response. For example, when you administer a sentence such as *Grover bites his peach*, if the child asks, "Whose?" do not give him or her the referent. Just ask, "What/who do you think?" If he or she persists in asking "Whose?" repeat the sentence. Try to encourage children to figure out the referent on their own.
- Recovering from child distraction. If the child becomes distracted, it may be necessary to discontinue temporarily the task administration until the child's interest in the task can be renewed. Simply play or talk with the child for a while, and then resume the task when the child seems willing to continue with it. Record some natural speech for a while during this break period because natural speech data are always valuable for a researcher (see Chapter 4). These data, however, should not be considered when scoring the EI task. Most 2- and 3-year-olds will have to be seen for a few shorter times rather than for one long session to cover all the stimulus sentences in an experiment.
- Enunciation. Sentences should be administered with a natural intonation and clear enunciation. The child must be able to hear clearly each word and morpheme in the sentence. Be sure to project your voice so that the children can hear every word you say. Individual sentences should be administered slowly so that all the words can be heard, including the function words (e.g., the connective *when* or conjunction *and*). Normal intonation patterns should still be used. Do not "drag out" the sentences.
- Intonation. Variation in intonation (e.g., in stress) can change the preferred interpretation of a sentence.[7] Therefore, a particular intonation should be established and standardized for a research study and practiced by the experimenter beforehand to be consistent. Avoid singsong patterns. Children can frequently imitate a singsong pattern more easily without actually comprehending the sentence and producing it at their level of understanding. Experimenters should establish and practice intonation for each experiment.
- Encouragement. Provide continual encouragement to the child. Children should always be told they are doing a good job and encouraged to imitate the sentence even though they may not be repeating the adult sentence exactly. In fact, it is important that the children feel good about themselves even when they are not able to imitate precisely. The children must feel they are doing well, even if the task is difficult for them. Use the child's name when praising. The experimenter must attempt to not systematically reinforce certain correct or incorrect responses.
- Researcher eye contact and reading battery sheet. Try not to look at the sentences too much; look at the child. Glance at the battery sheet to remind yourself of the sentence.
- Correcting researcher mistakes. If you make a mistake in administering the sentence, saying, "Mickey drinks his milk" instead of the correct battery sentence

---

7 For example, it may change the interpretation of a pronoun if you stress it. In *John thinks he is intelligent*, the pronoun *he* may refer to John or someone else, but if *he* is stressed, as in *John thinks HE is intelligent*, the referent of the pronoun has to be John.

Mickey drinks Donald's milk, make a note of it and go back to that sentence at the end of the battery and administer it correctly.
- <u>Contingency for incomplete session.</u> If the child does not complete the entire task in one session on one day, make sure you complete administering the remaining sentences as soon as possible. Too much delay will disqualify the data. There is no clear measure of what "too much delay" is, but the child should complete the task within a week.
- <u>Playback is only permissible at the session end.</u> Some children will imitate if they can hear their voices on tape. Children may be allowed to listen to their imitation on the recorder, but only during pretraining. Otherwise, the results will be contaminated.
- <u>Limited permissible word substitution.</u> If specific lexical items in your model sentences appear to be problematic for a child, you may substitute a word (preserving word length, syllable length, and all experimental variables—whatever the experiment is testing). If possible, try to change only one word.

6.1.7 Summary of the Elicited Imitation Task

This section provided the details for using the EI task in conjunction with experimental designs to elicit significant language production as data. Systematic design and administration techniques can ensure validity, reliability, and interpretability of data collected using this task.

6.2 The Elicited Production Task

6.2.1 What Is the Elicited Production Task?

Another technique commonly used to elicit language production in linguistic studies is often simply termed *elicited production* (EP), though it may take several forms. It is designed to reveal subjects' grammar by having them produce specific words or sentence types. In EP tasks, the researcher designs a set of contexts or situations that are intended to prompt subjects to produce the structures under investigation; therefore, the task may take different forms depending on the target structure and the situation: One may ask the subject to complete a sentence orally or in written form, or one may ask the subject to say something to a puppet or to answer questions about the images shown, and so forth.

6.2.2 Background Information: The Elicited Production Task

This technique is mostly used to test hypotheses regarding subjects' grammars in controlled experimental settings. One of the first studies that used EP and the most well known is Berko's 1958 study on children's acquisition of morphology. She showed children different drawings to have them produce different grammatical morphemes (e.g., past tense *–ed*, the plural *–s*) attached to novel words (words that do not exist in English but that conform to the structure of regular English words). For example, she showed children a drawing of a bird-like animal (see Figure 6.1) and said, "This is a wug." She then showed them another picture of two of these animals and said, "These are two . . . ," expecting the children to finish the utterance.

The uniqueness of the EP is that it allows the experimenter to elicit close to natural speech production in experimental settings without modeling the subject's responses (unlike EI). If a certain structure repeatedly appears in a child's elicited utterances, researchers using this task infer that it is part of that child's competence (Thornton, 1996).

6.2.3 Why Choose the Elicited Production Task?

EP tasks are suitable for children over the age of 3;0 and adults. Some experimenters have used it with younger children (age 2;06); however, at younger ages it becomes more challenging to keep the child focused on the experimental context. Whether this methodology can be used with younger children depends largely on the type of structure being studied. It is important when designing EP studies to make sure the interaction makes communicative sense. For instance, if we are asking the child to produce the answer to a question, the child must think we do not know the answer to the question, as in normal conversational situations. Ambridge and Rowland (2013) reported that even 2-year-olds can tell what the speaker's prior knowledge is. Pragmatic considerations such as this are important in any experimental situation, but they may be especially important in EP because many of the researcher–subject interactions in EP studies are presented as conversations.

6.2.3.1 Advantages

According to Thornton (1996), the following are the advantages of using an EP task:

- It is very close to natural speech because the subject's speech is not modeled.
- It enables the experimenter to control the meaning that is to be associated with the targeted utterance.
- The experimenter can try to provoke sentences corresponding to complex syntactic structures and/or ones that rarely occur in natural speech.
- A robust data sample of targeted structure can be gathered in one session.
- Controls can be added to test a particular scientific hypothesis. It can help us know what subjects can say and what they cannot say.

Fig. 6.1: "Wug" image for children's acquisition of morphology. From "The Child's Learning of English Morphology," by J. Berko, 1958, *Word*, *14*, p. 154. Copyright 1958 by Jean Berko. Reprinted with permission.

6.2.3.2 Disadvantages

- Using an EP task cannot guarantee that the participant will produce utterances the experimenter expects.
- It cannot ensure what the subject is attempting to say in a given context (as opposed to EI).
- The exact interaction between experimenter and participant is sometimes difficult to replicate.

6.2.4 Properties of Elicited Production Data

- The data produced can be compared with other data. EP is mostly used in cross-sectional studies in which significantly large amounts of participants are administered the same tasks. Because the researcher can control extraneous variables, the data can be compared across subjects.
- It is not scarce. Because the researcher controls the design of the task, he or she can decide how many utterances will be collected from each subject. It depends on the length of the batteries used in each study, but it is possible to collect significant amounts of occurrences of a particular structure in a single recording session.
- It can be considered as representative of the subject's competence. If a certain structure is repeatedly occurring in a subject's speech, it can be considered part of his or her grammar.

6.2.5 Collection of Elicited Production Data: Specific Procedures

When capturing EP data, similar procedures to the ones followed for EI must be considered. As with EI, it is necessary to keep in mind the importance of the recording equipment for capturing data in these tasks. High-quality voice recordings are necessary to retrieve the child's answers. In EP, a video recording of the task is also recommended; it will be helpful in recovering the context of each utterance (e.g., the picture the child was looking at) when transcribing.

One may use storybooks, pictures, props, or puppets in EP tasks. They let the child engage in "the game." The use of puppets may be helpful because children may feel comfortable talking to puppets. Common techniques for using puppets are telling the child that the puppet is too shy to talk to the experimenter or that the puppet cannot hear well and that the experimenter cannot speak loudly enough. This also eliminates the "you tell the puppet" reaction in the child (Thornton, 1996).

Blume (2002) used a storybook to elicit answers to questions varying in tense and aspect in Spanish about specific activities (e.g., ¿Qué está haciendo el perrito? 'What is the doggy doing?' and ¿Qué hacía la tortuga? 'What did the turtle do?'), with 2- and 3-year-olds. When asking questions in past tense, she selected a particular character that appeared on page 20, for example, and asked ¿Qué está haciendo el gato aquí?

'What is the cat doing here?' and then turned back the pages to page 5 where the same character appeared and said *Ahora, vamos a ver qué pasó antes. ¿Qué hacía el gato* 'Now, let's see what happened before. What did the cat do here?'.

In another task, (Blume & Rayas, 2016), the researchers showed English-speaking and Spanish-speaking children images of common places (e.g., a swimming pool, a bedroom, a bathroom, a kitchen) and asked them about their activities there (e.g., "What do you do here?") to elicit verbs describing habitual events.

When stories are used, it is recommended to mix the characters. Batman, Cinderella, and Shrek can appear in the same story. This will prevent the child from assuming the outcome of the story (Thornton, 1996). The puppets, storybooks, and props must be previously prepared, and the experimenter should have a script to ensure that the interaction with each child will be the same. However, small deviations from the script may be acceptable from subject to subject; for example, if after providing an answer a child continues talking about a related issue, the researcher should not interrupt him or her.

If pictures or objects are used, children should be tested on their names in a pretraining session. Otherwise, it will be impossible to distinguish whether the child is not responding because she or he lacks the grammatical knowledge or because she or he does not know the name of the place, the object, or the character.

It is not recommended that the same story be repeated more than twice. If a child fails to answer after the second attempt, move on. However, it is better to use a filler (i.e., a nonexperimental stimulus to which the child can easily give an appropriate answer) before the next utterance so that the child does not feel like she or he is failing in the game.

The experimenter must control his or her speech during pretraining and task administration. The child should not hear the target responses modeled in the experimenter's speech.

> Example 4.
> *Researcher*: what do you do in this place? do you **swim** here?
> *Subject*: yes, I swim here.

If the answer was modeled by the experimenter, it should not be considered in the analysis. If the researcher realizes he or she has made this mistake, he or she should make a note and repeat the same structure at the end of the experimental task.

6.2.6 Variations on the Elicited Production Task

Various approaches to attempting to elicit structured production from children exist, modified by the researcher's questions. In one approach (Potts, Carlson, Cocking, & Copple, 1979), a cloze procedure was integrated with an experimental design of stimulus sentences and pictures providing a context appropriate to a particular question (a *cloze procedure* refers to the deletion of certain words in a text; the text is then presented as a fill-in-the-blank test to participants). For example, in testing syntactic and semantic knowledge of reciprocals in language, children were asked to complete a structured interview question, as follows:

Example 5.
   Researcher: *Sometimes when dogs see other dogs, they bark. These dogs are barking at _____.*
   Child's anticipated response: *Each other.*

6.3 Other Tasks: Picture Description and Narrative Tasks

A picture description task is often used clinically to elicit speech, such as in the "Cookie Theft" picture task in the Boston Diagnostic Aphasia test or the frog story used in many studies of first, second, and bilingual language acquisition (Mayer & Mayer, 1975; Sánchez, 2006). These are well-known materials that consist of a single picture depicting a situation (cookie theft) or a set of pictures that narrate a single story (frog story). Such a task allows the researcher or clinician to deduce language and speech from a subject in a fairly natural situation. The subject may simply be asked to "describe everything going on in the picture," that depicts some event. Subjects' responses can then be analyzed for both their cognitive component (did they understand the gist of the event described in the picture?) and for their linguistic component (e.g., to what degree complex sentences are used). Although useful in their naturalness and ease of administration, the difficulty of such tasks for research purposes is that there are no common standards for administration, transcription, or analyses and interpretation of such data. Similar approaches have been used with children, (e.g., in the frog stories; R. A. Berman & Slobin, 1994). General procedures for natural speech assessment can be applied here.

6.4 Summary

Various approaches have been developed for eliciting language production data for research purposes. These range from naturalistic collections of speech to experimentally designed tasks. We have used the EI task to exemplify how standards can be developed to align this task with experimental methods and, thus, strengthen data reliability, replicability, and interpretation in pursuit of specific research questions. Many of these standards can be generalized to other EP tasks, each of which has its advantages and disadvantages.

7 Experimental Tasks for Generating Language Comprehension Data

Our knowledge of language allows us to map language from its form to its meaning. In comprehending language, we must integrate our knowledge of all formal aspects of language (i.e., its sound system, syntax, lexicon) to interpret that language. Testing a subject's language knowledge through a test of language comprehension, however, is complex, especially because language comprehension always involves much more than grammatical competence. Hearers must relate the sentence they hear to what they know and believe about reality in the world and in that particular testing situation. Experimental designs and test contexts must try to factor out grammatical knowledge from these other factors (Garrett, 1981; Lust, Chien, & Flynn, 1987; Saddy, 1992; Swinney, 2000; Townsend & Bever, 2001; Zurif, 1983). At the same time, a subject's interpretation of a sentence is determined to some degree by the linguistic structure of that sentence. Therefore, we can get evidence for the subject's knowledge of that linguistic structure through tests of language comprehension, just as we do on the basis of language production (e.g., Chapter 6, this volume). With careful experimental designs, we may use these tasks to assess what aspects of language knowledge a subject may or may not have.

7.1 The Act-Out "Toy Moving" Task

One technique for eliciting and assessing language comprehension behavior is the act-out task. It can be effective, especially when applying the experimental method of scientific inquiry for the study of language acquisition.

7.1.1 What Is the Act-Out Task?

7.1.1.1 Act-Out Task Description

The *act-out task* (AO) is sometimes referred to as a *toy-moving task*. The subject is given a specific set of dolls and props and asked to show the researcher (by moving the dolls and props) how he or she interprets a sentence—a "little story"—you read aloud, as in Examples 1 and 2, as follows.

>Example 1. *The chicken who touched the tissue bumped Ernie* (Flynn & Lust, 1980).

Example 2. *Fozzie tickled Big Bird when he dropped the cat* (Lust, Solan, Flynn, Cross & Schuetz, 1986).

The main purpose of this method is to elicit and assess a subject's language comprehension in a way that is simple and observable. Sentences administered as stimuli in the AO task can be designed to vary systematically in specific syntactic and semantic factors so that one can assess the role of these factors in affecting or determining the child's comprehension. They can also be designed to be compared with experimental sentences used in other tasks, tests of production such as elicited imitation, or tests of comprehension such as the truth-value judgment task, thus providing converging evidence with other tasks. Essentially, the participant in this task who demonstrates a particular AO behavior when interpreting a sentence can display a construction of the subject–predicate relations of the sentence, as well as other semantic aspects varied in the design, (e.g., potential co-reference between pronouns and antecedents which the sentence may involve; see Example 2).

7.1.1.2 Logical Structure of the Act-Out Task

The psycholinguistic structure of the AO task requires the following from the adult or child subject: The participant must (a) hear the stimulus sentence (e.g., Example 1), analyze it, and perceive it; (b) represent it in memory and store it over time while he or she engages in the AO task; (c) interpret its meaning, or at least a possible meaning; (d) assess the given physical situation and the materials available for interpretation; (e) consider the viability of an interpretation in terms of this physical context; (f) physically represent this meaning isomorphically through physical behaviors with the dolls and props (Lust et al., 1987). The AO task is, therefore, a cognitively complex task. It requires the subject to hold the interpretation of the model sentence in working memory, decode the sentence, and plan the actions that will result in depicting a possible meaning of the sentence, given the immediate pragmatic context (note that, as for the elicited imitation task, decoding a sentence requires reconstructing it).

7.1.2 What Are Act-Out Data?

AO data are not specifically linguistic data. They consist of the subject's physical behaviors (i.e., toy and prop moving) observed as his or her response to each stimulus sentence. Different aspects of this behavior can be subsequently analyzed for "correctness" or other specific properties of comprehension in which the researcher is interested, for example (see Chapter 10). Verbal comments made during AO behavior are not directly, immediately involved in the task, although they can be subsequently analyzed. However, the participant's AO behavior may have linguistic significance. To the degree that language comprehension requires grammatical knowledge, certain AO behaviors reveal grammatical competence (e.g., Lust et al., 1987). If a subject's AO behavior is influenced by the linguistic structure of the stimulus sentences, we can assume that such behavior reveals knowledge of the linguistic factors involved in these structures.

7.1.3 The Act-Out Task: Background Information

The AO task has long been used to study first and second language acquisition (e.g., Flynn, 1987; Sinclair & Bronckart, 1972), as well as the comprehension abilities of aphasic patients (e.g., Saddy, 1992; Zurif, 1983). Some of the grammatical forms studied include pronouns, relative clauses, passive sentences, questions, and prepositions. Readers may be interested in seeing prior research in which this method has been applied to get a better understanding of it. Some research studies that applied the AO method are listed in Table 7.1 (for details of these references, see the References section of this volume; for a review, see Goodluck, 1996).

Tab. 7.1: Examples of Studies Using the Act-Out Task

Authors	Study subject	Language	Year
Chan, Meints, Lieven, & Tomasello	Word order	English	2010
C. Chomsky	English control structures	English	1969
Sherman & Lust	Control structures	English	1987
Flynn & Lust	Relative clause	English	1980
Foley, Núñez del Prado, Barbier, & Lust	Sloppy identity	English	1997, 2003
Goodluck	English null/PRO anaphora	English	1987
Goodluck & Solan	Principle C and c-command	English and French	1995
Guo, Foley, Chien, Lust, & Chiang	Sloppy identity	Chinese	1996
Guo, Foley, Chien, Chiang, & Lust			1997
Lust & Clifford	3-D study: Factors involved in anaphora interpretation	English	1986
Lust, Solan, Flynn, Cross, & Schuetz	Null/PRO anaphora	English	1986
Sinclair & Bronckart	Word order	French	1972
Somashekar et al.	Hindi relative clause acquisition	Hindi	1997

7.1.4 Why Choose the Act-Out Task?

You might choose the AO task if you were interested in whether a subject could understand a particular grammatical construction, (e.g., sentences with relative clauses, as in Example 1) or how a subject might interpret a sentence that is constrained against a certain interpretation in adult grammar or is ambiguous. This task is appropriate for working with very young children or other special populations (e.g., cognitively impaired or aphasic subjects) for whom other more complex experimental situations may not be appropriate (e.g., tasks that require the subject to orally produce a statement). Finally, you might choose this task if you were seeking to find converging evidence through different methods (e.g., combining a production task with a comprehension task).

7.1.5 Properties of the Act-Out Task

7.1.5.1 Advantages

- The AO task is simple to set up and administer. No particular equipment or lab setting is needed; therefore, it can be used in various field situations.
- The task is accessible to very young children. They are asked to "play with toys." At the same time, versions of the AO task can be used with adults (converting toys to objects).
- The task is sensitive to fine-grained syntactic distinctions. Experimental sentences can be precisely varied and manipulated, allowing specific experimental hypotheses to be tested.
- The task is nonintrusive. It allows subjects to provide any interpretation they want, without the researcher giving them a set of adult-predetermined possible interpretations. This is important because children—and impaired subjects—may have grammars that deviate from those of nonimpaired adults in ways that the researcher may have not imagined. The task does not depend on prior adult representations of a sentence's meaning. Unlike, for example, the picture judgment task, it allows the child to create his or her own interpretations of a sentence, which the adult may not have predetermined as an option.
- The task can also be used in standardized ways across languages and cultures in various field situations.

7.1.5.2 Disadvantages and Limitations

- All interpretations tested in the AO task must be possible to act out. Subjects must make their interpretations observable by acting them out motorically. There are certain kinds of structures (e.g., questions) and certain kinds of predicates (e.g.,

want, hope, be happy) that cannot be acted out. How would one act out a sentence such as "He thinks you are smart"? Both the verb *think* and the adjective *smart* are difficult to represent by moving toy and props.
- Certain interpretations may be available to the subject, but he or she may choose not to act them out (this same problem arises with natural speech and elicited production data). Thus, if one is testing ambiguous sentences, depending on the research design, one may observe the subject's preferred interpretation in his or her AO behavior but possibly not alternative interpretations that are acceptable to the subject but not preferred.
- Behaviors in the AO task may be prone to certain response biases; for example, the subject may act out the easiest solution, one that is readily available in the physical context. Subjects may, for example, always choose a doll on the right side of them, or they may choose the doll nearest them. It is, therefore, important to place the dolls and props at the same distance from the subject. Subjects are also sometimes prone to a "bird-in-the-hand" strategy, so the researcher must tell the subject to put back the dolls and props in their original location after acting out each structure.
- Behaviors in the AO task can be difficult to transcribe and interpret, requiring meticulous design of stimulus sentences, detailed transcriptions, and detailed coding criteria (see Section 10.4.2).
- Some researchers attempt to avoid motoric behaviors in estimating children's language knowledge (e.g., Hamburger & Crain, 1982). They observe that children's motoric behaviors provide a confounding variable in assessments of children's language knowledge. Thus, they favor tasks in which the child must only respond *yes* or *no* to acceptable interpretations of sentences (see for example Section 7.2.1).

7.1.5.3 Types of Act-Out Data

The AO task may be given in a more free form in which a set of dolls and props are made freely available to the child (Lust, Solan, Flynn, Cross, & Schuetz, 1986), or it may be applied in a more structured form in which the experimental context is pre-structured to constrain behaviors in certain ways (Foley, Núñez del Prado, Barbier, & Lust, 1997, 2003). We provide examples of each type next.

7.1.6 Procedures of the Act-Out Task: How Does One Capture Act-Out Data?

7.1.6.1 What Is Your Purpose? The Role of the Researcher

The role of the experimenter must be to induce the subject's natural interpretations and behaviors in response to the stimulus sentences without researcher influence.

7.1.6.2 Recording Devices

Although most elicitation techniques face similar issues regarding the use of recording devices, some techniques require special care. In this case, when a researcher decides to apply the AO task, there are unique considerations. Although many AO tasks were administered in the past with only manual written transcriptions of observed behaviors, video recording can be essential. Video recordings allow analysis and reanalysis of subjects' AO behaviors, which are often difficult to analyze, especially in the case of children. They provide reliability and authenticity of the AO data. Video recording must be done carefully to capture all the subject's movements with all the dolls and props used in the task.

7.1.6.3 Recording Situations

As with all experimental research methods, the child must be in a quiet place where there is little or no interference from the environment. At least one transcriber must be present to capture the child's responses to the AO task. One person should be responsible for the video recordings.

7.1.6.4 Design of Act-Out Studies

Like all experimental methods, the success of the AO task is based on the strength of the experimental design. The precise design of the experimental sentences is critical (see the principles of sentence design described in Chapters 5 and 6; see also Ambridge & Rowland, 2013).

A. Choice of the Lexicon

Unlike the elicited imitation task, in which the lexicon in stimulus sentences can be allowed to vary freely, in the AO task, sentences must be designed to include a lexicon that refers to a specific set of dolls and props that you have established the subject will use. Verbs in sentences must be physically "act-outable" by the subject with the particular dolls, and they must be clearly observable, not vague (e.g., *Bert liked Ernie* is not possible, and *Bert told Ernie* is often difficult to see). Verbs such as *pushed*, *ate*, or *jumped* are easily observable.

B. Design Caveats

All the experimental standardizations previously described for production studies should be followed here. The AO task requires making additional design decisions about the materials to be used:

- More than three dolls at a time may create cognitive overload for a young child or an impaired subject. Thus, many AO studies present the subject with only three dolls at a time.
- Props used must be restricted in number; three appears workable. No small props, which could be dangerous, are allowed when working with children because they could be swallowed.
- Sentence length can be about the same as in an elicited imitation study with children of a similar age. Pretesting to determine the appropriate length for a research study and an age group is advisable.
- Replication items can be put into a second battery of sentences. Dolls and props can be changed so that different dolls and props appear in each battery set, allowing the child to think it is a "new story" and not realize the structures are being replicated. The researcher often works with a set of six dolls, three for Battery A and three for Battery B.
- As with all tasks, the subject's pragmatic assumptions about the task must be understood (see Hamburger & Crain, 1982, for an example of this concern with the AO task). For example, in a test of a subject's relative clause knowledge, if the subject does not expect there to be more than one horse in an example such as *The horse that is brown wins the race*, it is possible that the task may be viewed as pragmatically infelicitous to the subject.

7.1.7 Collection of Act-Out Data: Specific Procedures

A set of materials (dolls and props), as well as appropriate recording equipment, must be designed, tested, and readied. This is in addition to the experimental test batteries and other research materials that should be prepared in an experimental folder to be taken to the field.

7.1.7.1 Administrative Steps With Children

Because the AO task involves a set of dolls and props, it is essential that you first ascertain that the subject knows the name of each of these. If need be, these should be taught to the subject. A set of "pretraining" sentences should be designed and the subject should be tested on them first before proceeding to the experimental sentences. The pretraining sentences should not contain any of the material that is used in the experimental sentences, but should get the subject used to the task and to the type and length of sentences to be used in the experiment. The experimental batteries should then be administered in random order one by one. The subject should be unaware of the shift from pretraining to experimental sentences. When administering the task, the same standardized procedures of administration should be followed. We briefly review these here.

- The experimenter should administer each sentence once and then allow adequate time for the subject to respond. The experimenter should not say or do anything, if possible, between the administration of the sentence and the subject's response.
- As in other tasks, if the subject asks questions about the meaning of the sentence, the experimenter might say, "Whatever you think" (or should indicate that it is the subject's decision, and whatever the subject does is correct). You are always testing for what is in the subject's mind, not what is in yours.
- If the subject appears not to be listening or to have lost attention, or if the subject requests another repetition of the sentence, the administrator may repeat the sentence once. Further repetitions should not be given, and the data scored should be based on the subject's response to the first administration of the sentence or, if not this, to the second. Data will be discounted in scoring if the experimenter has repeated the sentence more than twice.
- As with all experimental tasks, the subject's response must be based on the whole stimulus sentence administered at one time. The subject should be dissuaded from beginning the AO behavior before the experimenter has provided the whole sentence.
- If a child's AO behaviors include only part of the sentence (i.e., one clause in a complex sentence), the child may be asked, "Is there more?" If he or she does not provide more, the data consist of whatever the child has chosen to act out. If you do not follow this principle, you will not know that subjects' responses are to their representation of the full structure you have presented. Adequate time—which may be surprisingly long from an adult perspective—must be provided to the child without adult interference of any sort.
- The child should always be encouraged. Whatever the child does constitutes the actual data. Never should a child be corrected or influenced by an experimenter in an experimental task.

Administration of the AO task depends on the precise design of each study. However, general principles will be established regarding the materials with which the subject is working. For example, left-right position or the physical position of the doll or props the subject may be using should be controlled in their presentation to the subject and in their availability during the task. After each AO behavior, the dolls and props must be returned to their original position to ensure that the response to each experimental sentence starts from the same point, thus, enabling comparisons across conditions. Procedures for administration of the AO task must be standardized and recorded for each particular study so that they can be replicated. These procedures must address the precise set up of the physical dolls, props, and context of the task as well as the manner of administration for each of the stimulus sentences.

7.1.7.2 Structured Form of Act-Out Tasks

Depending on the research question, a more structured form of the AO task may be developed. For example, in a study designed to test children's interpretation of the ambiguity in sentences such those as in Example 2, children were presented with a set of three dolls and structured options for interacting with them. As in Figure 7.1, each doll was introduced as having a plate on which there were three objects. Each plate had a picture identifying its owner.

Example 3: *Bert bites his banana and Oscar does too.*

The question here was whether children would realize the ambiguity in these sentences (e.g., does Oscar bite his own banana, or Bert's, or someone else's; see Foley et al., 1997, 2003). By giving the child three structured options (three dolls to work with, e.g., Bert, Oscar, Fozzie Bear, and objects belonging to each doll) researchers could then observe whether the child had each doll bite their own banana, or each bite one of them (e.g., Bert's); all choices were equally available. This restricted the behavioral choices by the child to those that were critical to the research design. In other words, did children understand the ambiguity of the sentence? Did they have a preferred interpretation? (See Section 10.4.2 for transcription and scoring examples for this study.)

7.1.8 Summary of the Act-Out "Toy-Moving" Task

The use of the AO task to test language comprehension is best applied when one is participating in the experimental method of scientific inquiry. Stimulus sentences can be designed factorially as they are in tasks eliciting language production. Systematizing data collection methods can help to provide reliable data for interpretation. (See Section 10.4.2 for examples of transcription and analyses protocols for this type of task.)

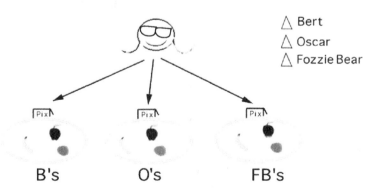

Fig. 7.1: A structured form of act-out task.

7.2 The Truth–Value Judgment Task

7.2.1 What Is the Truth–Value Judgment Task?

The *truth–value judgment task* (TVJ) provides another means for testing a subject's comprehension of language. The purpose of this task is to test a subject's comprehension by systematically isolating possible predetermined interpretations, exposing these to the subject, and evaluating whether he or she accepts these interpretations. As with other tests of comprehension, this task may be combined with other tasks (e.g., with a test of production or another test of comprehension) to provide converging evidence for a hypothesis tested.

Two main types of the TVJ task have been developed in the field. In the *dynamic type* (e.g., Crain & Thornton, 2000), the researcher physically acts out an interpretation of a sentence (using props) in front of the subject, and the subject is asked whether this behavior is a true representation of a sentence he or she hears. For instance, to test children's knowledge of pronoun interpretation, sentences such as those in Examples 4a and 5a are read (by a puppet) while the adult performs a behavior such as those in Example 4b and 5b with dolls and props (Crain & McKee, 1985).

Example 4. (a) *When HE stole the chicken, the LION was inside the box.*
(b) The experimenter shows the lion in the box stealing the chicken.
Example 5. (a) *HE ate the hamburger when the SMURF was inside the fence.*
(b) The experimenter shows the Smurf inside the fence eating the hamburger.

One version of this dynamic experimenter–AO type of TVJ task involved reinforcement: Children were told that if what the puppet said was true, they were to reward him (i.e., feed him a cookie); if not, they were to punish him (i.e., feed him a rag; Crain & McKee, 1985; Crain & Thornton, 2000; Gordon, 1996). In another type of the TVJ task, pictures are drawn and presented to the subject, and the subject is asked whether the picture is a true interpretation of the sentence (Chien & Lust, 2006; Chien & Wexler, 1987a, 1987b, 1990; Eisele & Lust, 1996). In Figure 7.2, children are tested for whether they will accept different interpretations of a sentence such as those in Example 6 by presenting them with two interpretations.

Example 6. *Lion cleans his window, and Rabbit does too.*

These structures are often called *sloppy identity sentences* because the referent of *his* is undetermined.

Figure 7.2 gives an example of the different interpretations of this sentence: *strict* and *sloppy* interpretations. Figure 7.2 (a(ii)) shows both animals cleaning their own windows, the *sloppy* interpretation, whereas in Figure 7.2(a (i)), both clean the same window, the *strict* interpretation (Foley et al., 2003).

a. True pictures
    (i) Strict   (ii) Sloppy

b. False pictures
    (i)   (ii)

Fig. 7.2: Truth–value judgment task. Pictures for "Lion cleans his window and Rabbit does too." From "Knowledge of Variable Binding in VP–Ellipsis: Language Acquisition Research and Theory Converge," by C. Foley, Z. Núñez del Prado, I. Barbier, and B. Lust, 2003, *Syntax*, *6*, p. 64. Copyright 2003 by John Wiley and Sons. Reprinted with permission.

False pictures (with false predicates), as in Figure 7.2(b), are necessary to ascertain that the subject's *yes* or *no* responses are veridical. The TVJ task (either type) requires the subject to make a binary or bipolar judgment—*yes* or *no* (or "not silly" or "silly")— if the sentence is believed to be true or false, respectively. Subjects are requested to judge whether a statement can accurately describe a particular situation or not.

7.2.1.1 Studying Language Acquisition Through a Truth–Value Judgment Task

Unlike in the AO task, in a TVJ task the researcher provides the subject with a predetermined interpretation of a sentence, and the subject is asked to judge whether the interpretation of the sentence presented by the researcher is true (or not false). In this sense, this task reverses the AO task in which a subject is asked to provide an interpretation for a sentence. Here, subjects do not spontaneously generate interpretations for sentences they hear, but certain interpretations are preselected by the experimenter. The task attempts to see whether the subject will find them possible.

7.2.1.2 Logical and Cognitive Structure of the Truth-Value Judgment Task

The TVJ task requires complex cognitive computation by subjects. In either form of the TVJ task, subjects must perceive a situation (either presented via an action by the dynamic experimenter-AO type [Crain & McKee, 1987] or via a picture) and then interpret this situation. They must hear a sentence presented orally and interpret it. Finally, they must relate the interpretation of the sentence heard to the interpretation of the situation just perceived. Many aspects of the sentence and the picture or demonstrated event may be considered in these interpretations. Because all sentences and all situations may be ambiguous (an infinite set of interpretations are always possible), the subject must consider whether the perceived situation fits a "possible" interpretation of the sentence. Then the sentence–situation match can be judged as true or false. Thus, the subject's sense of "truth" must be engaged. The TVJ task assumes

> that the child has some conception of the notion of truth in the sense of a correspondence between what is said and the situation referred to. Crucially, this requires the child to have an idea of what was said—that is, to construct a valid interpretation of the sentence via the parsing mechanisms, grammar, pragmatic assumptions, semantic entailments, and so on, that are available to her at that point in development. (Gordon, 1996, p. 212)

Grammatical factors may be involved in this decision (certain sentences may not allow a possible interpretation because the grammar for the language does not allow them). At the same time, pragmatic factors are also involved. If particular actions are pragmatically "unlikely" given a particular context, the sentence–situation match may be rejected as false.

The TVJ task has sometimes been confused with a grammaticality judgment (GJ) task (see Chapter 8). However, it is not a GJ task, but a task that tests the subject's comprehension. The subject is asked to interpret sentences and judge whether selected interpretations are possible. It does not require subjects to have metalinguistic knowledge, as does a GJ task (it does not require subjects to think about or talk about their grammatical knowledge of language, but only to apply this knowledge in interpreting a particular situation): "The task does not require the child to bring any of these processes to consciousness in any explicit way" (Gordon, 1996, p. 212).

7.2.2 What Are Truth-Value Judgment Data?

The TVJ task represents a type of method that reduces the overt behavior required from subjects (subjects do not have to engage their own motoric activity, as in the AO task, or their own vocal productions, as in language production tasks). The subject has only to indicate *yes* or *no* to the situation the experimenter presents. The data collected are thus a set of binary *yes* or *no* responses (acceptance or nonacceptance of a situation, given a particular sentence). In this way, because the "correct choice" data are only digital and binary, the analyses of these data must consist of a comparison of results against chance.

7.2.3 The Truth–Value Judgment Task: Background Information

After an experiment with the dynamic experimenter–AO type of the TVJ task provided interesting results (Crain & McKee, 1987), Chien adopted the picture judgment type of this task (Chien & Wexler, 1987a, 1987b, 1990). She did this to control the situation being presented to the child and apply it more thoroughly to experimental design methods that would more easily allow replication. For example, in the dynamic form, it is difficult to define, control, and repeat the exact set of actions provided over and over again by the researcher, both within a subject's session and across subjects tested. In the Cornell Language Acquisition Lab, the picture judgment form of the TVJ task has been favored for this reason (see Gordon, 1996, for a review).

7.2.4 Why Choose the Truth–Value Judgment Task?

You might choose this task if you were particularly interested in testing possible interpretations of a sentence that a subject had not spontaneously provided or if you were interested in whether the subject obeyed certain constraints against possible interpretations that you presented to him or her. Some examples of previous uses of this method are shown in Table 7.2.

7.2.5 Properties of Truth–Value Judgment Data

7.2.5.1 Advantages

- Once an experiment using the TVJ task has been designed, the task is easy to administer. It requires no specific linguistic training. The data are simple (binary *yes* or *no* responses) and easy to score and summarize.

Tab. 7.2: Examples of Studies Using a Truth Value Judgment Task

Authors	Study name	Language	Year
Crain & McKee	Acquisition of structural restrictions on anaphora	English	1985
Eisele & Lust	Knowledge about pronouns: A developmental study using a truth value judgment task	English	1996
Orfitelli & Hyams	Null subjects	English	2012
Pouscoulous, Noveck, Politzer, & Bastide	Processing costs in implicature production	English	2007

- The task also allows the researcher to investigate (a) interpretations other than those the subject might have spontaneously produced (that may simply reflect a "preferred interpretation" by the subject, not the only one she or he thinks is possible) and (b) hypothesized grammatical (or other) constraints on sentence interpretation. For example, Crain and McKee (1987) tested children's interpretations of sentences such as those in Examples 4 and 5 because they were interested in children's interpretations of pronouns such as *he* in these sentences. They wanted to know whether children would interpret *he* in Example 4 the same way they interpret *he* in Example 5. If they did, they would be violating a grammatical principle, Principle C of the Binding Theory in Universal Grammar, which says that a referring expression such as the noun *Smurf* should not be bound by another element (in this case the pronoun *he*) and, therefore, cannot co-refer with it (see Eisele & Lust, 1996; Lust, Eisele, & Mazuka, 1992). Chien and Wexler (1987a, 1987b) tested whether children would interpret the pronoun *him* in the same way they interpret the pronoun *himself* in another experiment using a similar method, thus testing another grammatical constraint reflecting another principle of the Binding Theory in the theory of Universal Grammar.
- The TVJ task can be used with impaired populations and/or second language learners, whose lack of productive spoken competence may hide greater grammatical knowledge, or with an adult control group.

7.2.5.2 Disadvantages and Limitations

- Because the cognitive act involved in the TVJ task is complex, all these factors (grammatical, pragmatic, cognitive) are involved in determining the subject's response to the task. The researcher must attempt to factor out these sources in interpreting the behavior and in designing the experimental stimuli. For example, subjects may be responding to any aspect of the picture or scene they have been shown (e.g., the position or specific act of the agent shown when they accept or reject a sentence).
- Because the form of the behavior gathered in this task is a "forced choice" binary response, there is no linguistic behavior that is directly gathered with this task. The researcher must infer the role of the grammatical component and other components involved. This inference is more indirect than with other methods that derive more specifically linguistic behavior.
- Because in a TVJ task the researchers predesign the sentence interpretations with which they want to test the subject, spontaneous interpretations the experimenters have not thought of will not be discovered, in contrast to the AO task.
- As with all methods, the TVJ task is more accessible as a test of certain types of sentences than others. For example, it is not clear how it could be used to test a subject's knowledge of the syntax of question formation.

- Children, especially young children, may become bored with the task over time. They may develop a response set, answering *yes* or *no* to all questions. They may often favor a *yes* response as a response set that favors agreement with the person testing them.

7.2.5.3 Age of Suitability for the Truth–Value Judgment Task

Studies have worked with groups of children 3;0 years old and older. Adult control groups have also been tested. Younger children show more acceptance of false pictures and a tendency to say *yes* (e.g., Eisele & Lust, 1996). Some 2-year-olds have been tested (Crain & McKee, 1987), although there are no known large groups of subjects of this age.

7.2.6 Procedures of the Truth–Value Judgment Task: How Does One Capture Truth–Value Judgment Data?

7.2.6.1 What Is Your Purpose? The Role of the Researcher

The researcher should make sure that the subjects understand they have to judge whether a sentence matches an interpretation presented to them by actions or pictures and to answer *yes* or *no* accordingly. For example, in the picture judgment task, the researcher explains to the child that he or she will see a picture and that a "story" will be read for each picture. Sometimes the story will match the picture and others times it will not. The researcher explains that the subject's task is to determine whether the story matches the picture by saying *yes* or *no*. Some researchers favor the terms "silly" or "not silly." After the pretraining sentences, when the experimenter is certain that the subject understands the game, the experimental testing begins.

7.2.6.2 Recording Devices and Situations

Depending on the type of task, audiotaping or videotaping may be more or less important. In a picture judgment task, audio and videotaping are recommended although not necessary. However, videotaping is important for the dynamic type of the TVJ task. It can be handy for double-checking whether the researcher accidentally makes mistakes in acting out the sentence for the subject. The researchers can continually note on preprepared scoring forms which response the subject gave to which stimulus (*yes* or *no*). Spontaneous responses, as well as binary judgments, by the subject should be recorded.

7.2.6.3 Design of Truth-Value Judgment Studies

As with all tasks used experimentally, the success of the TVJ task depends on the strength of the experimental design. The precise design of the experimental sentences is critical; principles of sentence design hold. True and false pictures must be equalized and randomized, as well as true and false pictures not related to the experimental factors, such as false predicates. In addition, the precise design of the pictures or the experimenter behavior is critical (e.g., pictures should be clear and equally attractive, researchers should not smile only when the subject answers correctly).

A. Choice of the Lexicon

As in all comprehension tasks, the choice of the lexicon cannot vary freely. It must be adaptable either to an experimenter's AO behaviors, which are observable and interpretable by a subject, or adaptable to a picture drawing that can represent it.

B. Design Caveats

All the experimental standardizations described earlier should be followed here also (e.g., the intonation of the experimental sentences as they are read must be carefully designed and controlled). Pretesting sentences must be designed according to the experimental design, as with other tasks reviewed earlier. In addition, this task requires other special design components. For example, given that a subject may respond randomly *yes* or *no* or may adopt a response bias (i.e., saying *yes* to everything), the researcher's design must involve a set of "false" pictures (or situations) independent of the experimental design to test for the subject's willingness and ability to say *no* when necessary (e.g., Figure 7.2 (b)). The exact design of such false pictures is an issue for the design (i.e., whether the subject or the predicate is false). Data from such conditions are necessary to argue that the subject is willing and able to express dissent in situations that are clearly false. Such situations should also be built into the pretesting sentences. In addition, because every judgment about the truthfulness of a situation or picture will involve thought about the pragmatic context it involves, numerous replications of a sentence type with numerous examples of various interpretations must be provided. Presenting the sentence either before or after the picture may, in fact, influence the results differently than would simultaneous presentation, although this has not been tested yet to the best of our knowledge (Eisele & Lust, 1996).

C. Materials

In the case of the dynamic experimenter-AO form of the TVJ task, materials and props must be chosen with similar constraints as in the AO task. In the case of the picture judgment, pictures must be prepared in accord with the experimental design. In studies that tested children's knowledge of ambiguity, pictures were drawn that depicted each of the two critical types of interpretation possible for a sentence, such as that in Figure 7.2 (Foley et al., 2003; Guo, Foley, Chien, Lust, & Chiang, 1996). These pictures must be either drawn specifically for the research study or adapted from existing pictures. In the case of published pictures, copyright permission must be obtained if the study results are published and this publication involves reproduction of sample pictures.

7.2.7 Collection of Truth–Value Judgment Data: Specific Procedures

One picture (or one experimenter AO behavior) at a time is presented to the subject in conjunction with a sentence read by the experimenter.

- The experimenter must explain to subjects that they must say *yes* when the sentence matches the picture or the situation and *no* when it does not.
- A pretraining period should be included to ensure that the subject understands the task and is able to answer *no* to the false sentences.
- A set of materials (either dolls and props or pictures) must be prepared in keeping with the experimental design and readied before testing and then administered in random order in conjunction with the sentence stimuli.
- The picture and the sentence are presented at the same time.
- As in other tasks, the researcher should refrain from speaking between the administration of the stimuli and the subject's response.
- The researcher should give at most two repetitions of the stimulus sentence and encourage the participant to figure out the interpretation when the subject requests some help.

7.2.8 Summary of Truth–Value Judgment Task

The TVJ task tests a subject's comprehension of language on the basis of certain possible interpretations predetermined for testing. It can be easily administered, and its data can be easily transcribed. It is especially effective in targeting constraints in language knowledge (i.e., it allows specific testing of whether specific ungrammatical interpretations are allowed by the subject). To be effective, it requires a strong experimental design and numerous controls of the materials and sentences used. It requires statistical testing of *yes/no* responses against chance. It does not provide direct linguistic data but can usefully be combined with other comprehension or production tests. Research has shown that results from use of the TVJ and AO tasks cohere (see Eisele & Lust, 1996, for an example of converging results across the TVJ and other tests of language knowledge; see also Chapter 11, this volume).

7.3 Other Tasks: Picture Selection and "Questions After Stories" Tasks

Numerous possibilities exist for the researcher to develop tests of language comprehension; we review others next. The standards of administration reviewed in previous chapters should be followed in these tasks, as in others.

7.3.1 Picture Selection Task

In a picture selection or picture verification task, the subject is presented with two (or more) pictures at a time and is asked to choose the one that best matches the sentence (Chien & Wexler, 1987a, 1987b). Many of the design and interpretation issues that arise in the TVJ task arise here as well. See Serratrice (2007) for an example of the use of this type of task with 8-year-old bilingual children.

7.3.2 "Questions After Stories" Task

In the "questions after stories" approach, subjects are read narratives by the experimenter and then queried with specific questions to attempt to adduce different possible interpretations of the story and/or to evaluate whether certain interpretations do not occur (see de Villiers & Roeper, 1996, for an example and review of development of this method). In these cases, subjects must first process and interpret every aspect of the narrative (each sentence alone, as well as the discourse structure) as presented and then address the experimenter's question regarding the story; this complex cognitive process must affect their final response. All the cognitive components that occur in other tests of comprehension, such as the AO task or TVJ task, occur here as well. The results of this comprehension task are, thus, especially complex to analyze.

7.4 Summary

All tests of language comprehension, no matter how simple they may appear at first, are cognitively complex, both for the subject and for the researcher's analyses. They require not only formal grammatical knowledge but also a wide array of processing and pragmatic reasoning. They provide behavior as data that are not specifically linguistic. The researcher must factor out the many varied factors both in designing research using these tasks and in analyzing and interpreting data obtained from any comprehension task.

8 The Grammaticality Judgment Task

Linguists developing theories of language base these theories on their "intuitions" about what is grammatical. Linguists doing field work on another unknown language must ask "informants" for their intuitions about the language they are investigating. In both cases, the linguist or the informant is making a judgment about what is possible or impossible in the grammar of a language. The contrast between what is and is not allowed is critical. One does not know a language unless one knows both the infinite productivity and the infinite constraints the language system allows. Judgments must thus be attained for both of these grammatical components. These judgments are termed *grammaticality judgments*.

Although the grammaticality judgment (GJ) task is a basic method used in the field of linguistics, the task is difficult to administer and interpret even with adults (see Schütze, 1996). Although the GJ task has been used in the study of adult second language acquisition with some success, it is not easily accessible by children, especially in research studies requiring systematization and larger samples; thus, it is only rarely used with children, and we only briefly review it here.

8.1 Studying Language Acquisition Through a Grammaticality Judgment Task

8.1.1 What Is the Grammaticality Judgment Task?

8.1.1.1 Description

In a GJ task, a subject hears or reads a sentence and is asked to judge whether it is grammatical or not. The task is meant to elicit an informant's judgment on the potential grammar underlying the sentence, not on the meaning per se. The GJ task can be used to elicit judgments about various aspects of grammar. Through the design of this task, the researcher hopes to test whether the subject has knowledge of various grammatical constraints and of where the grammar is productive. For example, a sentence such as that in Example 1 is not possible grammatically. Example 2 shows a grammatically possible sentence.

Example 1. *Fish to likes Mary.
Example 2. *Mary likes to fish.*

Because in Example 1 the English grammatical word order and the phrase construction are "ungrammatical," it is assumed that an informant who knows this aspect of English grammar will reject sentences like that in Example 1 but accept sentences like that in Example 2. It is important not to confuse this task with a truth-value judgment (TVJ) task. The TVJ task tests language comprehension; in that task, as in other comprehension tasks, the subject is asked to judge potential meanings of sentences (see Chapter 7). In the GJ task, the participant is asked to judge the grammar. The sentence in Example 2 should be accepted whether true or not.

8.1.1.2 Logical and Cognitive Structure

The elicitation of a GJ is complex. Language knowledge is unconscious. It is tacit knowledge and usually not brought to consciousness, except by practicing linguists and psycholinguists. The GJ task requires informants to access *metalinguistic knowledge*, knowledge about their tacit knowledge of language.

To give a GJ, the informant must hear (or read) and register the sentence—that is, provide it with a form of cognitive representation available for "thinking about." To do this, the informant must reconstruct the sentence; this requires access to and integration of its grammatical aspects (i.e., syntax and semantics), as well as lexicon (note that this is the same cognitive subprocess that is involved in language production tasks such as elicited imitation or in comprehension tasks). The participant must map successfully between form and meaning. The informant who is judging grammaticality must consider whether the sentence he or she heard and represented could be used in various possible pragmatic contexts other than in the immediate situation. If a sentence is ungrammatical, it should not allow the hearer to map form to meaning in any context of use. The informant must thus both associate the sentence form with meaning to represent it and dissociate it from pragmatics of use in making a GJ.

The complexity of these cognitive subprocesses in making what appears to be a simple *yes/no* GJ underscores the fact that these judgments are difficult to elicit and to interpret even with adults in the same culture, and more so with adults in other cultures (e.g., while doing field work on an unstudied language) or with children. In all cases, it is particularly difficult to interpret a *no* judgment on a test sentence. Informants could be responding to a potential meaning they have accessed, a particular use of the lexicon, or other factors. It is for this reason that field linguists sometimes hold that a *yes* judgment is more informative. Grammatical sentences may be rejected, as in the case of N. Chomsky's (1957) famous example "Colorless green ideas sleep furiously" (p. 15), a sentence that is grammatical. However, counterevidence to a *no* judgment can be adduced (e.g., by asking why is this not possible), although it may not be sought for a positive *yes* judgment. At the same time, with children and with some cultures, informants may not want to offend the researcher by providing a *no* judgment.

8.1.2 What Are Grammaticality Judgment Data?

The data resulting from administration of the GJ task are simple on the surface. The data usually consist of binary *yes* or *no* judgments by the informant. These *yes*/*no* judgments are assumed to indicate whether the subject accepts the grammar of the stimulus sentence or not. Asking informants why they have made their judgment can extend data.

8.1.3 The Grammaticality Judgment Task: Background Information

Field workers have long been concerned with the complexities of eliciting judgments from informants (Harris & Voegelin, 1953) and continue to study this process today in attempts to foster its reliability and validity. When one is trying to characterize the underlying cognitive competence for language, linguists have to be concerned when their judgments are not shared by other linguists or nonlinguists (Schütze, 1996). With children, it is difficult to convey the idea of "being able to say" a sentence divorced from possible meaning or pragmatic relevance of the sentence, as Example 3 (taken from Lust, 2006, after an interview by S. Shattuck-Hufnagel and K. Long, personal communication, 1977, with a 5-year-old child, p. 131) illustrates:

> Example 3. *Researcher*: suppose I say this sentence: "Jessica are a girl." Is that OK?
> *Child*: well, I don't like you. (wailing)

This culminated in a long exchange, with the researcher attempting to explain to the child what was required by the task: not "simple repetition," not the meaning or pragmatic relevance of the individual sentence, but the grammar (in the case of this sentence, the grammar of English agreement, which requires "Jessica is a girl").

This problem was a major motivation for development of other tasks, such as natural speech observations, to study young children's language knowledge. Some researchers, however, have reported successful use of the GJ task with some children, especially those 4 years old and older (McDaniel & Smith Cairns, 1996). Others have searched for children's awareness of grammaticality through other methods, such as looking for children's "spontaneous repairs" in their natural speech (e.g., E. V. Clark & Andersen, 1979). Although the GJ task has been only rarely used with young children, it has more often been used in studies of second (or further) language acquisition with some success, often with written stimuli.

8.1.4 Why Choose the Grammaticality Judgment Task?

In the ideal world, the GJ task would access the grammatical system in the mind more directly than other tasks that test comprehension or production of language. This is its intent.

8.1.4.1 Advantages

- The GJ task is the most fundamental task used in theoretical linguistics—one through which a researcher hopes to access "intuitions" about the grammar of language in native speakers. It would be desirable to have the same tasks used by adults and children.
- It can be used with language learners, including children (usually after the age of 4;0), for comparison with other tasks.
- It can be used more easily with adult second language learners.
- It attempts to test knowledge of grammatical "constraints" (i.e., what is not possible in language in general or in a language in particular).
- The data produced are simple (i.e., binary *yes/no* judgments).

8.1.4.2 Disadvantages

- The GJ task cannot easily underlie experimental method. Linguists (especially those practicing generative grammar) usually gather grammaticality judgment data informally (based on themselves, colleagues, and other native speakers). Responses are usually not quantified unless the *yes* and *no* digital judgments are assumed as straightforward data.
- It is difficult to convey to the informant that the researcher is requesting a judgment about the grammar (e.g., the syntax) underlying the sentence, rather than the meaning or pragmatics of the sentence.[1] Thus, it may be difficult to determine from an informant's answer whether he or she is ruling in (or out) a sentence because of its grammar or semantics or by judging whether the sentence is appropriate for a particular given or imagined pragmatic context.
- Many additional complexities characterize the attempts to gather GJs from children. The researcher must evaluate children's *metacognitive abilities* (their ability to make metalinguistic judgments) and must get them to understand what a GJ is. Children cannot be expected to know what the term *sentence* means. They often view the question about language syntax as a question about other aspects of language (Berthoud-Papandropoulou, 1978; Papandropoulou & Sinclair, 1974; see L. Gleitman & Gleitman, 1970, for evidence on children's access of different levels of language knowledge).

---

[1] For example, Edward Sapir attempted different grammatical paradigms with informants, including some he knew to be grammatical, and received varied responses, such as, "We don't say that here" (e.g., Anderson, 1985).

- Different contexts can make a sentence seem "acceptable" or not. Acceptability and grammaticality need not be identical, and it is hard to pinpoint the difference between them experimentally.
- Subjects may be inconsistent in their responses. It is difficult to obtain a large group of comparable responses suitable for statistical analysis.
- Subjects may get tired and confused, and a *"yes* response" bias can occur.[2] For unsure subjects, it is advisable to look away after administering the sentence because subjects may be responding to what they think the experimenter wants to hear (i.e., Clever Hans effect).[3] Researchers must watch for these effects.

8.1.5 Procedures of the Grammaticality Judgment Task: How Does One Capture Grammaticality Judgment Data?

8.1.5.1 Role of the Researcher

As in all research tasks, your job is not to determine the subject's response, but to elicit it and record it. In some cases, children can judge correctly but give wrong reasons for their judgment. For example, they might claim that the ungrammatical sentence *The elephant are jumping* is wrong because elephants do not jump. Therefore, it is important for the experimenter to find ways to try to ascertain whether subjects (and especially children) are judging the form of a sentence and not the meaning. Even though a research project might be focused uniquely on child language, an adult control group should be included.

Therefore, when using the GJ task, the researcher may have to build in follow-up interventions with the participant to resolve the meaning of *yes* and *no* responses; for example, one may ask the subject to provide the corresponding correct form of the structure to find out what the participant thinks is the source of the ungrammaticality. This is illustrated in Example 4.

---

[2] A *yes response bias* exists when participants tend to answer *yes* regardless of the particular stimulus presented to them.
[3] The *Clever Hans* effect is a well-known effect in experimental psychology by which the participant guesses what the expected answer is from clues provided unintentionally by the experimenter (e.g., a smile, a more relaxed body). The effect is named after Clever Hans, a German horse in the early 1900s who was presented at street fairs claiming he could add numbers given to him by his owner; he answered by tapping his hoof the number of times that matched the result of the addition operation presented to him. It was later discovered that the horse responded to the facial expression and posture of the questioner, which got tenser as Clever Hans approached the intended number and relaxed once he had given the right answer.

Example 4. *Researcher*: is it correct to say, "Jessica are a girl."
Participant: no.
Researcher: what would you change to make "Jessica are a girl" a correct English sentence?

The researcher can then judge from the answer given to the second question whether the participant is judging the sentence by the correct grammatical criteria. Examples 5 through 8 illustrate possible answers to the question "What would you change to make 'Jessica are a girl' a correct English sentence?"

Example 5. *Participant*: Jessica is a girl.
Example 6. *Participant*: Jessica are girls.
Example 7. *Participant*: Jessica is a woman. My aunt Jessica is 70 years old!
Example 8. *Participant*: it would be better to say, "Jessica is a lady."

The researcher can then judge by this second answer that in Example 5 the participant has indeed identified the intended grammatical error but in Example 6 he or she has not because he or she is providing another ungrammatical structure as a solution. In Example 7, we can see that the participant is judging whether the sentence is a true statement rather than its grammaticality, and in Example 8, we can see that the speaker is judging the appropriateness of the sentence for a particular formal context. Therefore, these follow-up questions are fundamental for understanding the nature of the participant's response.

8.1.5.2 The Subject

This task has been found to be applicable to some children 4 years old and older, although some researchers have reported that it has been used successfully with some 3-year-olds and a few (older) 2-year-olds (McDaniel & Smith Cairns, 1996). Not all older children perform successfully on the task in terms of judging grammar, and most younger children do not. Both individual and developmental differences must be considered. Some children may grasp the task quickly, others may need more than one pretraining session, and others may never be amenable to the task—for example, the child who gave the response "Well, I don't like you."

8.1.5.3 Design of Grammaticality Judgment Sentences

Sentences for elicitation must obey all the general constraints we reviewed in Chapter 5 (e.g., constraints on length and structure to control variance across the target focus) and those that characterize the other tasks. Stimulus sentences can be designed factorially, as with any other task in an experimental design.

8.1.6 Collection of Grammaticality Judgment Data: Specific Procedures

As in the case of other tasks described in this manual, it is necessary to administer pretraining, practice, and pretest sentences to the child before presenting the experimental sentences.

8.1.6.1 Pretraining

Pretraining is essential in this task because many subjects may be preliterate or not accustomed to talking about language or thinking about it. In pretraining, it is advisable to include sentences that represent several grammatical distinctions. Otherwise, subjects might assume that the experimenter is interested in only one type of ungrammaticality, and this might generate a response bias. For these variations, when working with children, try to select grammatical structures that are acquired early. The purpose of including these extra sentences is to observe how children will judge them if they understand the task.

It is recommended to start the pretraining with declarative sentences even if the study is interested in other grammatical types (e.g., interrogatives). Declarative sentences are easier to judge, and they are more helpful in getting children focused on the task. Children may start providing answers to the interrogatives instead of judging their grammatical form if they do not understand the task. In the following quotations, ways of introducing the task to a child are suggested:

> In presenting the task initially, we start with words rather than with sentences. We point to a prop—say, a strawberry—and ask the subject whether the right word to describe it is *chair*. Most subjects catch on right away and say *no*. We then remind the subject that we will also say things the right way sometimes, and we name another object correctly. We go through as many single words as the subject needs to catch on, but few subjects have needed more than the initial two words. (McDaniel & Smith Cairns, 1996, p. 238)

Once subjects have focused on form at the word level, researchers move on to examples with sentences.

Example 9.

> Suppose that this lion goes to this water and starts drinking it, like this. Suppose that I want to *say* what's happening. I'm going to try to say it, and you tell me if I'm saying it the right way or the wrong way. *The lion drinking is.* (McDaniel & Smith Cairns, 1996, p. 238)

After the experimenter is convinced that language has been established as a topic, the task can be introduced.

8.1.6.2 Suggested Instruction to the Subject

McDaniel and Smith Cairns (1996) suggested that it may be possible to get children focused on the grammar of their language by having the experimenter discuss language acquisition with the subject and explain what linguistics is and what a linguist does. The experimenter can also bring up other languages if the subject speaks them or has heard them on television, in the community, and so forth.

The best way of introducing the GJ task is telling children they will hear several sentences (note that the child must understand what a sentence is) and that they should tell the experimenter whether the sentences sound like he or she is talking "right" or whether they sound like he or she is talking "wrong." The experimenter has to explain to the child that sometimes he or she will say the sentences right, and sometimes he or she will say them wrong. An advisable strategy for presenting the task is telling the child that he or she and the experimenter will both pretend that the experimenter does not know or speak the child's language, and the child has to help the experimenter learn it.

Some researchers use puppets to present the sentences because children might be uncomfortable telling an adult that he or she is wrong. Some experimenters prefer using a puppet to introduce the task and asking the child to say whether the puppet is talking the right or wrong way. Another strategy that can be used is to tell the child that the puppet does not know how to speak the language or is just learning to speak the language that the child speaks and that the child's task is to teach the puppet how to speak it.

Narration (what the experimenter says while setting the appropriate context with the props) should be minimal and not divert the child from the task. Narration should also include all the lexical items of the test sentence but not include the sentence to be judged. Because children especially may find it unnatural to judge the form of the sentences, rather than the meaning, McDaniel and Smith Cairns (1996) suggested the first items of the pretest can be ill-formed words (e.g., *childs*, *goed*), after which the experimenter can proceed to complete sentences. They suggested that subjects can be coaxed to understand that a sentence such as *This is the boy what Grover talked to* is wrong because of grammar rather than meaning.

8.1.6.3 Presenting the Experimental Sentences

The following are examples of suggested forms the experimenter can use to present the test sentences (from McDaniel & Smith Cairns, 1996, p. 238):

- "Does it sound right or wrong to say . . . ?"
- "Does this sentence sound good or bad?"
- "Is this the right way or the wrong way to say it in English?"

- "How about ... ?"
- "Is it OK to say ... ?"

With children, it is not advisable to use the form "Can you say ... ?" (frequently used by linguists with adult informants) because it can be interpreted as a request for repetition. Furthermore, even though most of these forms are beginnings of interrogatives, it is important not to use interrogative intonation at the end of the test sentence unless the child is asked to judge interrogatives.

8.2 Summary

The GJ task is only rarely used with young children, given its cognitive complexity and the difficulty in interpreting the *yes/no* (or *right/wrong*) responses produced in the task, even with adults. It is especially difficult to adopt experimental designs that require standardized designs and methods of administration and analyses. However, it remains a privileged methodology in linguistics and assessments of adult second language acquisition, and some success has been reported with children, especially those 4 years old and older.

For an in-depth description of the GJ task as it has been used historically in linguistics and for detailed recommendations about constructing GJ tasks for adults, see Schütze (1996). For a fuller explication of attempts to use it in child language research, see McDaniel and Smith Cairns (1996) and L. Gleitman and Gleitman (1970) and (1979). As with all tasks, validity of task (i.e., whether the task is truly tapping grammatical knowledge) can best be assessed through converging evidence across tasks. The other tasks described in this manual all assess grammatical knowledge underlying observed behaviors participants produce (e.g., methods of language production and language comprehension).

III Managing and Interpreting Speech Data

9 Creating the Data II: Begin Data Processing

9.1 How to Use Data When Studying Language Acquisition

Each language elicitation task generates data that must be transcribed, coded, or scored. These codings or scorings must then be analyzed.[1] Only then can they be interpreted and used by the researcher to evaluate hypotheses regarding what the subject knows. Data must be "created" from the behaviors in each of the tasks administered. Chapter 3 summarized basic steps of the complex data creation process. In this chapter, we introduce more specific aspects of language data creation. We consider processes by which raw data are converted to data that can be studied scientifically; scientific principles must be applied at each stage of this process. Each task generates a different form of behavior (e.g., language production or language comprehension tasks, naturalistic/observational or experimental tasks). Therefore, each requires a slightly different series of data creation steps. We sketch only most basic principles and procedures here, concentrating on the first stage, data transcription.

The most fundamental type of behavior involving language is language production. As we have seen in preceding chapters, language can be naturally produced (as in natural speech samples) or experimentally induced by the researcher through an experimental task that elicits language production. Transcribing, coding, and analyzing language production data must integrate specifically linguistic methods of analysis with general principles of scientific methods in the behavioral sciences. Tests of language comprehension may not involve linguistic behavior directly at all—behaviors can be acted out with dolls, or *yes/no* responses can be elicited on truth-value judgment tasks. These require different forms of transcription, coding, and analysis but similar scientific principles and standardized procedures for data management and processing.

9.2 Data Transcription

The first step in the data creation process requires transcribing the behaviors resulting from the task that has been administered. *Transcription* involves writing down what has been observed—what has been performed by the subject/participant and heard

---

[1] See, for example, Grenoble and Furbee (2010), where among other relevant chapters, the one by Lust, Flynn, Blume, Westbrooks, and Tobin deals specifically with language acquisition data.

or seen by the researcher. These recordings provide the basis for what is studied to test the hypotheses being investigated in the research. The researcher must attempt to make this transcription, which records the subject's behavior, as descriptively accurate as possible, without insinuation of the researcher's intuitions or intentions regarding these behaviors, which may undermine the scientific method (see, e.g., the discussion of the Clever Hans phenomenon in H. Gleitman, Fridlund, & Reisberg, 2000).

Oral language production (speech) results in sound waves (perturbations in the air); this is the most basic source of language data. Before these raw data can be analyzed in a research study, they must be transcribed. Transcription is a fundamental but complex challenge (see Edwards 1992a, 1992b; Edwards & Lampert, 1993; Demuth 1996). It "is not a direct mirror of reality; it is a translation of a selected set of spatiotemporally organized oral and gestural events into a written medium with properties of its own" (J. A. Edwards, 1992b, p. 367). For an introduction to speech transcription see Rice (2011).

9.2.1 Introduction to Speech Transcription

9.2.1.1 Capturing the Data

When you transcribe the speech you hear, you transform the sounds of a speaker into a written form to "capture" the language and convert it to a form that you and others can study as scientific data. You perform a *transformation*—converting an aural medium to a written medium. You also perform a *cognitive act* by writing down what you think you heard the speaker say. Different people often think they hear different things from the same speaker's utterance. For this reason, creating an authenticated reliable transcript that is appropriate for scientific study is difficult. In the end, we try to know what a speaker said and how he or she said it as precisely as possible, using different principles to obtain this result.

9.2.1.2 Basic Principles

Generally, you will transcribe speech which has been collected on a recording—audio, video, or both. In some cases, researchers attempt to transcribe speech by hand as it is spontaneously uttered by a child. Without an accompanying audio and/or video recording, however, these data cannot be validated, replicated, or subject to reanalysis. A good transcription should be accurate and detailed, not only in terms of the language produced but also regarding the context of the situation or the context for the utterance the subject is producing (e.g., if the subject says, "What's that?" you should include a comment saying what he or she is referring to, if possible).[2] The following principles guide the process of transcription.

- Transcribe what the subject says, not what you think the subject is trying to say. Write down only what you hear, not what you would like to hear.

    Example 1. The child has said, "Uh wanna hear."
    DO NOT write, "I want to hear," because this is NOT what the child said.

- At the same time, you must provide additional information in the form of separate "comments" about the subject's language (i.e., what you think he or she was trying to say). For example, if the child utters "Mommy up," the researcher may comment that he or she believed the child was asking "Mommy, please pick me up" or "Mommy get up," and so forth. This is often called *rich interpretation*. Good transcriptions have multiple comments, including possible interpretations of what the subject said.
- Be accurate and precise. Do not hesitate to consult others on your research team when you are unsure.
- In a running record of your comments, you should mention any special aspects of your decisions about your transcription that you think are not straightforward and where you have made an individual decision.
- The most scientifically sound transcripts have had their reliability checked by more than one researcher, and records will be kept on points of disagreement (see Section 9.2.4).

9.2.1.3 Parts of a Transcript

1. *Session.* Each transcription should record one meeting or session with the subject at a time.
2. *Utterance.* Transcripts are analyzed in terms of utterances. For this reason, it is critical to try to approach systematicity in the coding of utterances. An utterance, however, is extremely difficult to code. An utterance is different from a sentence. A sentence is an abstract grammatical concept, whereas an utterance is an act of speech. It is a linear string of speech that may or may not be a complete phrase or sentence. Utterances are units of behavior. Sentences, like other categories, such as nouns, verbs, and so forth, are units of linguistic knowledge. By their analyses of speakers' utterances, researchers attempt to evaluate their linguistic knowledge.

---

[2] In our Data Transcription and Analysis Tool we have a specific field for this called *utterance context.*

The basic transcription unit in a written transcript is the utterance (see more in Section 9.2.1.4).
3. *Transcript.* A transcript is an utterance-by-utterance record of the session, including all subject utterances plus all relevant interlocutor utterances.
4. *Turn.* A turn may consist of several utterances that define one speaker's part in the discourse or interaction. In the following example, the child (S) initiates a discourse by producing the following utterances.

Example 2. S: let's see.
    S: what's this?   (the subject is looking at a black plastic object)

There are two utterances in this turn; thus, the two utterances have to be written on different lines.

9.2.1.4 What Constitutes an Utterance?

When transcribing subjects' natural speech, you have to record their utterances so they can be analyzed for their linguistic properties (e.g., the transcripts of "good" and "poor" natural speech samples in Chapter 4). In transcribing a natural speech sample, one of the most fundamental decisions is deciding how to break the sample into utterances. Speech samples are often evaluated in terms of number of utterances or proportions of number of utterances. When there are discrepancies among transcripts, it is often because researchers have not made the same decisions about utterances.

Analyzing subjects' linguistic knowledge will necessitate analyzing their sentence structure. A sentence may correspond to an utterance, but it need not. Because they are not linguistic categories, utterances are notoriously difficult to define. We must ask first: What constitutes an utterance? We might mistakenly assume that pauses or speech breaks always distinguish utterances. However, this is not always true. We often break our utterances midstream, as do children or adults or aging subjects coping with some form of pathology. The decision about what constitutes an utterance in a sample will include your analysis of timing (significance of pauses) and your analysis of the structure of the expression.

An utterance is a unit of behavior that has boundaries. In the clearest case, these boundaries are marked by pauses or an intervening utterance by someone else. Often it functions as a phonological or semantic unit (i.e., it has a distinct intonational pattern and meaning). An utterance may be as small as a single word and as long as a complex sentence—anything that is set off by intervening interlocutor utterances, intonation, and pausing. These carry equal weight. If the speech is set off by pauses and has its own intonation contour, it is a separate utterance. A change of intonation with an intervening pause indicates a new utterance. For example, the researcher will have to decide whether speech such as the following should be transcribed as one utterance or two:

> Example 3. The woman was eating her lunch . . . and she was thinking about her plan.

Characterizing utterances is always difficult in a transcription, but it is especially difficult with children or those with impaired speech. Some children speak slowly, and sometimes what may seem like a pause is just slow speech; you have to judge subject-by-subject and utterance-by-utterance. A semantic unit may mark an utterance, but very young children often break up larger semantic units (e.g., sentences or propositions) into parts, such as nouns, verbs, and prepositional phrases.

These criteria for evaluating what constitutes an utterance may be helpful. You may also find it useful to consult guidelines developed by the University of Chicago's "Language Development Project" (https://ldp.uchicago.edu/). In the end, there is no one correct way to define *utterance*. In spite of all attempts at standardization, this decision often relies on a researcher's judgment. Thus, it is essential that adapted criteria be articulated and available for others to use to aid replicability. An utterance will become a record in a central database; therefore, the formatting of a transcript must be tailored to the database adopted. Different formats will be favored by different databases and different search functions connected with them.

9.2.1.5 Step-by-Step Procedures for Speech Transcription

1. If you are using audio (or video) cassette tape (which may be necessary in some forms of field work in which digital electronic resources are not available), remove the "tabs" from tape before starting to use the tape to prevent the tape from being recorded over.
2. Before listening to an audio file, copy it and label it according to guidelines. The copy should consist of a digital file stored in a separate place and possibly also a physical file (e.g., backup drive, CD, DVD). If you are using a digital recorder, follow the instructions for "uploading digital audio files" to your computer or server. Transcribe from the original recording.
3. Organize the transcribing machine or computer software and earphones (earphones will improve audio quality).
4. Start by entering all metadata as indicated by the structure of your database (see Chapter 14 for an example).
5. Save your file in your personal folder and other backup devices while you are still working with it. Once it is finished, save it under the corresponding project file in the server and the backup drive. Name the document with the subject's ID and session number (see Chapter 3).

6. Before you begin to transcribe, listen to a few minutes of the sample to get a sense of the context and to accustom yourself to the people who are speaking. After listening to a section of the sample, return to the starting point and transcribe each utterance. Standardize transcription symbols. Appendix A provides basic transcription symbols.[3]
7. You may have to listen to an utterance several times to understand precisely what the subject said.
8. When the subject is a child or a new adult subject not familiar with the researcher or the situation, some researchers omit first utterances of a sample when a natural speech sample is being collected to insure that the subject's language has reached a productive level. Some subjects will have reached this stage before beginning to record. In principle, in our labs, we transcribe the session from the beginning (assuming preliminary "warm-up" sessions).
9. It is advisable to transcribe a speech sample as soon as possible after the data are collected so that the context is still clear in mind.
10. Use systematic codes, noting where the speech is unintelligible, or you are unsure (see Appendix A).
11. Your transcription of a subject's speech is central. However, the surrounding language by interlocutors should also be recorded, especially when this is relevant to your research question. Depending on your research question, the surrounding language by persons other than your subject may or may not be critical to record on the first pass. In the transcription of a young child's natural speech, the interlocutor's language is frequently essential to understand what the child means.
12. When an adult or another interlocutor adds speech not directly relevant to the child's speech and there is not sufficient time to transcribe all this, transcribe adult utterances immediately preceding the child's utterance and mark the transcript to show where there was more additional speech of the interlocutor that was not transcribed. These data can thus be accessed for future research purposes.
13. During the child's speech, an adult who worked with the child may have added his or her interpretation of what he or she believed the child was trying to say. This can be useful; however, you must be careful not to let the adult's interpretation of an utterance fully or automatically determine your transcription of what the child actually said.
14. Many researchers find it easiest to transcribe a continuous sample of speech in a word processing format such as Word before transferring the data to a database. If you are transcribing into a word processing document and subsequently transferring to a database, follow the procedures provided by each database to facilitate transfer of your data into the database.

---

[3] Different databases may require distinct transcription symbols. See the CHILDES CHAT transcription system, for example (http://childes.psy.cmu.edu/manuals/CHAT.pdf).

9.2.1.6 Summary of Dos and Don'ts of Speech Transcription

- Do transcribe only what you hear.
- Do not transcribe what you think the child is trying to say (although you may note that in your comments).
- Do be accurate and as precise as possible.
- Do ask questions if you need help.
- Do conduct a reliability check on your transcript (see Section 9.2.4).

9.2.2 Specific Linguistic Principles of Speech Transcription

In addition to consulting principles of language transcription that apply the scientific method, it is necessary also to consult specific linguistic principles of phonetics for the sounds you hear most precisely. In the case of children's language (i.e., language that is still developing) or the language of multilingual speakers and impaired populations, phonetic transcription is important because their language may deviate from the standard adult norm. Thus, knowledge of phonetics is advisable. Knowledge of phonetics requires considerable training, however. In many cases, it is important to involve a team of researchers including a person (or persons) trained in phonetics. Although a first pass at a good speech transcript can sometimes be made without involving phonetic representation, these transcripts can subsequently be subjected to a "phonetic edit," where further phonetic detail is added.

9.2.2.1 The Role of Phonetics

Phonetics is that branch of linguistics concerned with the sounds of languages of the world, their production, and their perception.

> Phonetics is concerned with describing the speech sounds that occur in the languages of the world. We want to know what these sounds are, how they fall into patterns and how they change in different circumstances. Most importantly, we want to know what aspects of the sounds are necessary for conveying the meaning of what is being said. The first job of a phonetician is, therefore, to try to find out what people are doing when they are talking and when they are listening to speech. (Ladefoged, 1993, p. 1)

Phoneticians are linguists who "can describe speech, who understand the mechanisms of speech production and speech perception, and who know how languages use these mechanisms" (Ladefoged, 1993, p. 25). For more refined forms of speech transcripts, transcription involves phonetic transcription, not only orthographic transcription. *Orthography* is another word for *spelling*, which we use in everyday writing and may not correspond to the actual sounds of a word (e.g., *laugh* has no [g] or [h] sounds because the letters *gh* are pronounced as [f] in English). Many researchers transcribe English child speech using only English spelling. English spelling, however, may not veridically capture what the child or subject said. If we are interested in the aspects of child language that are still developing, it is critical that transcription is as precise as possible.

9.2.2.2 International Phonetic Alphabet Transcription

We use the International Phonetic Alphabet (IPA) for representing sounds precisely (see Appendix B).[4] However, learning to use the IPA requires special training. Transcribers use this when in doubt about what they hear for particular unidentifiable words or when the subject has made a deviation from an adult standard form or when their particular research project concerns the phonology of the subject's knowledge of language. You need not transcribe whole utterances in this format unless your research project specifically involves a phonological study. In this case, phonetic transcription is critical.

> Example 4. uh wanna hear.
> IPA transcription where relevant: [ə wanə] hear.

Often a first transcription is done with English orthography, and a researcher who is trained in the IPA then provides a partial (as shown in example 4) or complete "phonetic edit" on the final transcript.

9.2.2.3 Types of Phonetic Transcription

Phoneticians distinguish between a *broad transcription* (one that uses a simple set of symbols) and a *narrow transcription* (one that shows more phonetic detail, often by using additional symbols). In *cross-linguistic transcriptions*, because various languages must be transcribed and compared, any and all relevant IPA symbols must be used for greatest accuracy. You have to focus on contrastive sounds within the language that you are transcribing. Ultimately, when you do cross-linguistic transcriptions, you will be developing your transcription on the basis of your knowledge of the language you are working with and your knowledge of phonetics.

---

4 Specific International Phonetic Alphabet (IPA) fonts may be needed for transcription depending on your text processor. Make sure you have the necessary fonts installed; you may have to update them with each new version of your text processor or operating system. A good system is provided by the SIL font page (http://www.sil.org/resources/software_fonts/search?f[0]=field_sf_category%3A36519). Alternatively, you can use an online IPA font and then copy your text into Word (e.g., http://ipa.typeit.org/).

For language-specific phonetic symbols, you may consult the International Phonetics Association's (1999) *Handbook of the International Phonetic Association*. It contains common phonetic symbols from a variety of languages for standard dialects. It may be a useful resource for those who are just beginning and want to make sure they are dealing with the most relevant symbols in the language they are studying.

Researchers trained in IPA transcription may provide a final phonetic edit on a transcript using the following steps:

1. Obtain the appropriate audio files.
2. Obtain the nonphonetic transcript.
3. Paste the contents into a Word document, and paste all the lines in table format. You can edit the transcript in this table format to keep it organized.
4. Open the sound files in Praat or other acoustic software.[5]
5. Select smaller segments of time in this software, and edit a printed copy of the transcript. Listen to the sound files as you are reading the transcript, locating discrepancies between standard adult pronunciations and the subject's speech. For areas of unclear speech, use spectrograms (e.g., in Praat) to analyze the sounds visually using acoustic cues to derive your transcription. For example, if you are not sure whether there is a stop, look for a closure on the spectrogram; if you are unsure of voicing, look for a voicing bar in the bottom of the spectrogram.
6. Once you have finalized editing on the printed copy of the transcript, edit the electronic transcript that you saved as a Word document.[6]
7. Do a final run-through listening to the audio files. Have at least one other person cross-check your transcript with the sound files. Make any necessary revisions. Retain records on reliability checking.
8. Save your work on the server under the appropriately labeled folder for your project.

9.2.2.4 Valuable Resources

Beginners on the subject can consult any introductory linguistics textbook that includes a section on phonetics and phonology (e.g., O'Grady & Archibald, 2009, *Contemporary Linguistics*; see also Weisler & Milekic, 2000, *Theory of Language*). Introductory textbooks dedicated to phonetics and phonology include Ladefoged and Johnson's (2014) *A Course in Phonetics*. However, there is no substitute for a course in linguistics to prepare for this dimension of language transcription.

---

[5] Software such as Praat (http://www.praat.org) makes acoustic analysis of speech possible. Make sure you select "Open as a long sound file" to open files large in length. Zoom in on specific areas to see the respective spectrograms for analysis.

[6] In Praat, original transcriptions will be in blue, editing will be in square brackets in red. Editing will use an SIL IPA font.

9.2.3 Procedures for Transcribing Elicited Imitation Data

All the principles and procedures for transcribing speech sketched earlier should be followed in the case of speech elicited through either natural speech observational methods or experimental methods using tasks such as elicited imitation (EI) or elicited production or others. Different procedures can be adopted, however. For example, in the case of EI, the stimulus uttered as a model for reproduction (i.e., interlocutor or experimenter utterances) will have been standardized and administered consistently throughout the experiment and across all children in the study. EI data will result from an experimental design in which model stimulus sentences have been factorially designed (see Appendix 9.1 for an example of such sentence design for a study on the acquisition of relative clauses). Thus, preset templates for recording the subject's speech in response to these stimuli can be developed. See Appendix 9.2 for an example of a transcript form for EI used in one experiment in language acquisition. In accord with the principles described in earlier chapters, all EI transcripts should have their reliability checked by at least one other transcriber. The following step-by-step guidelines may be helpful.

9.2.3.1 Steps for Transcribing Elicited Imitation Data

1. Transcription templates (see Appendix 9.2) should be designed for your experimental study and prepared in advance. These can order your data by battery administration order (which is randomized), and they should be coded by experimental factor so they can be sorted by factor for subsequent analysis. Transcribers can enter data onto the transcription templates provided for the experimental study. On this sheet, the experimental model sentence administered will be prerecorded. There will be blank lines for the subject's response to each administered sentence, which should give you enough room to record everything the child said relevant to that administered sentence.
2. If you are transcribing data from an EI task or some other elicitation task, listen to each test sentence individually. Stop the audio file after each sentence. For each test sentence write down exactly what the child said. If something is unclear, replay the audio file and listen again. Include all stops, starts, hesitations, questions, and so forth.
3. Note how many repetitions of each experimental sentence are administered in parentheses after the test sentence. When the experimenter repeats a sentence, write "REPEAT" in capital letters.
4. Use the symbols in Appendix A to mark unclear speech, starts, stops, or overlapping speech.
5. In an EI task, if an adult says exactly what is on the transcription sheets, you do not have to transcribe the adult speech. If the adult makes any changes, note exactly what the changes are (including starts, stops, etc.).
6. If the experimenter makes additional comments, write what the experimenter says in parentheses.

7. You only have to write what is important for the test. If the child gets distracted and the experimenter discusses matters besides the test sentence, you do not need to record this.
8. All transcriptions should be checked for reliability by at least one other transcriber in accord with the procedures described next.

9.2.4 Reliability Checking

All transcriptions of speech data (whether naturalistic or experimentally derived data, such as through EI or other language production tasks) must be checked for reliability before they can become reliable scientific data. Because each transcription of speech by a hearer represents an interpretation of the continuous speech stream uttered by a speaker, it is possible, and more than likely, that any two transcribers (hearers) will produce different transcriptions of the speech they hear. For reliable analyses of speech (for scientific study), it is necessary that a single reliable transcript of speech be available. The transcriber must reliably identify the units (phonological, syntactic, semantic) that characterize the speech he or she hears.

9.2.4.1 Forms of Reliability Checking

There are three forms of reliability checking for a speech transcript:

- Two (or more) different transcribers each transcribe the same speech sample independently, without initial communication between them. The resulting speech transcriptions are compared.
- One transcriber at a later time reviews the transcription of a first transcriber, in the presence of the audio record of the original speech. This second transcriber makes a decision about what constitutes the "true" or "valid" transcript of the speech being studied.
- A third approach combines the previous two. Two transcribers transcribe the same speech sample independently, and a third transcriber later reviews each transcript. Finally, using the acoustic analysis of the audio sample plus their judgment, the team creates a third, "reliable" transcript.

9.2.4.2 Resolving Discrepancies

When speech transcriptions differ, the differences must be resolved so that we achieve a single transcript for scientific study. Discrepancies may be resolved in several ways:

- Both transcribers listen to the tape again together, discussing the discrepancies and coming to an agreed conclusion regarding the true or "right" transcription

of the speech. In some cases, one transcriber will have simply missed certain aspects of the speech and, on review, will realize this.
- For the remaining discrepancies, it may be useful to consult the acoustic properties of the speech being transcribed. Acoustic analyses will bear on how the speech should be analyzed and transcribed. For example, it may help resolve whether the child said, *I can* or *I can't* or *pad* versus *bad*. Acoustic analyses, however, require prior training. When researchers work in interdisciplinary teams, this type of analysis can be carried out by the linguists in the team, who can provide the information to developmental psychologists. The psychologists then can use the information in speech therapy or other ways.

When transcribers do not have specialized training in acoustic analyses of speech, they may simply make a note in their transcription pointing out that acoustic analyses might be useful there to resolve the transcription of an utterance for which the transcription was indeterminate. Some transcription discrepancies may not be resolvable. In some cases, it may be simply impossible to determine what the subject actually said or what he or she intended to say. In these cases, it is important that the final "reliable" transcript record this conclusion.

9.2.4.3 Step-by-Step Reliability Checking

1. Produce a copy of the transcript, and meet with the first transcriber to compare your transcripts.
2. Carefully examine every utterance:
   Check both subject and interlocutor's utterances.
   Check punctuation and markings.
   Enter any additional subject utterances or important interlocutor utterances not previously recorded.
3. In case of discrepancy, listen to the tape again together.
4. If you agree on the utterance change, change it.
5. If the discrepancy continues, one utterance should be written in the utterance field, and alternative utterances should be indicated in the comments.
6. Date the changes you have made.
7. Write your name as reliability checker each time you check a transcript for reliability.
8. Update the subject's transcript every time changes are made.

9.2.4.4 Reliability Checking History

Records on reliability determination should be recorded and saved as part of the history of the speech transcription. Future researchers using the speech data will benefit from this as much as from any particular transcription of speech.

9.2.5 Transcription Tips for Data Resulting From Other Language Behaviors and Other Tasks

In this chapter, we have concentrated on transcribing and processing language production data. When other language behaviors have been elicited (e.g., various forms of language comprehension), similar principles must be developed. For each task, such as the act-out task, reliable transcription of observed behaviors must be established, transcription criteria must be articulated and standardized to assure replicability, and finally, templates for data entry into a database must be established. Transcribing data from tests of comprehension or grammaticality judgment tasks involve the principles we have reviewed in this chapter. However, in these cases, the behaviors produced may not involve speech. Thus, the behaviors to be transcribed and subsequently analyzed may be essentially nonlinguistic. We provide two examples next.

9.2.5.1 Act-Out Task Testing Language Comprehension

In *a free-form act-out task*, behaviors to be recorded and transcribed are motoric behaviors—actions with the dolls and props after a model stimulus sentence. These behaviors follow administered sentences that the subject is asked to interpret and act out, which are designed with regard to a factorial experimental design with appropriate controls (e.g., length; see Chapter 7). The sample sentence designs in Appendix 9.1 and the transcription template in Appendix 9.2 are also applicable to the act-out task.[7] Appendix 9.3 shows an example of a transcript of one child's behaviors in the act-out task used in an experiment on acquisition of relative clauses. Behaviors in such free-form versions of the act-out task can be difficult to describe and interpret. Particular criteria for interpretation must be developed for each study.

The behavioral transcription of an act-out task can be simplified in a *structured* form of the act-out task (see Chapter 7). For example, in one study that used this type of structured task (Foley, Núñez del Prado, Barbier, & Lust, 1997), the subject was given several restricted options for restricted behaviors, thus simplifying the transcription process and facilitating the analysis of results to follow.[8]

---

[7] Sample sentence designs and a transcription sheet template from a study using the act-out task (Flynn & Lust, 1980) can be found online at http://pubs.apa.org/books/supp/blume/
[8] A detailed transcription sheet for the structured form of the act-out task used in this study can be found online at http://pubs.apa.org/books/supp/blume/

9.2.5.2 Truth–Value Judgment Task Testing Language Comprehension

A task such as the truth–value judgment task (see Chapter 7) requires only *yes/no* responses from subjects regarding whether they consider a sentence acceptable or not, given a particular picture or scenario. In this case, because the data are not linguistic and responses are binary, transcription is simple. At the same time, the researcher has to construct a transcript template, given the experimental design of the study. Responses have to be coded by factor to prepare for subsequent statistical analyses.[9]

9.3 Summary

In this chapter, we have sketched a number of principles and examples of procedures necessary for creating reliable transcriptions from observed language data. We have stressed that this is a complex and challenging process. These transcriptions are the first stage of converting raw data to data ready for analysis and interpretation. Unless these transcriptions are high quality and reliable, all further analyses will be weakened. All dissemination of data based on such transcriptions will be unreliable. The principles and procedures we have exemplified here will hopefully advance the scientific quality of the research process in this area.

---

[9] A sample transcription sheet from a study using the truth–value judgment task (Foley, Núñez del Prado, Barbier, & Lust, 1997) can be found online at http://pubs.apa.org/books/supp/blume/

Appendix 9.1
Experimental Sentences by Factor: Relative Clause, Elicited Imitation Task[1]

Imitation: Experimental Sentences by Design

Lexically Headed	
I. Lexically Headed	
Object Subject	Object Object
Big Bird pushes the balloon which bumps Ernie. (A3)	Ernie touches the balloon which Big Bird throws. (A5)
Kermit the Frog bumps the block which touches Ernie. (B2)	Scooter grabs the candy which Fozzie Bear eats. (B4)
II. Indefinite Headed	
Ernie pushes the thing which touches Big Bird. (A1)	Cookie Monster eats the thing which Ernie kicks. (A2)
Scooter hits the thing which touches Kermit the Frog. (B1)	Fozzie Bear kisses the thing which Kermit the Frog hits. (B6)
Free Relatives/Headless	
III. Headless	
Cookie Monster hits what pushes the Big Bird. (A4)	Cookie Monster pushes what the Big Bird throws. (A6)
Kermit the Frog pushes what touches Scooter. (B5)	Fozzie Bear hugs what Kermit the Frog kisses. (B3)

Sentence Batteries (Randomized)

Pretraining sentences:

1. Fozzie kisses Scooter.
2. Kermit Frog jumped up, and Fozzie sat down.
3. Ernie fell down when he turned around.
4. Fozzie Bear gives something to Scooter.

Battery A:

1. Ernie pushes the thing which touches Big Bird.
2. Cookie Monster eats the thing which Ernie kicks.
3. Big Bird pushes the balloon which bumps Ernie.
4. Cookie Monster hits what pushes Big Bird.

---
[1] Data from Flynn and Lust (1980).

5. Ernie touches the balloon which Big Bird throws.
6. Cookie Monster pushes what the Big Bird throws.

Battery B:

1. Scooter hits the thing which touches Kermit Frog.
2. Kermit Frog bumps the block which touches Fozzie.
3. Fozzie Bear hugs what Kermit the Frog kisses.
4. Scooter grabs the candy which Fozzie Bear eats.
5. Kermit the Frog pushes what touches Scooter.
6. Fozzie kisses the thing which Kermit Frog hits.

Appendix 9.2
Transcription Sheets: Relative Clause, Elicited Imitation Task

Subject's ID _____   Date _____
Transcriber _____   Transcriber 2 _____
Age _____

Practice sentences:

1. Fozzie kisses Scooter.

2. Kermit Frog jumped up, and Fozzie sat down.

3. Ernie fell down when he turned around.

4. Fozzie Bear gives something to Scooter.

Experimental sentences:

Battery A

1. Ernie pushes the thing which touches Big Bird. (IH, S)

2. Cookie Monster eats the thing which Ernie kicks. (IH, O)

3. Big Bird pushes the balloon which bumps Ernie. (H, S)

4. Cookie Monster hits what pushes Big Bird. (-H, S)

5. Ernie touches the balloon which Big Bird throws. (H, O)

6. Cookie Monster pushes what the Big Bird throws. (-H, O)

Battery B

1. Scooter hits the thing which touches Kermit Frog. (I, S)

2. Kermit Frog bumps the block which touches Fozzie. (H, S)

3. Fozzie Bear hugs what Kermit the Frog kisses. (-H, O)

4. Scooter grabs the candy which Fozzie Bear eats. (H, O)

5. Kermit the Frog pushes what touches Scooter. (-H, S)

6. Fozzie kisses the thing which Kermit Frog hits. (I, O)

Note. Relative clause type: H = lexically headed; I = indefinite "thing" head; -H = headless. Data from Flynn and Lust (1980).

Appendix 9.3
Transcription Example: Act-Out Responses in the Act-Out Task

Metadata

Subject ID: BS120875
Gender: F
Age: 3;9
Experimenters: S. Flynn and T. Clifford
Date of testing: 9/25/07
Place: [Include school or day care here, but remove if this document becomes public.]
Battery order: Act-out task, then elicited imitation
Comprehension: Act-out task
Experimenter's sentence is in bold. Child's behavior according to transcriber present at the time is below. Here the subject is referred to as *Child* instead of *S* (subject) to avoid confusion with the doll *S* (Scooter).
Dolls are: Battery A: Big Bird (BB), Ernie (E), Cookie Monster (CM)
              Battery B: Scooter (S), Fozzie Bear (FB), Kermit the Frog (KF)

Lexically Headed

Object Subject Relative Clause

1. **Big Bird touches the tissue which bangs Ernie. (A5)**
   Child takes BB and lays him on the tissue.
2. **Scooter throws the tissue which hits Fozzie Bear. (B4)**
   Child puts tissue to KF's mouth and then puts tissue to S's hand.

Object Object Relative Clause

1. **Ernie touches the candy which Big Bird holds. (A2)**
   Child puts candy in BB's hand and has E touch the candy while in BB's hand.
2. **Fozzie Bear kicks the balloon which Scooter hugs. (B2)**
   Child puts balloon into S's arm and then puts balloon to FB's mouth and makes kiss noise.

Empty Headed/Thing Head

Object Subject Relative Clause

1. **Ernie hugs the thing which hits Cookie Monster. (A4)**
   Child says, "What is it going to be?"
   Child picks up BB and puts BB's beak to floor.
2. **Scooter hits the thing which touches Kermit Frog. (B1)**
   Child says, "KF." Child throws balloon on KF and then S touches the balloon.

Object Object Relative Clause

1. **Cookie Monster hits the thing which Ernie throws. (A6)**
   Child puts balloon in E's hand and has him throw it; then puts CM to the balloon.
2. **Kermit Frog grabs the thing which Scooter kisses. (B5)**
   Child puts tissue to KF's hand and then puts tissue to S's mouth.

Headless

Object Subject Relative Clause

1. **Big Bird kisses what touches Cookie Monster. (A1)**
   Child picks up BB and has BB kiss CM's foot.
2. **Fozzie Bear touches what hits Kermit the Frog. (B6)**
   Child puts tissue to FB's hand and then has FB throw the tissue to KF and hit FB.

Object Object Relative Clause

1. **Cookie Monster eats what the Big Bird kisses. (A3)**
   Child picks up CM and (starts talking) kisses BB's foot.
2. **Scooter pushes what Kermit the Frog scratches. (B3)**
   Child puts block to KF's hand and then makes KF scratch balloon, then puts balloon to S's mouth.

10 Creating the Data III: Preparing for Data Analysis

Once raw data are prepared, as described in Chapters 3 and 9, we must analyze these data. We want to discover what the subject knows about language and how this knowledge changes over time. Thus, our choices for data analyses must allow us to approach these questions. When data are generated through any of the types of tasks sketched in the previous chapters, these data must be transcribed and coded or scored, and then these codings or scorings must be analyzed. Only then can they be interpreted and used by the researcher to evaluate hypotheses regarding what the subject knows.

10.1 Speech as Data for Analysis

Speech does not become research data until the audio recording has been transcribed, the transcription has been checked for reliability, and the audio recording and final transcript have been archived (see Chapters 3 and 9). Until these steps have been taken, speech is simply equivalent to whatever we continually hear each other say every day. Speech data include an immense amount of variation that cannot be controlled. Characteristically, transcripts show that no two hearers will necessarily hear and understand any particular stretch of speech in exactly the same way. Thus, it is essential that there be precise, systematic, and standardized procedures for capturing the collected data from the recording to render it suitable for scientific inquiry.

The next research step after transcription, described in Chapter 9, involves coding the transcribed data in a way that is systematic and replicable. *Coding* data means characterizing them in ways that prepares them for analysis. Different forms of software can be used for registering this coding, but the most important aspect of coding is the researcher's conceptual description of the data collected. Specific coding systems must be developed based on the researcher's leading question. However, certain general coding procedures can be adopted.

10.2 Natural Speech as Data

Natural speech is especially difficult not only to transcribe but also to code. Without established procedures, we cannot even guarantee that any two researchers will divide the speech sample up into independent utterances in the same way.

10.2.1 Which Utterances Do We Code in a Natural Speech Sample?

Before reading this section, please review the definition of *utterance* in Chapter 9. When coding utterances, we only code complete utterances, for which the meaning is fairly clear. For this reason, some utterances in a transcript may not be coded at all, except for marking them as "incomplete" or "unclear." Of course, these decisions depend on the research questions being asked.

10.2.2 Beginning to Analyze Pragmatics of Language Use: Speech Acts and Speech Modes

The first, most general, broadest characterization of natural speech usually involves consideration of the speech act for which an utterance is being used. Sentences are uttered by speakers in certain contexts to communicate certain intentions. *Speech act theory* concerns utterances (i.e., individual behaviors with language). Each utterance reflects a speech act—that is, the use of language for a particular intention (Matthews, 1997). Linguists working in the area of pragmatics have attempted to characterize the distinct types of communicative use of utterances—that is, the different "speech acts" of utterances. Remember the difference between a sentence and an utterance (see Chapter 9): A *sentence* is a linguistic unit, determined in terms of formal structure, and an *utterance* is a behavioral unit; it is determined in terms of meaning, intention, and occurrence in real time.

10.2.2.1 Speech Acts

Judging and categorizing a speech act is complex and requires careful analysis of the surrounding context of the utterance, both the linguistic context and the pragmatic or concrete context. The same utterance can be used to convey different speech acts, according to context. For example, the utterance *The window is open* could be the following:

- an observation and related assertion; or
- a subtle expression of a wish that someone would close the window and, therefore, an indirect way of asking someone to close the window; or
- an imperative (i.e., a direct way of asking someone to close the window, etc.).

Table 10.1 shows some examples of speech acts with various examples of possible structures for each one.

Tab. 10.1: A Preliminary Typology for Coding Basic Speech Acts

Type	Examples
Declarative/assertive. The utterance is an affirmation or negation.	- *I've had enough.* - *The truck is red.* - *I don't like pizza.*
Question. The utterance requests information.	- *Can I go out to play?* - *I can go out to play?* - *Do you want to play?* - *What is this?* - *Is this a van or a truck?*
Imperative. The utterance is an order for someone to do or not do something.	- *Go away.* - *Give me more milk.* - *Don't climb on that chair.*
Promise	- *I will come tomorrow.* - *I will try.*
Wish or request. The utterance expresses a request, a vocative, or a wish.	- *I want more milk.* - *Pass the salt, please.* - *Mom!* (as in calling her)
Expressives or exclamations. Any word or nonword with exclamatory intonation (unless it can also be classified as any of the other speech acts).	- *Oh, no!* - *Whoa!*
Politeness	- *Thank you.* - *Please.*
Greetings. The utterance's purpose is greeting or saying goodbye.	- *Hi.* - *Goodbye.* - *See you soon.*
Naming. The utterance purpose is to name one or more entities.	- *Truck, boat, shoe* - *What is this? A shoe.* (Here, the first utterance would be classified as question and the second one as naming. Note that if the utterance is *It is a shoe*, it includes naming, but the utterance is an assertion.)
Counting. The speaker is saying numbers in a sequence.	
Singing. The utterance is part of a song.	
Yes/no/OK. The utterance is formed only by *yes, no, OK*, or their equivalents in other languages.	
Other. None of the above.	
Unclear. The utterance could be a type other than those listed, and the context does not disambiguate it.	

Depending on the research question, a researcher may choose to analyze only sentences or utterances that occur in certain speech acts. Thus, coding transcriptions in terms of speech acts can provide a foundation by which future more specific analyses can be directed and calibrated. For background on the area of pragmatics, including the study of speech acts, see Sadock (2006), Verschueren (1999), and Horn and Ward (2006). For background on the study of pragmatics in the child, see E. Clark (2016). For an instrument to assess pragmatic competence, see Dewart and Summers (1988).

10.2.2.2 Speech Modes

Speech mode refers to the context of the utterance, where we indicate, for example, whether the utterance was spontaneous, was produced as a response to somebody else's utterance, or was a repetition, either of oneself or another. When one is analyzing a subject's knowledge of language, it is useful to distinguish these various speech modes before beginning analysis of sentence structure. Table 10.2 presents categories for coding modes of speech.

Tab. 10.2: Codings for Types of Speech Mode

Context type	Code for the type of context for the utterance	
	Spontaneous	The subject's utterance is not triggered by something in the context.
	Responsive	The subject's utterance is triggered by something in the context.
Responsive context	Code for the type of responsive context for the utterance	
	Repetition	The subject is repeating an utterance or part of an utterance present in the discourse.
	Answer to question	The subject is answering a question.
Type of repetition	Code for the type of repetition	
	Self repetition	The subject repeats an utterance or part of an utterance said by him or herself.
	Other repetition	The subject repeats an utterance or part of an utterance said by another person.
Type of question	Code for the type of question the answer is an answer for	
	Answer—*wh*	The child answers a question headed by a *wh*-word.
	Answer—*y/n*	The child answers a question that can be answered by *yes* or *no*.
	Other answer	The child answers a question that is not a *wh*-question or a *y/n*-question (e.g., "Do you want cake or ice cream?").

10.2.3 Beginning to Analyze Sentence Structure

The sentences that underlie utterances have syntactic structure, and we want to understand this structure to assess knowledge of language. Syntactic structure analyses vary in terms of type and complexity depending on the questions that lead each research project. In contrast to experimental research in which specific hypotheses regarding linguistic structure are tested as hypotheses through experimental designs, much research on syntactic knowledge in child language acquisition has been based on analyses of natural speech data.

Regardless of the specific question for which one may conduct analyses of natural speech, it is useful first to calibrate and structure the data in terms of the properties described in Sections 10.2.1 and 10.2.2. For example, in a study of early speech of 2-year-olds, some researchers may only be interested in which of the child's utterances are sentences to analyze early sentence structure. In more advanced research questions, one may wish to divide simple and complex sentences, types of questions, types of embedding, types of ellipsis, use of morphology, or verb inflection, among other things. More advanced research questions require more precise analyses of each of these domains. It will be helpful to look at the initial codings shown in Exhibit 10.1 before proceeding to more specific analyses.

For each particular research study, whether based on experimental methods or natural speech observations, data coding and coding criteria must be established and made available for replication and collaboration to be possible. No matter how simple or complex the research question, the fundamental data must be calibrated. Otherwise, analyses will not be comparable. For example, if different researchers do not code utterances in the same way, results of further coding analyses on the basis of "percent of utterances" will not be comparable. We suggest the guidelines in Exhibit 10.1 for basic codings, but different researchers will select different codings as supplements to these depending on their research question.

In all cases, coding decisions must be articulated, archived, and shared if collaborative data are desired. See, for example, Valian, Solt, and Stewart (2008) and Pine and Martindale (1996) for examples of detailed studies of young children's natural speech. Here, investigation of young children's knowledge of abstract phrase structure including determiners (e.g., *a* and *the* in English) produces different results based on different coding criteria. See also Lust (1981) and Ardery (1980) for examples of investigations of young children's natural speech with regard to children's higher order knowledge of coordinate syntax. Here, investigations provide different conclusions depending on coding criteria adopted.

10.2.4 Mean Length of Utterance: Analyses of Utterance Length

Since the early days of the study of early language acquisition based on natural speech as data, researchers have applied a measure to code children's language development,

Exhibit 10.1: Guidelines for Coding Sentences

(a) Is this a sentence? The first step is to decide whether the utterance is a sentence. We may define *sentence* as any complete utterance containing a (null or overt) verb.
- We assume there is a null verb when the subject is clearly attempting or intending a sentence but leaving the verb out. This is common in young children. The structure must have a noun phrase and some sort of complement—for example, *the car red, the car very fast, I cake*. The context should make fairly clear what verb (or type of verb) is missing.
- When you are not sure it is a sentence with a null verb, you should mark the structure as not being a sentence, but mark as unclear.

(b) Is the verb overt? Is the verb in the sentence overt or not?
(c) What is the sentence type?

Simple. The sentence only has one clause—that is, one verb (null or overt).[1]
- *Daddy cake for baby.*
- *Daddy bought cake for baby.*
- *I like cake.*
- *Daddy bought a big chocolate cake with pink flowers.*
- *John and Mary bought a cake at the corner bakery.*

Complex. The sentence has two or more clauses—therefore, two or more verbs.
- *Daddy bought a cake to bring to Grandma's house.*
- *The cake Daddy bought was big.*
- *If Daddy buys a cake I will eat it up.*
- *Daddy wants me to go.*

Coordinate. These are two or more sentences joined by a conjunction.
- *John bought a cake, and Mary did too.*
- *John bought a cake, and Mary bought flowers.*
- *Daddy bought a cake, and I ate it all.*

---

[1] *Clause* is a descriptive term used to refer, minimally, to a construction consisting of a verb phrase with its arguments, although some of these elements may be elided, especially in child speech. For more detailed definitions of *clause*, see Bright (1992), Crystal (1987), Carnie (2002), and Haegeman and Guéron (1999).

---

termed *mean length of utterance* (MLU; see R. Brown, 1973, pp. 53–59, Tables 7 and 8, for example). MLU consists of counting the length of each of the subject's utterances and dividing the total unit count by the total number of the subject's utterances. Because children in the early stages of language development show a gradual expansion in length of utterances, and children develop language at different rates, psycholinguists often attempt to measure language development in terms of MLU. Roger Brown (1973) began to define "stages" of grammatical development on the basis of MLU expansion. The measure is applicable to earliest stages of speech development because, as R. Brown's early work showed, by the time an MLU reaches 3.5, speech begins revealing properties of recursion, the onset of limitless length. Nevertheless, some researchers have found effectiveness up to MLU 4.5 (see, e.g., Blake, Quartaro, & Onorati, 1993). The measure has been widely applied to natural speech samples but can also be applied to language data elicited through experimental designs. Example 1 shows hypothetical child early utterances with the number of morphemes each utterance has in parentheses.

Example 1

Me up (2)
Baby want*s* milk (4, the word *wants* has two morphemes, *want* and -*s*)
Truck fall (2)
MLU computation: total 8/3 utterances = 2.2

MLU is frequently measured in terms of morphemes, under the assumption that a larger percentage of morphemes per utterance indicates a higher stage of grammatical development. Thus, in Example 1, *wants* would have been coded as two morphemes because the inflection -*s* would have counted as one unit. To fully define *morpheme*, however, we must consult the grammatical system of a language. The early proposal for MLU analysis (R. Brown, 1973) was not consistent on morphological analysis (i.e., in specifying which is complex—for example, it did not distinguish between *come* and *came*; irregular forms of verbs were considered a single morpheme in MLU counts).

MLU in morphemes is difficult, perhaps impossible, to use in providing comparisons across languages because all languages differ in their morphological systems, some being morphologically much richer than others. The length constraint is accordingly realized differently across languages in early child speech. It has been suggested that "It seems advisable to regard MLU as a purely intralinguistic device, allowing comparisons of the same child's language over time, and between children acquiring the same languages" (Hickey 1991, p. 569). MLU has been investigated in many languages: Hebrew (Dromi & Berman, 1982), Dutch (Arlman-Rupp, van Niekerk de Haan, & van de Sandt-Koenderman, 1976), Irish (Hickey, 1991), Mohawk (Feurer, 1980), Finnish (Kunnari, 2002), and Mayan (P. Brown, Pfeiler, de León, & Pye, 2013). See Pye, Pfeiler, and Pedro (2013) and Peters (1997) for an overview. When working across languages, MLU is sometimes measured in terms of syllables or words or content words (see Devescovi et al., 2005; Rollins, Snow, & Willett, 1996; or P. Brown, Pfeiler, de León, & Pye, 2013). See also Pye's (2009) *Minimal Coding Procedure* for an approach to a morphologically complex and rich set of four Mayan languages.

10.2.5 Establishing Shared Criteria for Mean Length of Utterance Computation

The MLU measure can be advanced by the adoption of standardized and shared coding criteria. Appendix 10.1 provides an example of shared criteria in collaborative research

---

[1] An example of Spanish MLU criteria can be found online at http://pubs.apa.org/books/supp/blume

involving English.[1] Such shared criteria can strengthen replicability and interpretability of MLU coding whether applied to natural or experimentally derived speech data.

10.2.6 Conclusions About Mean Length of Utterance

MLU must be considered as only a general measure of speech, one that does not necessarily convey specifically linguistic insight into the nature of a subject's language and that is particularly difficult to apply in cross-linguistic investigations. It need not correlate directly with age or with grammatical development (see, e.g., Klee & Fitzgerald, 1985; Conant, 1987). It can be useful, however, early in the development of speech production, especially within a language and within a child, for tracking children's language development and for calibrating with the field, where the measure is widely used. It can be integrated with experimental designs, where it is used to group subjects in a more precise way than age (e.g., Lust, 1977). The measure has also been used in the study of language impairment (e.g., Eisenberg, Fersko, & Lundgren, 2001; Leonard, 1998; Scarborough, Rescorla, Tager Flusberg, Fowler, & Sudhalter, 1991), bilingualism, and second language acquisition. The usefulness of MLU coding can be advanced by the adoption of precise coding criteria within each language.

10.3 Preparing Coding for a Database

Before coded data can be analyzed, summarized, and interpreted, it must be prepared for entry into a structured database. This process varies in part according to the database chosen and the type of questions that are asked of the data by the researcher. For example, in the case of natural speech data, the Child Language Data Exchange System of data representation and dissemination has developed a particular database entry system which is well described in MacWhinney (1991, 1999) and MacWhinney and Snow (1990).[2] A consistent system of annotation, at least for initial stages of data representation, is necessary for data sharing and collaborative research on such data.[3] The Data Transcription and Analysis (DTA) Tool uses the transcription system described here. After entering the appropriate metadata in the database, the researcher can transcribe utterance-by-utterance directly in the DTA Tool or import a transcription in Word by pasting it into a window in the database.

---

2 In particular, see their CHAT (http://childes.psy.cmu.edu/manuals/CHAT.pdf) and CLAN (http://childes.psy.cmu.edu/manuals/CLAN.pdf) systems for data coding.
3 See Pareja-Lora, Blume, and Lust (2016; and http://quijote.fdi.ucm.es:8084/LLOD-LSASummerWorkshop2015/Home.html) for results of a recent workshop directed at articulating and confronting issues involved in the establishment of principles and procedures in this area of "linked open data" in the language sciences, which can cross labs, institutions, languages, and disciplines.

10.4 Analyzing Experimental Data

The following sections focus briefly on introducing initial processes for managing data arising from different forms of tasks used with experimental designs and preparing them for subsequent analyses. These experimental tasks induce language behaviors to test language production or comprehension. Many of the principles and procedures described earlier for natural speech data can be applied to and supplement many tasks that generate speech data using experimental designs. However, many tests of language comprehension can elicit behaviors that are not essentially linguistic and require distinct forms of transcription, coding, and analysis.

Tasks that provide more direct linguistic data in experimental designs are elicited imitation (EI) and elicited production (EP) tasks, which induce language production; tasks accessing linguistic knowledge more indirectly, indicating language comprehension, are the act-out (AO) and truth-value judgment (TVJ) tasks. We offer introductory guidelines on how to transcribe and score such experimental data. Such procedures must be modified for each particular research project, depending on the question being investigated.

10.4.1 Tests of Language Production

10.4.1.1 Elicited Imitation

A. Transcription

Because of the nature of EI data and the experimental designs with which it is used, it is especially essential that the subject's language be precisely transcribed and scored. Most of the principles for speech transcription are identical to those for transcribing natural speech data (see Chapter 9). In one sense, it is easier to transcribe EI data precisely because one knows the model the subject is attempting to produce in their speech (i.e., the model the researcher has administered in the task). It is best to transcribe EI data as soon as possible after data collection because this is the easiest time to remember what the subject said and how the session went. As with natural speech data, to assure reliability of EI transcription, EI data should be independently transcribed and scored by a second experimenter. As reviewed in Chapter 9, all discrepancies must be resolved by listening to the file again and recording this in the data history.

B. Coding and Scoring

Because of the nature of EI data, coding and scoring a subject's response in this task can be complex. Many of the basic coding principles applied in the study of natural speech data (as described earlier) can be applied in coding EI data (e.g., whether the subject's response involves a sentence). Each experimental design varies certain factors to test them; EI data must be analyzed in terms of these experimental factors. However, in each research study, the researcher must further decide what must be scored and coded, given the experimental design and the hypothesis. Not only does each experimental study search for certain phenomena to test certain hypotheses but the subject may also produce language that has not been anticipated. In each study, researchers code and score whether a sentence model is repeated successfully. However, certain changes of the model sentence may not be significant, depending on the research project. For example, in a study investigating whether a subject controls the grammar for coordinate sentence structure, it may not be critically important to the hypothesis if a subject changes a word such as *a* or *the* in the model sentence or phonologically distorts pronunciation of a word. At the same time, in other studies, these changes may be critical (e.g., in a study designed to study a subject's noun phrase or determiner phrase knowledge).

For each study, precise scoring criteria must be established and standardized. In each experimental study using a task such as EI, the researcher scores both the sentences that are correctly reproduced and the deformations or "errors" made in the reproduction.[4] Discovering the deformations is as important as discovering the variation in the correct reproductions of the sentences. Each experimental study must provide specific coding instructions; these codings provide scoring instructions that will allow replication. The same data will not allow replication if they are coded differently.

For each child, a scoring sheet is set up to assess the subject's response to the model sentence.[5] The scoring sheet is arranged by factor (three types of relative clause structure in the model) and subject or object gaps in the model. A horizontal line is established for every item in every condition and its replication. For example, the sample scoring sheet available online records scoring for determinate lexically headed relatives with subject gaps in accord with the design. Each sentence is analyzed by factorial condition for both correctness (Column 1) or types of deformations of the model in which the researcher is interested (Columns 3–28). Recording of coding and scoring data, when arranged in such a template, allows the researcher to enter the data into a database suitable for statistical analyses or for qualitative analyses of utterances with particular structural deformations of the model.

To advance replicability and scientific validity, scoring criteria must be established to define what constitutes "correctness" in each particular research study and which deformations are of interest for the study. Appendix 10.2 provides an example

---

4 Although the term *error* is frequently used, a more suitable term is *deformation* or *reformation* because, as discussed in Chapter 6, these deformations are viewed as providing essential information on the subject's theory of grammar for the language. In that sense, they are not errors within the subject's system.

5 A sample scoring sheet designed to capture results of an elicited imitation task used to test knowledge of relative clause structure (Flynn & Lust, 1980) can be found online at http://pubs.apa.org/books/supp/blume

of such criteria used in conjunction with the scoring sheet template available online (http://pubs.apa.org/books/supp/blume).

C. Analyses

Results from an EI task are analyzed quantitatively and qualitatively. For quantitative results, statistical analyses of results from an experimental design in a research study (see Appendix 10.2) assess the number of correct imitations (or matches) across sentences in contrast to coding for incorrect imitations or "deformations," which vary in critical grammatical factors specified by the coding criteria. The researcher can ask whether subjects are significantly more successful at reproducing sentences with certain types of relatives as opposed to others, given the experimental design (see Chapter 5).

For qualitative results, analyses of changes that subjects make to the model sentence are critical. These errors or mismatches (deformations or reformations) provide evidence of the subject's analysis and reconstruction of the model sentence. Linguistic analysis can be brought to bear on the nature of these mismatches. For example, in the study in Appendix 10.2 (see also Chapter 9), child subjects not only were more successful at reproducing sentences with headless relative clause types (e.g., *Fozzie Bear hugs what Kermit the Frog kisses*), but they also frequently changed other types of relative clause structures to this headless form in their deformations. Thus, both quantitative and qualitative data can be analyzed with regard to leading hypotheses that the experiment was designed to test.

10.4.1.2 Elicited Production

A. Transcription

The EP task (see Chapter 6) provides data close to natural speech data, although it is led by experimental design and specific research questions in conjunction with this design. Therefore, data are transcribed, coded, and scored by principles and procedures similar to those used for both natural speech and experimentally derived EI data. As in EI, the researcher's utterances are, for the most part, fixed.

B. Coding and Scoring

Unlike with natural speech data, it may not be necessary to score all responses from the subject. For example, the researcher may be looking for a particular verb form, so only the verb forms produced by the subject are scored in terms of whether they produced the verb form expected by the experimenter (e.g., *is swimming*) or a form that deviates from it (e.g., *swimming, swims, swam*; Blume, 2002). These deviations are then scored in terms of the exact changes produced (e.g., did the subject change the tense or the aspect of the verb? did the subject produce a nonfinite verb when the experimenter expected him or her to produce a finite form, etc.). As with EI data, the changes that are significant, and those that are not, depend on the coding criteria established for a particular study in terms of research design and hypotheses.

C. Analyses

Results from EP tasks, like those from EI tasks, are analyzed quantitatively and qualitatively. For quantitative results, in the case of EP tasks and their experimental designs, the number of responses that provide matches to the expected answer rather than those that do not are analyzed quantitatively and may then be subjected to statistical tests. For qualitative results, analyses again may take into account spontaneous changes that children make in their expected answer. As with EI, these "errors" can provide evidence of the subject's grammatical development. Linguistic analyses can provide interpretation of these changes.

10.4.2 Comprehension Tasks

Various tasks that test for a subject's comprehension of language typically do not involve speech directly. The behaviors to be analyzed are primarily nonlinguistic. Each task requires its own methods for coding and scoring transcribed behavioral data.

10.4.2.1 Act-Out Task

A. Transcription

As we saw in Chapter 9, because of the unique interactive nature of the AO method of elicitation, a transcriber (or preferably more than one) must capture the AO behavior of each child after each sentence administered. Prepared transcription sheets can be provided to assist the researcher, and subsequently the coder, to prepare for subsequent analyses. Research using the AO task must establish procedures to elicit data in a form that can be efficiently and reliably scored and analyzed. Otherwise, the process of analysis and scoring following transcription can be time consuming and difficult. Having two transcribers of observed behaviors and two transcriptions that can be compared helps resolve indeterminacy in the data recorded (see Chapter 9). Thus, when researchers move to coding, scoring, and analyzing the data, they may have more than one transcription and a video recording from which to work. Good quality standards for design and administration of AO tasks (see Chapter 7) can significantly aid the complex transcription and scoring procedures necessitated by this task.

B. Coding and Scoring

Standardized scoring criteria for interpreting AO behaviors should be established in writing for the research study concerned. On the basis of these criteria, reliability of scoring and replicability of the research can be tested. Dependent variables that are measured can include not only scoring of behaviors as correct or incorrect but also specific aspects of the data that involve the hypothesis being studied. Data resulting from tests of language comprehension, such as the AO task, can be analyzed factorially in terms of experimental research design, as we saw with data from tests of language production earlier. Specific aspects of the behavior can be analyzed as well as correct or incorrect scoring, in keeping with the research experimental design—for example, amount of co-reference judgments between pronouns and their antecedents or amount of particular interpretations for an ambiguous sentence, and so forth. For example, in a study testing a subject's knowledge of sentences such as *Big Bird touched his apple, and Ernie did too*, the researcher can investigate whether the Big Bird doll and the Ernie doll both touch their own apple or both touch one apple (testing ambiguity). In a sentence such as *Big Bird turned around when he jumped up*, the researcher can observe whether the subject had Big Bird both turn around and jump up (co-reference) or had another doll jump up. The transcription of the AO behaviors must allow the researcher to assess the data for whichever measures may be crucial to the research hypotheses.

As with language production measures, scoring sheets can be created in a template representing the experimental design, based on established scoring criteria. These scoring sheets, created for each subject, establish the data in a format ready for entry into a database and statistical analyses.[6] When more "structured" forms of the AO task are given (see Chapter 7), coding and analysis of AO data can be greatly simplified. The transcription sheets can sometimes initially establish the factorial basis for scoring, as we saw in Chapter 9 (Sloppy Identity Study; Foley et al., 2003).[7]

10.4.2.2 Truth-Value Judgment Task

A. Transcription

Because the data are simple in the TVJ task (i.e., digital and binary *yes* or *no* responses by a subject), a transcription sheet, structured in accord with randomized sentence batteries, can be prepared in keeping with the study, with simple check boxes for

---

[6] A sample scoring sheet for an act-out task used in a test of comprehension of relative clauses, providing converging evidence with that from a language production test of this study (Flynn & Lust, 1980), can be found online at http://pubs.apa.org/books/supp/blume

[7] See also the sample transcription sheet for the act-out task used in this Sloppy Identity study, which is available online at http://pubs.apa.org/books/supp/blume

each sentence.[8] Space should be allowed for recording any spontaneous comments offered by the subject in response to a sentence during task administration. Although a researcher or a researcher's assistant can simply mark the subject's *yes* or *no* response on the transcription sheet, greater reliability is achieved if the session is audio or video recorded so that the data can be checked for reliability before scoring. This also aids in the collection of possible spontaneous comments by children, which may be relevant to their interpretation, providing insights the experimenter had not conceived of before the study.

B. Coding and Scoring

Some researchers (e.g., Crain & Wexler, 1999) have suggested that there should be no variance on a task like the TVJ task (i.e., on the researcher's hypothesis that if there is a grammatical constraint, the child should never accept a situation or picture that conveys an interpretation which offends this grammatical constraint). However, as we have suggested elsewhere (Lust, Flynn, Foley, & Chien, 1999), behavioral and pragmatic variance always interacts with the display of grammatical knowledge through behavioral tasks (see Eisele, 1988; Eisele & Lust, 1996). As we have argued, grammatical knowledge may be discrete and not subject to continuous variance; in contrast, behaviors occur in real time and are continuously variable. As in all behavioral tests, all analyses must evaluate the significant effect of experimental factors against a baseline of variance on performance on the task. Pragmatic and other factors, as well as linguistic factors, determine each response. For example, not only children but also adults may reject a picture that is apparently grammatically possible because it is not pragmatically felicitous (Eisele & Lust, 1996) in the context given. For example, when asked to judge pictures for the sentence *Big Bird held the apple when he touched the pillow*, adults significantly rejected a picture in which someone other than Big Bird was touching the pillow (non-co-reference), an interpretation that is grammatically possible but assumedly pragmatically less felicitous in this situation.

In the TVJ task, because the data are binary (i.e., *yes/no*), all results must be statistically evaluated against the possibility of "chance" occurrence. Quantification of results requires such statistical testing for each condition in the experimental design. The researcher must decide how to use or not use data from subjects who demonstrate chance responding or who demonstrate a response bias (e.g., always *yes*) across the task, and the researcher should report such in subsequent report preparation. False negative pictures or situations have been included in the design of such tasks (see Chapter 7) to assess the possibility for such biased or chance responding; thus, statistical analyses should involve a comparison of data

---

[8] See, for example, the sample transcription sheet for the truth-value judgment task, available online at http://pubs.apa.org/books/supp/blume

from these conditions as well. Researchers must continually investigate the factors involved in their stimulus (e.g., the picture presented as well as the sentence administered), which may involve not only various grammatical factors but also pragmatic ones as well. Because the observed response, the dependent variable in analyses, is only *yes* or *no*, the behavior does not inform the researcher of the cognitive source of the response by the subject.

10.5 Summary

The principles and procedures that have been reviewed in this chapter can significantly aid in the processing of raw and transcribed data, moving them reliably along the "data pipeline" to ready them for analyses and interpretation. We have exemplified such principles and procedures here in only a few examples of tasks that can be potentially used to assess a subject's language production and/or comprehension. Hopefully, they can be usefully extended to others.

Appendix 10.1
English Mean Length of Utterance Criteria

General Mean Length of Utterance Criteria

Some researchers base mean length of utterance (MLU) on only 100 utterances or take out the first page of the transcript or the first 15 utterances. We use all utterances available except those in Items 1 through 7.

Do Not Count

Utterances

1. All unclear utterances, including
   - Totally unclear utterances: *XXX* (code as Unclear/Fragment under SpeechAct)
   - Partially unclear utterances: *XX the cat, I need that XX* (code as Unclear/Fragment under SpeechAct)
2. Do not count fragments when they are caused by an interruption from another speaker:[1]

   Child: I want^

   Adult: come here

3. Do not count singing, recitation or memorized expressions, repetitions of number series, fragments of stories (in which the child repeats what an adult said or where it is clearly memorized). (See Sentis, 1979; Herrera & Pandolfi, 1984.)

Words

4. Do not count fragments of words when an interlocutor gives a clue to the child:

   Adult: what is this?

   Adult: this is a chi . . . ?

   Child: cken

---

[1] Notice the symbol is "^" and not ">," which marks self interruption. These symbols are usually confused.

5. Do not count fillers such as *um* and *oh*.
6. Do not count *no, yes, hi,* and so forth.

Do Count

Utterances

7. When you understand a sentence except for one word (that may be a nonsense word, as underlined in the example), code the rest of the utterance and count the unclear word as 1 word, 1 morpheme, and X number of syllables.

   For example:
   It is raining <u>na</u>? → *na* = 1 syllable, 1 morpheme, 1 word (Total for utterance = 5 syllables [it-is-rai-ning-<u>na</u>], 5 morphemes [it-is-rain-ing-na], 4 words [it-is-raining-na])
   It is raining <u>napa</u>? → *napa* = 2 syllables, 1 morpheme, 1 word (Total for utterance = 6 syllables [it-is-rai-ning-na-pa], 5 morphemes [it-is-rain-ing-napa], 4 words [it-is-raining-napa]
   It is raining <u>na pa</u>? → *Unclear* Do not count this at all because there is more than one unintelligible word.

8. Count fragments when they are caused by a break-off. They count as 1 utterance.

   Child: I want> have to clean.

   Just count the correction; that is, count only the morphemes, syllables, and so forth, of *have*. In the case where there is repetition of a part of the utterance, as follows:

   Child: I want> I have to clean.

we code the utterance as if it were *I have to clean*. We just count one subject.

9. Count all exact and inexact imitations of the interlocutor's utterance (other-rep) and all exact and inexact self imitations (self-rep).

Words

10. Count words repeated for emphasis.
    No, no, no. We would not count these because we do not count *no* at all.
    Look, aunt, that, there, there. Count both *there*.
    I don't want, I don't want. Count these as 2 different utterances.

11. Stuttering: Count the word once in the most complete form for morphemes, syllables, and words (see Sentis, 1979).

Special Types of Words

12. Compound proper names are counted as 1 morpheme, 1 word, X number of syllables.
    Mary Ann → (compound first name), 3 syllables, 1 morpheme, 1 word
13. Count all compound words as you would for an adult.
    telephone → 3 syllables (te-le-phone), 2 morphemes (tele-phone), 1 word
    television → 4 syllables (te-le-vi-sion), 2 morphemes (tele-vision), 1 word
    birthday → 2 syllables (birth-day), 2 morphemes (birth-day), 1 word
    seesaw → 2 syllables (see-saw), 2 morphemes (see-saw), 1 word
14. Consider the contractions *don't* and *he'll* as having two roots, and thus count as 2 morphemes.
15. Onomatopoeias: Do not count except when they are a motherese word.

    Adult: make the car move.

    Child: ¡brr... brr... pum! (car sound). [This isn't coded.]

    Adult: what's that?

    Child: it's a wow-wow (*wow-wow* = motherese word for *dog*.). [This is coded: Wow-wow = 2 syllables, 1 morpheme, 1 word.]

16. When the child pronounces two words as one:

    Whathat (*what that*)

    count them as 2 different words.

English-Specific Guidelines

17. Prepositions. All prepositions have just 1 morpheme in English. Count syllables according to the particular preposition.
18. Number. Count as 1 morpheme the plural ending *-s* or *-es*. Singulars are not given points because the child is not adding morphemes to them. For example,
    cats → 1 syllable (cats), 2 morphemes (cat-s), 1 word
    foxes → 2 syllables (fo-xes), 2 morphemes (fox-es), 1 word
19. Count interrogative words and relative pronouns *what, who, which, that, where* → 1 syllable, 1 morpheme, 1 word.

Inflection and Agreement: Verbs

Nonfinite Forms

- Infinitives can appear accompanied by the preposition *to* or without it.
  to sing → 2 syllables (to-sing), 2 morphemes (to-sing), 2 words
  sing → 1 syllable (sing), 1 morpheme (sing), 1 word
- Gerunds
  singing → 2 syllables (sin-ging), 2 morphemes (sing-ing), 1 word
  studying → 3 syllables (stu-dy-ing), 2 morphemes (study-ing), 1 word
  discovering → 4 syllables (dis-co-ve-ring), 2 morphemes (discover-ing), 1 word
- Past participles
  sung → 1 syllable (sung), 1 morphemes (sung), 1 word
  studied → 2 syllables (stu-died), 2 morphemes (studi-ed), 1 word
  eaten → 2 syllables (ea-ten), 2 morphemes (eat-en), 1 word

Finite Forms

Indicative
- Present
  (I/you/we/you/they) *eat* → 1 syllable (eat), 1 morpheme (eat), 1 word
  (he/she/it) *eats* → 1 syllable (eats), 2 morphemes (eat-s), 1 word
  (I/you/we/you/they) *dance* → 1 syllable (dance), 1 morpheme (dance), 1 word
  (he/she/it) *dances* → 2 syllables (dan-ces), 2 morphemes (dance-s), 1 word
- Past
  (I/you/ he/she/it/we/you/they) *ate* → 1 syllable (ate), 1 morpheme (ate), 1 word
  (I/you/ he/she/it/we/you/they) *danced* → 1 syllable (danced), 2 morphemes (danc-ed), 1 word
- Future (follow the same guidelines as for *would, can, could*, etc.)
  (I/you/ he/she/it/we/you/they) *will eat* → 2 syllables (will eat), 2 morphemes (will eat), 2 words
  (I/you/ he/she/it/we/you/they) *will dance* → 2 syllables (will dance), 2 morphemes (will dance), 2 words

Imperative
look → 1 syllable (look), 1 morpheme (look), 1 word

Verb *to be*
- Present
  am → 1 syllable, 1 morpheme, 1 word
  are → 1 syllable, 1 morphemes, 1 word
  is → 1 syllable, 1 morpheme, 1 word

- Past
  was → 1 syllable, 1 morpheme, 1 word
  were → 1 syllable, 1 morpheme, 1 word

Verb *to have*
- Present
  have → 1 syllable, 1 morpheme, 1 word
  has → 1 syllable, 1 morpheme, 1 word
- Past
  had → 1 syllable, 1 morpheme, 1 word

Derivational Morphology

Diminutives. Count the diminutive morphemes *–y* and *–ie* as 1 morpheme.
doggy → 2 syllables (do-ggy), 2 morphemes (dog-y), 1 word
horsie → 2 syllables (hor-sie), 2 morphemes (hors-ie), 1 word

Appendix 10.2
Scoring Criteria: Relative Clause[1]

Correct–Incorrect Data

1. Alteration of the original sentence structure was scored as incorrect.
   Examples:
   (a) Clause reversal
       Stimulus: Cookie Monster eats the thing which Ernie kicks.
       Imitation Response: Ernie kicks the thing which Cookie Monster eats.
   (b) Omissions of a clause
       Stimulus: Cookie Monster pushes what the Big Bird throws.
       Imitation Response: Big Bird throws.
   (c) Conflation to a single clause
       Stimulus: Big Bird pushes the balloon which bumps Ernie.
       Imitation Response: Big Bird pushes Ernie.
   (d) Change in relative pronoun other than *which/that* substitution.
       Stimulus: Cookie Monster eats the thing which Ernie kicks.
       Imitation Response: Cookie Monster eats the thing what Ernie kicks.

2. Major changes in the constituents of the sentence were scored as incorrect.
   Examples:
   (a) Change in noun phrase (NP)
       Cookie Monster → Big Bird
   (b) Change in predicate
       Stimulus: Fozzie Bear hugs what Kermit the Frog kisses.
       Imitation Response: Fozzie Bear kisses what Kermit the Frog kisses.

3. Requirement of repetition of the original sentence after the original presentation was scored as incorrect. Take the first response but allow one repetition if
   (a) there is no response by child, or
   (b) the child asks for a repetition if they have given no response.

---

[1] Data from Flynn and Lust (1980).

4. Changes that were scored as correct:
   (a) *That* substitution for *which*
   (b) Tense changes
   (c) Omission or addition of possessive marker or determiner
   (d) "In class" word substitution that are close semantically or phonological similarities

   Semantically similar examples:

   - *touches/pushes*
   - *hits/pushes*
   - *bumps/touches*
   - *bumps/hits*

   Phonologically similar examples:

   - *kiss/kick*

   Do not count as correct substitutions that result from repetition or movement of the second verb
      Examples:
      Stimulus: Fozzie kisses the thing which Kermit Frog hits.
      Imitation Response: Fozzie hits the thing which Kermit Frog hits.
      Or
      Imitation Response: Fozzie hits the thing which Kermit Frog kisses.
   (e) Additions to original sentence that produce no change in meaning

5. Allow self-corrections where there is a pause.
      Stimulus: Cookie Monster pushes what the Big Bird throws.
      Imitation Response: Cookie Monster pushes which ... what the Big Bird throws.
      But count as incorrect if no pause:
      Imitation Response: Cookie Monster pushes which/what the Big Bird throws.

Error/Deformation Scoring

Code deformations are made on the model sentence in terms of the theoretical purpose of the study.

1. Structural errors
   Examples:
   (a) Conversion of head type in a relative clause
   (b) Change of grammatical relations

2. Other. For example, in this study the subsequent analysis of children's imitation errors showed that
   - the largest proportion of structural errors across all relative types involved the head or comp, signifying that head type is a significant variable in the acquisition errors.
   - errors that changed grammatical relations across clauses occurred far less often.
   - the structural preference for headless relatives was supported in error analysis by the high amount of conversion of the relative pronoun *which* in either the Type I determinate headed or Type II nondeterminate headed relatives to the pronoun *what*, which had been used in the headless relative. About 80% to 90% of subordinate clause errors or about 25% of Type I and II items shifted from *which* to *what*.

3. E. Ernie touches the balloon which Big Bird throws.
   S. Ernie touches the thing what Big Bird throws. (5;01) (Flynn and Lust, 1980, p. 37).
   - All the head type conversions for Type II nondeterminate-headed relatives and half the conversions of Type I determinate-headed relatives were conversions to free relatives.
   - Conversions of the free relative head type were mostly (93%) conversions to *thing* headed Type II relatives; the highest proportions of these occurred in the oldest age group.
   - Errors such as exemplified in Items 6 and 7 confirm children's general difficulty with differentiation and ordering of the head NP and complementizer in relatives.

4. E. Fozzie kisses the thing which Kermit Frog hits.
   S. Fozzie Bear kisses which the thing the thing that Kermit Frog hits. (3;09)

5. E. Cookie Monster eats the thing which Ernie kicks.
   S. Cookie Monster eats the thing that about Ernie kicks. (4;03) (Flynn and Lust, 1980, p. 37).

11 Interpreting the Data: Scientific Inference

After producing a reliable set of data through the use of scientific methods such as the ones described in preceding chapters, the researcher is now ready to interpret these data. However, the relation between data and interpretation is not direct, and the researcher must make inferences about the meaning of these data.

Interpreting subject language data is challenging. A first challenge involves dealing with general variability (related to sampling error, measurement error, or individual differences, as discussed in Chapter 5). Other challenges are more specific to the field of child language acquisition. One such challenge has to do with the complex nature of what has to be acquired—that is, language, which involves multiple domains, including grammar, phonology, semantics, and pragmatics. Although a research project may aim to investigate the development of a specific area within a given language domain such as grammar (e.g., development of grammatical categories), one cannot simply assume this develops in isolation from everything else. Development of any given aspect of language is likely to be, to some extent, affected by development in other areas and/or domains of language, as well as by development in the child's integration of these domains (Lust, 2006; Valian & Aubry, 2005). For instance, research on the acquisition of grammatical categories initially proceeded under the assumption that this particular aspect of syntax could be studied meaningfully apart from the study of other aspects of development. However, evidence now indicates that the development of grammatical categories is affected by development in other areas of syntax such as sentential structural complexity (Bloom, 1970; Dye, Foley, Blume, & Lust, 2004), as well as phonology (Demuth, 2007; Demuth & Tremblay, 2008; Dye, 2011) and pragmatics (Sorace, Serratrice, Filiaci, & Baldo, 2009). Furthermore, language interacts with other mental functions, including short-term and long-term memory systems, attention, perception, and motor functions. Indeed, evidence shows the development of grammatical categories is influenced by the developing working memory, in addition to other factors (Valian & Aubry, 2005).

Another major challenge in interpreting child language data has to do with the complexities involved in assessing a developing and changing organism. In this context, one expects to encounter even more variability than when studying adults. In children, everything is developing: both that which is being studied and everything else (i.e., including extraneous factors). Especially challenging is the development of various language abilities, which may proceed at different rates across individuals (Shaffer

---

This chapter was contributed by Cristina D. Dye, PhD, Center for Linguistics and Language Sciences, Newcastle University, Newcastle upon Tyne, England, and Claire A. Foley, PhD, Department of Slavic and Eastern Languages and Literatures, Boston College, Boston, MA.

& Kipp, 2007). For example, evidence shows that at early periods, some children may be more advanced in utterance length although their pronunciation and intelligibility is less advanced, whereas others may appear to show the opposite pattern, making faster progress on their pronunciation although utterance length is delayed (E. Bates, Dale, & Thal, 1995).

Studies often attempt to make inferences regarding what a child "knows" about language on the basis of behavioral data, which constitutes the results of observation or experiment. However, the link between behavior and competence is complex, abstract, and indirect (Lust 1999, 2006; see also Chapters 7 and 8, this volume). Adding to the inferential challenge are the complexities of linguistic theories of language knowledge, which help to define *competence* and must be related to empirical observations.

In this chapter, we introduce some of the complexities involved in scientific inference based on empirical results in language acquisition research, as well as a set of means for strengthening this inference (i.e., of producing sound interpretation as opposed to speculation). The interpretation of results must be guided by the way in which the study was set up, its research question(s) and hypothesis, the modality (comprehension vs. production) of the task used, any assumptions or limitations associated with the task itself, any controls built into the study, the type of analyses conducted, and findings from previous research. This is actually rather helpful. Unlike reading tea leaves or other nonscientific forms of interpretation, when interpreting results, much more information is available to guide and facilitate interpretation. In addition, it is not always the case that all interpretations are equally plausible. To avoid an overinterpretation of results or unjustified conclusions, a number of steps can be taken. Considering the questions in each of these steps is helpful for the proper interpretation of results. The first half of this chapter considers several constraints guiding inference in language acquisition studies: original hypothesis, inferences from sample to populations, and how the type of study and data guide the interpretations. The second half reviews ways that acquisition researchers can strengthen inference: alternative explanation elimination, linking findings, interpreting across multiple languages and methods.

11.1 The Original Hypothesis: Was It Supported?

Results must be interpreted with regard to the hypothesis the study initially set out to test. Chapter 5 discussed the specific steps and protocols involved in setting up a scientific study. In particular, we have seen that a scientific study begins with the formulation of a hypothesis (whether derived from a theoretical model or based on previous empirical observations) for which a suitable experiment is then designed. Thus, a strong basis for interpreting results is created because it allows for confirmatory analysis (Diggle & Chetwynd, 2011). Using statistical procedures, we can determine whether the null hypothesis that observations were due to chance alone may be rejected. If so, we may then accept that the research hypothesis is supported. It is worth stressing here that results cannot be interpreted with regard to hypotheses that were not tested in the study or hypotheses that emerged only after inspection of the data. Starting the process of interpretation with the data (instead of the initial hypothesis) would preclude the possibility of disconfirmation (and may overrate the occasional chance associations in the study).

11.2 Inference From Sample to Population: Are the Results Generalizable?

The distinguishing mark of scientific research is the goal to make inferences that go beyond the particular data collected. In any scientific study regardless of the field, the ultimate goal is to discover something that is true that holds for a population of subjects and/or items. For example, a study may investigate a research question about Spanish-speaking toddlers' performance on relative clauses. Although because of time, financial, or other constraints, any given study can only investigate a sample (e.g., 30 toddlers), what we are interested in is the population from which the sample was drawn—the ultimate goal is to be able to generalize the results obtained from the sample to the population. But how does one go from the results from the sample (which has been measured) to drawing conclusions about the full population (which cannot be measured)? How does one go from conclusions about what is known to conclusions about what is unknown? Almost 300 years ago, David Hume (1739/2000) argued that it was impossible, but, fortunately, this formidable leap is now achievable.

Statistical procedures allow for making inferences of this nature. The data are used to calculate statistics for the sample, which are then used through the appropriate statistical test (e.g., t-test) to draw probability conclusions about the population parameters. Thus, provided that statistical procedures have been carefully followed throughout the study (including issues regarding randomization, and independence; e.g., Diggle & Chetwynd, 2011), we can generalize our results to the entire population, making claims regarding, for example, Spanish-speaking toddlers in general rather than just the 30 tested in our study. The same holds with regard to stimuli, for example, if we wish to claim that our results hold for relative clauses in general (with respect to both types and tokens), rather than just the ones tested in our study.

Replication of research findings contributes to claims of generalizability. When different researchers with different samples obtain the same findings, the credibility of the conclusions is enhanced. Indeed, the importance of replication has received increased attention in recent years, including a crowd-sourced empirical effort to estimate the reproducibility of a sample of studies from three prominent scientific journals wherein researchers followed a structured protocol for designing and conducting a close replication of a key effect from the selected articles (see Open Science Collaboration, 2012, in press, and see https://osf.io/ezcuj/wiki/home/).

11.3 The Type of Study and Data Guide the Interpretation of Results

Interpreting the results of a given study is to some extent guided by the type of study and/or data. Next, we summarize a set of issues related to study and data type that have to be considered in interpreting results.

11.3.1 Interpreting Experimental Versus Observational Studies

The way results are interpreted depends on whether the data were collected through observation or experimentation. Observational studies (described in Chapters 1 and 4) are fundamentally different from experimental studies (described in Chapters 1, 5–8, 14). In an observational study, the researcher notes a certain behavior (e.g., the child's production of correct verb forms or sentences) without interfering (i.e., manipulating or controlling). In contrast, in an experimental study, the researcher manipulates one or more independent variables (e.g., verb type, sentence type) while controlling a set of potentially confounding variables (e.g., length in syllables) to determine whether this manipulation leads to variation in the behavior of interest—that is, the dependent variable (e.g., amount of correctly produced verb forms). If variation in the manipulated variable leads to variation in the dependent variable, with potential confounds being controlled, it is possible in principle to infer a causal relationship. Because observational studies are not controlled and because a given set of observations is compatible with more than one explanation, cause and effect relations cannot be inferred from observational studies.[1] Results from observational studies may be used, for example, to help formulate hypotheses to be tested in future studies. Experimental results, in comparison with observational results, allow for more precise interpretation and stronger conclusions.

Observational studies also differ from experimental studies in the nature of their reproducibility. Any specific natural speech sample includes a specific context, which is not reproducible. That is, the child is in a particular place, at a particular time, thinking and talking about particular issues, with particular people. Although natural

---

[1] Note that this holds regardless of the type of statistical test used to analyze the observational data, even if using inferential statistics (e.g., t-tests, chi-square tests). Establishing causation has to do with the way the study was set up, not with the type of statistical tests used.

speech findings may be "reproducible" on one level, such that different researchers with different samples may see the same trends, the conditions of observation will necessarily vary in a way that experimental conditions need not vary.

Furthermore, although observational studies help us discover what a child produces, they do not help us know what the child cannot produce or what else the child can but did not produce during a given observation. Karl Popper (1934) famously argued that it is logically impossible to verify the truth of a statement such as *all swans are white* or *there are no black swans* by means of repeated observations of white swans (but it is possible to falsify it by a single observation of a black swan). The absence of a particular linguistic form or structure in a child's spontaneous speech sample may be associated with various factors, including lack of linguistic competence, lack of exposure to the construction, lack of appropriate discourse or pragmatic context in the sample, or simple lack of occurrence in the finite amount of time during which the child was observed (Stromswold, 1996; Tomasello & Stahl, 2004). For example, whereas early studies claimed that forms involving a nonfinite verb preceded by a subject pronoun (*il ouvrir*) were not found in the speech of children acquiring French (Rizzi, 1993), these forms were documented in a subsequent study involving more detailed analysis, including spectral analysis (Dye, 2011).

Likewise, within an observational study, interpreting what a given child utterance was "intended" to mean can be difficult. Although methods such as "rich interpretation" have been developed, wherein the context of natural speech is carefully considered to determine what a child's utterance means and what its structure likely is (e.g., Bloom, 1970), this process remains subjective, and inferences must be qualified appropriately. Experimental studies using methods such as elicited imitation allow stronger conclusions to be drawn regarding a child's intended utterance, and thus its meaning and potential underlying structure because the experiment provides the target form (see Chapter 6). For example, an elicited imitation study (discussed in Section 11.7.1) found that children omitted expletive subjects (e.g., *It was raining*) more often than pronoun subjects in imitating sentences in which other variables were held constant, allowing the study authors to draw stronger inferences about grammatical knowledge underlying language performance (Valian, Hoeffner, & Aubry, 1996).

11.3.2 Interpreting Studies With Independent Versus Quasi-Independent Variables

Many analyses test for differences across two or more groups of stimuli or participants. One consideration relates to the nature of the independent variable. With experimental studies, inference of causality may be possible when the independent variable is a true independent variable (i.e., can be manipulated or participants can be randomly assigned to its different levels of a variable), such as verb type or sentence type, for example. When the independent variable is only a quasi-independent variable such as age or sex (i.e., it cannot be manipulated, or participants cannot be randomly assigned to its different levels; see more on this in Chapter 5), claims have to be qualified appropriately. For example, when investigating differences in language performance between monolingual versus bilingual children, even if a statistically significant group difference is found, it cannot be interpreted as explaining the difference in performance.

11.3.3 Interpreting Correlations

Some analyses investigate relations among variables. In such studies, there are limits on inferences that can be drawn from correlations. For example, results in a study may show a statistically significant correlation between two variables, A and B. It does not follow that A causes B, because correlation does not mean causation. If variable A increases as B increases, it does not necessarily mean A causes B. There may well be a third variable which affects both A and B. Yet another possibility is that it may be a case of reversed causation, with B causing A. This point is typically discussed in introductory-level statistics textbooks (e.g., Solso & MacLin, 2002).

11.3.4 Interpreting Comprehension Versus Production Studies

There are differences in the inferences that can be drawn from comprehension and production studies. Much of the early literature in the field was devoted to the study of language production. As more methods became available, it became possible to investigate comprehension as well, including at very early periods (i.e., even before the onset of production). Because perception studies have shown evidence that at least some linguistic abilities develop early on (Jusczyk, 1997) and because production has often been argued to lag behind comprehension (e.g., E. V. Clark & Hecht, 1983, but see also Sundara, Demuth, & Kuhl, 2011, for contrasting evidence), claims based on production data alone need proper qualification (e.g., the data indicate that the construction under investigation was not observed in production, in the sample observed).

At the same time, it is important to keep in mind that comprehension data, though obtainable at earlier ages or from younger children, in no way provide any more direct evidence regarding competence than do production data (see Chapter 7). Beyond the issue of the comprehension–production lag, production and comprehension studies by their nature require researchers to consider different sets of questions bearing on inference as they interpret data sets. For example, for production data, it is important to consider what is known about the target utterance and what the context of the utterance is. See Section 11.7 for a discussion of the different questions raised in production and comprehension studies.

11.3.5 Task-Specific Constraints or Assumptions Guiding Interpretation

Often the particular task or methodology used in a given study imposes its own constraints and assumptions regarding the interpretation of results. For example, act-out tasks, because of their nature, are less amenable to drawing conclusions about which sentence interpretation for a given stimulus is not accessible to the subject. One can only assume that the interpretations are accessible. Certain interpretations may be available to the subject, but he or she may choose not to act them out (a problem that also arises with spontaneous speech and elicited production data). Tasks involving grammaticality judgments assume metalinguistic abilities on the part of the children. Because such abilities are themselves subject to development (Shaffer & Kipp, 2007), the interpretation of results regarding early linguistic competence has to take this into account and properly qualify the results. Truth–value judgment tasks assume that the child has some conception of truth in the sense of a correspondence between what is said and the situation referred to (i.e., they are predicated on the child's sense of "truth"; see Chapter 7).

Techniques used with infants, such as high-amplitude sucking or preferential listening/looking, can test discrimination between two or more types of linguistic stimuli. However, they may not tell us why or how children accomplish the discrimination, and thus interpreting results obtained with these techniques has to be couched within these constraints. Data from electrophysiological techniques such as electroencephalography and functional brain imaging (e.g., functional magnetic resonance imaging and near infrared spectroscopy) are becoming more popular because they can minimize overt behavior and detect language-dependent patterns of brain activity; however, they often lend themselves more easily to interpretations with regard to processing rather than competence (for application of such methods to child language research, see Friederici & Thierry, 2008). We return to some of these points in Section 11.7.2.

11.4 Eliminating Alternative Explanations

Having proposed an explanation for a new set of results, our next step is to consider any alternative explanations and discuss why these might be invalid or less suitable. The more alternative explanations eliminated, the stronger your inference. For example, it is worth considering whether results could be due to experimental or statistical confounds, such as when the absence of an expected effect cannot be explained by a lack of power or floor or ceiling effects (see Solso & MacLin, 2002). In general, discussion of the various controls built into the study should allow for at least some alternative explanations to be ruled out (especially those related to task-specific strategies). Demonstrating that these alternative explanations are not feasible strengthens inference.

Similarly, debating alternative theoretical interpretations of a study can strengthen inference. For a concrete illustration, the reader is referred to Santelmann, Berk, Austin, Somashekar, and Lust (2002) for a review of a range of accounts for the observation that in English in some *yes/no* questions, children do not invert the subject and auxiliary verb. The authors pointed out that in some studies claiming a delay in development of inversion in question formation, no distinction is drawn between utterances with overt verbal inflection (e.g., *Dat's the owner?* for the target utterance *Is that the owner?*) and those without overt inflection (e.g., *Dem baby puppies?*). By discussing the theoretical claim that inversion is delayed developmentally and introducing this distinction between utterances with and without overt verbal inflection, the authors can specify precisely the reasons their data are incompatible with most of the theories considered.

11.5 Linking to Previous Findings in the Field

It is always valuable to interpret and discuss new results in the context of previous results in the area investigated. As noted earlier, previous results may have led to the hypothesis being tested in the new study. In these cases, discussing other results can demonstrate the progression of discovery in an area of research. Often, the new results taken in conjunction with results from previous literature may reveal something that does not necessarily follow from the current results alone. Making this link further strengthens the interpretation of the current results and helps readers see the big picture.

When the new results contrast with previously published results, it is useful to discuss why we think this might be. For example, one may consider whether there were differences between the new study and previous studies with regard to participants (e.g., sample size, age, socioeconomic status, IQ, mean length of utterance [MLU]), the modality of the study (e.g., comprehension vs. production), or the administration of the task (auditory vs. visual presentation). It is useful to identify such differences and speculate on how they might account (at least partially) for differences from previous results. This is where speculation is appropriate.

11.6 Interpreting Results Across Multiple Child Languages

Further strengthening inference about grammatical knowledge underlying language behavior are cross-linguistic studies. When underlying knowledge can be argued to characterize acquisition in typologically or historically unrelated languages, it can be related to aspects of acquisition that are argued to be universal (e.g., a theory of universal grammar; N. Chomsky, 1986; Lust, 2006). Studies of acquisition of the same area of knowledge in different languages can provide evidence for what is under development and for the nature of cross-linguistic variation (e.g., Lust, 1986, 1987; Lust, Hermon, & Kornfilt, 1994; Lust, Suñer, & Whitman 1994). In particular, cross-linguistic research can compare languages that share a particular feature, but differ in another. Studying the course of development across two or more languages can contribute to "factoring out" what may be universal and what is specific to individual languages (Lust 1999, 2006).

11.7 Interpreting Results Across Multiple Methods

Inference is strengthened when evidence regarding a given question is available as a result of using multiple methods. First, multiple studies using different methods can yield converging evidence—findings from different sets of data that point to the same conclusion:

> Research findings are more informative and more persuasive when researchers take the time to demonstrate that their results are robust across variations in methods, procedures, subject populations, and estimation techniques and therefore are more worthy of dissemination to the field. (Duncan, Engel, Claessens, & Dowsett, 2014, p. 2419)

Evidence obtained across different tasks makes it possible to infer with more certainty that the results obtained are real and are not related to task effects.

Second, evidence obtained using one method may complement evidence obtained from another. When available, evidence from different tasks helps achieve a deeper and more comprehensive picture of underlying competence because each method reveals different dimensions of knowledge. The strengths of one method may complement the limitations of another, and vice versa. Next, we illustrate these points with examples of converging evidence from previous studies. The studies were selected to illustrate a range of methodologies and the ways the evidence they uncover may converge on one hand and be complementary on the other. We refer to evidence obtained through use of two types of production tasks (11.7.1), two types of comprehension tasks (11.7.3), and a comprehension and a production task (11.7.2 and 11.7.4). One of these pairs also compares evidence obtained across experimental and observational studies (11.7.1). For each pair, we discuss the results from the first method and some of the inferences permitted and then discuss the results from the second method, highlighting how the study expands on the first and what can be inferred about language knowledge.

11.7.1 Interpreting Spontaneous Speech and Elicited Imitation Data

Spontaneous speech and elicited imitation offer strong potential for converging and complementary evidence. Spontaneous speech may yield child utterances that researchers never imagined, leading to theories about children's grammatical systems.

At the same time, even with careful attention to context, the target utterance may not be known. As discussed in Chapter 6, elicited imitation provides a way to study production when the target is known. Furthermore, it allows the precise manipulation of grammatical factors to test hypotheses that may have arisen through the study of spontaneous speech.

For example, a study of early production of overt subjects in the spontaneous speech of young children reported that in the spontaneous speech of children acquiring English, the percentage of utterances with verbs that also include overt subjects increases over development, from an average of 69% of utterances in the youngest age group (mean age 2;0, mean MLU 1.77) to an average of 95% in the oldest (mean age 2;7, mean MLU 4.22; Valian, 1991). From the English spontaneous speech data alone, it was not possible to determine whether the change from lower MLU to higher MLU resulted from a change in grammatical knowledge or a change in performance capacity. For example, one grammatical hypothesis is that children's early grammars permit null subjects (e.g., in English, *Plays with kitty* instead of *She plays with kitty*). In contrast, one performance hypothesis is that the omission of subjects is likelier with heavier cognitive processing demands.

The alternative explanations can be investigated to some degree using additional spontaneous speech data. For example, if rates of children's subject production for English (which does not permit null subjects) are higher than those at similar developmental stages for a language that does permit null subjects, this suggests knowledge of language-specific constraints on subject omission. Valian (1991) did, in fact, report such data: In a parallel analysis of spontaneous speech in the acquisition of Italian, which permits null subjects, percentages of utterances with overt subjects were much lower at each developmental point than in English. The inference from the full natural speech data set was that performance constraints were influencing subject omission, though the method did not provide a way to test alternative hypotheses by design.

By using elicited imitation, Valian, Hoeffner, and Aubry (1996) were able to investigate ways in which the two theoretical accounts made different predictions. They reasoned that if omission of subjects at low MLU in English were due to the children's hypothesis that their grammar permitted null subjects, they should omit expletive subjects (e.g., in "It rained yesterday") more often than pronominal subjects because expletive subjects are not present in the adult grammars of languages like Italian. In contrast, under this hypothesis, at higher MLU stages when children's inclusion of subjects in spontaneous speech approaches that of adults, expletive subjects would not be predicted to be omitted more than pronominal subjects.

The results of the experiment both corroborated and extended earlier findings. First, they showed that children omitted more subjects in elicited imitation at earlier points in development, replicating the spontaneous speech finding. At the same time, children with both lower and higher MLUs omitted expletive subjects more than they omitted pronominal subjects; there was no differential effect. This finding would not be predicted under the hypothesis that null subjects were permitted by the children's grammar, but it is consistent with a performance explanation for omission of overt subjects. This finding would be difficult to uncover in spontaneous speech; in the spontaneous speech study, children produced few expletive subjects at any age. The imitation results helped determine the extent of different influences on production, thereby helping strengthen inferences from the observation study.

11.7.2 Interpreting Elicited Imitation and Act-Out Data

Considering results across production and comprehension experiments permits a fuller set of inferences about knowledge than would be possible with just one task modality alone. For example, the act-out task (see Chapter 7) may provide information about children's preferred interpretation of a structure whereas the elicited imitation task (see Chapter 6) may strengthen inferences from an act-out study by providing a way to tease apart factors that may be influencing interpretation. In turn, the act-out task may be further manipulated to see whether factors revealed as significant in elicited imitation are, in fact, determining interpretation.

This potential dynamic relationship between act-out and elicited imitation is illustrated by a study of young English-acquiring children's knowledge of the interpretation of elements with different forms in the subject position of embedded clauses (Cohen Sherman & Lust, 1993). The study investigated three contexts: complement clauses with a non-overt subject (technically termed *PRO*), which require an infinitival verb; complement clauses with a pronoun, requiring a tensed verb; and coordinated clauses, which require a tensed verb, as shown in Table 11.1.

The interpretation of *PRO* in the infinitival contexts of A and C in Table 11.1 requires knowledge of the language-specific lexical items *told*, *reminded*, and *promised*—specifically that *told* and *reminded* require the main clause object to serve as the

Tab. 11.1: Example Sentences for Control and Coordinate Structures

	Clause with *PRO* subject	Clause with lexical pronoun subject
Object control	A. John$_i$ told/reminded Tom$_j$ PRO$_{*i,j,*k}$ to leave.	B. John$_i$ told/reminded Tom$_j$ that he$_{i,j,k}$ will leave.
Subject control	C. John$_i$ promised Tom$_j$ PRO$_{i,*j,*k}$ to leave.	D. John$_i$ promised Tom$_j$ that he$_{i,j,k}$ will leave.
Coordinate	E. The turtle$_i$ tickles the skunk$_j$, and $_{i,*j}$ bumps the car.	F. The turtle$_i$ tickles the skunk$_j$, and he$_{i,j,k}$ bumps the car.

Note: The subscripts *i*, *j*, and *k* are *referential indices*, a notational aid to describe whether elements may refer to the same individual. For example, if *John* and *he* bear the same referential index *i*, this notes that they may co-refer; if the index is marked with an asterisk, **i*, this signals that they may not refer to the same individual. For an introduction to the syntax of *PRO*, see Carnie (2013, pp. 430–450). From "Children Are in Control," by J. C. Sherman and B. Lust, 1993, *Cognition, 46*, pp. 47–48. Copyright 1993 by Elsevier. Adapted with permission.

antecedent (i.e., to "control") for *PRO* and that *promised* requires main clause subject control. In contrast, the pronominal form in B and D is not similarly constrained, although its interpretation may be subject to pragmatic influence. Coordinate sentences, as in E and F, permit both null and lexical subjects but, unlike control structures, include a tensed verb in both cases. The authors hypothesized that if universal grammar constrains children's grammars, they should show sensitivity to the distribution of *PRO* versus lexical pronouns, allowing A to D but ruling out sentences in which *PRO* appears with a tensed verb (e.g., **John reminded Tom that* PRO *will leave*) or in which a pronoun appears with a nonfinite verb (e.g., **John reminded Tom him to leave*). Further, they hypothesized that children should be aware that the interpretation of *PRO* is constrained, as in A and C, in ways that interpretation of the lexical pronoun is not, as shown in B and D. These hypotheses concern the accessibility in children's grammars of an abstract relationship between embedded verb tense and the form of an element in embedded subject position and the integration of lexical knowledge with grammatical constraints on embedded subject interpretation.

Their elicited imitation data showed that the most common error was conversion of clause type wherein children converted both subjects and verbal inflection (i.e., children frequently converted structures like A to B and vice versa but rarely changed either subjects or verbal inflection without making the required change in the other). In contrast, in their imitations of the coordinate structures in E and F, children changed the proform (*PRO* or the pronoun) but not tense, suggesting that they distinguish the coordinate subject position from the control domain where *PRO* appears.

Act-out results from the same study revealed a significant contrast between pronoun and infinitival complement sentences. Sentences were presented to children with two different pragmatic leads, one corresponding to the subject, and one to the object (e.g., *This is a story about Tom* or *This is a story about Billy*). Results showed that for pronoun sentences, children chose the subject as antecedent for the pronoun significantly more when the pragmatic lead included the subject noun phrase and similarly chose an object antecedent more when the pragmatic lead included the object noun phrase. In contrast, the pragmatic lead did not influence children's choice for infinitival complement sentences.

Taken together, the findings from the elicited imitation and act-out data offered a fuller picture of competence than either one could by itself. Although the production data suggested that children are sensitive to the distribution of *PRO*, the comprehension data suggested that they knew that "control" of *PRO* could not be overridden by pragmatics (unlike interpretation of the lexical pronoun, which can).

11.7.3 Interpreting Act-Out and Truth–Value Judgment Data

Used together, two experimental tests of comprehension permit exploration of different dimensions of interpretation. The act-out method can uncover what interpretation

Tab. 11.2: Example Verb Phrase Ellipsis Sentences

Two-object sloppy interpretation (grammatical)	A. O bites O's apple, and B bites B's apple.	ii jj
One-object strict interpretations (grammatical)	B. O bites O's apple, and B bites O's apple.	ii ji
	C. O bites B's apple, and B bites B's apple.	ij jj
	D. O bites E's apple, and B bites B's apple.	ik jk
Example two-object interpretation that is ungrammatical	E. *O bites O's apple, and B bites E's apple.	ii jk

Note: From "Knowledge of Variable Binding in VP–Ellipsis: Language Acquisition Research and Theory Converge," by C. Foley, Z. Núñez del Prado, I. Barbier, and B. Lust, 2003, *Syntax*, 6, p. 53. Copyright 2003 by John Wiley and Sons. Adapted with permission.

is possible and most accessible. Truth–value judgment tasks can investigate whether one or more of a range of interpretations is possible.[2] For example, both types of tasks were used in work probing the comprehension of ambiguous verb phrase ellipsis structures such as *Oscar bites his apple, and Bert does too* by children acquiring English (Foley, Núñez del Prado, Barbier, & Lust, 2003). In adults, this structure permits the two-object interpretation shown as A in Table 11.2 (which has been termed the *sloppy* interpretation) and the one-object *strict* interpretation shown as B to D in Table 11.2. Other logically possible combinations of subject and possessor in the two clauses are not accepted as possible by adults, as shown in E in Table 11.2 (Foley et al., 2003).

According to linguistic theory, the two-object sloppy interpretation involves variable binding[3] of each object pronoun by the local subject, and the one-object strict interpretation requires pragmatic motivation for its representation. The authors reasoned that the capacity for variable binding, which in linguistic theory is considered to be part of universal grammar, should be observed early on, whereas pragmatic knowledge, which is not part of universal grammar, should develop over time. Thus, they predicted that (a) the sloppy interpretation should be accessible at the earliest stages of language acquisition; (b) because of its hypothesized links to the discourse, the degree to which the strict interpretation is selected should be subject to pragmatic influence; and (c) the ungrammatical interpretations should be ruled out from the earliest stages of language acquisition.

---

[2] It is important to note that a truth–value judgment response cannot be viewed as an absolute determinant of whether an interpretation is possible. It may reflect the respondent's preference for one interpretation over another (see Eisele & Lust, 1996).

[3] Here, *variable binding* refers to constraint on interpretation of one element (the pronoun) by an element in a particular syntactic configuration with respect to the variable (the subject).

The experimental design included two pragmatic factors predicted to influence choice of interpretation: self-orientation of predicate and alienability of object. For example, structures with a non-self-oriented predicate and an alienable object, such as *Fozzie Bear rolls his orange, and Oscar does too*, were predicted to be most likely to yield a strict interpretation whereas structures with a self-oriented predicate and inalienable object, such as *Oscar scratches his arm, and Fozzie Bear does too*, would be less likely to trigger a strict interpretation.[4]

Behaviors produced as responses to the act-out stimuli (from 86 children aged 3;0–7;11) were coded as correct if they corresponded to one of the interpretations shown in A to D in Table 11.2 and as incorrect if they did not (e.g., if an act-out response corresponded to an ungrammatical interpretations such as the one shown in E in Table 11.2). Act-out findings showed that across age groups, children spontaneously demonstrated significantly more sloppy interpretations than strict both overall and in every age group. A within-participant analysis further showed that 31% of children spontaneously showed both sloppy and strict interpretations in their act-out responses, whereas 51% of children showed only sloppy interpretations, and 7% showed only strict. Act-out responses were influenced by the pragmatic factors (e.g., with the highest number of strict interpretations shown for non-self-oriented actions with alienable objects). Children only rarely showed ungrammatical interpretations such as the one shown as E in Table 11.2 for pronoun sentences.

The study also included a truth–value judgment experiment with a subset of 35 children, in which 74% of children accepted pictures corresponding to both sloppy and strict interpretations, whereas 26% accepted sloppy only, and none accepted strict only interpretations. Results from the truth–value judgment task both converged with and complemented the act-out findings. Findings from both methods supported the prediction that the two-object sloppy interpretation should be accessible from the earliest stages. However, because the act-out method allowed choice of interpretation, the truth–value judgment results provided an important way to determine whether both interpretations were accessible from the youngest ages. Together, the methods permitted a fuller set of inferences about which interpretations were permitted, preferred, and excluded by children for the structures investigated.

11.7.4 Interpreting Preferential Looking and Elicited Imitation Data

For very young children, preferential looking (see Chapter 13) provides a window into perception, whereas elicited imitation can be used to test for differences in pro-

---

[4] In addition to control structures with intransitive verbs and transitive verbs whose objects did not involve possession, the design included sentences with indefinite and definite articles instead of possessive pronouns. These sentences with articles, unlike the pronoun sentences, theoretically permitted the full range of interpretations.

duction across contexts. Sundara, Demuth, and Kuhl (2011) investigated 2-year-olds' performance with the third person singular morpheme -s on verbs in sentence-final position compared with verbs in sentence-medial position. This study was designed to determine whether sentence-position effects could be explained by perceptual factors. The study compared 22- and 27-month-olds' perception and elicited production of the morpheme in the two positions. The authors assessed perception by measuring looking and listening times to a screen display of a cartoon paired with a grammatical versus an ungrammatical sentence (e.g., *She eats now* vs. *She eat now*).

Results showed that children at both ages demonstrated sensitivity to the presence or absence of this inflectional morpheme in sentence-final, but not sentence-medial, position. Children were also more accurate at producing third person singular -s sentence finally, and production accuracy was predicted by vocabulary measures as well as by performance on the perception task. Taken together, results across the two methods indicated that children's more accurate production of third person singular -s in sentence-final position cannot be explained by articulatory factors alone but that perceptual factors play an important role in accounting for early patterns of production. Together, findings from the two methods permitted inferences about a close connection between perception and production of verbal agreement in 2-year-olds.

11.8 Summary

In this chapter, we have seen that the interpretation of results is guided and, to some extent, constrained by the way in which a study is set up. Interpretation is guided and constrained by the study's research question hypotheses, the modality (comprehension vs. production) of the task used, any assumptions or limitations associated with the task itself, the type of analyses conducted, and the degree to which the findings are generalizable. We have reviewed ways to strengthen the inferences possible from a language acquisition study, including eliminating alternative explanations for findings, linking findings to those from previous studies in the field, and comparing findings from studies that used different methods. Consideration of constraints on inference and the ways inference can be strengthened may enable researchers to characterize more precisely and understand how language is developing in the context of the many other domains of a child's development.

IV Special Considerations in Language Acquisition Research

12 Assessing Multilingual Acquisition

In this chapter, we review challenges one meets when working cross-linguistically and when assessing bilingual populations. We start by defining bilingualism. We then review the challenges of classifying bilingual speakers. Finally, we briefly review methods that are commonly used to assess bilingual children's and adults' degree of bilingualism and to test different aspects of their linguistic knowledge; some of these methods have already been introduced in this manual.

12.1 Bilingual and Second Language Speakers

There are millions of bilingual people across the world. Even though for decades monolingualism was seen as the norm and bilingualism was seen as problematic for society and as a potentially damaging condition for children, we know now that most people across the world are bilingual (or multilingual). We also know that they do not experience any disadvantage for knowing more than one language. The misconception that bilingualism could cause cognitive disadvantages was based on the finding that lower scores were obtained by bilingual children in IQ tests due to methodological issues in testing (J. Edwards, 2006). Those early results were taken as an indication that bilingualism was detrimental, which led many teachers and doctors to tell parents their children would be confused if exposed to more than one language and that they would not learn any language properly. Later research proved that these lower scores were due to the fact that children were tested in their weaker or second language rather than their native language (Hakuta, 1986). As we have stressed in this manual, methodology is fundamental in language research, and one should be especially cautious about the effects of methodology on results when working with bilingual populations that may already be at a disadvantage for other reasons (e.g., immigrant status, lack of education that supports their first language, low socioeconomic status).

Linguists and other professionals interested in language study bilinguals because

- they represent the majority of speakers of the world, and our knowledge of speaker competence and performance would be quite incomplete if we did not take into account the majority of the population;
- studying bilinguals allows us to understand better the great capacity of our mind to acquire not just one language but also more than one;
- the understanding of bilingual populations is fundamental to understand their educational needs; and

- we have to be able to tell apart speakers with language deficits from those who are in the process of acquiring a second language. Too many children are referred to language therapy across the world just because they have not yet mastered their second language.

12.2 Bilingual, Multilingual, and Second Language Acquisition

In our field, the term *bilingual* refers to people who may know two or more languages (i.e., multilingual people), and the term *second language* (or *L2*) refers to any languages acquired after the first language, even if they are truly the speaker's third or fourth language. *First language* (or *L1*) refers to the first language acquired by a person, his or her *native language* or *mother tongue*. In the case of simultaneous acquisition since birth speakers are said to have two (or more) first languages. We will continue the tradition here.

12.3 Challenges Due to the Characteristics of Bilingual Populations

The scientific study of bilingualism started with diary studies of children acquiring two languages simultaneously (i.e., usually not distributed, and many of them are versions of other previous manuals Leopold, 1970; Ronjat, 1913) and has flourished in recent decades to include children learning many languages, studied through different methods and integrating bilingual and second language acquisition. As we will see, however, studying bilingualism is complicated due to the many factors affecting bilingual/L2 acquisition.

When we study monolingual children and adults, we assume they started first language acquisition at the same developmental stage, both cognitively and physically[1] and ended at a similar level of language competence and proficiency (i.e., whatever is normal for a "native speaker"). Monolingual speakers are compared with bilingual speakers in most studies dealing with bilingual speakers. An interesting fact is that it is increasingly difficult to find truly monolingual children and adults for research purposes because most people in the world know a second language, at least to some degree. In fact, in many studies comparing bilingual with monolingual populations,

---

[1] This is without taking into account cases in which children were raised in exceptional circumstances (e.g., Curtiss, 1977; Itard, 1962; Skuse, 1993) or cases of deaf speakers who did not get access to a first language from birth (e.g., Boudreault & Mayberry, 2006; Curtiss, 1989; Grimshaw, Adelstein, Bryden, & MacKinnon, 1998; Newport, 1990).

the monolingual control group may be formed by speakers who are not truly monolingual but who have had much less exposure to the second language than the bilingual group (de Groot, 2011, pp. 16–17). There is also some debate about which is the best control group for second language speakers, with some researchers advocating to compare second language speakers with bilingual speakers instead of monolingual speakers, assuming there is an effect of bilingualism and that, therefore, monolinguals should not be the yardstick by which to measure second language acquisition (Unsworth & Blom, 2010).

We cannot assume that all bilingual speakers start at the same initial state or that their end states are the same or necessarily similar to those of monolinguals in any of their languages. One main difference among bilingual speakers is the age at which they started acquiring their languages. Some bilinguals may have been exposed to two (or more) languages from birth, in which case we speak of *bilingual first language acquisition* and *simultaneous bilinguals* as having two (or more) first languages. Other bilinguals learned a second language after they acquired some of their first language. These *successive* or *sequential bilinguals* may have started learning their L2 during childhood or as adults, which may have consequences for their language proficiency. Age of acquisition effects are usual in second language acquisition, with speakers who started learning a second language at a young age generally achieving a higher level of proficiency than those speakers who started learning it at an older age; there is debate in the field about how to account for these age effects (Bialystok & Hakuta, 1999; J. S. Johnson & Newport, 1989).

Nevertheless, the relationship between age of acquisition and language proficiency is not a straightforward one. Many factors besides age interfere, and simultaneous bilinguals are not always more proficient than sequential bilinguals. For example, Kim, Park, and Lust (2016) studied four Korean–English bilingual children. Two of the children were simultaneous bilinguals, and the other two were successive bilinguals. Their results suggested that differences between simultaneous and successive bilinguals were not just explained by age of acquisition and that the children developed their language subskills differently.

Another main issue with bilinguals is the quantity and type of input they may get in each of their languages, which affects their language proficiency and dominance. Even simultaneous bilinguals may receive more input in one language than the other (e.g., if one of their languages is a majority language and the other one is a minority language, or if they are in a one-parent/one-language situation and one parent has more time to spend with the child than the other). In some households, both languages are spoken, but only a grandparent may speak the minority language or the only source for the majority language may be the child's older sibling.[2] Many adults

---

[2] Bhatia and Ritchie (2006) reminded us that this is already a simplification because in some communities a child may hear four to five languages only at home.

and children hear (and use) different languages in different situations: one language at home and another at school or work. In other cases, both languages are spoken in the wider community, but input may vary as to the amount of code switching[3] heard because some communities reject or restrict code switching and other communities embrace it and use it daily and everywhere. It is well known that the amount of input has an effect on the child's ultimate attainment in the language (De Houwer, 2007), especially in language production. There is little research, however, on the effects of input source (one-parent/one-language vs. more than one member of the family speaking both languages, code-switched input vs. a strict separation of languages) on children's language (Huerta-Macías, 1981; Quay, 2008).

Most studies have focused on the acquisition and use of two L1s or one L2. However, an emerging area is exploring *language attrition*, the loss of a language due to lack of use (Montrul, 2008; Polinsky, 2011). This may happen when adult or child bilinguals immigrate and lose contact with their L1 community or when internationally adopted children do not maintain their first language. Language attrition may be gradual and slow in the first case, though internationally adopted children may experience dramatic losses in a short time (Nicoladis & Grabois, 2002; Isurin, 2000). A different but related case is that of heritage speakers[4] who may experience attrition of their first language or who may not have acquired all the characteristics of the standard variety of their language, in which case some researchers speak of *incomplete acquisition* (Montrul, 2002; Polinsky, 2006; Silva-Corvalán & Montanari, 2008; but see Putnam & Sánchez, 2013, for a critique of this view).

Given the heterogeneity of bilingual speakers, many studies in the field, both of bilingual children and adult second language speakers, have been conducted as case studies. A *case study* is a longitudinal study of one speaker (although in the case of children, some case studies have included two siblings) whose language development is described in detail. Although they provide detailed and rich data, the results are not generalizable.

12.4 Issues in Defining Bilinguals

Research on speakers of more than one language has traditionally been divided into two different subfields: *bilingualism*, research on which has mainly dealt with child bilinguals and adult bilinguals who are fairly proficient in all their languages and who usually are immersed in at least one of their languages; and *second language*

---

[3] *Code switching* refers to the use of two languages in an utterance such as *I want you to come **para que me ayudes*** 'I want you to come so that you (can) help me' or ***La*** 'house' ***está bien*** big and comfortable 'The house is very big and comfortable.'

[4] The term *heritage speaker* (Wiley & Valdés, 2000) is used mainly to describe bilingual speakers in the United States who learned a language other than English at home but who have been immersed in English since childhood. Some are just receptive bilinguals, and others are fluent in both languages but not in all domains.

acquisition, research on which has usually dealt with speakers who learn a second language in adulthood through instruction rather than immersion (Cook, 2008). However, the lines between bilingual and second language speakers are blurry; there is truly a continuum between incipient second language learners and bilinguals who live life fully in two languages (Austin, Blume, & Sánchez, 2015). The growing area of research on child second-language acquisition has helped close the gap between the two areas (Austin, Blume, & Sánchez, 2013; Lakshmanan, 2009).

The field's and the general public's opinion has moved from the expectation that a bilingual is a perfectly proficient speaker in both languages in all areas of communication to the belief that from the moment one is exposed to a second language, one becomes an incipient bilingual. Hoff and Rumiche (2012) reported that when recruiting child subjects for bilingual studies, they have to turn down parents who believe their children are becoming bilingual only through watching bilingual TV programs. These authors discussed at length differences in language exposure requirements for bilingual subjects participating in research. Hoff and Rumiche require children to have at least 10% exposure to the second language, such exposure coming from conversations in which the child participates. Other researchers require at least 20% exposure to the second language because a study by Pearson, Fernández, Lewedeg, and Oller (1997) that found that children exposed to less than that amount of the second language are reluctant to produce it. Still other researchers require an equal amount of exposure to both languages, though this may limit the number of participants available in many populations (Bosch & Sebastián-Gallés, 2002).

12.4.1 Age of Acquisition

The term *simultaneous bilingual* may be used for children who learned two languages from birth and who therefore have two first languages. *Successive* or *sequential bilinguals* is used for speakers who acquired first a (first) language and later acquired one or more second languages.

Who then are simultaneous bilinguals? It depends on who you ask. For a child to be considered a simultaneous bilingual, according to De Houwer (1990), he or she has to be exposed to the second language not more than a week after birth (and exposure to the first language), and he or she had to be addressed in both languages almost every day. Children who acquire a second language after birth but before age 3;00 are referred to as *early bilinguals*, with usually no explanation on where the cut off point is between simultaneous and early bilinguals. De Houwer (2005) is the exception: She proposed that early second language acquisition starts between 1;06 and 4;00. That leaves us with the problem of not having a good term for children who were exposed to a second language later than 1 week after birth but before age 1;06 or for those who do not have regular input from both languages but who are not exposed to one language only.

One important factor is that given that some structures appear later than others in child language, children who acquire a second language (even after age 3;00) may have not acquired some structures in their L1 (e.g., passives, constraints on the interpretation of pronouns); thus, in those areas, sequential bilinguals may actually experience simultaneous acquisition (Lakshmanan, 2009). The term *late bilingual* is reserved for people learning a second language after puberty because studies have found age effects in ultimate attainment after this age (J. S. Johnson & Newport, 1989).

12.4.2 Language Dominance

Another important factor in defining bilinguals is language dominance. Some speakers appear to have equal knowledge of their languages and are referred to as *balanced bilinguals* (although it is improbable that truly balanced bilinguals exist; see Cutler, Mehler, Norris, & Segui, 1989). When the speaker has more knowledge of one language than the other, we say he or she is a *dominant bilingual*, and we specify the language (e.g., "English-dominant Spanish–English bilingual"). The order in which languages are listed for a bilingual indicates the order of acquisition—for example, a "Spanish–English bilingual" is assumed to be a person who learned Spanish first and English later. In some studies, however, the order refers to language dominance, so a "Spanish–English bilingual" refers to a person who is Spanish dominant, regardless of age of Spanish acquisition.

Determining language dominance is not easy. In adult bilinguals and older children, language dominance may be measured by various tests that C. Baker (2011) described as follows:

- For reaction time in word association tasks, the bilingual is asked to provide a word (e.g., *shoe*) associated with a stimulus word (e.g., *foot*). The test is done in the two languages of the bilingual, and the speed at which he or she answers in each language (the reaction time) is measured and compared. The language for which reaction times are shorter is considered the dominant language.
- To determine quantity of reactions in a word association task, the speakers are asked to provide as many words as possible to a stimulus word in 1 minute. The number of words in each language is compared, and the language with more words is considered dominant.
- In word detection tasks, the bilingual speaker is shown a nonsense word (e.g., *dansonodend*; C. Baker, 2011, p. 25) and asked to extract from it words in both his or her languages (i.e., *dans, ans, de, en* for French; *no, nod, node, ode, end* for English; and *an, son,* and *on* for both languages). These types of words are dif-

ficult to construct, and they depend on the languages' phonology or orthography being similar.
- Time taken to read words in both languages.
- Amount of language mixing in speakers' productions.

These tests measure language competence, but they also are dependent on language processing, and they test only specific aspects of a language. However, they are conveniently easy and fast to administer and score, so they provide a quick way to assess language dominance.

For younger child bilinguals, language dominance is deduced from a questionnaire such as the ones we describe next, which are filled in by caregivers, or by calculating scores on tasks such as the ones we describe in Section 12.6, Measuring Bilingualism. One important issue, as C. Baker (2011) reminded us, is that dominance is variable. Not only can someone's language dominance change with time, but it can also vary according to context, even at a fixed point.

> Dominance will vary by domain and across time, being a constantly shifting personal characteristic. It is possible to be approximately equally proficient in two languages, yet one may be dominant. Speed of processing may provide evidence about balance but not about dominance in actual language use, in different sociocultural contexts and over time (Valdés & Figueroa, 1994). (C. Baker, 2011, p. 25)

12.4.3 Language Competence and Language Proficiency

Sometimes determining language dominance is not enough, and one has to discover how much knowledge the speaker has acquired of his or her languages. Knowledge can be defined in terms of language competence or language proficiency. *Language competence* is understood as formal competence, as knowledge of the abstract rules of grammar. *Proficiency* includes competence but goes beyond it and is sometimes called *communicative competence* (Hymes, 1967, 1972); that is, it includes the capacity to use language in socially acceptable ways, using the right language for a determined socioeconomic class and being able to reach goals by using appropriate discourse (Canale, 1983; Canale & Swain, 1980). We restrict ourselves here to language competence because we have to measure competence to be able to measure proficiency.[5] When measuring competence, ideally, one would study the speaker in all the main aspects of linguistic knowledge (phonology, lexicon, morphology, syntax, semantics) in oral production and comprehension as well as in writing and reading modes (when

---

[5] Proficiency has proven difficult to define and measure because it involves many aspects of language that interact with each other (Butler & Hakuta, 2006; Canale & Swain, 1980; Hernandez-Chavez, Burt, & Dulay, 1978; Hymes, 1972).

applicable). In reality, that is not the case because prescreening speakers for research would take more time than actually conducting research with them. We discuss in the following sections some common assessment tools. In the case of bilinguals, it is important to measure both production and comprehension because a speaker may be able to understand much more of his or her less dominant language than he or she is able to show in production. Speakers who can understand a language but not speak it are called *receptive bilinguals*.

Another related issue involves what we call a *native speaker*. The term is used to refer to someone who learned a language as an L1 or someone who has the same competence or proficiency as a native speaker. In the first sense, we have to define how early someone has to acquire a language to be considered a native speaker. In the second sense, we have to define what the level of competence of a native speaker should be. Native speakers may vary in their command of different language areas (e.g., some have more vocabulary and some less, some know how to read and write and some do not). The issue gets more complicated when we look at bilinguals.

12.5 Interacting Variables

Even simultaneous bilinguals may not be equally proficient in all areas due to input and domains of learning and use. It has been shown that people's performance varies according to where they are speaking, through what medium they are speaking, to whom they are speaking, their purpose, and so forth (C. Baker, 2011). This is obviously related in part to language input. Some bilinguals use both languages in all contexts, and some use them in completely different spheres (e.g., home vs. work or school, with older relatives vs. peers); some get input in one of the languages from only a restricted number of speakers or from nonnative speakers. All of this has consequences for the bilingual's vocabulary acquisition and use as well as on his or her knowledge of particular structures that may be more frequently used in some contexts than in others.

All create challenges for researchers working with bilingual populations. It is difficult to generalize results from one population (or indeed a single case) to a larger population. It is also difficult to find comparable populations across studies. A frequent finding is that people who volunteer for research tend to have better education and, therefore, more income than people who do not volunteer. This is especially important when conducting studies on bilingualism in which the bilingual population may be a minority group, with lower income and education level than the average monolingual population. These conditions may, in turn, affect language development and views on bilingualism. It also means that researchers have to make a greater effort to recruit minority populations and that socioeconomic status and educational level have to be controlled for when comparing bilingual populations (Hoff & Rumiche, 2012).

The first step to being able to study bilingual speakers and to disentangle the effects of the factors affecting their competence (e.g., age, level of education, socioeconomic status) is to have enough information about each of the speakers we test to see what variables we might want to control in our studies and with which speakers we can compare them. Grosjean (2006) reviewed how researchers described their participants in several studies and concluded that not enough information was given about them for other researchers to be able to judge whether participants from two different studies were comparable. He also found that insufficient factors were considered when selecting participants for a study (e.g., researchers grouped participants according to age of acquisition but did not consider how frequently they used each language), and different criteria, assessment, and data collection tools were used to select participants. He believed that this state of affairs was one possible explanation for the lack of converging results in studies on bilingualism and L2 acquisition.

Grosjean (2008) also suggested that when studying bilingual speakers, one should collect and report information on (a) language history and language relationship (age of acquisition, contexts of acquisition, skills acquired, language use), (b) language stability (languages still being acquired, interference), (c) function of languages (purposes and contexts of use for each language), (d) language proficiency in the four skills, (e) language modes (i.e., a bilingual mode occurs when the speaker uses his or her two languages and a monolingual mode when he or she uses one; Grosjean, 1999), and (f) biographical data. Next, we review some of the instruments available to gauge a person's level of bilingualism, among them a multilingualism questionnaire developed in our lab (available online at http://pubs.apa.org/books/supp/blume) that tries to gather much of this relevant information.

12.6 Measuring Bilingualism

12.6.1 Indirect Measures of Bilingualism

The best way to gather the information prescribed by Grosjean (2008) is to follow a bilingual person around for some days and observe his or her performance in each language in various contexts and with different interlocutors. However, that is usually impossible, so researchers rely on reports by the bilingual speaker (when he or she is old enough) or the bilingual child's caretaker to obtain information.

12.6.1.1 Caretaker Reports of Overall Language Exposure and Use

The most common report type is a questionnaire, such as the one we describe in this section. Other methods described later include diary reports and estimates of vocabulary comprehension and production.

A. Questionnaires

There are many bilingualism questionnaires (e.g., Bosch & Sebastián-Gallés, 2002; Lanza, 1988; Li, Sepanski, & Zhao, 2006; Luk & Bialystok, 2013; Marian, Blumenfeld, & Kaushanskaya, 2007; Zúñiga, Sánchez, & Zacharías, 2000). Some are published as independent sources or appendices to journal articles and books, some are used in independent labs and usually not distributed, and many of them are versions of other previous manuals (e.g., Weber-Fox & Neville's 1996 questionnaire is based on Lanza's 1988 questionnaire). Some questionnaires are more extensive than others, but most tend to be fairly short (i.e., two to four pages long).[6] We describe here the one we use at our labs, the Virtual Center for Language Acquisition (VCLA) Multilingualism Questionnaire, as an example of a long and detailed questionnaire originally based on Weber-Fox and Neville's (1996) questionnaire and developed over 10 years with the contribution of the VCLA members.[7] The questionnaire requests information from the caretaker in five parts: (I) information about the child (e.g., name, date of birth, sex, age, birth order, education, possible health and hearing problems, present and past residence, levels of shyness); (II) information about the child's language, including child language use and exposure to language, as well as caretaker assessments of the child's proficiency across both language production and comprehension; (III) family background (e.g., basic caregiver information, residence, employment, language proficiency and use, literacy); (IV) the child's and family's code switching; and (V) the child's reading and writing ability, if applicable. This questionnaire takes from 30 minutes to 1 hour to complete. When using questionnaires, it is advisable for researchers to meet with parents and help them fill out the questionnaire. We, and other researchers in the field, have found that in this way incomplete or contradictory answers can be avoided. Time spent with the parent while filling in the questionnaire is also fruitful because children are frequently present, and this gives the child one is going to record some time to get acquainted with the researchers.

---

6 A good description and comparison of all questionnaires is a task that we should undertake in our standardization of research methods in our field.
7 The Virtual Center for Language Acquisition Multilingualism Questionnaire, as well as a detailed history of its development, is available online at http://pubs.apa.org/books/supp/blume

B. Language Diaries

Although diary studies were used as the first method for documenting bilingual development, the method has been further developed by De Houwer and Bornstein (2003) and is described in Hoff and Rumiche (2012). Parents are asked to keep a record of the child's language exposure for 7 weeks, but each week they report on only one particular day. They report on the language used, the people who interacted with the child, and the activities performed for 30-minute periods from early morning to late at night.[8] Hoff and Rumiche (2012) reported that parents of 4-year-olds felt they could not complete the diary because they no longer spent the whole day with the child. Therefore, the diary was substituted with an over-the-telephone interview with the parents 1 day of the week for 7 weeks.

12.6.1.2 Caretaker Reports on Vocabulary Measures

The MacArthur-Bates Communicative Development Inventories (CDI; Fenson et al., 2007) assess the linguistic and communicative development of the child by having parents mark the words they believe the child understands and produces. It is divided into two parts. The first, subtitled "Words and Gestures," is for children 8 to 15 months of age, and the second part, "Words and Sentences," is for 16- to 30-month-old children. It has been adapted for 54 languages, including American Sign Language. Obviously, its utility depends on whether the caretaker can give an accurate report of the child's language. Nevertheless, the results on the CDI show strong correlations between gestures, vocabulary, grammar, and socioeconomic level. This is, then, an important instrument, but it also has some limitations: It is useful only for very young children, it measures mostly vocabulary, and there is no version created specifically for bilingual children. Researchers then have to convince parents to check a somewhat lengthy vocabulary list twice. Another problem reported by Hoff and Rumiche (2012) is that some versions (e.g., English and Spanish) were normed with populations from different socioeconomic status groups and, therefore, the percentile scores are not comparable across languages.

---

[8] A similar record is included in the VCLA Multilingualism Questionnaire, but parents are asked to fill it out at once instead of on 1 day per week; thus, it may reflect language distribution in typical weeks, and therefore, it may provide a picture of what caretakers consider a typical week, although the language diary provides more precise data about specific days, some of which may not be typical. The language diary, however, has the advantage of being able to provide information to cross-check caretakers' beliefs—which may not always be accurate—about the amount of time children interact in each language.

12.6.2 Direct Methods for Assessing Bilingualism

Direct assessment of bilinguals in which the child is tested rather than relying on caretaker assessment is also possible, and all the methods described in this manual can be adapted for bilingual populations. Recently, a new approach has exemplified the use of one direct language production task we reviewed earlier (elicited imitation) with a controlled cross-linguistic design to assess the quantity and quality of bilingualism in young children (see Section 12.7, Using Multiple Methods to Assess Bilingualism). We focus here on methods used more generally.

12.6.2.1 Natural Speech

The natural speech method (see Chapter 4) is frequently used to assess bilingual children, though it is not used as frequently with adults. Depending on the goals of research, speakers may be recorded in situations in which they use both their languages (e.g., with a bilingual researcher who uses both languages during conversation) or with a monolingual speaker in each language.[9] When working in the home setting with children, it is important to get the person who is the main source of the target language to interact with the child whenever possible.

12.6.2.2 Norm-Referenced Tests

Some norm-referenced assessment tools exist that can be used for assessing language development, although they are mostly English tests translated into other languages, and most have Spanish versions only.

A. The Peabody Picture Vocabulary Test
Another way language knowledge is measured is by assessing a person's vocabulary comprehension using the Peabody Picture Vocabulary Test (Dunn & Dunn, 2007), which can be given to speakers from 2 to 90 years of age. In this test, a bilingual speaker is shown a page with four pictures and asked to point to the one named by

---

9 In these situations, some researchers have the child interact with a bilingual interlocutor who is a new acquaintance for the child and who pretends to be monolingual. However, this should be avoided because bilingual children can usually tell easily whether their interlocutor understands their languages.

the researcher. For bilinguals, the test has to be administered twice, once in each language. The concepts represented increase gradually in difficulty, and the test is stopped when the person makes eight consecutive errors. This test has English and Spanish versions and, thus, it can be used with bilingual children; however, the English version was updated and the Spanish version was not.

B. Expressive One-Word Picture Vocabulary Test

In the Expressive One-Word Picture Vocabulary Test (Brownell, 2000), the child is shown pictures, and he or she is asked to produce a name for the picture shown. This test has a version normed with Spanish–English bilinguals in the United States. Children are asked to name the picture in the dominant language, and if they cannot name it, they are asked to name it in their other language. Used that way, it allows for conceptual scoring of vocabulary but does not let us know how many words the child knows in each independent language (or in both). Hoff and Rumiche (2012) reported that they use this task in both languages to assess vocabulary knowledge.

C. Preschool Language Scales, Fifth Edition

The Preschool Language Scales (5th ed.; Zimmerman, Steiner, & Pond, 2002) can be used from birth till age 7;11. It measures language comprehension and production and focuses on four language aspects: language precursors (attention, vocal development, social communication), semantics (vocabulary and concepts), structure (morphology and syntax), and integrative thinking abilities. It includes drawings and props for concepts not easily depicted in pictures (e.g., a ball, a soft cloth, five blocks, crayons) that are used to test the children; for example, crayons are used to see whether the child can recognize the colors named by the researcher; a bear, three plastic cups, and fake ice-cubes are used to test comprehension of verbs (e.g., *put, pour*) and possessives (*Which is your cup?*); the bear, a cloth, a duck, and a box are used to test prepositions (e.g., *Take the blanket off the bear, Put the bear in the box*). Drawings are used to ask the child to point to items (e.g., *his shoes* vs. *her shoes*).

12.7 Using Multiple Methods to Assess Bilingualism

One common finding among researchers working on bilingualism is that the instruments we have to measure bilingualism are limited, and they can only give us a partial picture of the bilingual person's competence. Problems exist with several of the available tests; some of which we mentioned earlier. Hoff and Rumiche (2012) gave a concrete example:

> As with all tests in two languages, there is noncomparability. At many age levels there are items that have no equivalent in the other language. For example, one of the categories at the 2;6 to 2;11 level in the Spanish version is "understands several pronouns (*me, mi, tú, tu*)." There is no clear counterpart to this in English. Another related problem is that when the same categories are in the Spanish and English versions, they may appear at different age levels across the two versions. For example, items that are designed to tap children's understanding of the part/whole relationships (e.g., *the door of the car*) are in the 2;6 to 2;11 group on the English version, but their equivalents (e.g., *la puerta del carro*) are a 3;0 to 3;11 category in the Spanish version . . . the test was designed for monolingual English- and Spanish-speaking populations. We found that we cannot control what language a child will use to answer questions. We do not want to assume that a child is incapable of answering in Spanish just because she chooses to answer a question posed in Spanish in English. ("Preschool Language Scale—4," para. 1).

Therefore, it is fundamental to use more than one method to assess bilinguals (Flege, MacKay, & Piske, 2002) and to test bilinguals with direct measures in addition to indirect measures. We show here an example of a study that used the elicited imitation (EI) task (described in Chapter 6) to corroborate data on bilingual development provided by parents through questionnaires.[10] Lust et al. (2014) compared data collected via the caretaker-derived VCLA Multilingualism Questionnaire with results from an EI task focused on the production of coordinate sentences in both languages. The subjects were two 4-year-old Korean–English bilinguals closely matched on background. The EI task revealed significant differences between the two children in the quantity and quality of their bilingualism in both their first and second languages, which the questionnaire data did not reveal. The test revealed not only small differences in the children's production of English coordinate sentences (which matched differences in proficiency ratings in the questionnaires and differences in exposure to English) but also differences in their production of the same structures in Korean that were not predicted by proficiency ratings or amount of input reports from the questionnaire. Pease-Álvarez, Hakuta, and Bayley (1996) also found that answers by the participants and their parents in interviews predicted less Spanish proficiency for their 8- to 10-year-old Spanish–English bilingual participants than direct testing showed.

As we mentioned previously, many of the norm-referenced tests exist only in English or, at most, in English and Spanish. That is not the only complication when conducting research with bilingual populations. When testing speakers of indigenous languages or illiterate speakers, the number of available tests is even fewer, and researchers have to be creative. Sánchez (2006), for example, discussed possibilities

---

10 For other examples of bilingual assessment using elicited imitation, see Berkes and Flynn (2012); Amaro, Flynn, and Rothman (2012); Flynn (1987); and West (2014).

for developing data collection methods and assessment tools that are comparable and culturally and cognitively appropriate for bilingual children living in rural communities who speak a minority language and have low levels of literacy in Peru. In communities such as this, narrations and guided conversations can be used to assess language competence. Valdés and Figueroa (1994) also warned against the use of self-rating instruments in cases such as these, given that speakers have limited access to different registers, and recommended that questionnaires be used only in conjunction with other instruments.

12.8 Attaining Comparative Cross-Linguistic Measures

It is well known that bilingual speakers' languages differ in many respects. One of the areas in which differences are frequently found is the lexicon; most speakers have a larger and more productive vocabulary in one language than in the other. This difference may be especially noticeable in bilingual children (Hoff et al., 2012). At the same time, vocabulary development correlates with later linguistic development, and therefore, teachers and parents worry when a child's vocabulary seems relatively small; many bilingual children are referred to a language therapist when they are not truly language delayed. Therefore, Bedore, Peña, García, and Cortez (2005) proposed that bilingual children have to be assessed differently from monolingual children to see whether they display any developmental delay. The vocabulary of a bilingual person in one of his or her languages does not necessarily match item-by-item his or her vocabulary in the other language; Pearson, Fernández, and Oller (1995) calculated that translation equivalents (i.e., words referring to the same object in two languages, such as *gato* 'cat' and *cat*) form only about 30% of children's vocabulary before age 2;00, which means these children have a name for the majority of their lexical items in one language only. If one counts the concepts children know regardless of the language in which they know the word for the concept (this is called *conceptual scoring*), bilingual children's scores are in the average range for the monolingual children.

Another frequently used measure of language development is mean length of utterance (MLU). Because languages differ in terms of average number of morphemes per word, it is often impossible to compare MLU measures cross-linguistically; a Spanish-speaking child will have a larger MLU than an English-speaking child of the same age and level of development because Spanish has on average more morphemes per word than English. MLU in morphemes is also not useful when dealing with code-switching data. When working cross-linguistically or with bilingual children, researchers usually compare MLU in words (MLU-w). MLU is just a broad measure of language development and should also be compared with other measures, but MLU-w correlates well with age, can be used with code-switching data, and is useful to identify developmental differences. (Gutiérrez-Clellen, Restrepo, Bedore, Peña, & Anderson, 2000).

Sánchez (2006) commented about the creation of cross-linguistic instruments for culturally diverse communities:

> In the case of language assessment of Quechua- and Aymara-speaking children, the team... encountered a major problem in developing aural comprehension items... deciding whether the texts would be first generated in the common majority language (Spanish) and later translated into Quechua or Aymara, or whether they would be generated in one of the indigenous languages and then translated into the other indigenous language and Spanish. The differences in grammatical structure at the sentential level and in textual structure at the discourse level made the choice even more difficult because the translations had to be as close as possible to the original text while respecting the textual structure associated to narratives in each language tradition. The team decided to have different items generated in one of the three languages and then translated into the others to minimize the effect of a one-way translation practice in all items. To preserve the cultural and environmental appropriateness of the test, the team also decided to incorporate elements of the children's environment such as pet animals and traditional short stories. Translating the texts was particularly difficult because there were only few bilingual indigenous researchers and educators who were available to work with us generating items. The situation was further complicated by the fact that cross-linguistic validity between the texts generated in the two indigenous languages could be checked by only one of the consultant educators who is trilingual in Quechua, Aymara, and Spanish. This educator was also the person who recorded the texts in the three languages to minimize the effect that differences in the recording may have had in the results of the sample group. (p. 138)

12.9 Testing Bilingual Speakers

The study of language in bilingual minds has followed different directions and used specific research methods. The description of those methods and an overview of the findings in this area would take a whole book on its own and goes well beyond the goals of this manual. Many of the techniques used require sophisticated machinery (e.g., eye-trackers, magnetic resonance imaging machines) and specific training, and we will not be able to cover them here. Nevertheless, we hope the scientific method we have explained and the methods we have described can serve as a strong foundation for readers to understand these other more technically demanding methods. In this section, we touch on the relevant areas of research and point the reader toward some relevant resources. De Groot's (2011) book, *Language and Cognition in Bilinguals and Multilinguals,* provides a detailed and exhaustive review of the techniques and main findings in the field. Austin et al. (2015) provided a more concise review of the main theoretical issues and results in this area.

There is a prolific area of studies on bilingual language processing in real time and the amount of influence of one language on the other during processing, especially with regard to access to lexical items, using techniques such as eye tracking (see Chapter 13 and also Dussias & Sagarra, 2007; Marian & Spivey, 2003), picture naming and lexical decision tasks (Costa, Miozzo, & Caramazza, 1999; Loebell & Bock, 2003; Nicoladis, 2006; Serratrice, 2007), masked priming (Gollan, Forster, & Frost, 1997), and reaction time measures (Costa, Caramazza, & Sebastián-Gallés, 2000; Tse & Altarriba, 2012). From a neurological point of view, the structure of brains and the activation of different brain regions has been studied comparing bilinguals with monolinguals using methods such as positron emission tomography, functional magnetic resonance imaging, magnetoencephalography, and electroencephalography (see Posner & Raichle, 1994, for a good description of these techniques; Kuhl & Rivera-Gaxiola, 2008, for their use in research with children; and Mechelli et al., 2004, for an example in their use in studying bilinguals). Another area of research has looked at language separation in children (Austin, 2010; Meisel, 1986; Paradis & Genesee, 1996), the influence of one linguistic system on another (Hulk & Müller, 2000; Müller & Hulk, 2001; Paradis & Navarro, 2003; Sánchez, 2004; Sorace, 2000), and language change and language attrition (Cuza & Frank, 2011; Montrul, 2004, 2009; Polinsky, 2006, 2007, 2011; Silva-Corvalán, 1994), using the methods already reviewed in this manual.

12.10 Summary

In this chapter, we reviewed the many complexities involved in studying subjects who speak more than one language or who are acquiring more than one language at once. We reviewed the various methodological approaches that have been taken to try to characterize different types of bilingual speakers and to assess their competence. We also provided the reader with a description of the main topics in the study of bilinguals and referred to further reading.

Grosjean (1989) claimed that "the bilingual is not two monolinguals in one person" (p. 1). As we have seen throughout this chapter, bilingual speakers differ from monolingual speakers in more than one respect. As we pointed out in the previous chapter, gathering data through different methods and seeing whether the data converge is the most effective way to draw scientifically sound conclusions. This was again highlighted in this chapter: The complexity of bilingual speakers requires us to assess bilinguals and to study their linguistic and neurological characteristics through more than one method to get a more accurate picture of the bilingual experience.

13 Introduction to Infant Testing Methods in Language Acquisition Research

This chapter provides an introductory review of the principles underlying research on infant language acquisition and outlines some of the main methodologies in this field, while referring readers to more specialized bibliographical sources as well as video and graphic demonstrations available on the web (see Appendix 13.1).

The ever-growing incorporation of *infant testing methods*[1] (ITMs) in language acquisition research is part of a broader process in developmental science in recent decades, in which classic approaches to studying the child (e.g., Piagetian) have been accompanied and at times even replaced by ITMs. ITMs provide a powerful empirical tool to study the child's cognitive and socioemotional capabilities in their earliest forms through the infant's repertoire of physiological and motor responses. In fact, this line of research has shed light on early learning and cognitive patterns not only in infants but also in newborns and even fetuses.

The use of ITMs, which are based on discrete, nonlinguistic, and motor behaviors and measures—for example, looking, listening, sucking, heart rate, respiration—has enabled scholars in the field to uncover infants' often surprising linguistic knowledge, already apparent during the so-called preverbal stages in language development. It is important to note that although certain ITMs (e.g., high-amplitude sucking, head turn preference) have been specifically developed for testing ongoing debates in the field of language acquisition, other infant paradigms are less suitable for testing language-related issues (e.g., violation of expectation).

13.1 Background

The development of ITMs and their application in language acquisition research has been affected by two major advancements in the developmental and language sciences from the 1960s on. First, following the "cognitive revolution" and the weakening of the behaviorist influence on the field, the common view regarding infants' capabilities and skills among early language and cognition researchers drastically

---

[1] Jusczyk (1997) included an appendix (pp. 233–250) that also provides a good description of these methods.

This chapter was contributed by Yarden Kedar, PhD, Department of Early Childhood Education, Beit Berl College, Kfar Saba, Israel.

http://dx.doi.org/10.1037/15968-014
Research Methods in Language Acquisition: Principles, Procedures, and Practices, by M. Blume and B. C. Lust
Copyright © 2017 by the American Psychological Association and Walter de Gruyter GmbH. All rights reserved.

changed. That is, the infant was no longer perceived as a passive, ignorant agent but as a sophisticated, attentive learner (Lust, 2006).

Second, N. Chomsky's (1957) hypothesis of an innate, biological language infrastructure in the human species inspired extensive research with children. Specifically, the empirical goal in the emerging science of developmental psycholinguistics has been to find evidence that during the earliest stages of language development, young children already adhere to innate constraints and principles such as those predicted by N. Chomsky (e.g., Can we actually identify and track down the process of parameter setting in children as they begin to master their native tongue?). This exciting debate eventually led to the development and application of several empirical methods and tools with the purpose of examining the earliest forms of (covert) linguistic knowledge and online computation of linguistic stimuli in infants (in fact, from prenatal stages on). Nowadays, sophisticated ITMs are applied in a comparative cross-linguistic framework (i.e., exploring and comparing the initial stages in the acquisition of language in monolingual and multilingual communities) to study specific aspects of early language (i.e., phonology, syntax), and this line of research now also includes the use of neuroscience methods.

13.2 Rationale

The ITMs presented in this chapter share a common critical assumption: By meticulously documenting and analyzing infants' physiological and behavioral responses to a carefully designed task, we can infer something about their cognitive and linguistic knowledge at a given developmental stage. This assumption simultaneously highlights the key pros and cons of ITMs. On one hand, it refers to new and exciting research opportunities that became possible by applying such methods—in particular, testing much younger child populations and focusing on their online processing patterns rather than delayed speech responses (as discussed in the previous chapters in this manual). On the other hand, these studies have always been questionable in some sense and often accused of "rich interpretation" because it is not clear what can—and cannot—be deduced on the basis of infant or fetus performances on such tasks. For example, if an infant tested on a preferential looking task (details discussed later) directs his or her gaze toward an image projected on the right monitor in front of him or her rather than the one on the left, the overt behavior which he or she exhibits is not informative, nor is it linguistic in essence. Nonetheless, we infer that this subtle motor response relates to a significant, often complex cognitive process in his or her mind.

To reach such a conclusion, we must design our task in a strict manner that would make alternative hypotheses for explaining the infant's behavior unlikely. First, we must take into account the specific qualities of the linguistic stimuli. For example, are we using real words and/or gibberish words in our task? How will the sentences or words be recorded and edited? Did we take into account their phonological composition in terms of consonant–vowel structure? Are we using natural speech? If so, whose voice would we use, and how would we ask our speaker to utter the words (e.g., in motherese? or perhaps in adult-directed speech?)? If not, would we use unnatural, digitized speech samples? Second, we must be aware of nonlinguistic features of the stimuli and the infant's general cognitive capabilities and limitations at a specific age tested (e.g., Does the infant know the objects presented to her on the basis of her previous experience? Can we expect him or her to be able to focus on a scene for several seconds and memorize it?). Third, we must carefully plan and control the manner by which these stimuli are presented to the infant and our coding scheme for analyzing the infant's responses, among many other empirical considerations.

Before we review the main ITMs used in child language research in detail, let us further discuss some additional characteristics and scientific dilemmas that are associated with these methodologies. First, as with any empirical investigation, we must be clear about the exact knowledge that we are after on a given task, and we must assess what is possible for a particular age range. Thus, our task must involve a theory of what our measures supposedly reflect in terms of infants' knowledge about language. That is, are we seeking evidence that will demonstrate that the infant is capable of detecting a particular linguistic stimulus or that he or she can discriminate among certain elements and perhaps categorize them into distinct linguistic types or that he or she prefers one type of stimulus over another in a given linguistic context?

Second, ITMs have allowed scholars to investigate to some extent the critical issue of continuity in child language. Because ITMs can be applied at any point after birth (and, in fact, even prenatally), these methods have the potential "to begin mapping a continuous developmental course in language knowledge from birth" (Lust, 2006, p. 136). Hence, an experiment in which infants are found to treat differently two or more types of linguistic stimuli would demonstrate that at least some linguistic features enter into the data that the infant is accessing and storing and that such covert processes are not dependent on speech production. At the same time, such isolated results cannot typically support the claim that infants' underlying representation or processing of a given linguistic structure is fully available (i.e., adultlike) at such early stages or that nothing develops in this respect. As the field advances, a comparative, cross-linguistic approach accompanied by the use of an array of fine-tuned online measures and methods seems to be a promising avenue for a more precise understanding of the nature and scope of infants' early representation of language.

The third issue that is briefly mentioned here concerns the novelty versus familiarity debate, which has been crucial in the design and interpretation of studies using ITMs. Do infants prefer familiar or novel stimuli? And do infants' novelty and familiarity preferences remain fixed beyond different circumstances and developmental stages? This intriguing debate is beyond the scope of this chapter (see de Groot, 2011, and Fennell, 2012, for a detailed discussion). Still, it is important to keep in mind its main outcomes: A preference for novel items does seem to exist in infants in most cases and guides their behavioral responses to different stimuli. In addition, some scholars argue that the infant's particular preference it is not important, but the fact that he or she responds differently to particular stimuli is. The debate is not settled: The "classic" attentional shift (from familiar to novel) is not always found and actually changes over time in many cases to familiarity preference and vice versa (Fennell, 2012; Slater, 2004).

13.3 Task Demands

ITMs require a special lab setup. In a typical infant study, the child is first familiarized with the lab setting and the experimenters as part of a play session. Next, the child and the parent enter the experimental room, where the test occurs. To avoid a Clever Hans effect (see Chapter 8), parents would typically be asked to wear darkened sunglasses and/or headphones to avoid affecting their infant's looking and/or listening patterns. Infants are seated on their parent's lap so that their eyes directly face the monitors in front of them. Before the experimenter leaves the experimental room, parents are reminded to remain neutral and to avoid talking to their infant during the entire test session.

Infant studies typically have a much larger attrition rate than do other types of studies discussed in this manual. This should not be a surprise because we are dealing with a very young population who often cannot complete the task due to fussiness or inattentiveness (for various reasons) during most or all of the test session. Historically, since the first psychological experiments with infants, there has been an ongoing transition from manipulation of the task by hand and offline coding by experimenters, to the application of video and computerized tools, with minimal or no human intervention at all in running the experiment and coding the data. This makes data collection easier, "cleaner," and most important, much more accurate (compare, for example, the first habituation studies with current experiments with infants in which computer-monitored eye tracking is used).

As is demonstrated in detail next, ITMs can be classified in several ways, such as the modality (one or more) that is being accessed, task demands (e.g., detection, discrimination), and specific measures used (e.g., infants' overall looking time to target during the entire test session vs. their latency to target). One interesting aspect in this typology of ITMs concerns the infant's degree of involvement in the task. That is, although in some of these methods the infant only passively sees or listens to a stimulus, in other experimental settings, the infant takes a more active role in the task (e.g., sucking rate controls the specific sound he or she would hear).

13.4 Infant Testing Methods in Language Acquisition Research

13.4.1 Habituation

The term *habituation* refers to a notable decline in an organism's response due to repeated presentations of a certain stimulus that it is capable of perceiving. This phenomenon has been long documented in humans as well as nonhuman species (including the most simple, single-celled life forms) essentially in every sensory modality and is considered a key component of nonassociative learning and memory processes (e.g., Jennings, 1906; Kandel & Schwartz, 1982). In the field of developmental psychology, habituation is regarded not only as a successful method used with newborns, infants, and toddlers up to about two years of age but also as an underlying principle that most ITMs build on to some extent. In particular, habituation in human infants is realized in most cases by presenting the children with a visual target and recording them as they decrease their looking time across trials as long as no other (new) stimulus is presented.

Infants' rate of habituation was initially the sole focus of researchers, who used habituation as a basic measure of learning. In another line of studies (e.g., Fantz, 1964), two stimuli were contrasted, one familiar (constant, presented again and again) and the other novel (changing on every trial). With the progression of trials, infants fixated for much longer times on the side in which a new stimulus was presented, hence demonstrating that they discriminated the familiar and novel stimuli. In most recent studies, however, a typical habituation procedure would involve both a habituation and a dishabituation phase. That is, an infant would first be habituated to a particular visual stimulus. When the infant's looking time reached a predetermined criterion (e.g., when his or her overall mean looking time during the last three trials had decreased to less than 50% of the overall mean looking time recorded during the first three trials—when the infant was supposedly still more interested in the stimulus), the test phase would begin. The test phase would typically present the familiar stimulus again, followed in the next trial with a different, novel stimulus (or a series of novel stimuli). If infants distinguished the novel stimulus from the familiar one, we would expect a significant increase in the time the infant dedicated to examining the novel stimulus in contrast to the familiar stimulus. In this case, we would say that the infant had *dishabituated* on detecting a new stimulus. The attentional shift in response to a substantial change in one or more characteristics of a stimulus has also been validated in the brain (Turk-Browne, Scholl, & Chun, 2008).

In language acquisition research, the use of habituation procedures with infants who do not express themselves verbally has greatly contributed to our understanding of infants' representation of language in several domains of language knowledge (speech perception, word learning, syntax). A typical experiment with preverbal infants that involves habituation necessitates the manipulation of both the visual and auditory modalities. That is, the visual target would often be accompanied by an auditory stimulus that is played back in the background, either simultaneously or antecedently to the visual stimulus. The underlying rationale in such studies is that infants may link linguistic form (e.g., syllable, word, sentence) to meaning (i.e., visual referent such as an object or a dynamic event). In addition, language acquisition researchers have expanded the classic habituation design to explore particular types of language processing and representation in infants. One prominent example of such innovative use of the basic habituation procedure is the *Switch Design* developed by Werker, Cohen, Lloyd, Casasola, and Stager (1998). In their study, infants had to link a novel linguistic label (e.g., *lif, neem*) with an unfamiliar visual object. Infants were first habituated to two different pairings between a (non-English) word and an object. The test phase explored whether infants detected a switch in the word–object pairing. In yet another line of research, scholars claimed to have matched infants' auditory (and visual) processing measures in habituation tasks as reliable predictors of delays or impairments in language and cognition in early childhood (e.g., Benasich & Tallal, 2002).

13.4.2 High-Amplitude Sucking

The high-amplitude sucking (HAS) technique, which is based on measuring variations in infants' sucking rate and strength in response to different acoustic stimuli (and is, therefore, labeled *nonnutritive sucking*), has been used extensively in infant studies in the last few decades and has provided valuable insights regarding infants' sound detection capabilities as well as their acoustic preferences during the first days (in fact, hours) of life. This reliable paradigm is unique among the array of infant methods that have been used in the last 50 years or so in two senses. First, as described later, not only does the infant's response patterns (i.e., sucking) reveal his or her detection and discrimination competences but we can also get a sense of his or her preferences in an active manner. That is, in certain variations of this procedure, the infant him- or herself determines (or "chooses") which sounds will be played back by speeding up or slowing down his or her sucking rate. Second, by exposing newborns to distinct sounds and syllables shortly after birth—with both familiar (e.g., heard "in the womb" during the prenatal period) and novel items presented—the HAS paradigm has also enabled researchers to test empirically and confirm the stimulating idea according to which learning in general, and phonetic development in particular, is a process that begins already during prenatal stages.

In a typical HAS experiment, infants are positioned in a reclined baby seat and wear headphones through which the auditory stimuli are presented to them. When in a peaceful mood, infants are given a sterilized rubber or silicone pacifier to suck on. This artificial nipple is connected to a pressure transducer and computer software that continuously measures infants' sucking rate and controls the stimuli presentation according to these measurements. The procedure typically begins by obtaining a baseline of sucking while infants are attentive and calm (i.e., not sleeping, eating, or in distress) and have not had any exposure to the sounds that are part of the experimental design. During the subsequent *familiarization* phase, infants listen to a set of acoustic stimuli (e.g., nonlinguistic sounds, syllables, words, or even whole paragraphs). These sounds are only presented to infants once they produce a series of high-amplitude sucks. After a while, infants typically become habituated to the specific sound(s) they were listening to, as indicated by a gradual decrease in their sucking rate. When a predetermined habituation criterion is reached, a new auditory stimulus is played back and, hence, the *test* phase begins. If infants perceive this new stimulus as different from those presented during familiarization, they typically begin to suck faster and stronger again, hence demonstrating their discrimination of the auditory change.

13.4.3 Head-Turn Preference Procedure

Unlike most ITMs, the head-turn preference procedure (HPP) has been specifically designed to explore and measure infants' speech perception in terms of discrimination and categorization of various kinds of acoustic stimuli, optimally between 6 and 9 months of age (e.g., Saffran, Aslin, & Newport, 1996). However, as E. K. Johnson and Zamuner (2010) explained, the method is suitable for both (slightly) younger as well as older infants and toddlers. Hence, as soon as infants have mastered sufficient muscle control for head turns, typically around 4.5 months, the HPP can be used empirically (Mandel, Jusczyk, & Pisoni, 1995; Nazzi, Jusczyk, & Johnson, 2000). HPP designs have been successfully carried out with 18-month-olds (Santelmann & Jusczyk, 1998) and even older toddlers (e.g., Nazzi, Paterson & Karmiloff-Smith, 2003). As with the HAS procedure, in the HPP, it is essentially the infant who "decides" how long he or she will listen to the acoustic stimuli. Unlike the HAS procedure, however, the HPP allows the use of considerably longer samples of speech.

In a typical HPP experiment, the infant sits on her or his caregiver's lap in front of a light or a video monitor. On each of the side walls in the three-sided testing booth, there is a blinking light that is visible to the child, with a loudspeaker mounted underneath. Both lights on the sides are of the same color and different from the one that is located at the center in front of the infant. As in most ITM settings now, the entire session is videotaped. The experiment commences with the center light flashing at a constant rate (or some image or video appearing on the video monitor) until the child's attention is drawn to midline. At that point the center light is turned off and (only) one of the lights on the sides begins to flash. Once the infant turns her or his head considerably enough in that direction (according to a predetermined criterion), an auditory stimulus is played back (e.g., /ba/, /ba/, /ba/). This stimulus stops only when the infant looks away for a certain amount of time (e.g., more than 2 seconds) or (in some cases) if the infant seems to be "stuck" in one direction only for a long time and the designated time for a trial ends. In another version of the HPP that has contributed to some of the most exciting findings in the field of early speech perception, Werker, Gilbert, Humphrey, and Tees (1981) used an animated toy (a dancing bear) as a visual reinforcer instead of a simple light. The toy bear was located at the side of the room and was lit up and visible to the child only when a change in the auditory stimulus had occurred. If the infant was capable of perceiving that change, he or she quickly learned to turn his or her head toward the toy immediately following the change in sound and in anticipation for the "bear show." In contrast, an infant who did not discriminate among the sounds that were played back to him or her would turn his or her head toward the animated toy only after it had already became visible.

13.4.4 The Intermodal Preferential Looking Paradigm

On the basis of the seminal empirical designs and results presented by Fantz (1958) and Spelke (1979), Golinkoff, Hirsh-Pasek, Cauley, and Gordon (1987) developed the *Intermodal Preferential Looking Paradigm* (IPLP; Hirsh-Pasek & Golinkoff, 1996). This innovative empirical paradigm has been used intensively in the last 3 decades to explore both cognitive and language development in children from about six months to about three years of age. In particular, in the field of language acquisition, the IPLP has been highly successful in highlighting covert linguistic capabilities in preverbal infants and young children in a wide range of language domains, such as speech perception, word learning, word categorization, and sentence computation (Golinkoff, Ma, Song, & Hirsh-Pasek, 2013).

The rationale of the paradigm is that "infants will prefer to watch the screen that matches the linguistic stimulus more than the screen that does not" (Hirsh-Pasek & Golinkoff, 1996, p. 61). Thus, unlike habituation-based procedures that depend on the infant's ability to detect (i.e., dishabituate to) a novel stimulus, the IPLP builds on the assumption that if infants already possess certain knowledge of language, they should use the linguistic input they receive during the test to orient toward a matching display rather than a nonmatching display.

The typical IPLP procedure introduces pairs (usually more than just one pair across trials) of visual stimuli (images, dynamic animations, or video clips) that are designed to be equally attractive and that are constituted from about the same colors, patterns, size, and so on. On each trial, a pair of images is presented simultaneously to the infant (i.e., side-by-side on two TV screens). After a familiarization trial, in which the images are typically presented either with no language at all or with only some general reference to the visual imagery (e.g., *Wow! Look at this!*), a test trial presents the images again, this time, however, accompanied by an acoustic stimulus—either single words or short utterances—that relates to the visual content that is shown on one of the screens but not the other (e.g., Kedar, Casasola, & Lust, 2006).

The original paradigm has been extended over the years to several related yet different empirical designs that are distinguished by their manipulation of stimulus presentation, data coding, and data analysis, among other experimental criteria. One such variation of the IPLP is the *Split-Screen* technique in which both images are presented on a single screen that is split in the middle (Hollich, Rocroi, Hirsh-Pasek, & Golinkoff, 1999). This setup minimizes the infant's need to turn her or his head from side to side and is especially useful with younger infants and in studies that combine the split-screen procedure with *Event-Related Potential* (ERP) measurements (i.e., sensitive electrophysiological brain measurements in which head movements are forbidden).

An automatic, technology-based, and highly accurate method that often uses the rationale and measures of the IPLP is *Eye Tracking*. In this technique, eye movements are analyzed automatically by specialized software, which provides detailed information about the specific time course of the experiment. This allows researchers to capture not only the group averages of infants assigned to different experimental conditions but also to pursue individual differences in language processing efficiency among infants (discussed later in more detail). Similarly, the *Looking-While-Listening* (LWL) variation of the IPLP is not as automatic and accurate as eye tracking, but nevertheless constitutes a low-cost alternative with similar effects. Thus, LWL is based on real-time coding of the time course of the infant's gaze patterns toward the visual stimuli as a function of particular accompanying speech (Fernald, Zangl, Portillo, & Marchman, 2008). Because the infant's gaze patterns toward the visual stimuli are time locked to the speech signal and coded frame-by-frame, LWL supports high-resolution measures of the infant's processing to the speech samples, rather than relying on summary measures of the infant's looking preferences throughout the entire trial (Fernald, Swingley, & Pinto, 2001).

13.4.5 Eye Tracking

Using the relatively new eye-tracking technology with infants and young children for experimental purposes has provided developmental researchers with a much greater level of precision in comparison with other ITMs in terms of tracking and recording the child's online processing of visual stimuli. Furthermore, because eye movements and fixations are recorded so effectively, researchers can pinpoint specific parts or areas of the stimulus the infant scanned during a trial and plot the infant's fixations on the target in a continuous manner (i.e., in milliseconds, as the sentence or word that is played back unfolds). Moreover, the eye-tracking technique enables the use of multiple measures. In language acquisition research, the visual stimuli are also accompanied and time locked to the infant's processing of a linguistic stimulus. For example, in a sentence computation study, one may mark several pivotal measurement points. The child's looking patterns will then be analyzed according to different time points that correspond with critical sentential locations in the test sentences.

In a typical developmental eye-tracking setup, the child is seated in a dimly lit room in front of the eye tracker's camera (that is adjusted relative to its head position), looking at the computer screen ahead. A video-based desk-mounted eye tracker is set on remote recording mode, which allows monocular recording without head stabilization. As soon as the child is seated comfortably and is attentive, built in programs provided with the eye tracker are used for calibration and validation purposes (five points in a random sequence, for children). At this stage, the consecutive presentation of the experimental trials begins. In essence, all aspects of the eye-tracking experimental procedure are "hands-free"; that is, the actual recording, coding, and data summary and analysis are computerized. Specifically, the software provides data on the number, duration, and onset of the subject's fixations, as well as on the accurate position of the eye gaze for each fixation.

13.5 Summary

The introduction of ITMs to language and cognitive development research in the last few decades has had a fundamental impact on these fields. The empirical dilemma described earlier still remains, namely, the uncertainty regarding the infant's actual representation of the linguistic domain under investigation. We have nonetheless now reached a new level of understanding regarding the child's representation, processing, and beginning knowledge of language at the earliest stages of life. This positive trend is now being strengthened by the incorporation of neuroscience methods in developmental science. The integration of the behavioral ITMs discussed earlier with brain-imaging methods such as Magnetoencephalography (MEG); functional Magnetic Resonance Imaging (fMRI; e.g., Perani et al., 2011); Near-Infrared Spectroscopy (e.g., Bortfeld, Wruck, & Boas, 2007); and Event-Related Potentials (ERPs; see de Haan, 2013, for a review) has opened up a new and exciting vision for the field so that we can now examine and associate in vivo the relation between the child's linguistic computations and visual orientation to referents and the respective neurological patterns of these in the brain (and, in addition, assimilating knowledge derived from lesion studies). In the last few years, a promising direction in the field that has been made conceivable through the use of ITMs and neuroscience methods with infants is the focus on the predictive value of infant perception and computation of speech for detecting in advance major language impairments and cognitive difficulties (e.g., Marchman & Fernald, 2008; Molfese & Molfese, 1985).

Appendix 13.1
Recommended Resources on Infant Testing Methods

Several online materials provide examples of infant testing methods. The following are links to infant lab websites that provide videos and illustrations of these methods.

- Rutgers University's Infancy Studies Laboratory (April Benasich): http://babylab.rutgers.edu/HOME.html
- Stanford University's Language Learning Lab Center for Infant Studies (Anne Fernald): https://web.stanford.edu/group/langlearninglab/cgi-bin/
- University of British Columbia's Infant Studies Centre (Janet F. Werker): http://infantstudies.psych.ubc.ca/
- University of Arizona's Child Cognition Lab (Rebecca Gomez): http://web.arizona.edu/~tigger/infantstudies.html
- Harvard University's Laboratory for Developmental Studies (Jesse Snedeker): https://software.rc.fas.harvard.edu/lds/

The following sites have links to useful videos.

- Patricia Kuhl (2010), The Linguistic Genius of Babies: http://www.ted.com/talks/patricia_kuhl_the_linguistic_genius_of_babies.html
- Janet Werker, Infant Speech Perception: https://www.youtube.com/watch?v=CSMjKDZvNWA
- Peter Jusczyk, Three Procedures for Investigating Infant Speech Perception and Language Development: https://www.youtube.com/watch?v=EFlxiflDk_o
- University of Maryland's Project on Children's Language Learning: Research Methods, with short explanations on several methods, some of which have video links: http://ling.umd.edu/research/acquisition_lab/methods/

14 Conclusions and Proceeding to the Future

In this research methods manual, we have attempted to provide a brief introduction to principles and procedures we hope will exemplify strong and sound research practices for the empirical study of language acquisition. Thus, we hope to have strengthened the scientific foundations of our field. Our goal has been to provide an introduction to every stage of what Leek and Peng (2015) termed the "data pipeline," shown in Figure 14.1 (from Leek & Peng, 2015, p. 612). Like Leek and Peng, we have recognized that the quality of every stage of this pipeline is crucial to the final scientific value of the research process, and we have provided examples of attempts to strengthen each stage (see also Lust, Flynn, Blume, Westbrooks, & Tobin, 2010). In doing so, we have addressed certain current pressing challenges in the language sciences and have laid the groundwork for possible advancements in the future. We have stressed the need for deeper integration of experimental methods in the field of language acquisition to enable hypothesis testing. At the same time, we have introduced ways in which observational methods (e.g., the study of "natural speech" in the child) can be strengthened, thus providing a potential research source for rich description and hypothesis generation.

Our emphasis has been on the primary research process. We realize that secondary research methods (which use and reuse primary research results) may be widely necessary and valuable in the field of language acquisition research; witness, for example, the thousands of subsequent secondary research studies that have been conducted over decades on the basis of the original transcripts of the three children, Adam, Eve, and Sarah, studied in the seminal work by Roger Brown at Harvard. Many researchers do not have the interdisciplinary training for experimental methods, the ability to form collaborative interdisciplinary teams, or the practical resources for the long and complex process primary research requires. Our hope is that by strengthening primary research methods through principles and procedures such as those we have suggested in this manual, the quality of secondary research will also be strengthened and supported.

14.1 Data Management

As we have seen, tracking the data pipeline from its inception to the collection of raw data and the reporting of final results and interpretation yields a massive data management challenge for the researcher. To render this problem tractable, we

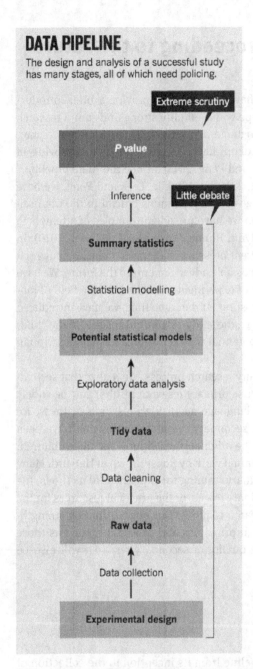

Fig. 14.1: Data pipeline. From "Statistics: P Values Are Just the Tip of the Iceberg," by J. T. Leek and R. D. Peng, 2015, *Nature*, *520*, p. 612. Copyright 2015 by Macmillan. Reprinted with permission.

have recommended the continuous creation and recording of metadata at every stage along the research pipeline, including the first steps of a research project.[1] We have identified necessary components of this metadata, and we have offered an example of an infrastructure for supporting this process (See section 14.7.1.3). This infrastructure may help to guide the researcher through the primary research process. The process we have recommended and the particular data creation procedures and database structure we have modeled may provide a useful framework and examples that other labs may build on.

14.2 Replicability

The principles for data management we have introduced are not simply "bookkeeping" mechanisms. In fact, they can transform the research process in a way that affects the conduct of primary research and has widespread consequences. For example, as we discussed in Chapters 5 and 11, replicability is a keystone of sound research, yet it is a constant challenge. The social sciences, like other sciences, are now confronting the fact that many apparently sound research studies are not replicable, causing what has been termed a *replication crisis* (Bohannon, 2015a, 2015b; Schooler, 2014). Because reproducibility is a crucial aspect of strong science, we must ask how this challenge can be addressed. Failure to replicate can involve each and every step of the research pipeline. For example, variation in population characteristics, tasks chosen, stimuli used, and coding and scoring criteria can and do cause variability in results. As Grosjean (2006) and Chapter 12 in this volume show, these issues are perhaps even more challenging when studying multilingual language acquisition.

The principles and procedures we hope to have set in place through this manual may help to address the replication challenge. First, by precise specification of every aspect of metadata along the research pipeline, including, for example, entry of every aspect of research design into an "experiment bank" infrastructure such as we have drafted, replication becomes more achievable. Second, however, no two "replications" need provide exactly the same results. The principles and procedures we have drafted here can help to identify the exact source of nonreplication; in doing so, they contribute positively to the research process by their identification of intervening factors in the effects being studied (see Schooler, 2014, on this issue).

---

[1] Note that it is essential to begin at the first stages of the research process. If not, researchers may, for example, be left with dispersed unlabeled files of collected data that they must then go back and try to identify precisely. Issues about how stimuli were created and what controls were adopted and why may become important at the end of the research process when research results are interpreted. Without records, researchers will rarely remember their motivation for every design decision they made.

14.3 Collaboration

At the same time, the principles and procedures we have drafted in this manual will, we hope, strengthen foundations for collaborative research. We have suggested that interdisciplinary teams provide crucial collaborations to support scientifically sound and significant research results. For example, psychologists trained in experimental methods and/or in developmental science can collaborate with linguists informed by linguistic theory to drive hypothesis formation. Researchers across languages can work together on calibrated data. Large interdisciplinary questions may become more accessible to scientific advance: What universal linguistic, social, or cultural properties underlie language acquisition? How can multiple languages be acquired simultaneously or successively?

14.4 Shared Data

We hope that the data management principles and procedures and the infrastructure we have introduced will provide a stronger foundation for data sharing. As we have seen, only if data at every stage in the pipeline are managed and archived systematically for access, can data be shared (e.g., even across collaborators working on the same data). At the same time, this foundation leads to several challenges in the future. For example, by U.S. White House Executive Order, government-supported data must be made available in open format. Considering the data pipeline, we can see that this laudable order immediately raises the issue of the point at which data are considered to be ready for sharing. We have seen that the data creation process, beginning even before raw data collection, will be long and complex before it can achieve scientific worth. In addition, we have seen in regard to primary research that data generation is as important as data analysis; its methods of collection can affect the quality of all work along the pipeline. It is necessary for every step of this process, including data generation, to be recognized as an inherent component of the research process. See, for example, Poldrack and Poline (2015), who suggested that "data generation" publications be valued as much as data interpretation.

14.5 Toward the Future

14.5.1 Specialized Software

We hope that the general principles and procedures we have introduced will facilitate the integration of shared data with specialized software programs for more specialized analyses in the language acquisition field (e.g., for phonology or morphology;

see, e.g., Warner, 2012). In the same way, we hope that they will facilitate integration with many diverse methodologies for assessing language acquisition and knowledge across the life span (e.g., eye tracking methods; see, e.g., Speer, 2012). Similarly, they may facilitate integration with new attempts to facilitate data collection and annotation (e.g., ELAN [https://tla.mpi.nl/tools/tla-tools/elan/] a tool created to facilitate transcription and morphological and phonetic coding by The Language Archive initiative from the Max Planck Institute [https://tla.mpi.nl/]).

14.5.2 When Shared Data Becomes "Big Data"

Sharing data can lead to large datasets that can aid in the advancement of science. At the same time, if data are not calibrated in some way, if secure storage and access methods do not exist, and if annotations across data sets are not linked, researchers are not able to query and retrieve data within or across data sets. Both technical and conceptual challenges exist.

The field of linguistics has recently highlighted "Linguistic Theory in a World of Big Data" in a summer 2015 Linguistic Institute. Linked Open Data in Linguistics (LLOD) represents the attempt to serve this interest in data integration by harnessing Internet and cloud resources, developing both infrastructure and technologies necessary for an "open data" agenda.[2] LLOD refers to the program of rendering language data in a form which can be accessible, interconnected, and released under an open license, fostering collaboration and interoperability of these data. For a series of papers regarding the extension of LLOD to potential application in language acquisition, see http://quijote.fdi.ucm.es:8084/LLOD-LSASummerWorkshop2015/Home.html.

14.6 Building a New Culture of Collaboration

Although we have stressed the necessarily collaborative nature of research on language acquisition, we recognize that the "culture of collaboration" is not only not widespread but also not easily achieved. In addition to personal challenges, issues of intellectual property rights and coauthorship must be resolved (e.g., Borgman, 2007; Gewin, 2015; Ledford, 2008).

We hope that the principles and procedures we have drafted in this manual will facilitate potential integration across scholars, data sets, and laboratories by articulating shared best practices, systematizing metadata standards, and building a framework

---

[2] See, for example, the Third Linked Data in Linguistics workshop (http://linguistics.okfn.org/2014/05/13/third-workshop-on-linked-data-in-linguistics-reykjavik-27th-may-2014/) organized by the Working Group on Open Data in Linguistics (http://linguistics.okfn.org/).

for calibrating varying database structures now in existence in different labs. Now, "data curation should be viewed as a necessary cost of research. Creative data generation should be a source of scholarly esteem and a criterion for promotion" (Boulton, 2012, p. 441).

14.7 Building Infrastructure for Collaboration

It is now necessary to develop interdisciplinary collaborative networks built on a functional infrastructure that can sustain collaborative data creation and data sharing and analyses. Several groups have initiated work to create such infrastructure. For example, in addition to the Virtual Center for the Study of Language Acquisition (VCLA) and its Virtual Linguistic Laboratory (VLL), which we discuss in more detail later, MetaLab (http://metalab.Stanford.edu) is creating research tools for aggregating data across research studies in the language acquisition literature. Databrary (https://nyu.databrary.org) is developing a video data library for developmental science. Data on the Mind: Center for Data-Intensive Psychological Science, at the University of California, Berkeley, is evaluating technologies for the collection of behavioral data and potentially data-intensive online databases.

Several sites are now creating data archives. In addition to the Child Language Data Exchange System database (CHILDES; http://childes.psy.cmu.edu/) at Carnegie Mellon, which has stored and disseminated transcripts of the language of many children, The Language Archive at the Max Planck Institute for Psycholinguistics (https://tla.mpi.nl/) maintains a large database of resources on languages worldwide and is establishing principles and procedures for open access. The Tromso Repository of Language and Linguistics (http://opendata.uit.no) is working to provide a repository of data sets and materials for linguistic research.

14.7.1 Components for Building a Virtual Linguistic Laboratory

As mentioned in Chapter 1, this manual is one of several resources developed by the VCLA to contribute to the training of new language researchers and to facilitate the collection, storage, analysis, and sharing of scientifically sound language acquisition data. In this section we briefly introduce what has been developed as a VLL.[3] The VLL provides an Internet portal directed at teaching students about the available

---

[3] The companion website for this book provides images of the Virtual Linguistic Laboratory (VLL) to illustrate better what Internet portals like the VLL look like (http://pubs.apa.org/books/supp/blume). These images demonstrate the portal's landing page, a list of learning topics, learning modules, a discussion board, cyber tools to aid learning and research, a data sample, and the Data Transcription and Analysis Tool, all of which relate to the discussion in this section.

methodologies they can use, as well as other tenets of scientific research with human subjects, children in particular. Certain techniques and tools developed at the Cornell Language Acquisition Laboratory with the VCLA are briefly described—these include the development of the Data Transcription and Analysis Tool. For potential international use, these materials have been partially translated into Spanish as well. We present a description of these materials here as an example of an Internet resource that has been created and can now be further developed. The examples here may provide a model for other developments in the field.

14.7.1.1 Resources for Educators

The VLL portal, in conjunction with this manual, can provide a valuable resource for institutions and individuals who wish to start a course on methods for the study of language acquisition or who seek to complement their existing courses (http://www.clal.cornell.edu/vll; Blume & Lust, 2012). The VCLA has created a sequence of three courses (three semesters) dedicated to this topic. The first course is an introduction to the basic methods for collecting, managing, analyzing, and interpreting acquisition data, and the two following courses support the development of original research by students. These courses can be taught either synchronously or asynchronously with other institutions using the materials available from the Internet. For this purpose, the VLL makes available the following types of pedagogical materials.

A list of learning topics organized in logical sequence covers the basics of research with human subjects, methods of obtaining child data, and issues of data management, among others. Each learning topic contains

- prepared class presentations for the use of instructors;
- readings from relevant articles and books, classified by topic;
- an archive of assignments that have been used and revised through each iteration of the course sequence;
- learning modules or collections of written, audio, and video materials containing actual child data and other research materials designed to introduce students to the aspects of research with hands-on experience;
- templates to support the research process (e.g., a template for the creation of a research proposal; see Appendix C);
- this volume, available from the VLL portal, which can be used in conjunction with each research topic;
- semester-long and/or weekly syllabi from previous versions of the relevant courses taught at various institutions, archived for future use and adaptation;
- a discussion board, equipped with wiki capabilities for students to share their work and opinions; this part of the portal also holds profiles from all institutions, professors, and students involved in a VLL-based course currently and in the past;

- certain cybertools made available through the VLL portal, which currently include a Data Transcription and Analysis Tool, its user's manual, and an introductory virtual workshop that teaches its capabilities in an interactive way (for a further description of this cybertool and its potential use for both education and research purposes, see Blume, Flynn, & Lust, 2012; Blume, Foley, Whitlock, Flynn, & Lust, 2016; Pareja-Lora, Blume, & Lust, 2013); and
- continual web conferences across institutions that can cultivate the collaborative and/or cross-linguistic approach to research. Different institutions offering the same course in the same semester can communicate through regular web conferences, where students from across the country and the world can communicate their opinions, pose questions, and present their projects to peers. Recordings of these Web conferences are also stored in the VLL for members to view.

14.7.1.2 Learning Modules

For most of the research methods that have been described in this manual, the VLL contains a complementary learning module with video or audio data illustrating the relevant task in practice. The data in these modules can be transcribed, scored, and otherwise used by students to have a closer experience with the task of a real researcher. The data samples in the learning modules are often part of a published research project, and students are provided with materials used by the researchers themselves, such as blank transcription forms, scoring criteria, and blank summary tables, to gain practice in each step and to test published results for replication. These modules also contain follow-up questions for students to answer after they have completed the applied part of the task.

14.7.1.3 Data Transcription and Analysis Tool

The VLL portal links to a cybertool component of the VCLA resources: the Data Transcription and Analysis (DTA) Tool. Even though this cybertool can be introduced in an early course in research methods, its use can lead the student or new researcher into new, original research. Thus, a subsequent course can focus on use of the DTA Tool to guide students in the primary research process. The tool can facilitate and structure the original documentation of any new experiment (or study). An experiment bank structure in this tool provides the metadata fields for documentation of every aspect of a new experiment or other research project. It requests researcher information, project description, hypotheses and motivations, and details of experimental design, as well as a bibliography. This provides the basis for ultimate replication of the study and for ultimate collaboration on the project and its data. It then provides a structure for the researcher to assist him or her in creating metadata files necessary for the representation of collected data according to project, subject, and session.

Collected data, when a project is conducted, can be linked to the cybertool in the form of video clips or audio samples, transcriptions, or other external documents along the whole data creation path. The cybertool provides electronic coding forms, which allow both systematized calibration of new language data and the possibility of customizing codings specific to new research projects, and it allows queries for desired codes, subjects, and sessions. Statistical analysis, data summaries, interpretation, and conclusions can be linked. Projects are stored in a standardized format to facilitate their retrieval, intelligibility, and sharing capabilities. A more detailed description of the DTA Tool can be found in the *DTA Manual*, available on the VLL portal.

The VLL portal and its associated tools can provide a useful complement to this manual. Adaptation of the DTA Tool or other such tool can assist the new researcher in conducting new research in a scientific framework. At the same time, such a tool, used in conjunction with the principles introduced in this manual, can transform the primary research process. Research projects will be available for replication by the researcher, who may want to conduct cross-linguistic extensions or other extensions of his or her study, and by others, thus greatly increasing scientific worth. By using a cybertool such as the DTA Tool, research data can be structured in such a way that they can be rendered available for collaborative research (across individuals and/or institutions) in the future. When stored in the DTA Tool, data are automatically archived in a way such that the necessary metadata will be integrated for describing the provenance and nature of the archive. Reliability and replicability of research are ensured. The foundations for collaborative research are provided.

In summary, an Internet-based resource such as that exemplified by the VLL portal can integrate the use of this manual with materials both for teaching and for interactive student learning. It can also be useful for collaborative researchers who choose to share both methods and data such as described in the principles and procedures we have discussed in this manual.

14.8 Interdisciplinarity and Neuroscience Extensions

We have seen that the field of language acquisition is essentially interdisciplinary. Now, as results in the field of neuroscience begin to approach the study of language, it will become more necessary to extend this interdisciplinarity and achieve collaboration and requisite data sharing with and across the field of neuroscience as well, bridging social science and natural science dimensions. This integration will require confronting many structural and theoretical issues, including fundamental issues related to the bidirectional "causal links between psychological and biological processes" (e.g., Schwartz, Lilienfeld, Meca, & Sauvigné, 2016, p. 66). Given the massive database challenges that confront the field of neuroscience now—for example, the multiple parameters characterizing even one brain scan—we can only hope that the principles and procedures we have established for management and processing of behavioral data in this manual, culminating in a shared structured database, will aid and abet this ultimate integration.

14.9 Funding Infrastructure Development

Finally, it must be recognized that

> digital data are ephemeral, and access to data involves infrastructure and economic support.... Access to data requires that the data be hosted somewhere and managed by someone. Technological and human infrastructure supporting data stewardship is a precondition to meaningful access and reuse, as "homeless" data quickly become no data at all. (F. Berman & Cerf, 2013, p. 616)

In all sciences, researchers are struggling with the issue of who will pay for the infrastructure required to make research data widely available. University libraries are "natural foci for the stewardship of digital research data" (F. Berman & Cerf, 2013, p. 616), but they are in dire need of support. Several progressive libraries are now addressing this challenge (see, e.g., the Tromso Repository of Language and Linguistics and the Cornell University Library, now hosting the Cornell Language Acquisition database; see also Rieger & Long, 2015). As F. Berman and Cerf (2013) suggested, a wider sector of participation and support must now be constructed. Federal granting agencies must assist in integrating varied infrastructure attempts now developing across institutions.

14.10 A Closing Caveat

In closing, we may remember that no amount of methodology, including experimental, and no amount of "big data" can produce significant new and exciting research results in any field of science without the initial considerations before inception: insight, vision, and creativity (see G. Marcus & Davis, 2014; Ramon y Cajal, 1916, 1999; Wilson, 2013). Perhaps the greatest discoveries in the field of cognitive development arose from a research process that combined observational and experimental methods. For example, the observation of a young child tracking a ball rolling under a couch led to Piaget's discovery of the cognitive concept of *object permanence*, which subsequently triggered decades of research in the area of cognitive development.

The discovery involved a combination of astute behavioral observations and formal interdisciplinary theory construction (involving Piaget's collaboration with other scientists including logicians, mathematicians, and physicists) followed by a methodology for hypothesis testing that integrated observational and experimental methods, the *Clinical Method*. On the basis of this integrative combined theoretical and empirical methodology, behavioral predictions were made and tested, as in the "conservation" phenomenon. Piaget's robust discoveries, which were replicated widely under vastly varying conditions across the world and which triggered thousands of subsequent extensions and interpretations, were strong enough that to a large degree they did not require the "p-value" resulting from a statistical test, although they provided the foundation for decades of further research.

Appendix A: Transcription Symbols

Marking		Description
.	Statement	*Subject*: that's a car.
		Subject: daddy's coming.
?/¿?	Question	*Researcher*: whatcha doing?
		Subject: it fits?
		Researcher: ¿qué haces? 'What are you doing?'
		Subject: ¿me queda bien? 'It fits?'
!/¡!	Imperative/exclamative	look!/come here!/ wow!
		¡mira!/¡ven!/¡oh! 'look!/come!/ oh!'
>	Breakoff	*Child*: I wanna>I wanna go home.
^	Interruption	*Child*: I wanna^
		Mother: what's this here?
{ }	Simultaneous	*Child*: {what's} that?
		Mother: {look here}!
X	One unintelligible syllable	
&X	One unintelligible word	
XX	Part of utterance is unintelligible, unspecified length	
XXX	Entire utterance is unintelligible, unspecified length	
&	Partial understanding: Use where other part of word is understood (e.g., &*tion*)	
...	Pause or hesitation pause at beginning or end of utterance	
-	To mark a stutter	
ww	Indicates where interlocutor speech occurs, but where there is no transcription (e.g., interlocutors have been speaking for a long time among themselves without addressing the subject. In this case, one can abridge interlocutor speech by using "ww")	

Appendix B: The International Phonetic Alphabet

IPA Chart, http://www.internationalphoneticassociation.org/content/ipa-chart, available under a Creative Commons Attribution-Sharealike 3.0 Unported License. Copyright © 2015 International Phonetic Association.

THE INTERNATIONAL PHONETIC ALPHABET (revised to 2015)

CONSONANTS (PULMONIC) © 2015 IPA

	Bilabial	Labiodental	Dental	Alveolar	Postalveolar	Retroflex	Palatal	Velar	Uvular	Pharyngeal	Glottal
Plosive	p b			t d		ʈ ɖ	c ɟ	k ɡ	q ɢ		ʔ
Nasal	m	ɱ		n		ɳ	ɲ	ŋ	ɴ		
Trill	ʙ			r					ʀ		
Tap or Flap		ⱱ		ɾ		ɽ					
Fricative	ɸ β	f v	θ ð	s z	ʃ ʒ	ʂ ʐ	ç ʝ	x ɣ	χ ʁ	ħ ʕ	h ɦ
Lateral fricative				ɬ ɮ							
Approximant		ʋ		ɹ		ɻ	j	ɰ			
Lateral approximant				l		ɭ	ʎ	ʟ			

Symbols to the right in a cell are voiced, to the left are voiceless. Shaded areas denote articulations judged impossible.

CONSONANTS (NON-PULMONIC)

Clicks	Voiced implosives	Ejectives
ʘ Bilabial	ɓ Bilabial	ʼ Examples:
ǀ Dental	ɗ Dental/alveolar	pʼ Bilabial
ǃ (Post)alveolar	ʄ Palatal	tʼ Dental/alveolar
ǂ Palatoalveolar	ɠ Velar	kʼ Velar
ǁ Alveolar lateral	ʛ Uvular	sʼ Alveolar fricative

OTHER SYMBOLS

ʍ Voiceless labial-velar fricative
w Voiced labial-velar approximant
ɥ Voiced labial-palatal approximant
ʜ Voiceless epiglottal fricative
ʢ Voiced epiglottal fricative
ʡ Epiglottal plosive

ɕ ʑ Alveolo-palatal fricatives
ɺ Voiced alveolar lateral flap
ɧ Simultaneous ʃ and x

Affricates and double articulations can be represented by two symbols joined by a tie bar if necessary. t͡s k͡p

VOWELS

Front — Central — Back

Close: i•y — ɨ•ʉ — ɯ•u
        ɪ ʏ   ʊ
Close-mid: e•ø — ɘ•ɵ — ɤ•o
                  ə
Open-mid: ɛ•œ — ɜ•ɞ — ʌ•ɔ
          æ   ɐ
Open: a•ɶ — — ɑ•ɒ

Where symbols appear in pairs, the one to the right represents a rounded vowel.

SUPRASEGMENTALS

ˈ Primary stress   ˌfoʊnəˈtɪʃən
ˌ Secondary stress
ː Long   eː
ˑ Half-long   eˑ
˘ Extra-short   ĕ
| Minor (foot) group
‖ Major (intonation) group
. Syllable break   ɹi.ækt
‿ Linking (absence of a break)

DIACRITICS
Some diacritics may be placed above a symbol with a descender, e.g. ŋ̊

̥ Voiceless	n̥ d̥	̤ Breathy voiced	b̤ a̤	̪ Dental	t̪ d̪		
̬ Voiced	s̬ t̬	̰ Creaky voiced	b̰ a̰	̺ Apical	t̺ d̺		
ʰ Aspirated	tʰ dʰ	̼ Linguolabial	t̼ d̼	̻ Laminal	t̻ d̻		
̹ More rounded	ɔ̹	ʷ Labialized	tʷ dʷ	̃ Nasalized	ẽ		
̜ Less rounded	ɔ̜	ʲ Palatalized	tʲ dʲ	ⁿ Nasal release	dⁿ		
̟ Advanced	u̟	ˠ Velarized	tˠ dˠ	ˡ Lateral release	dˡ		
̠ Retracted	e̠	ˤ Pharyngealized	tˤ dˤ	̚ No audible release	d̚		
̈ Centralized	ë	̴ Velarized or pharyngealized	ɫ				
̽ Mid-centralized	ẽ	̝ Raised	e̝ (ɹ̝ = voiced alveolar fricative)				
̩ Syllabic	n̩	̞ Lowered	e̞ (β̞ = voiced bilabial approximant)				
̯ Non-syllabic	e̯	̘ Advanced Tongue Root	e̘				
˞ Rhoticity	ɚ ɑ˞	̙ Retracted Tongue Root	e̙				

TONES AND WORD ACCENTS

LEVEL		CONTOUR	
e̋ or ˥	Extra high	ě or ˩˥	Rising
é ˦	High	ê ˥˩	Falling
ē ˧	Mid	e᷄ ˦˥	High rising
è ˨	Low	e᷅ ˩˨	Low rising
ȅ ˩	Extra low	e᷈ ˧˦˧	Rising-falling
↓ Downstep		↗ Global rise	
↑ Upstep		↘ Global fall	

Appendix C: Outline for Preparation of Schematic Research Proposal

Include a title page with name of author and date.

I. Introduction

i. State the general area to be studied.
ii. State your leading question about language acquisition.
iii. Why are this area and this question important to the study of language acquisition?

II. Background

i. What critical study (or studies) have already been done in this area relative to your proposed study? (You may want to choose one study as a jumping off point.) State the main result of the study you choose.
ii. Critique why this background study is insufficient. What specific question(s) does it leave unresolved that you would like to study?
iii. Choose (at least) one of these specific questions you would like to pursue yourself.
iv. Have you yourself done a pilot study? If so, summarize the results.

III. Proposal

i. Question. What specific question would you address in your study? What claim about language acquisition will you evaluate?
ii. Rationale. What hypothesis (or hypotheses) will you test in your study to evaluate whether your claim is true? What alternative hypothesis would you be disconfirming?
iii. If your hypothesis is confirmed, what will this show about language acquisition?
iv. If your hypothesis is disconfirmed, what will this suggest about first language acquisition?

IV. Design

What is the design of your study? That is, what factors will you vary in your study? What kinds of manipulations or variations of factors would you test for to test your hypothesis (or hypotheses)? For example, what factors would you vary if you were presenting a child with different types of stimulus sentences (e.g., sentences spoken in motherese compared with sentences spoken in adult speech? Were ages varied comparing 2-year-olds to 3-year-olds to test a developmental hypothesis?) How would varying these factors allow you to confirm or disconfirm your hypothesis? What significant differences would you need to find to confirm or disconfirm your hypothesis? In particular, how could your hypothesis be disconfirmed by your data? Are your factors "between group" factors or "within subjects" factors? (See supplementary materials for definitions of these terms.)

V. Method

What methodology would you choose for your study to test your hypothesis (or hypotheses)? Why is this method the best for your purposes? (For example, will you test a child's language production or comprehension, and how? What task will you use—elicited imitation or act-out or truth-value judgment or another?)

  i. Controls. What kinds of factors do you have to control for in your study? How might you build these controls into your study? In other words, what types of effects would be likely to occur that would make your results appear to confirm or to disconfirm your hypotheses but are "confounding variables"? How can you rule them out by your design?
  ii. Subjects, participants, and groups. Describe the sample (population) you will test and explain why you have chosen this sample.

VI. Conclusions and Significance

How would your proposed research lead to a significant improvement over the original study (or studies), and how would it benefit the field of language acquisition? What future studies do you advise?

VII. Bibliography

See the human subjects guidelines and application forms, and attach a completed "Human Subjects" form to your proposal (https://www.osp.cornell.edu/ProposalPrep/default.html).

Suggested Readings

Part I: Fundamentals of Language Acquisition Research

Chapter 1. The Challenge of Studying Language

Baker, A., & Woll, B. (2008). *Sign language acquisition*. Amsterdam, Netherlands: John Benjamins.

Chomsky, N. (2006). *Language and mind* (3rd ed.). Cambridge, England: Cambridge University Press.

Larson, R. K., & Ryokai, K. (2010). *Grammar as science*. Cambridge, MA: MIT Press.

Mihalicek, V., & Wilson, C. (2011). *Language files: Materials for an introduction to language and linguistics*. Columbus, OH: Ohio State University Press.

O'Grady, W., Dobrovolsky, M., & Aronoff, M. (1989). *Contemporary linguistics: An introduction*. New York, NY: St. Martin's Press.

Yule, G. (2010). *The study of language* (4th ed.). Cambridge, England: Cambridge University Press. http://dx.doi.org/10.1017/CBO9780511757754

Chapter 2. Preparing to Work With Children, Schools, and Families

Bowern, C. (2010). Fieldwork and the IRB: A snapshot. *Language, 86,* 897–905.

Part II: Experimental and Observational Methods in Language Acquisition Research

Chapter 4. Studying Language Acquisition Through Collecting Speech

Ervin-Tripp, S. (2000). Studying conversation: How to get natural peer interaction. In L. Menn & N. B. Ratner (Eds.), *Methods for studying language production* (pp. 271–288). Mahwah, NJ: Erlbaum.

Pan, B. A., Perlmann, R. Y., & Snow, C. E. (2000). Food for thought: Dinner table as a context for observing parent–child discourse. In L. Menn & N. B. Ratner (Eds.), *Methods for studying language production* (pp. 205–224). Mahwah, NJ: Erlbaum.

Yin, R. K. (2009). *Case study research* (4th ed.). Los Angeles, CA: Sage.

Chapter 5. Introduction to Experimental Methods: Design and Analysis

Blom, E., & Unsworth, S. (Eds.). (2010). *Experimental methods in language acquisition research.* Philadelphia, PA: John Benjamins. http://dx.doi.org/10.1075/lllt.27

Bodemer, N., & Ruggeri, A. (2012, March 23). Finding a good research question, in theory. *Science, 335*(6075), 1439. http://dx.doi.org/10.1126/science.335.6075.1439-a

Carpenter, S. (2012, March 30). Psychology's bold initiative. *Science, 335*(6076), 1558–1561. http://dx.doi.org/10.1126/science.335.6076.1558

Coleman, E. B. (1964). Generalizing to a language population. *Psychological Reports, 14*, 219–226.

Creswell, J. W. (2009). *Research design.* Los Angeles, CA: Sage.

Gibson, E., & Fedorenko, E. (2010). Weak quantitative standards in linguistics research. *Trends in Cognitive Sciences, 14*, 233–234. http://dx.doi.org/10.1016/j.tics.2010.03.005

Greenwald, A. G. (2012). There is nothing so theoretical as a good method. *Perspectives on Psychological Science, 7*, 99–108. http://dx.doi.org/10.1177/1745691611434210

McCall, R. B., & Kagan, J. (2001). *Fundamental statistics for psychology* (8th ed.). Los Angeles, CA: Wadsworth-Cengage Learning.

Pearl, J. (2010). The foundations of causal inference. *Sociological Methodology, 40*, 75–149. http://dx.doi.org/10.1111/j.1467-9531.2010.01228.x

Shadish, W. R., Cook, T. D., & Campbell, D. T. (2002). *Experimental and quasi-experimental designs for generalized causal inference.* Boston, MA: Houghton Mifflin.

Smith, C. S., & van Kleeck, A. (1986). Linguistic complexity and performance. *Journal of Child Language, 13*, 389–408. http://dx.doi.org/10.1017/S0305000900008126

Chapter 6. Experimental Tasks for Generating Language Production Data

Eisenbeiss, S. (2009). Contrast is the name of the game: Contrast-based semi-structured elicitation techniques for studies on children's language acquisition. *Essex Research Reports in Linguistics, 57*(7), 1–27.

Gair, J., Lust, B. C., Bhatia, T. K., Sharma, V., & Khare, J. (1998). A Parameter-setting paradox: Children's acquisition of Hindi anaphora in "jab" clauses. In J. Gair (Ed.), *Studies in South Asian linguistics* (pp. 286–304). Oxford, England: Oxford University Press.

Lust, B. C., Bhatia, T. K., Gair, J., Sharma, V., & Khare, J. (1995). Children's acquisition of Hindi anaphora: A parameter-setting paradox. In V. Ghambir (Ed.), *Teaching and acquisition of South Asian languages* (pp. 172–189). Philadelphia, PA: Penn Press.

Lust, B. C., & Chien, Y. (1984). The structure of coordination in first language acquisition of Chinese. *Cognition, 17*, 49–83. http://dx.doi.org/10.1016/0010-0277(84)90042-8

Lust, B. C., Flynn, S., Chien, Y., & Clifford, T. (1980). Coordination: The role of syntactic, pragmatic, and processing factors in first language acquisition. *Papers and Reports on Child Language Development, 19*, 79–87.

Núñez del Prado, Z., Foley, C. A., Proman, P., & Lust, B. C. (1997). Subordinate CP and prodrop: Evidence for degree-n learnability from an experimental study of Spanish and English. In S. Somashekar, K. Yamakoshi, M. Blume, & C. A. Foley (Eds.), *Papers on language acquisition: Cornell University Working Papers in Linguistics* (pp. 141–159). Ithaca, NY: CLC.

Postman, W., Foley, C. A., Pactovis, J., Rothenstein, B., Kaye, M., Lowe, D., & Lust, B. C. (1997). Children's knowledge of verbal inflection and LF raising: New evidence from elicited production of VP ellipsis structures. *Cornell Working Papers in Linguistics*, *15*, 39–64.

Whitaker, H. (1976). A case of the isolation of the language function. In H. Whitaker & H. A. Whitaker (Eds.), *Studies in neurolinguistics* (Vol. 2, pp. 1–58). New York, NY: Academic Press. http://dx.doi.org/10.1016/B978-0-12-746302-5.50008-6

Chapter 7. Experimental Tasks for Generating Language Comprehension Data

Sinclair, H. (1976). Developmental psycholinguistics. In B. Inhelder, H. H. Chipman, & C. Zwingmann (Eds.), *Piaget and his school* (pp. 205–218). Berlin, Germany: Springer-Verlag. http://dx.doi.org/10.1007/978-3-642-46323-5_15

Chapter 8. The Grammaticality Judgment Task

Bader, M., & Haussler, J. (2010). Toward a model of grammaticality judgments. *Journal of Linguistics*, *46*, 273–330. http://dx.doi.org/10.1017/S0022226709990260

Dabrowska, E. (2010). Naïve vs. expert intuitions: An empirical study of acceptability judgments. *The Linguistic Review*, *27*, 1–23. http://dx.doi.org/10.1515/tlir.2010.001

Gleitman, L., & Gleitman, H. (1979). Language use and language judgment. In C. Fillmore, D. Kemler, & W. Wang (Eds.), *Individual differences in language ability and language behavior* (pp. 103–126). New York, NY: Academic Press.

Sprouse, J., & Almeida, D. (2013). The role of experimental syntax in an integrated cognitive science of language. In C. Boecks & K. K. Grohmann (Eds.), *The Cambridge handbook of biolinguistics* (pp. 181–202). Cambridge, England: Cambridge University Press. http://dx.doi.org/10.1017/CBO9780511980435.013

Part III: Managing and Interpreting Speech Data

Chapter 9. Creating the Data II: Begin Data Processing

Geisler, C. (2004). *Analyzing streams of language*. New York, NY: Pearson.

Sperber, D., & Wilson, D. (1995). *Relevance, communication and cognition*. Cambridge, MA: Blackwell.

Chapter 10. Creating the Data III: Preparing for Data Analysis

Austin, J. L. (1962). *How to do things with words*. Cambridge, MA: Harvard University Press.

Bavin, E., & Stoll, S. (Eds.). (2013). *The acquisition of ergativity*. Philadelphia, PA: John Benjamins. http://dx.doi.org/10.1075/tilar.9

Bickel, B., Comrie, B., & Haspelmath, M. (2008). *Leipzig glossing rules: Conventions for interlinear morpheme-by-morpheme glosses*. Retrieved from http://www.eva.mpg.de/lingua/resources/glossing-rules.php

Chen Pichler, D., Hochgesang, J., Lillo-Martin, D., & Quadros, R. (2010). Conventions for sign and speech transcription in child bimodal bilingual corpora in ELAN. *Language, Interaction and Acquisition, 1*, 11–40. http://dx.doi.org/10.1075/lia.1.1.03che

Green, G. (1989). *Pragmatics and natural language understanding*. Hillsdale, NJ: Erlbaum.

Katz, J. (1980). *Propositional structure and illocutionary force*. Cambridge, MA: Harvard University Press.

Kempson, R. (2003). Pragmatics: Language and communication. In M. Aronoff & J. Rees-Miller (Eds.), *The handbook of linguistics* (pp. 394–424). Cambridge, MA: Blackwell. http://dx.doi.org/10.1002/9780470756409.ch16

Levinson, S. (1983). *Pragmatics*. Cambridge, England: Cambridge University Press.

Searle, J. R. (1969). *Speech acts. An essay in the philosophy of language*. Cambridge, England: Cambridge University Press. http://dx.doi.org/10.1017/CBO9781139173438

Chapter 11. Interpreting the Data: Scientific Inference

Lust, B., & Mervis, C. A. (1980). Development of coordination in the natural speech of young children. *Journal of Child Language, 7*, 279–304. http://dx.doi.org/10.1017/S0305000900002634

Taper, M., & Lele, S. (2004). *The nature of scientific evidence*. Chicago, IL: University of Chicago Press. http://dx.doi.org/10.7208/chicago/9780226789583.001.0001

Part IV: Special Considerations in Language Acquisition Research

Chapter 12. Assessing Multilingual Acquisition

Anderson, R. T. (1996). Assessing the grammar of Spanish-speaking children: A comparison of two procedures. *Language, Speech, and Hearing Services in Schools, 27*, 333–344. http://dx.doi.org/10.1044/0161-1461.2704.333

Bergelson, E., & Swingley, D. (2012). At 6–9 months, human infants know the meanings of many common nouns. *Proceedings of the National Academy of Sciences of the United States of America, 109*, 3253–3258. http://dx.doi.org/10.1073/pnas.1113380109

De Houwer, A. (2009). *Bilingual first language acquisition*. Bristol, England: Multilingual Matters.

Dörnyei, Z. (2010). *Questionnaires in second language research: Construction, administration, and processing* (2nd ed.). Mahwah, NJ: Erlbaum.

Grosjean, F. (2010). *Bilingual: Life and reality*. Cambridge, MA: Harvard University Press. http://dx.doi.org/10.4159/9780674056459

Mackey, A., & Gass, S. (2005). *Second language research: Methodology and design*. Mahwah, NJ: Erlbaum.

Marchman, V. A., & Martine-Sussmann, C. (2002). Concurrent validity of caregiver/parent report measures of language for children who are learning both English and Spanish. *Journal of Speech, Language, and Hearing Research, 45*, 983–997. http://dx.doi.org/10.1044/1092-4388(2002/080)

Paradis, J., Emmerzael, K., & Duncan, T. S. (2010). Assessment of English language learners: Using parent report on first language development. *Journal of Communication Disorders, 43*, 474–497. http://dx.doi.org/10.1016/j.jcomdis.2010.01.002

Chapter 13. Introduction to Infant Testing Methods in Language Acquisition Research

Aslin, R. N. (2007). What's in a look? *Developmental Science, 10*, 48–53. http://dx.doi.org/10.1111/j.1467-7687.2007.00563.x

Aslin, R. N., Jusczyk, P. W., & Pisoni, D. B. (1998). Speech and auditory processing during infancy: Constraints on and precursors to language. In D. Kuhn & R. Siegler (Eds.), *Handbook of child psychology: Vol. 2. Cognition, perception, and language* (5th ed., pp. 147–198). New York, NY: Wiley.

Aslin, R. N., Pisoni, D. B., & Jusczyk, P. W. (1983). Auditory development and speech perception in infancy. In M. M. Haith & J. J. Campos (Eds.), *Handbook of child psychology: Vol. 2. Infancy and developmental psychobiology* (4th ed., pp. 573–687). New York, NY: Wiley.

Byers-Heinlein, K., & Werker, J. F. (2013). Lexicon structure and the disambiguation of novel words: Evidence from bilingual infants. *Cognition, 128*, 407–416. http://dx.doi.org/10.1016/j.cognition.2013.05.010

Colombo, J., McCardle, P., & Freund, L. (Eds.). (2008). *Infant pathways to language: Methods, models, and research directions*. New York, NY: Psychology Press.

Colombo, J., & Mitchell, D. W. (2009). Infant visual habituation. *Neurobiology of Learning and Memory, 92*, 225–234. http://dx.doi.org/10.1016/j.nlm.2008.06.002

DeCasper, A. J., & Spence, M. J. (1986). Prenatal maternal speech influences newborns' perception of speech sounds. *Infant Behavior & Development, 9*, 133–150. http://dx.doi.org/10.1016/0163-6383(86)90025-1

Eimas, P. D., Siqueland, E. R., Jusczyk, P., & Vigorito, J. (1971, January 22). Speech perception in infants. *Science, 171*(3968), 303–306. http://dx.doi.org/10.1126/science.171.3968.303

Houston-Price, C., & Nakai, S. (2004). Distinguishing novelty and familiarity effects in infant preference procedures. *Infant and Child Development, 13*, 341–348. http://dx.doi.org/10.1002/icd.364

Jusczyk, P. W., Pisoni, D. B., & Mullennix, J. (1992). Some consequences of stimulus variability on speech processing by 2-month-old infants. *Cognition, 43*, 253–291. http://dx.doi.org/10.1016/0010-0277(92)90014-9

Kemler Nelson, D., Jusczyk, P. W., Mandel, D. R., Myers, J., Turk, A., & Gerken, L. (1995). The head-turn preference procedure for testing auditory perception. *Infant Behavior & Development, 18*, 111–116. http://dx.doi.org/10.1016/0163-6383(95)90012-8

Mahr, T., McMillan, B. T. M., Saffran, J. R., Ellis Weismer, S., & Edwards, J. (2015). Anticipatory coarticulation facilitates word recognition in toddlers. *Cognition, 142*, 345–350. http://dx.doi.org/10.1016/j.cognition.2015.05.009

Nelson, D. G. K., Jusczyk, P. W., Mandel, D. R., Myers, J., Turk, A., & Gerken, L. (1995). The head-turn preference procedure for testing auditory perception. *Infant Behavior & Development, 18*, 111–116. http://dx.doi.org/10.1016/0163-6383(95)90012-8

Werker, J. F., & Tees, R. C. (1984). Cross-language speech perception: Evidence for perceptual reorganization during the first year of life. *Infant Behavior & Development, 7*, 49–63. http://dx.doi.org/10.1016/S0163-6383(84)80022-3

Chapter 14. Conclusions and Proceeding to the Future

Armstrong, S. (1994). *Using large corpora*. Cambridge, MA: Bradford Books.

Jasny, B., Chin, G., Chong, L., & Vignieri, S. (2011, December 2). Again and again and again . . . *Science, 334*(6060), 1225. http://dx.doi.org/10.1126/science.334.6060.1225

Rosch, E. (2002, August 18). Corpus linguistics. *The New York Times Magazine*, p. 14.

Westbrooks, E. L., Pantle, S., & Lowe, B. (2005). *Mann library manual of archiving practices*. Ithaca, NY: Cornell University.

References

Aitchison, J. (2011). *The articulate mammal: An introduction to psycholinguistics*. London, England: Taylor & Francis.

Altarriba, J., & Heredia, R. (Eds.). (2008). *An introduction to bilingualism: Principles and processes*. New York, NY: Erlbaum.

Amaro, J. C., Flynn, S., & Rothman, J. (Eds.). (2012). *Third language acquisition in adulthood*. Philadelphia, PA: John Benjamins. http://dx.doi.org/10.1075/sibil.46

Ambridge, B., & Rowland, C. F. (2013). Experimental methods in studying child language acquisition. *WIREs Cognitive Science, 4*, 149–168. http://dx.doi.org/10.1002/wcs.1215

American Psychological Association. (2010). *Ethical principles of psychologists and code of conduct (2002, Amended June 1, 2010)*. Retrieved from http://www.apa.org/ethics/code/index.aspx

Anderson, S. R. (1985). *Phonology in the twentieth century: Theories of rules and theories of representations*. Chicago, IL: University of Chicago Press.

Ardery, G. (1980). On coordination in child language. *Journal of Child Language, 7*, 305–320. http://dx.doi.org/10.1017/S0305000900002646

Arlman-Rupp, A. J. L., van Niekerk de Haan, D., & van de Sandt-Koenderman, M. (1976). Brown's early stages: Some evidence from Dutch. *Journal of Child Language, 3*, 267–274. http://dx.doi.org/10.1017/S0305000900001483

Austin, J. (2010). Rich inflection and the production of finite verbs in child language. *Morphology, 20*, 41–69. http://dx.doi.org/10.1007/s11525-009-9144-7

Austin, J., Blume, M., & Sánchez, L. (2013). Syntactic development in the L1 of Spanish–English bilingual children. *Hispania, 96*, 542–561. http://dx.doi.org/10.1353/hpn.2013.0091

Austin, J., Blume, M., & Sánchez, L. (2015). *Bilingualism in the Spanish-speaking world: Linguistic and cognitive perspectives*. New York, NY: Cambridge University Press. http://dx.doi.org/10.1017/CBO9780511844201

Baayen, R. H. (2008). *Analyzing linguistic data*. Cambridge, England: Cambridge University Press. http://dx.doi.org/10.1017/CBO9780511801686

Baayen, R. H., Davidson, D. J., & Bates, D. M. (2008). Mixed-effects modeling with crossed random effects for subjects and items. *Journal of Memory and Language, 59*, 390–412. http://dx.doi.org/10.1016/j.jml.2007.12.005

Baker, C. (2011). *Foundations of bilingual education and bilingualism* (5th ed.). Bristol, England: Multilingual Matters.

Baker, M. (2001). *The atoms of language*. New York, NY: Basic Books.

Barlow, M. (1996). Corpora for theory and practice. *International Journal of Corpus Linguistics, 1*, 1–37. http://dx.doi.org/10.1075/ijcl.1.1.03bar

Bates, D. (2005). Fitting linear mixed models in R. *R News, 5*, 27–30.

Bates, E., Dale, P., & Thal, D. (1995). Individual differences and their implications for theories of language development. In P. Fletcher & B. MacWhinney (Eds.), *The handbook of child language* (pp. 96–151). Oxford, England: Blackwell.

Bedore, L. M., Peña, E. D., García, M., & Cortez, C. (2005). Conceptual versus monolingual scoring: When does it make a difference? *Language, Speech, and Hearing Services in Schools, 36,* 188–200. http://dx.doi.org/10.1044/0161-1461(2005/020)

Benasich, A. A., & Tallal, P. (2002). Infant discrimination of rapid auditory cues predicts later language impairment. *Behavioural Brain Research, 136*(1), 31–49. http://dx.doi.org/10.1016/S0166-4328(02)00098-0

Berk, S. (1996). *What does why what trigger?* (Unpublished BA honors thesis). Cornell University, Ithaca, NY.

Berkes, E., & Flynn, S. (2012). Multilingualism: New perspectives on syntactic development. In T. K. Bhatia & W. C. Ritchie (Eds.), *Handbook of bilingualism and multilingualism* (pp. 137–167). Oxford, England: Blackwell. http://dx.doi.org/10.1002/9781118332382.ch6

Berko, J. (1958). The child's learning of English morphology. *Word, 14,* 150–177. http://dx.doi.org/10.1080/00437956.1958.11659661

Berman, F., & Cerf, V. (2013). Science priorities. Who will pay for public access to research data? *Science, 341,* 616–617. http://dx.doi.org/10.1126/science.1241625

Berman, R. A., & Slobin, D. I. (1994). *Relating events in narrative: A crosslinguistic developmental study.* Hillsdale, NJ: Erlbaum.

Berthoud-Papandropoulou, I. (1978). An experimental study of children's ideas about language. In A. Sinclair, R. J. Jarvella, & W. M. J. Levelt (Eds.), *The child's conception of language* (pp. 55–64). New York, NY: Springer.

Bhatia, T. K., & Ritchie, W. C. (Eds.). (2006). *The handbook of bilingualism.* Malden, MA: Wiley-Blackwell.

Bialystok, E., & Hakuta, K. (1999). Confounded age: Linguistic and cognitive factors in age differences for second language acquisition. In D. Birdsong (Ed.), *Second language acquisition and the critical hypothesis* (pp. 161–181). Mahwah, NJ: Erlbaum.

Biber, D., Conrad, S., & Reppen, R. (1998). *Corpus linguistics: Investigating language structure and use.* Cambridge, England: Cambridge University Press.

Bird, S., & Simons, G. (2001). The OLAC metadata set and controlled vocabularies. *Proceedings of the ACL/EACL Workshop on Sharing Tools and Resources for Research and Education, 15,* 7–18. http://dx.doi.org/10.3115/1118062.1118065

Blake, J., Quartaro, G., & Onorati, S. (1993). Evaluating quantitative measures of grammatical complexity in spontaneous speech samples. *Journal of Child Language, 20,* 139–152. http://dx.doi.org/10.1017/S0305000900009168

Bloom, L. (1970). *Language development: Form and function in emerging grammars.* Cambridge, MA: MIT Press.

Blume, M. (2002). *Discourse-morphosyntax interface in Spanish non-finite verbs: A comparison between adult and child grammars* (Unpublished doctoral dissertation). Cornell University, Ithaca, NY.

Blume, M., Flynn, S., & Lust, B. C. (2012). Creating linked data for the interdisciplinary international collaborative study of language acquisition and use: Achievements and challenges of a new Virtual Linguistics Lab. In C. Chiarcos, S. Nordhoff, & S. Hellmann (Eds.), *Linked data in linguistics: Representing and connecting language data and language metadata* (pp. 85–96). Heidelberg, Germany: Springer-Verlag.

Blume, M., Foley, C. A., Whitlock, J., Flynn, S., & Lust, B. C. (2016). *Principles and new cybertools for interlinking data in the study of language acquisition: Leveraging the advantages of a digital environment.* Manuscript in preparation.

Blume, M., & Lust, B. C. (2012). First steps in transforming the primary research process through a Virtual Linguistic Lab for the study of language acquisition and use: Challenges and accomplishments. *Journal of Computational Science Education*, *3*, 34–46.

Blume, M., & Rayas, M. (2016). *Aspectual ambiguity effects in the development of morphosyntax: English and Spanish constraints in speaking about habitual events*. Manuscript in preparation.

Bohannon, J. (2015a, December 18). Reproducibility in psychology. *Science*, *350*, 1459.

Bohannon, J. (2015b). Many psychology papers fail replication test. *Science*, *349*, 910–911. http://dx.doi.org/10.1126/science.349.6251.910

Borgman, C. (2007). *Scholarship in the digital age*. Cambridge, MA: MIT Press.

Bortfeld, H., Wruck, E., & Boas, D. A. (2007). Assessing infants' cortical response to speech using near-infrared spectroscopy. *NeuroImage*, *34*, 407–415. http://dx.doi.org/10.1016/j.neuroimage.2006.08.010

Bosch, L., & Sebastián-Gallés, N. (2002). Evidence of early language discrimination abilities in infants from bilingual environments. *Infancy*, *2*, 29–49. http://dx.doi.org/10.1207/S15327078IN0201_3

Boudreault, P., & Mayberry, R. I. (2006). Grammatical processing in American Sign Language: Age of first language acquisition effects in relation to syntactic structure. *Language and Cognitive Processes*, *21*, 608–635. http://dx.doi.org/10.1080/01690960500139363

Boulton, G. (2012). Open your minds and share your results. *Nature*, *486*, 441. http://dx.doi.org/10.1038/486441a

Bright, W. (1992). *International encyclopedia of linguistics*. New York, NY: Oxford University Press.

Brown, P., Pfeiler, B., de León, L., & Pye, C. (2013). The acquisition of agreement in four Mayan languages. In E. Bavin & S. Stoll (Eds.), *The acquisition of ergativity* (pp. 271–306). Philadelphia, PA: John Benjamins. http://dx.doi.org/10.1075/tilar.9.10bro

Brown, R. (1973). *A first language: The early stages*. Cambridge, MA: Harvard University Press. http://dx.doi.org/10.4159/harvard.9780674732469

Brownell, R. (Ed.). (2000). *Expressive one-word vocabulary test* (3rd ed.). Novato, CA: Academic Therapy.

Brysbaert, M. (2007). *The language-as-fixed-effect fallacy: Some simple SPSS solutions to a complex problem*. London, England: Royal Holloway, University of London.

Butler, Y. G., & Hakuta, K. (2006). Bilingualism and second language acquisition. In T. K. Bhatia & W. C. Ritchie (Eds.), *The handbook of bilingualism* (pp. 114–144). Malden, MA: Blackwell. http://dx.doi.org/10.1002/9780470756997.ch5

Canale, M. (1983). From communicative competence to communicative language pedagogy. In J. C. Richards & R. W. Schmidt (Eds.), *Language and communication* (pp. 2–27). London, England: Longman.

Canale, M., & Swain, M. (1980). Theoretical bases of communicative approaches to second language teaching and testing. *Applied Linguistics*, *1*, 1–47.

Carnie, A. (2002). *Syntax: A generative introduction*. Oxford, England: Blackwell.

Carnie, A. (2013). *Syntax: A generative introduction* (3rd ed.). Malden, MA: Wiley-Blackwell.

Chan, A., Meints, K., Lieven, E., & Tomasello, M. (2010). Young children's comprehension of English SVO word order revisited: Testing the same children in act-out and intermodal preferential looking tasks. *Cognitive Development*, *25*, 30–45. http://dx.doi.org/10.1016/j.cogdev.2009.10.002

Chien, Y., & Lust, B. C. (1985). The concepts of topic and subject in first language acquisition of Mandarin Chinese. *Child Development*, *56*, 1359–1375. http://dx.doi.org/10.2307/1130457

Chien, Y., & Lust, B. C. (2006). Chinese children's acquisition of binding principles. In P. Li, L. H. Tan, E. Bates, & O. J. L. Tzeng (Eds.), *Handbook of East Asian psycholinguistics: Vol. 1. Chinese* (pp. 23–38). Cambridge, England: Cambridge University Press.

Chien, Y., & Wexler, K. (1987a). Children's acquisition of the locality condition for reflexives and pronouns. *Papers and Reports on Child Language Development, 26,* 30–39.

Chien, Y., & Wexler, K. (1987b, October). *A comparison between Chinese-speaking and English-speaking children's acquisition of reflexives and pronouns.* Paper presented at the Boston University Conference on Language Development, Boston, MA.

Chien, Y., & Wexler, K. (1990). Children's knowledge of locality conditions in binding as evidence for the modularity of syntax and pragmatics. *Language Acquisition, 1,* 225–295. http://dx.doi.org/10.1207/s15327817la0103_2

Chomsky, C. (1969). *The acquisition of syntax in children from 5 to 10.* Cambridge, MA: MIT Press.

Chomsky, N. (1957). *Syntactic structures.* The Hague, Netherlands: Mouton.

Chomsky, N. (1964). Formal discussion of W. Miller and Susan Ervin, "The development of grammar in child language." *Monographs of the Society for Research in Child Development, 29,* 35–39.

Chomsky, N. (1981). *Lectures on government and binding.* Dordrecht, Netherlands: Foris.

Chomsky, N. (1986). *Knowledge of language: Its nature, origins, and use.* Portsmouth, NH: Greenwood.

Christensen, L. B. (2006). *Experimental methodology* (10th ed.). Boston, MA: Allyn & Bacon.

Christensen, L. B., Johnson, B., & Turner, L. A. (2014). *Research methods, design, and analysis* (12th ed.). Boston, MA: Allyn & Bacon.

Clark, E. (2016). *First language acquisition* (3rd ed.). Cambridge, England: Cambridge University Press.

Clark, E. V., & Andersen, E. S. (1979). Spontaneous repairs: Awareness in the process of acquiring language. *Papers and Reports on Child Language Development, Stanford University, 16,* 1–12.

Clark, E. V., & Hecht, B. F. (1983). Comprehension, production, and language acquisition. *Annual Review of Psychology, 34,* 325–349. http://dx.doi.org/10.1146/annurev.ps.34.020183.001545

Clark, H. H. (1973). The language-as-fixed-effect fallacy: A critique of language statistics in psychological research. *Journal of Verbal Learning & Verbal Behavior, 12,* 335–359. http://dx.doi.org/10.1016/S0022-5371(73)80014-3

Clear, J. H. (1993). The British National Corpus. In G. P. Landow (Ed.), *The digital word: Text-based computing in the humanities* (pp. 163–188). Cambridge, MA: MIT Press.

Cohen, J. (1988). *Statistical power analysis for the behavioral sciences* (2nd ed.). Hillsdale, NJ: Erlbaum.

Conant, S. (1987). The relationship between age and MLU in young children: A second look at Klee and Fitzgerald's data. *Journal of Child Language, 14,* 169–173. http://dx.doi.org/10.1017/S0305000900012794

Cook, V. (2008). Linguistic contributions to bilingualism. In J. Altarriba & R. R. Heredia (Eds.), *An introduction to bilingualism: Principles and processes* (pp. 245–264). New York, NY: Routledge.

Costa, A., Caramazza, A., & Sebastián-Gallés, N. (2000). The cognate facilitation effect: Implications for models of lexical access. *Journal of Experimental Psychology: Learning, Memory, and Cognition, 26,* 1283–1296. http://dx.doi.org/10.1037/0278-7393.26.5.1283

Costa, A., Miozzo, M., & Caramazza, A. (1999). Lexical selection in bilinguals: Do words in the bilingual's two lexicons compete for selection? *Journal of Memory and Language, 41,* 365–397. http://dx.doi.org/10.1006/jmla.1999.2651

Crain, S., & McKee, C. (1985). The acquisition of structural restrictions on anaphora. *Proceedings of NELS, 15,* 94–110.

Crain, S., & McKee, C. (1987, October). *Cross-linguistic analysis of the acquisition of coreference relation.* Paper presented at the Boston University Conference on Language Development, Boston, MA.

Crain, S., & Thornton, R. (2000). *Investigations in universal grammar.* Cambridge, MA: MIT Press.

Crain, S., & Wexler, K. (1999). Methodology in the study of language acquisition: A modular approach. In W. C. Ritchie & T. K. Bhatia (Eds.), *Handbook of child language acquisition* (pp. 387–425). San Diego, CA: Academic Press.

Crystal, D. (1987). *The Cambridge encyclopedia of language.* Cambridge, England: Cambridge University Press.

Curtiss, S. (1977). *Genie: A psycholinguistic study of a modern-day "wild child."* New York, NY: Academic Press.

Curtiss, S. (1989). The independence and task-specificity of language. In M. H. Bornstein & J. S. Bruner (Eds.), *Interaction in human development* (pp. 105–137). Hillsdale, NJ: Erlbaum.

Cutler, A., Mehler, J., Norris, D., & Segui, J. (1989, July 20). Limits on bilingualism. *Nature, 340,* 229–230. http://dx.doi.org/10.1038/340229a0

Cuza, A., & Frank, J. (2011). Transfer effects at the syntax-semantics interface: The case of double-que questions in Heritage Spanish. *Heritage Language Journal, 8,* 66–88.

Darwin, C. (1874). *The descent of man.* New York, NY: Heritage Press. (Original work published 1859)

de Groot, A. (2011). *Language and cognition in bilinguals and multilinguals.* New York, NY: Psychology Press.

de Haan, M. (Ed.). (2013). *Infant EEG and event-related potentials.* Hove, England: Psychology Press.

De Houwer, A. (1990). *The acquisition of two languages from birth: A case study.* Cambridge, England: Cambridge University Press. http://dx.doi.org/10.1017/CBO9780511519789

De Houwer, A. (2005). Early bilingual acquisition: Focus on morphosyntax and the separate development hypothesis. In J. Kroll & A. De Groot (Eds.), *The handbook of bilingualism: Psycholinguistic approaches* (pp. 30–48). New York, NY: Oxford University Press.

De Houwer, A. (2007). Parental language input patterns and children's bilingual use. *Applied Psycholinguistics, 28,* 411–424. http://dx.doi.org/10.1017/S0142716407070221

De Houwer, A., & Bornstein, M. (2003, April). *Balancing the tightrope: Language use patterns in bilingual families with young children.* Paper presented at the Fourth International Symposium on Bilingualism, Tempe, AZ.

Demuth, K. (1996). Collecting spontaneous production data. In D. McDaniel, C. McKee, & H. Smith Cairns (Eds.), *Methods for assessing children's syntax* (pp. 3–22). Cambridge, MA: MIT Press.

Demuth, K. (2007). Acquisition at the prosody–morphology interface. In A. Belikova, L. Meroni, & M. Umeda (Eds.), *Generative approaches to language acquisition North America* (pp. 84–91). Somerville, MA: Cascadilla Press.

Demuth, K., & Tremblay, A. (2008). Prosodically-conditioned variability in children's production of French determiners. *Journal of Child Language, 35,* 99–127. http://dx.doi.org/10.1017/S0305000907008276

Devescovi, A., Caselli, M. C., Marchione, D., Pasqualetti, P., Reilly, J., & Bates, E. (2005). A crosslinguistic study of the relationship between grammar and lexical development. *Journal of Child Language, 32,* 759–786. http://dx.doi.org/10.1017/S0305000905007105

de Villiers, J., & Roeper, T. (1996). Questions after stories: On supplying context and eliminating it as a variable. In D. McDaniel, C. McKee, & H. Smith (Eds.), *Methods for assessing children's syntax* (pp. 163–188). Cambridge, MA: MIT Press.

Dewart, H., & Summers, S. (1988). *The pragmatics profile of early communication skills.* Windsor, England: NFER Nelson.

Diggle, P. J., & Chetwynd, A. G. (2011). *Statistics and scientific method.* New York, NY: Oxford University Press. http://dx.doi.org/10.1093/acprof:oso/9780199543182.001.0001

Dromi, E., & Berman, R. A. (1982). A morphemic measure of early language development: Data from modern Hebrew. *Journal of Child Language, 9*, 403–424. http://dx.doi.org/10.1017/S0305000900004785

Duncan, G. J., Engel, M., Claessens, A., & Dowsett, C. J. (2014). Replication and robustness in developmental research. *Developmental Psychology, 50*, 2417–2425. http://dx.doi.org/10.1037/a0037996

Dunn, L., & Dunn, D. (2007). *Peabody Picture Vocabulary Test* (4th ed.). San Antonio, TX: Pearson Assessments.

Dussias, P. E., & Sagarra, N. (2007). The effect of exposure on syntactic parsing in Spanish–English bilinguals. *Bilingualism: Language and Cognition, 10*, 101–116. http://dx.doi.org/10.1017/S1366728906002847

Dye, C. D. (2011). Reduced auxiliaries in early child language: Converging observational and experimental evidence from French. *Journal of Linguistics, 47*, 301–339. http://dx.doi.org/10.1017/S002222671000037X

Dye, C. D., Foley, C. A., Blume, M., & Lust, B. C. (2004). *Mismatches between morphology and syntax in first language acquisition suggest a "syntax-first" model*. Retrieved from http://www.bu.edu/bucld/proceedings/supplement/vol28/

Edwards, J. (2006). Foundations of bilingualism. In T. K. Bhatia & W. C. Ritchie (Eds.), *The handbook of bilingualism* (pp. 7–31). Malden, MA: Blackwell. http://dx.doi.org/10.1002/9780470756997.ch1

Edwards, J. A. (1992a). Computer methods in child language research: Four principles for the use of archived data. *Journal of Child Language, 19*, 435–458. http://dx.doi.org/10.1017/S030500090001148X

Edwards, J. A. (1992b). Transcription of discourse. In W. Bright (Ed.), *International encyclopedia of linguistics* (pp. 367–371). New York, NY: Oxford University Press.

Edwards, J. A., & Lampert, M. (Eds.). (1993). *Talking data: Transcription and coding in discourse research*. Hillsdale, NJ: Erlbaum.

Egido, C. (1983). *The functional role of the closed class vocabulary in children's language processing* (Unpublished doctoral dissertation). MIT, Cambridge, MA.

Eisele, J. (1988). *Meaning and form in children's judgments about language* (Unpublished doctoral dissertation). Cornell University, Ithaca, NY.

Eisele, J., & Lust, B. C. (1996). Knowledge about pronouns: A developmental study using a truth value judgment task. *Child Development, 67*, 3086–3100. http://dx.doi.org/10.2307/1131768

Eisenberg, S. L., Fersko, T. M., & Lundgren, C. (2001). The use of MLU for identifying language impairment in preschool children: A review. *American Journal of Speech–Language Pathology, 10*, 323–342. http://dx.doi.org/10.1044/1058-0360(2001/028)

Fantz, R. L. (1958). Pattern vision in young infants. *The Psychological Record, 8*, 43–47.

Fantz, R. L. (1964). Visual experience in infants: Decreased attention to familiar patterns relative to novel ones. *Science, 146*, 668–670. http://dx.doi.org/10.1126/science.146.3644.668

Fennell, C. T. (2012). Habituation procedures. In E. Hoff (Ed.), *Research methods in child language: A practical guide* (pp. 1–16). Malden, MA: Wiley-Blackwell. http://dx.doi.org/10.1002/9781444344035.ch1

Fenson, L., Marchman, V. A., Thal, D. J., Dale, P. S., Reznick, J. S., & Bates, E. (2007). *MacArthur-Bates Communicative Development Inventories* (2nd ed.). Baltimore, MD: Paul H. Brookes.

Fernald, A., Swingley, D., & Pinto, J. P. (2001). When half a word is enough: Infants can recognize spoken words using partial phonetic information. *Child Development, 72*, 1003–1015. http://dx.doi.org/10.1111/1467-8624.00331

Fernald, A., Zangl, R., Portillo, A. L., & Marchman, V. A. (2008). Looking while listening: Using eye movements to monitor spoken language comprehension by infants and young children. In I. A. Sekerina, E. M. Fernandez, & H. Clahsen (Eds.), *Developmental psycholinguistics: On-line methods in children's language processing* (pp. 97–135). Amsterdam, Netherlands: John Benjamins. http://dx.doi.org/10.1075/lald.44.06fer

Feurer, H. (1980). Morphological development in Mohawk. *Papers and Reports on Child Language Development, 18*, 25–42.

Flege, J. E., MacKay, I. R. A., & Piske, T. (2002). Assessing bilingual dominance. *Applied Psycholinguistics, 23*, 567–598. http://dx.doi.org/10.1017/S0142716402004046

Flynn, S. (1986). Production vs. comprehension: Differences in underlying competencies. *Studies in Second Language Acquisition, 8*, 135–164. http://dx.doi.org/10.1017/S0272263100006057

Flynn, S. (1987). Contrast and construction in a parameter-setting model of L2 acquisition. *Language Learning, 37*, 19–62. http://dx.doi.org/10.1111/j.1467-1770.1968.tb01311.x

Flynn, S., & Lust, B. C. (1980). Acquisition of relative clauses: Developmental changes in their heads. *Cornell Working Papers in Linguistics, 1*, 33–45.

Foley, C. A., Núñez del Prado, Z., Barbier, I., & Lust, B. C. (1997). Operator-variable binding in the initial state: An argument from English VP ellipsis. *Cornell Working Papers in Linguistics, 15*, 1–19.

Foley, C. A., Núñez del Prado, Z., Barbier, I., & Lust, B. C. (2003). Knowledge of variable binding in VP-ellipsis: Language acquisition research and theory converge. *Syntax, 6*, 52–83. http://dx.doi.org/10.1111/1467-9612.00056

Friederici, A. D., & Thierry, G. (Eds.). (2008). *Early language development: Bridging brain and behaviour* (Vol. 5). Amsterdam, Netherlands: John Benjamins. http://dx.doi.org/10.1075/tilar.5.11fri

Fromkin, V. (Ed.). (2000). *Linguistics*. Boston, MA: Blackwell.

Garrett, M. F. (1981). Objects of psycholinguistic enquiry. *Cognition, 10*, 97–101. http://dx.doi.org/10.1016/0010-0277(81)90031-7

Garrett, M. F., & Sherman, J. C. (1989, January). *Molecular performance systems in normal and aphasic language*. Paper presented at the meeting of the American Association for the Advancement of Science, San Francisco, CA.

Gerken, L. (1991). The metrical basis for children's subjectless sentences. *Journal of Memory and Language, 30*, 431–451. http://dx.doi.org/10.1016/0749-596X(91)90015-C

Gerken, L., Landau, B., & Remez, R. (1990). Function morphemes in young children's speech perception and production. *Developmental Psychology, 26*, 204–216. http://dx.doi.org/10.1037/0012-1649.26.2.204

Gewin, V. (2015, July 8). Collaborations: Recipe for a team. *Nature, 523*, 245–247. http://dx.doi.org/10.1038/nj7559-245a

Gleason, J. B., & Ratner, N. B. (Eds.). (2012). *The development of language* (8th ed.). Boston, MA: Pearson/Allyn & Bacon.

Gleitman, H., Fridlund, A., & Reisberg, D. (2000). *Basic psychology*. New York, NY: Norton.

Gleitman, L., & Gleitman, H. (1970). *Phrase and paraphrase: Some innovative uses of language*. New York, NY: Norton.

Gleitman, L., & Gleitman, H. (1979). Language use and language judgment. In C. Fillmore, D. Kemler, & W. Wang (Eds.), *Individual Differences in Language Ability and Language Behavior* (pp. 103–126). New York, NY: Academic Press.

Golinkoff, R. M., Hirsh-Pasek, K., Cauley, K. M., & Gordon, L. (1987). The eyes have it: Lexical and syntactic comprehension in a new paradigm. *Journal of Child Language, 14*, 23–45. http://dx.doi.org/10.1017/S030500090001271X

Golinkoff, R. M., Ma, W., Song, L., & Hirsh-Pasek, K. (2013). Twenty-five years using the intermodal preferential looking paradigm to study language acquisition: What have we learned? *Perspectives on Psychological Science, 8*, 316–339. http://dx.doi.org/10.1177/1745691613484936

Gollan, T. H., Forster, K. I., & Frost, R. (1997). Translation priming with different scripts: Masked priming with cognates and noncognates in Hebrew–English bilinguals. *Journal of Experimental Psychology: Learning, Memory, and Cognition, 23*, 1122–1139. http://dx.doi.org/10.1037/0278-7393.23.5.1122

Goodluck, H. (1987). Children's interpretations of pronouns and null NPs: An alternative view. In B. C. Lust (Ed.), *Studies in the acquisition of anaphora: Vol. 11. Applying the constraints* (pp. 247–270). Boston, MA: Reidel.

Goodluck, H. (1996). The act out task. In D. McDaniel, C. McKee, & H. Cairns (Eds.), *Methods for assessing children's syntax* (pp. 147–162). Cambridge, MA: MIT Press.

Goodluck, H., & Solan, L. (1995). Principle C and c-command in children's grammar: A replication. *Cahiers Linguistiques d'Ottawa, 23*, 43–52.

Gordon, P. (1996). The truth-value judgment task. In D. McDaniel, C. McKee, & H. Smith Cairns (Eds.), *Methods for assessing children's syntax* (pp. 211–230). Cambridge, MA: MIT Press.

Grenoble, L. A., & Furbee, N. L. (Eds.). (2010). *Language documentation: Practice and values.* Philadelphia, PA: John Benjamins. http://dx.doi.org/10.1075/z.158

Grimshaw, G. M., Adelstein, A., Bryden, M. P., & MacKinnon, G. E. (1998). First-language acquisition in adolescence: Evidence for a critical period for verbal language development. *Brain and Language, 63*, 237–255. http://dx.doi.org/10.1006/brln.1997.1943

Grosjean, F. (1989). Neurolinguists, beware! The bilingual is not two monolinguals in one person. *Brain and Language, 36*, 3–15. http://dx.doi.org/10.1016/0093-934X(89)90048-5

Grosjean, F. (1999). The bilingual's language modes. In J. L. Nicol (Ed.), *One mind, two languages: Bilingual language processing* (pp. 1–25). Oxford, England: Blackwell.

Grosjean, F. (2006). Studying bilinguals: Methodological and conceptual issues. In T. K. Bhatia & W. C. Ritchie (Eds.), *The handbook of bilingualism* (pp. 32–63). Malden, MA: Blackwell. http://dx.doi.org/10.1002/9780470756997.ch2

Grosjean, F. (2008). *Studying bilinguals.* Oxford, England: Oxford University Press.

Guo, F., Foley, C. A., Chien, Y., Chiang, C.-P., & Lust, B. C. (1997). A cross-linguistic study of Chinese and English children's first language acquisition of VP ellipsis structures. In S. Somashekar, K. Yamakoshi, M. Blume, & C. A. Foley (Eds.), *Cornell Working Papers in Linguistics: Papers on Language Acquisition* (Vol. 15, pp. 160–176). Ithaca, NY: Cornell Linguistics Circle, Cornell University, Department of Linguistics.

Guo, F., Foley, C. A., Chien, Y., Lust, B. C., & Chiang, C. (1996). Operator variable binding in the initial state: A cross linguistic study of VP ellipsis structures in Chinese & English. *Cahiers de Linguistique Asie Orientale, 25*, 3–34.

Guo, G., & Zhao, H. (2000). Multilevel modeling for binary data. *Annual Review of Sociology, 26*, 441–462. http://dx.doi.org/10.1146/annurev.soc.26.1.441

Gutiérrez-Clellen, V., Restrepo, M. A., Bedore, L., Peña, E., & Anderson, R. (2000). Language sample analysis in Spanish-speaking children: Methodological considerations. *Language, Speech, and Hearing Services in Schools, 31*, 88–98. http://dx.doi.org/10.1044/0161-1461.3101.88

Haegeman, L., & Guéron, J. (1999). *English grammar: A generative perspective.* Malden, MA: Blackwell.

Hakuta, K. (1986). *Mirror of language: The debate on bilingualism*. New York, NY: Basic Books.

Hale, J. T. (2014). *Automaton theories of human sentence comprehension*. Chicago, IL: University of Chicago Press.

Hamburger, H., & Crain, S. (1982). Relative acquisition. In S. A. Kuczaj, II (Ed.), *Syntax and semantics: Vol. I. Language development* (pp. 245–274). Hillsdale, NJ: Erlbaum.

Harris, Z., & Voegelin, C. F. (1953). Eliciting in linguistics. *Southwest Journal of Anthropology, 9*, 59–75.

Hernández-Chávez, E., Burt, M., & Dulay, H. (1978). Language dominance and proficiency testing: Some general considerations. *NABE Journal, 1*, 41–54.

Herrera, M. O., & Pandolfi, A. M. (1984). El índice PLE como criterio para analizar el lenguaje infantil [The MLU index as a criterion to analyze child language]. *Revista de Lingüística Teórica y Aplicada, 22*, 65–75.

Hickey, T. (1991). Mean length of utterance and the acquisition of Irish. *Journal of Child Language, 18*, 553–569. http://dx.doi.org/10.1017/S0305000900011247

Hirsh-Pasek, K., & Golinkoff, R. (1996). The intermodal preferential looking paradigm reveals emergent language comprehension. In D. McDaniel, C. McKee, & H. Smith Cairns (Eds.), *Methods for assessing children's syntax* (pp. 105–124). Cambridge, MA: MIT Press.

Hockett, C. F. (1997). Approaches to syntax. *Lingua, 100*, 151–170. http://dx.doi.org/10.1016/S0024-3841(96)00041-1

Hoff, E. (Ed.). (2012). *Research methods in child language: A practical guide*. Malden, MA: Wiley-Blackwell.

Hoff, E., Core, C., Place, S., Rumiche, R., Señor, M., & Parra, M. (2012). Dual language exposure and early bilingual development. *Journal of Child Language, 39*, 1–27. http://dx.doi.org/10.1017/S0305000910000759

Hoff, E., & Rumiche, R. L. (2012). Studying children in bilingual environments. In E. Hoff (Ed.), *Research methods in child language: A practical guide* (pp. 300–316). Malden, MA: Wiley-Blackwell. http://dx.doi.org/10.1002/9781444344035.ch20

Holland, A. L., Boller, F., & Bourgeois, M. (1986). Repetition in Alzheimer's disease: A longitudinal study. *Journal of Neurolinguistics, 2*, 163–176. http://dx.doi.org/10.1016/S0911-6044(86)80010-0

Hollich, G., Rocroi, C., Hirsh-Pasek, K., & Golinkoff, R. (1999, April). *Testing language comprehension in infants: Introducing the split-screen preferential looking paradigm*. Poster presented at the meeting of the Society for Research in Child Development, Albuquerque, NM.

Horn, L., & Ward, G. (Eds.). (2006). *The handbook of pragmatics*. Malden, MA: Blackwell. http://dx.doi.org/10.1002/9780470756959

Huerta-Macías, A. (1981). Code-switching: All in the family. In R. P. Durán (Ed.), *Latino language and communicative behavior* (pp. 153–160). Norwood, NJ: Ablex.

Hulk, A., & Müller, N. (2000). Bilingual first language acquisition at the interface between syntax and pragmatics. *Bilingualism: Language and Cognition, 3*, 227–244. http://dx.doi.org/10.1017/S1366728900000353

Human Subject Research. (n.d.). In *Wikipedia*. Retrieved August 3, 2016 from https://en.wikipedia.org/wiki/Human_subject_research

Hume, D. (2000). *A treatise of human nature*. New York, NY: Oxford University Press. (Original work published 1739)

Hymes, D. H. (1967). Models of the interaction of language and social setting. *Journal of Social Issues, 23*, 8–38. http://dx.doi.org/10.1111/j.1540-4560.1967.tb00572.x

Hymes, D. H. (1972). On communicative competence. In J. B. Pride & J. Holmes (Eds.), *Sociolinguistics: Selected readings* (pp. 269–293). Harmondsworth, England: Penguin.

International Phonetics Association. (1999). *Handbook of the International Phonetic Association*. Cambridge, England: Cambridge University Press.

Isurin, L. (2000). Deserted islands or a child's first language forgetting. *Bilingualism: Language and Cognition, 3*, 151–166. http://dx.doi.org/10.1017/S1366728900000237

Itard, J. M. G. (1962). *The wild boy of Aveyron* (G. Humphrey & M. Humphrey, Trans.). New York, NY: Appleton-Century-Crofts.

Jennings, H. S. (1906). *Behavior of the lower organisms*. New York, NY: Columbia University Press.

Johnson, E. K., & Zamuner, T. S. (2010). Using infant and toddler testing methods in language acquisition research. In E. Blom & S. Unsworth (Eds.), *Experimental methods in language acquisition research* (pp. 73–94). Amsterdam, Netherlands: John Benjamins. http://dx.doi.org/10.1075/lllt.27.06joh

Johnson, J. S., & Newport, E. L. (1989). Critical period effects in second language learning: The influence of maturational state on the acquisition of English as a second language. *Cognitive Psychology, 21*, 60–99. http://dx.doi.org/10.1016/0010-0285(89)90003-0

Joos, M. (1950). Description of language design. *Journal of the Acoustical Society of America, 22*, 701–707. http://dx.doi.org/10.1121/1.1906674

Jusczyk, P. W. (1997). *The discovery of spoken language*. Cambridge, MA: MIT Press.

Kandel, E. R., & Schwartz, J. H. (1982). Molecular biology of learning: Modulation of transmitter release. *Science, 218*, 433–443. http://dx.doi.org/10.1126/science.6289442

Kedar, Y., Casasola, M., & Lust, B. (2006). Getting there faster: 18- and 24-month-old infants' use of function words to determine reference. *Child Development, 77*, 325–338. http://dx.doi.org/10.1111/j.1467-8624.2006.00873.x

Kim, A., Park, A., & Lust, B. (2016). Simultaneous vs. successive bilingualism among preschool-aged children: A study of four-year-old Korean–English bilinguals in the U.S.A. *International Journal of Bilingual Education and Bilingualism*. http://dx.doi.org/10.1080/13670050.2016.1145186

Klee, T., & Fitzgerald, M. D. (1985). The relation between grammatical development and mean length of utterance in morphemes. *Journal of Child Language, 12*, 251–269. http://dx.doi.org/10.1017/S0305000900006437

Kuhl, P., & Rivera-Gaxiola, M. (2008). Neural substrates of language acquisition. *Annual Review of Neuroscience, 31*, 511–534. http://dx.doi.org/10.1146/annurev.neuro.30.051606.094321

Kunnari, S. (2002). Word length in syllables: Evidence from early word production in Finnish. *First Language, 22*, 119–135.

Labov, W., & Labov, T. (1978). Learning the syntax of questions. In R. N. Campbell & P. T. Smith (Eds.), *Recent advances in the psychology of language: Formal and experimental approaches* (pp. 1–44). New York, NY: Plenum Press. http://dx.doi.org/10.1007/978-1-4684-2532-1_1

Ladefoged, P. (1993). *A course in phonetics*. London, England: Harcourt Brace.

Ladefoged, P., & Johnson, K. (2014). *A course in phonetics* (7th ed). Stamford, CT: Cengage.

Lakshmanan, U. (2009). Child second language acquisition. In W. C. Ritchie & T. K. Bhatia (Eds.), *The new handbook of second language acquisition* (pp. 377–399). Sheffield, England: Emerald.

Lanza, E. (1988). Language strategies in the home: Linguistic input and infant bilingualism. In A. Holmes, E. Hansen, J. Gimbel, & J. N. Jørgensen (Eds.), *Bilingualism and the individual* (pp. 69–84). Clevendon, England: Multilingual Matters.

Lasnik, H., & Crain, S. (1985). On the acquisition of pronominal reference. Review of L. Solan, "Pronominal reference: Child language and the theory of grammar." *Lingua, 65*, 135–154. http://dx.doi.org/10.1016/0024-3841(85)90024-5

Lawler, J., & Dry, H. A. (Eds.). (1998). *Using computers in linguistics: A practical guide*. New York, NY: Routledge.

Ledford, H. (2008). Collaborations: With all good intentions. *Nature, 452*, 682–684. http://dx.doi.org/10.1038/452682a

Leek, J. T., & Peng, R. D. (2015). Statistics: P values are just the tip of the iceberg. *Nature, 520*, 612. http://dx.doi.org/10.1038/520612a

Leonard, L. (1998). *Children with specific language impairment*. Cambridge, MA: MIT Press.

Leopold, W. F. (1970). *Speech development of a bilingual child: A linguist's record*. New York, NY: AMS Press.

Li, P., Sepanski, S., & Zhao, X. (2006). Language History Questionnaire: A Web-based interface for bilingual research. *Behavior Research Methods, 38*, 202–210. http://dx.doi.org/10.3758/BF03192770

Loebell, H., & Bock, K. (2003). Structural priming across languages. *Linguistics, 41*, 791–824. http://dx.doi.org/10.1515/ling.2003.026

Luk, G., & Bialystok, E. (2013). Bilingualism is not a categorical variable: Interaction between language proficiency and usage. *Journal of Cognitive Psychology, 25*, 605–621. http://dx.doi.org/10.1080/20445911.2013.795574

Lust, B. C. (1977). Conjunction reduction in child language. *Journal of Child Language, 4*, 257–287. http://dx.doi.org/10.1017/S0305000900001653

Lust, B. C. (1981). Coordinating studies of coordination: A reply to Ardery. *Journal of Child Language, 8*, 457–470. http://dx.doi.org/10.1017/S0305000900003299

Lust, B. C. (Ed.). (1986). *Studies in the acquisition of anaphora: Vol. 1. Defining the constraints*. Dordrecht, Netherlands: Reidel.

Lust, B. C. (Ed.). (1987). *Studies in the acquisition of anaphora: Vol. 2. Applying the constraints*. Dordrecht, Netherlands: Reidel.

Lust, B. C. (1999). Universal Grammar: The strong continuity hypothesis in first language acquisition. In W. C. Ritchie & T. K. Bhatia (Eds.), *Handbook of child language acquisition* (pp. 111–156). New York, NY: Academic Press.

Lust, B. C. (2006). *Child language: Acquisition and growth*. Cambridge, England: Cambridge University Press. http://dx.doi.org/10.1017/CBO9780511803413

Lust, B. C., Chien, Y., & Flynn, S. (1987). What children know: Comparisons of experimental methods for study of first language acquisition. In B. C. Lust (Ed.), *Studies in the acquisition of anaphora: Vol. 2. Applying the constraints* (pp. 271–356). Dordrecht, Netherlands: Reidel.

Lust, B. C., & Clifford, T. (1986). The 3-D study: Effects of depth, distance and directionality on children's acquisition of anaphora. In B. C. Lust (Ed.), *Studies in the acquisition of anaphora: Vol. I. Defining the constraints* (pp. 203–244). Dordrecht, Netherlands: Reidel.

Lust, B. C., Eisele, J., & Mazuka, R. (1992). The binding theory module: Evidence from first language acquisition for Principle C. *Language, 68*, 333–358. http://dx.doi.org/10.2307/416944

Lust, B. C., Flynn, S., Blume, M., Park, S. W., Kang, C., Yang, S., & Kim, A.-Y. (2014). Assessing child bilingualism: Direct assessment of bilingual syntax amends caretaker report. *The International Journal of Bilingualism, 20*, 153–172. http://dx.doi.org/10.1177/1367006914547661

Lust, B. C., Flynn, S., Blume, M., Westbrooks, E., & Tobin, T. (2010). Constructing adequate language documentation for multifaceted cross-linguistic data: A case study from a virtual center for study of language acquisition. In L. A. Grenoble & N. L. Furbee (Eds.), *Language documentation: Practice and values* (pp. 127–152). Philadelphia, PA: John Benjamins. http://dx.doi.org/10.1075/z.158.11lus

Lust, B. C., Flynn, S., & Foley, C. A. (1996). What children know about what they say. In D. McDaniel, C. McKee, & H. Smith-Cairns (Eds.), *Methods for assessing children's syntax* (pp. 55–76). Cambridge, MA: MIT Press.

Lust, B. C., Flynn, S., Foley, C. A., & Chien, Y. (1999). How do we know what children know? Establishing scientific methods for the study of first language acquisition. In W. C. Ritchie & T. K. Bhatia (Eds.), *Handbook of child language acquisition* (pp. 427–456). San Diego, CA: Academic Press.

Lust, B. C., Hermon, G., & Kornfilt, J. (1994). *Syntactic theory and first language acquisition: Cross-linguistic perspectives: Vol. 2. Binding, dependencies, and learnability.* New York, NY: Psychology Press.

Lust, B. C., Solan, L., Flynn, S., Cross, C., & Schuetz, E. (1986). Acquisition of null and pronominal anaphora in English by L1 learners. In B. C. Lust (Ed.), *Studies in the acquisition of anaphora: Vol. 1. Defining the constraints* (pp. 245–277). Dordrecht, Netherlands: Reidel.

Lust, B. C., Suñer, M., & Whitman, J. (1994). *Syntactic theory and first language acquisition: Cross-linguistic perspectives: Vol. 1. Heads, projections, and learnability.* New York, NY: Psychology Press.

MacWhinney, B. (1991). *The CHILDES Project: Tools for Analyzing Talk.* Hillsdale, NJ: Erlbaum.

MacWhinney, B. (1999). The CHILDES System. In T. K. Bhatia & W. C. Ritchie (Eds.), *Handbook of child language acquisition* (pp. 457–491). San Diego, CA: Academic Press.

MacWhinney, B., & Snow, C. (1990). The Child Language Data Exchange System: An update. *Journal of Child Language, 17,* 457–472. http://dx.doi.org/10.1017/S0305000900013866

Mandel, D. R., Jusczyk, P. W., & Pisoni, D. B. (1995). Infants' recognition of the sound patterns of their own names. *Psychological Science, 6,* 315–318. http://dx.doi.org/10.1111/j.1467-9280.1995.tb00517.x

Marchman, V. A., & Fernald, A. (2008). Speed of word recognition and vocabulary knowledge in infancy predict cognitive and language outcomes in later childhood. *Developmental Science, 11,* F9–F16. http://dx.doi.org/10.1111/j.1467-7687.2008.00671.x

Marcus, G., & Davis, E. (2014, April 7). Eight (no, nine!) problems with big data. *The New York Times.* Retrieved from http://www.nytimes.com/2014/04/07/opinion/eight-no-nine-problems-with-big-data.html

Marcus, M. P., Santorini, B., & Marcinkiewicz, M. A. (n.d.). *Building a large annotated corpus of English: The Penn Treebank.* Retrieved from https://catalog.ldc.upenn.edu/docs/LDC95T7/cl93.html

Marian, V., Blumenfeld, H. K., & Kaushanskaya, M. (2007). The Language Experience and Proficiency Questionnaire (LEAP-Q): Assessing language profiles in bilinguals and multilinguals. *Journal of Speech, Language, and Hearing Research, 50,* 940–967. http://dx.doi.org/10.1044/1092-4388(2007/067)

Marian, V., & Spivey, M. (2003). Competing activation in bilingual language processing: Within- and between-language competition. *Bilingualism: Language and Cognition, 6,* 97–115. http://dx.doi.org/10.1017/S1366728903001068

Matthews, P. H. (1997). *The concise Oxford dictionary of linguistics.* Oxford, England: Oxford University Press.

Maxwell, S. E., & Delaney, H. D. (2004). *Designing experiments and analyzing data: A model comparison perspective* (Vol. 1). Mahwah, NJ: Erlbaum.

Mayer, M., & Mayer, M. (1975). *One frog too many.* New York, NY: Penguin.

McDaniel, D., McKee, C., & Smith Cairns, H. (Eds.). (1996). *Methods for assessing children's syntax.* Cambridge, MA: MIT Press.

McDaniel, D., & Smith Cairns, H. (1996). Eliciting judgment of grammaticality and reference. In D. McDaniel, C. McKee, & H. Smith Cairns (Eds.), *Methods for assessing children's syntax* (pp. 233–254). Cambridge, MA: MIT Press.

Mechelli, A., Crinion, J. T., Noppeney, U., O'Doherty, J., Ashburner, J., Frackowiak, R. S., & Price, C. J. (2004). Neurolinguistics: Structural plasticity in the bilingual brain. *Nature, 431*, 757. http://dx.doi.org/10.1038/431757a

Meisel, J. M. (1986). Word order and case marking in early child language. Evidence from simultaneous acquisition of two first languages: French and German. *Linguistics, 24*, 123–183. http://dx.doi.org/10.1515/ling.1986.24.1.123

Menn, L., & Ratner, N. B. (Eds.). (2000). *Methods for studying language production*. Mahwah, NJ: Erlbaum.

Molfese, D. L., & Molfese, V. J. (1985). Electrophysiological indices of auditory discrimination in newborn infants: The bases for predicting later language development? *Infant Behavior & Development, 8*, 197–211. http://dx.doi.org/10.1016/S0163-6383(85)80006-0

Montrul, S. (2002). Incomplete acquisition and attrition of Spanish tense/aspect distinctions in adult bilinguals. *Bilingualism: Language and Cognition, 5*, 39–68. http://dx.doi.org/10.1017/S1366728902000135

Montrul, S. (2004). Subject and object expression in Spanish heritage speakers: A case of morpho-syntactic convergence. *Bilingualism: Language and Cognition, 7*, 125–142. http://dx.doi.org/10.1017/S1366728904001464

Montrul, S. (2008). *Incomplete acquisition in bilingualism: Re-examining the age factor*. Amsterdam, Netherlands: John Benjamins. http://dx.doi.org/10.1075/sibil.39

Montrul, S. (2009). Knowledge of tense-aspect and mood in Spanish heritage speakers. *The International Journal of Bilingualism, 13*, 239–269. http://dx.doi.org/10.1177/1367006909339816

Moskowitz, L. (2000). *Summary of my research experience for HD 401 and my teaching experience for HD 403*. Unpublished manuscript, Department of Human Development, Cornell University, Ithaca, NY.

Müller, N., & Hulk, A. (2001). Cross-linguistic influence in bilingual language acquisition: Italian and French as recipient languages. *Bilingualism: Language and Cognition, 4*, 1–21. http://dx.doi.org/10.1017/S1366728901000116

Nazzi, T., Jusczyk, P. W., & Johnson, E. K. (2000). Language discrimination by English-learning 5-month-olds: Effects of rhythm and familiarity. *Journal of Memory & Language, 43*, 1–19. http://dx.doi.org/10.1006/jmla.2000.2698

Nazzi, T., Paterson, S., & Karmiloff-Smith, A. (2003). Early word segmentation by infants and toddlers with Williams syndrome. *Infancy, 4*, 251–271. http://dx.doi.org/10.1207/S15327078IN0402_06

Newport, E. (1990). Maturational constraints in language learning. *Cognitive Science, 14*, 11–28. http://dx.doi.org/10.1207/s15516709cog1401_2

Nicoladis, E. (2006). Cross-linguistic transfer in adjective–noun strings by preschool bilingual children. *Bilingualism: Language and Cognition, 9*, 15–32. http://dx.doi.org/10.1017/S136672890500235X

Nicoladis, E., & Grabois, H. (2002). Learning English and losing Chinese: A case study of a child adopted from China. *The International Journal of Bilingualism, 6*, 441–454. http://dx.doi.org/10.1177/13670069020060040401

O'Grady, W., & Archibald, J. (2009). *Contemporary linguistics* (6th ed.). New York, NY: Bedford/St. Martin's.

Open Science Collaboration. (2012). An open, large-scale, collaborative effort to estimate the reproducibility of psychological science. *Perspectives on Psychological Science, 7*, 657–660. http://dx.doi.org/10.1177/1745691612462588

Open Science Collaboration. (in press). Maximizing the reproducibility of your research. In S. O. Lilienfeld & I. D. Waldman (Eds.), *Psychological science under scrutiny: Recent challenges and proposed solutions*. New York, NY: Wiley.

Orfitelli, R., & Hyams, N. (2012). Children's grammar of null subjects: Evidence from Comprehension. *Linguistic Inquiry, 43*, 563–590. http://dx.doi.org/10.1162/ling_a_00106

Osgood, C. E., & Sebeok, T. A. (1965). *Psycholinguistics. A survey of theory and research problems*. Bloomington: Indiana University Press.

Papandropoulou, I., & Sinclair, H. (1974). What is a word? Experimental study of children's ideas on grammar. *Human Development, 17*, 241–258.

Paradis, J., & Genesee, F. (1996). Syntactic acquisition in bilingual children: Autonomous or interdependent? *Studies in Second Language Acquisition, 18*, 1–25. http://dx.doi.org/10.1017/S0272263100014662

Paradis, J., & Navarro, S. (2003). Subject realization and crosslinguistic interference in the bilingual acquisition of Spanish and English: What is the role of the input? *Journal of Child Language, 30*, 371–393. http://dx.doi.org/10.1017/S0305000903005609

Pareja-Lora, A., Blume, M., & Lust, B. C. (2013). Transforming the Data Transcription and Analysis Tool metadata and labels into a linguistic linked open data cloud resource. In C. Chiarcos, P. Cimiano, T. Declerck, & J. P. McCrae (Eds.), *2nd Workshop on linked data in linguistics representing and linking lexicons, terminologies and other language data* (pp. 34–43). Retrieved from http://anthology.aclweb.org//W/W13/W13-55.pdf

Pareja-Lora, A., Blume, M., & Lust, B. C. (2016). *Development of linguistic linked open data resources for collaborative data-intensive research in the language sciences*. Manuscript submitted for publication.

Pearson, B. Z., Fernández, S., & Oller, D. K. (1995). Cross-language synonyms in the lexicons of bilingual infants: One language or two? *Journal of Child Language, 22*, 345–368. http://dx.doi.org/10.1017/S030500090000982X

Pearson, B. Z., Fernández, S. C., Lewedeg, V., & Oller, D. K. (1997). The relation of input factors to lexical learning by bilingual infants (ages 10 to 30 months). *Applied Psycholinguistics, 18*, 41–58. http://dx.doi.org/10.1017/S0142716400009863

Pease-Álvarez, L., Hakuta, K., & Bayley, R. (1996). Spanish proficiency and language use in California's Mexicano community. *Southwest Journal of Linguistics, 15*, 137–151.

Perani, D., Saccuman, M. C., Scifo, P., Anwander, A., Spada, D., Baldoli, C., . . . Friederici, A. D. (2011). Neural language networks at birth. *Proceedings of the National Academy of Sciences of the United States of America, 108*, 16056–16061. http://dx.doi.org/10.1073/pnas.1102991108

Peters, A. (1997). Language typology, prosody and the acquisition of grammatical morphemes. In D. Slobin (Ed.), *The crosslinguistic study of language acquisition* (Vol. 5, pp. 136–197). Hillsdale, NJ: Erlbaum.

Piaget, J. (1968). *Le structuralisme*. Paris, France: Presses universitaires de France.

Pine, J. M., & Martindale, H. (1996). Syntactic categories in the speech of young children: The case of the determiner. *Journal of Child Language, 23*, 369–395. http://dx.doi.org/10.1017/S0305000900008849

Pinhas, J., & Lust, B. C. (1987). Principles of pronoun anaphora in the acquisition of oral language by the hearing impaired. In B. C. Lust (Ed.), *Studies in the acquisition of anaphora: Vol. 2. Applying the constraints* (pp. 189–224). Dordrecht, Netherlands: Reidel.

Poldrack, R. A., & Poline, J.-B. (2015). The publication and reproducibility challenges of shared data. *Trends in Cognitive Sciences, 19*, 59–61. http://dx.doi.org/10.1016/j.tics.2014.11.008

Polinsky, M. (2006). Incomplete acquisition: American Russian. *Journal of Slavic Linguistics, 14*, 191–262.

Polinsky, M. (2007). Reaching the end point and stopping midway: Different scenarios in the acquisition of Russian. *Russian Linguistics, 31*, 157–199. http://dx.doi.org/10.1007/s11185-007-9011-2

Polinsky, M. (2011). Reanalysis in adult heritage language. *Studies in Second Language Acquisition, 33*, 305–328. http://dx.doi.org/10.1017/S027226311000077X

Popper, K. (1934). *The logic of scientific discovery*. London, England: Hutchinson.

Posner, M. I., & Raichle, M. E. (1994). *Images of mind*. New York, NY: Scientific American Books.

Potts, M., Carlson, P., Cocking, R., & Copple, C. (1979). *Structure and development in child language*. Ithaca, NY: Cornell University Press.

Pouscoulous, N., Noveck, I., Politzer, G., & Bastide, A. (2007). A developmental investigation of processing costs in implicature production. *Language Acquisition, 14*, 347–375. http://dx.doi.org/10.1080/10489220701600457

Putnam, M., & Sánchez, L. (2013). What's so incomplete about incomplete acquisition? A prolegomenon to modeling heritage language grammars. *Linguistic Approaches to Bilingualism, 3*, 476–506. http://dx.doi.org/10.1075/lab.3.4.04put

Pye, C. (2009). *Minimal coding page*. Retrieved from http://pyersqr.org/minimal

Pye, C., Pfeiler, B., & Pedro, P. M. (2013). The acquisition of extended ergativity in Mam, Q'anjob'al and Yucatec. In E. Bavin & S. Stoll (Eds.), *The acquisition of ergativity* (pp. 307–336). Philadelphia, PA: John Benjamins. http://dx.doi.org/10.1075/tilar.9.11pye

Quay, S. (2008). Dinner conversations with a trilingual two-year-old: Language socialization in a multilingual context. *First Language, 28*, 5–33. http://dx.doi.org/10.1177/0142723707083557

Quené, H., & van den Bergh, H. (2004). On multi-level modeling of data from repeated measures designs: A tutorial. *Speech Communication, 43*, 103–121. http://dx.doi.org/10.1016/j.specom.2004.02.004

Quené, H., & van den Bergh, H. (2008). Examples of mixed-effects modeling with crossed random effects and with binomial data. *Journal of Memory and Language, 59*, 413–425. http://dx.doi.org/10.1016/j.jml.2008.02.002

Quirk, R. (1992). On corpus principles and design. In J. Svartvik (Ed.), *Directions in corpus linguistics. Proceedings of Nobel Symposium 82 Stockholm, 4–8 August 1991* (pp. 457–470). Berlin, Germany: Mouton de Gruyter.

Raaijmakers, J. G. (2003). A further look at the "language-as-fixed-effect fallacy." *Canadian Journal of Experimental Psychology/Revue Canadienne de Psychologie Expérimentale, 57*, 141.

Raaijmakers, J. G., Schrijnemakers, J., & Gremmen, F. (1999). How to deal with "the language-as-fixed-effect fallacy": Common misconceptions and alternative solutions. *Journal of Memory and Language, 41*, 416–426. http://dx.doi.org/10.1006/jmla.1999.2650

Ramón y Cajal, S. (1916). *Reglas y consejos sobre investigación científica: Los tónicos de la voluntad* (4th ed.). Madrid, Spain: Fortanet.

Ramón y Cajal, S. (1999). *Advice to a young investigator*. (N. Swanson & L. W. Swanson, Trans.). Cambridge, MA: MIT Press.

Rice, K. (2011). *Fieldwork*. Retrieved from Oxford Bibliographies website: http://dx.doi.org/10.1093/obo/9780199772810-0015

Riches, N. G., Loucas, T., Baird, G., Charman, T., & Simonoff, E. (2010). Sentence repetition in adolescents with specific language impairments and autism: An investigation of complex syntax. *International Journal of Language & Communication Disorders, 45*, 47–60. http://dx.doi.org/10.3109/13682820802647676

Rieger, O., & Long, E. (2015, July). *Addressing sustainability issues: University library role*. Paper presented at The Linguistic Society of America Summer Institute, Chicago, IL. Retrieved from http://quijote.fdi.ucm.es:8084/LLOD-LSASummerWorkshop2015/Program.html

Rizzi, L. (1993). Some notes on linguistic theory and language development: The case of root infinitives. *Language Acquisition, 3*, 371–393. http://dx.doi.org/10.1207/s15327817la0304_2

Rollins, P., Snow, C. E., & Willett, J. (1996). Predictors of MLU: Semantic and morphological development. *First Language, 16*, 243–259. http://dx.doi.org/10.1177/014272379601604705

Ronjat, J. (1913). *Le développement du langage observé chez un enfant bilingue* [The development of language as observed in the bilingual child]. Paris, France: Champion.

Rosenthal, J. (2002, August 18). Corpus linguistics. *The New York Times*. Retrieved from http://www.nytimes.com/2002/08/18/magazine/18ONLANGUAGE.html

Saddy, D. (1992). Islands in an aphasic individual. In H. Goodluck & M. Rochemont (Eds.), *Island constraints: Theory, acquisition and processing* (pp. 399–417). Dordrecht, Netherlands: Kluwer. http://dx.doi.org/10.1007/978-94-017-1980-3_15

Sadock, J. (2006). Speech acts. In L. R. Horn & G. Ward (Eds.), *The handbook of pragmatics* (pp. 53–73). Malden, MA: Blackwell. http://dx.doi.org/10.1002/9780470756959.ch3

Saffran, J. R., Aslin, R. N., & Newport, E. L. (1996). Statistical learning by 8-month-old infants. *Science, 274*, 1926–1928. http://dx.doi.org/10.1126/science.274.5294.1926

Sánchez, L. (2004). Functional convergence in the tense, evidentiality and aspectual systems of Quechua–Spanish bilinguals. *Bilingualism: Language and Cognition, 7*, 147–162. http://dx.doi.org/10.1017/S136672890400149X

Sánchez, L. (2006). Bilingualism/second-language research and the assessment of oral proficiency in minority bilingual children. *Language Assessment Quarterly, 3*, 117–149. http://dx.doi.org/10.1207/s15434311laq0302_3

Santelmann, L., Berk, S., Austin, J., Somashekar, S., & Lust, B. (2002). Continuity and development in the acquisition of inversion in yes/no questions: Dissociating movement and inflection. *Child Language, 29*, 813–842. http://dx.doi.org/10.1017/S0305000902005299

Santelmann, L., & Jusczyk, P. W. (1998). Sensitivity to discontinuous dependencies in language learners: Evidence for limitations in processing space. *Cognition, 69*, 105–134. http://dx.doi.org/10.1016/S0010-0277(98)00060-2

Scarborough, H., Rescorla, L., Tager Flusberg, H., Fowler, A., & Sudhalter, V. (1991). The relation of utterance length to grammatical complexity in normal and language-disordered groups. *Applied Psycholinguistics, 12*, 23–45. http://dx.doi.org/10.1017/S014271640000936X

Scholz, R. W., & Tietje, O. (2002). *Embedded case study methods*. Los Angeles, CA: Sage.

Schooler, J. W. (2014). Metascience could rescue the "replication crisis." *Nature, 515*, 9. http://dx.doi.org/10.1038/515009a

Schütze, C. (1996). *The empirical base of linguistics: Grammaticality judgments and linguistic methodology*. Chicago, IL: University of Chicago Press.

Schwartz, S. J., Lilienfeld, S. O., Meca, A., & Sauvigné, K. C. (2016). The role of neuroscience within psychology: A call for inclusiveness over exclusiveness. *American Psychologist, 71,* 52–70. http://dx.doi.org/10.1037/a0039678

Sentis Bahamondes, F. (1979). Aplicación de los índices del desarrollo lingüístico a la evaluación gramatical infantil [Application of linguistic development indices to the evaluation of child grammar]. *Signos, 11,* 73–83.

Serratrice, L. (2007). Cross-linguistic influence in the interpretation of anaphoric and cataphoric pronouns in English–Italian bilingual children. *Bilingualism: Language and Cognition, 10,* 225–238. http://dx.doi.org/10.1017/S1366728907003045

Shaffer, D., & Kipp, K. (2007). *Developmental psychology: Childhood and adolescence.* Belmont, CA: Thomson Wadsworth.

Sherman, J. C., & Lust, B. (1993). Children are in control. *Cognition, 46,* 1–51. http://dx.doi.org/10.1016/0010-0277(93)90021-M

Sherman, J. C., & Lust, B. C. (1987). Syntactic and lexical constraints on the acquisition of control in complement sentences. In B. C. Lust (Ed.), *Studies in the acquisition of anaphora: Vol. 1. Defining the constraints* (pp. 279–308). Dordrecht, Netherlands: Reidel.

Silva-Corvalán, C. (1994). *Language contact and change: Spanish in Los Angeles.* New York, NY: Oxford University Press.

Silva-Corvalán, C., & Montanari, S. (2008). The acquisition of *ser, estar* (and *be*) by a Spanish–English bilingual child: The early stages. *Bilingualism: Language and Cognition, 11,* 341–360. http://dx.doi.org/10.1017/S136672890800357X

Simons, G., & Bird, S. (2000a). *Requirements on the infrastructure for open language archiving.* Retrieved from http://www.language-archives.org/documents/requirements.html

Simons, G. F., & Bird, S. (2000b). *The seven pillars of open language archiving: A vision statement.* Retrieved from https://www.researchgate.net/publication/241702040_Building_an_Open_Language_Archives_Community_on_the_OAI_foundation

Simons, G., & Bird, S. (2001). *OLAC protocol for metadata harvesting.* Retrieved from http://www.language-archives.org/OLAC/protocol.html

Sinclair, H., & Bronckart, J. (1972). S.V.O. a linguistic universal? A study in developmental psycholinguistics. *Journal of Experimental Child Psychology, 14,* 329–348. http://dx.doi.org/10.1016/0022-0965(72)90055-0

Skuse, D. H. (1993). Extreme deprivation in early childhood. In D. Bishop & K. Mogford (Eds.), *Language development in exceptional circumstances* (pp. 29–46). Hove, England: Erlbaum.

Slater, A. (2004). Novelty, familiarity and infant reasoning. *Infant and Child Development, 13,* 353–355. http://dx.doi.org/10.1002/icd.356

Slobin, D., & Welsh, C. (1968). Elicited imitation as a research tool in developmental psycholinguistics. In C. A. Ferguson & D. Slobin (Eds.), *Studies of child language development* (pp. 485–497). New York, NY: Holt, Rinehart & Winston.

Solso, R. L., & MacLin, M. (2002). *Experimental psychology: A case approach* (7th ed.). Boston, MA: Allyn & Bacon.

Somashekar, S., Lust, B. C., Gair, J., Bhatia, T. K., Sharma, V., & Khare, J. (1997). Principles of pronominal interpretation in Hindi "jab" clauses: Experimental test of children's comprehension. In S. Somashekar, K. Yamakoshi, M. Blume, & C. A. Foley (Eds.), *Papers on Language Acquisition: Cornell University Working Papers in Linguistics* (pp. 65–87). Ithaca, NY: CLC.

Sorace, A. (2000). Differential effects of attrition in the L1 syntax of near-native L2 speakers. In S. C., Howell, S. A. Fish, and T. Keith-Lucas (Eds.), *Proceedings of the 24th Annual Boston University Conference on Language Development* (pp. 719–725). Somerville, MA: Cascadilla Press.

Sorace, A., Serratrice, L., Filiaci, F., & Baldo, M. (2009). Discourse conditions on subject pronoun realization: Testing the linguistic intuitions of older bilingual children. *Lingua, 119*, 460–477. http://dx.doi.org/10.1016/j.lingua.2008.09.008

Speer, S. (2012). Eye movements as a dependent measure in research on spoken language. In A. Cohn, C. Fougeron, & M. Huffman (Eds.), *The Oxford handbook of laboratory phonology* (pp. 580–592). Oxford, England: Oxford University Press.

Spelke, E. S. (1979). Perceiving bimodally specified events in infancy. *Developmental Psychology, 15*, 626–636. http://dx.doi.org/10.1037/0012-1649.15.6.626

Sportiche, D., Koopman, H., & Stabler, E. (2014). *An introduction to syntactic analysis and theory*. Oxford, England: Wiley-Blackwell.

Sprouse, J., Wagers, M., & Phillips, C. (2012). A test of the relation between working memory capacity and syntactic island effects. *Language, 88*, 82–123. http://dx.doi.org/10.1353/lan.2012.0004

Stromswold, K. (1996). Analyzing children's spontaneous speech. In D. McDaniel, C. McKee, & H. Smith Cairns (Eds.), *Methods for assessing children's syntax* (pp. 23–53). Cambridge, MA: MIT Press.

Sundara, M., Demuth, K., & Kuhl, P. K. (2011). Sentence-position effects on children's perception and production of English third person singular –s. *Journal of Speech, Language, and Hearing Research, 54*, 55–71. http://dx.doi.org/10.1044/1092-4388(2010/10-0056)

Swinney, D. (2000). Understanding the behavioral-methodology/language-processing interface. *Brain and Language, 71*, 241–244. http://dx.doi.org/10.1006/brln.1999.2259

Thornton, R. (1996). Elicited production. In D. McDaniel, C. McKee, & H. Smith Cairns (Eds.), *Methods for assessing children's syntax* (pp. 77–102). Cambridge, MA: MIT Press.

Tomasello, M., & Stahl, D. (2004). Sampling children's spontaneous speech: How much is enough? *Journal of Child Language, 31*, 101–121. http://dx.doi.org/10.1017/S0305000903005944

Townsend, D., & Bever, T. (2001). *Sentence comprehension*. Cambridge, MA: MIT Press.

Trochim, W. (2001). *The research methods knowledge* (2nd ed.). Cincinnati, OH: Atomic Dog.

Tse, C., & Altarriba, J. (2012). The effects of first- and second-language proficiency on conflict resolution and goal maintenance in bilinguals: Evidence from reaction time distributional analyses in a Stroop task. *Bilingualism: Language and Cognition, 15*, 663–676. http://dx.doi.org/10.1017/S1366728912000077

Turk-Browne, N. B., Scholl, B. J., & Chun, M. M. (2008). Babies and brains: Habituation in infant cognition and functional neuroimaging. *Frontiers in Human Neuroscience, 2*, 16.

Unsworth, S., & Blom, E. (2010). Comparing L1 children, L2 children and L2 adults. In E. Blom & S. Unsworth (Eds.), *Experimental methods in language acquisition research* (pp. 201–222). Amsterdam, Netherlands: John Benjamins. http://dx.doi.org/10.1075/lllt.27.12uns

Valdés, G., & Figueroa, R. A. (1994). *Bilingualism and testing: A special case of bias*. Norwood, NJ: Ablex.

Valian, V. (1991). Syntactic subjects in the early speech of American and Italian children. *Cognition, 40*, 21–81. http://dx.doi.org/10.1016/0010-0277(91)90046-7

Valian, V., & Aubry, S. (2005). When opportunity knocks twice: Two-year-olds' repetition of sentence subjects. *Journal of Child Language, 32*, 617–641. http://dx.doi.org/10.1017/S0305000905006987

Valian, V., Hoeffner, J., & Aubry, S. (1996). Young children's imitation of sentence subjects: Evidence of processing limitations. *Developmental Psychology, 32*, 153–164. http://dx.doi.org/10.1037/0012-1649.32.1.153

Valian, V., Solt, S., & Stewart, J. (2008). Abstract categories or limited-scope formulae? The case of children's determiners. *Journal of Child Language, 35*, 1–36.

Van de Sompel, H., & Lagoze, C. (2001). *The open archives initiative protocol for metadata harvesting.* Retrieved from http://www.openarchives.org/OAI/1.1/openarchivesprotocol.html

Verschueren, J. (1999). *Understanding pragmatics.* London, England: Arnold.

Vinther, T. (2002). Elicited imitation: A brief overview. *International Journal of Applied Linguistics, 12*, 54–73. http://dx.doi.org/10.1111/1473-4192.00024

Warner, N. (2012). Methods for studying spontaneous speech. In A. Cohn, E. Fougeron, & M. Huffman (Eds.), *The Oxford handbook of laboratory phonology* (pp. 621–633). Oxford, England: Oxford University Press.

Weber-Fox, C. M., & Neville, H. J. (1996). Maturational constraints on functional specializations for language processing: ERP and behavioral evidence in bilingual speakers. *Journal of Cognitive Neuroscience, 8*, 231–256. http://dx.doi.org/10.1162/jocn.1996.8.3.231

Weisler, S., & Milekic, S. (2000). *Theory of language.* Cambridge, MA: MIT Press.

Werker, J. F., Cohen, L. B., Lloyd, V. L., Casasola, M., & Stager, C. L. (1998). Acquisition of word-object associations by 14-month-old infants. *Developmental Psychology, 34*, 1289–1309. http://dx.doi.org/10.1037/0012-1649.34.6.1289

Werker, J. F., Gilbert, J. H. V., Humphrey, K., & Tees, R. C. (1981). Developmental aspects of cross-language speech perception. *Child Development, 52*, 349–355. http://dx.doi.org/10.2307/1129249

West, D. E. (2014). Assessing L2 lexical versus inflectional accuracy across skill levels. *Journal of Psycholinguistic Research, 43*, 535–554. http://dx.doi.org/10.1007/s10936-013-9268-0

Wiley, T., & Valdés, G. (2000). Heritage language instruction in the United States: A time for renewal. *Bilingual Research Journal, 24*, iii–v. http://dx.doi.org/10.1080/15235882.2000.10162770

Wilson, E. (2013). *Letters to a young scientist.* New York, NY: Liveright.

Zimmerman, I., Steiner, V., & Pond, R. (2002). *Preschool Language Scale* (4th ed.). San Antonio, TX: The Psychological Corporation.

Zúñiga, M., Sánchez, L., & Zacharías, D. (2000). *Demanda y necesidad de educación bilingüe* [Demand and need for bilingual education]. Lima, Peru: Ministerio de Educación del Perú-GTZ-KfW.

Zurif, E. B. (1983). Aspects of sentence processing in aphasia. In M. S. Kennedy (Ed.), *Psychobiology of language* (pp. 188–194). Cambridge, MA: MIT Press.

Index

Act-out toy-moving task, 137–145
– advantages and disadvantages of, 140–141
– data collection in, 143–145
– interpretation of data from, 221–224
– overview, 137–138
– preparation of data from, 198–199
– procedures in, 141–143
– properties of data from, 138–139, 142
– transcription example from, 185–186
– transcription of data from, 179
– uses of, 139
Adult participation permission letters, 31–33
Ambridge, B., 78, 132
Analysis of variance (ANOVA), 109–111
Analytic method, 13
Annotation systems, 194
ANOVA (analysis of variance), 109–111
AO task. See Act-out toy-moving task
Arguments (noun phrases), 27
Attention, 211
Aubry, S., 220
Audio recordings. See also Linguistic data
– overview, 57–60, 62, 65–68
– transcription of, 168, 171. See also Transcription
– of truth-value judgment task, 151
Austin, J., 218, 244

Backup data, 62, 64
Baker, C., 234, 235
Balanced bilinguals, 234
Batteries, 59
Bayley, R., 242
Bedore, L. M., 243
Behavioral units, 25
Berk, S., 88–89, 125, 218
Berko, J., 132
Berman, F., 268
Between-subjects factorial design, 99
Between-subjects variables, 97
Bhatia, T. K., 231n2
"Big data," 263, 268
Bilingualism research, 229–245
– challenges with, 230–232
– and elicited imitation task, 121
– interacting variables in, 236–237

– on language performance, 216
– measures used in, 237–241, 243–244
– overview, 229–230
– and replicability, 261
– terminology of, 230, 232–236
– testing bilingual speakers in, 244–245
– use of multiple methods in, 241–243
Bilinguals
– Balanced bilinguals, 234
– Dominant bilinguals, 234
– Early bilinguals, 233
– First language acquisition of, 231
– Late bilinguals, 234
– Receptive bilinguals, 236
– Sequential bilinguals, 231
– Simultaneous bilinguals, 231
– Successive bilinguals, 231
Bloom, L., 75
Blume, M., 125, 134
Books, use in research, 85–86
Bornstein, M., 239
Boston Diagnostic Aphasia test, 136
Brain research, 217, 245
Broad transcription, 174
Brown, Roger, 74, 78n6, 259

Caretaker reports, 238, 239
Carnegie Mellon Child Language Data Exchange System. See Child Language Data Exchange System
Casasola, M., 251
Case studies, 232
Cauley, K. M., 254
CDI (Communicative Development Inventories), 239
Cerf, V., 268
Certification courses, 30
Chien, Y., 149, 150
Child Abuse History Certification, 41
Child Language Data Exchange System (CHILDES), 19n15, 62n7, 73, 194, 264
Child safety and care, 45–47
Chomsky, N., 104, 121, 156, 248
CLAL. See Cornell Language Acquisition Laboratory
Clark, H. H., 108, 109

Clauses, 26–27
– main, 27
– relative, 94–96, 98–105, 107, 179, 207–209
– root, 27
– subordinate, 26–27, 209
Clever Hans effect, 159, 250
Closed-class vocabulary, 121
Cloze procedure, 135–136
Code switching, 232, 243
Coding
– of act-out toy-moving task data, 199
– defined, 20, 187
– of elicited imitation task data, 195–197
– of elicited production task data, 197–198
– and intermodal preferential looking paradigm, 255
– of natural speech data, 187–192
– of truth–value judgment task data, 200–201
Cognitive acts, 150, 168
Cohen, L. B., 251
Collaboration, 262–267
– importance of, 262
– infrastructure for, 264–267
– new culture of, 263–264
Collaborative Institutional Training Initiative, 30
Communicative competence, 235
Communicative Development Inventories (CDI), 239
Competence
– communicative, 235
– language, 212, 235–236
Complete counterbalancing technique, 113–117
Computational linguistics, 71
Computer corpora, 71
Conceptual scoring, 243
Confirmatory analysis, 212–213
Confounding variables, 102–104
Consent, informed, 30, 34–35
Cornell Language Acquisition Laboratory (CLAL)
– labeling and storage at, 67
– metadata at, 64
– overview, 7
– regulations and permissions at, 33
– triggered natural speech task used by, 88
– use of elicited imitation task by, 120–121
– use of truth–value judgment task in, 149
Cornell University
– Institutional Review Board of, 30
– Research Data Management Group, 50

Corpus, 19, 73
Corpus linguistics, 71
Correlations, 216
Cortez, C., 243
Counterbalancing, 98, 104, 113–117
A Course in Phonetics (P. Ladefoged & K. Johnson), 175
Criminal history, 41
Crosslinguistic research
– comparative measures in, 243–244
– data interpretation with, 218–219
– on infants, 248
– transcriptions in, 174
Cross-sectional studies, 18
Cultural considerations, 46, 156. *See also* Bilingualism

Data. *See* Linguistic data
Data analysis. *See also* Data interpretation
– of elicited imitation task data, 197
– of elicited production task data, 198
– of natural speech data, 91
– in observational research, 23
– as step in experimental method, 20–21
Databrary, 264
Data collection
– considerations with methods for, 24
– future directions for, 263
– of natural speech data. *See* Natural speech data
– overview, 19–20, 23
– post-raw, 52
– preparation for, 54–60
– pre-raw, 52
– successful, 51–52
Data creation process, 20
Data interpretation, 211–225
– across multiple child languages, 218–219
– across multiple methods, 219–225
– elimination of alternative explanations in, 217–218
– generalizability in, 213–214
– overview, 21, 211–212
– and previous research, 218
– and support for hypothesis, 212–213
– and type of research, 214–217
Data management, 259–261
Data on the Mind: Center for Data-Intensive Psychological Science, 264

"Data pipeline," 259–261
Data preparation, 187–201. See also Transcription
– for entry into structured databases, 194
– of experimental data, 195–201
– of natural speech data, 187–194
– overview, 187
Data Transcription and Analysis (DTA) Tool, 51, 194, 265–267
Day care centers
– general principles for working with, 42
– making research visits to, 42–43
– natural speech samples from, 77
De Groot, A., 244
De Houwer, A., 233, 239
Delaney, H. D., 111
Demuth, K., 225
Department of Human Services, 41
Dependent variables
– in act-out toy-moving task data, 199
– concepts related to, 101–102
– independent variables' effects on, 107
– overview, 96–99
Descriptive hypothesis, 16
Determiner phrases, 27
Developmental considerations
– and data interpretation, 211–212
– with elicited imitation task, 123
– with habituation, 251
Diary studies, 239
Digital recorders, 57
Disabilities, 47
Documentation
– of experimental research, 112
– of metadata, 54
– overview, 30
Dolls
– in act-out toy-moving task, 137–138, 141–145
– in elicited imitation task, 125
– pretend play with, 86
Dominant bilinguals, 234
DTA. See Data Transcription and Analysis Tool
Dutch, 193
Dynamic truth-value judgment task, 146

Early bilinguals, 233
EE (experimental error), 108
Effect size, 105
EI task. See Elicited imitation task

ELAN, 73
Electroencephalography, 217, 245
Electrophysiological techniques, 217
Elicitation techniques, 17–18. See also specific techniques
Elicited imitation (EI) task, 119–131
– advantages and disadvantages of, 122–124
– capturing data with, 124–127
– conclusions drawn from, 215
– interpretation of data from, 219–222, 224–225
– overview, 119–120
– preparation of data from, 195–197
– procedures in, 128–131
– properties of data from, 120
– sample transcription sheet for, 183–184
– transcription of data from, 175–177
– uses of, 120–122
Elicited production (EP) task, 131–136
– advantages and disadvantages of, 132, 134
– capturing data with, 134–135
– overview, 131
– preparation of data from, 197–198
– properties of data from, 134
– uses of, 132, 134
– variations of, 135–136
Empirical methods
– overview, 13
– and theory, 11
EP task. See Elicited production task
Ethnicity, 46
Event-related potential, 254
Experimental error (EE), 108
Experimental research, 93–112
– common statistical analyses in, 107–111
– data interpretation in, 214–215
– design of, 95–104
– documentation and publication of, 112
– and importance of statistics, 106–107
– observational methods vs., 13–15
– preparation of data in, 195–201
– procedures in, 106
– research combining observational method and, 268
– research questions and hypotheses in, 94–95
– sample selection in, 105
– steps in, 15–22
– task selection in, 104–105

Experimental tasks for eliciting language comprehension data, 18, 137–154
- act-out toy-moving task, 137–145
- picture selection task, 154
- questions after stories task, 154
- truth-value judgment task, 146–153

Experimental tasks for eliciting language production data, 18, 119–136
- elicited imitation task, 119–131
- elicited production task, 131–136
- picture description and narrative tasks, 136

Explanatory hypothesis, 16
Expressive One-Word Picture Vocabulary Test, 241
External handheld microphones, 57
Extraneous variables, 102–103
Eye tracking, 244, 255–256

Factorial design, 99
Families
- general principles for working with, 42
- making contact with, 36, 40–42

Fantz, R. L., 254
Fernández, S. C., 233, 243
Figueroa, R. A., 243
Fingerprint-based federal criminal history, 42
Finnish, 193
First language acquisition research, 121, 230. *See also* Bilingualism research; Language acquisition research
Free-form act-out tasks, 179
French, 215
F-test, 107–111
Functional brain imaging, 217, 245

García, M., 243
Generalizability, 19, 21, 22, 213–214
Generative linguistics, 71
Gilbert, J. H. V., 253
GJ task. *See* Grammaticality judgment task
Golinkoff, R. M., 254
Gordon, L., 254
Government-supported data, 262
Grammatical categories, 211
Grammaticality judgment (GJ) task, 155–163
- advantages and disadvantages of, 157–159
- overview, 155–156
- procedures of, 159–163

- properties of data from, 157
- uses of, 157

Grammatical theory, 13, 24
Grosjean, F., 237, 245, 261

Habituation, 250–252
Hakuta, K., 242
Handbook of the International Phonetic Association, 174
HAS (high-amplitude sucking), 252–253
Head-turn preference procedure (HPP), 253–254
Hebrew, 193
Heritage speakers, 232
Hierarchical linear model, 111
High-amplitude sucking (HAS), 252–253
Hirsh-Pasek, K., 254
Hoeffner, J., 220
Hoff, E., 239, 241, 242
Home visits, 42–43, 61
HPP (head-turn preference procedure), 253–254
Hume, David, 213
Humphrey, K., 253
Hypotheses
- and data interpretation, 212–213
- descriptive, 16
- in experimental research, 94–95
- explanatory, 16
- predictive, 16

Hypothesis testing
- in experimental research, 95–96
- overview, 13, 19

Incomplete counterbalancing technique, 113–117
Incomplete language acquisition, 232
Independent variables
- data interpretation with, 215–216
- and effects on dependent variables, 107
- overview, 96–99

Infants, 18, 217
Infant testing methods (ITMs), 247–257
- eye tracking, 255–256
- habituation, 250–252
- head-turn preference procedure, 253–254
- high-amplitude sucking, 252–253
- intermodal preferential looking paradigm, 254–255

– overview, 247–248
– rationale of, 248–250
– resources on, 257
– task demands of, 250
Inference, scientific, 213–214, 219. *See also* Data interpretation; Hypotheses
Informed consent, 30, 34–35
Infrastructure, 264–268
Institutional review board requirements, 30
Insurance requirements, 30
Interdisciplinarity, 262, 267–268
Intermodal preferential looking paradigm, 254–255
International Phonetic Alphabet (IPA), 174, 273–274
International Phonetics Association (IPA), 174–175
Intonation, 130, 170
Inversion, 17
IPA. *See* International Phonetic Alphabet; International Phonetics Association
Irish, 193
Islands (syntax), 24
ITMs. *See* Infant testing methods

Johnson, E. K., 253
Johnson, K., 175
Joos, M., 12

Kim, A., 231
Knowledge, metalinguistic, 156
Korean, 231, 242
Kuhl, P. K., 225

Labeling, of data, 49–50, 64–68
Labov, T., 88
Labov, W., 88
Ladefoged, P., 175
Language acquisition research, 11–28. *See also specific headings*
– challenges with, 11–12
– questions in, 3
– and scientific method, 12–25
– types of linguistic data in, 11, 25–28
Language and Cognition in Bilinguals and Multilinguals (A. De Groot), 244
The Language Archive, 73, 263, 264
Language attrition, 232, 245
Language change, 245

Language competence, 212, 235–236
Language comprehension
– and data interpretation, 216
– elicitation techniques for. *See* Experimental tasks for eliciting language comprehension data
– observational research on, 14
Language diaries, 239
Language discrimination, 18
Language dominance, 234–235
Language production
– and data interpretation, 216
– elicitation techniques for. *See* Experimental tasks for eliciting language production data
– observational research on, 14
Language proficiency, 235–236
Language separation, 245
Late bilinguals, 234
Leek, J. T., 259
Legal requirements, 30
Lewedeg, V., 233
Lexical decision tasks, 245
Linguistic data, 49–68
– analysis of. *See* Data analysis
– backing up of, 62, 64
– collection of raw. *See* Data collection
– complexity of creating, 49
– creation of, 61–63
– labeling and storage of, 49–50, 64–68
– and metadata. *See* Metadata
– and preliminary assumptions, 50–51
– preparing for collection of, 54–60
– shared, 262, 263
– steps following collection of, 61–68
– transcription of. *See* Transcription
– types of, 11, 25–28
Linguistics, 71. *See also specific headings*
Linguistic stimuli, 17
Linguistic units, 26
Linked Open Data in Linguistics (LLOD), 263
Lloyd, V. L., 251
Longitudinal research designs, 18–19
Looking-while-listening (LWL), 255
Lust, B. C., 94, 218, 231, 242
LWL (looking-while-listening), 255

Magnetoencephalography, 245
Main clauses, 27
Masked priming, 245

Max Planck Institute Language Archive. *See* The Language Archive
Maxwell, S. E., 111
Mayan languages, 193
McDaniel, D., 162
Mean length of utterance (MLU), 191–194, 202–206, 220, 243–244
Memory
– interaction of language and, 211
– working, 138
Metacognitive abilities, 158
Metadata
– collection of, 52–54
– and data management, 261
– defined, 20, 49
– entering of subject and session, 64
– overview, 19
MetaLab, 264
Metalinguistic knowledge, 156
Microphones, 57, 58. *See also* Recording devices
Milekic, S., 26
Minimal Coding Procedure (C. Pye), 193
Mixed-effects modeling, 111
Mixed factorial design, 100
MLU. *See* Mean length of utterance
Model sentences. *See* Stimulus sentences
Morphemes, 27, 121, 132, 193, 225
Morphology, 131–133
Moskowitz, Lauren, 84–88
Mother tongue. *See* First language acquisition research
Motor functions, 141, 211
Multilevel modeling, 111
Multilingual acquisition, 229. *See also* Bilingualism

Narrative tasks, 136
Narrow transcription, 174
National Institutes of Health, 30, 50
National Science Foundation (NSF), 50
Native language acquisition. *See* First language acquisition research
Native speakers, 236
Naturalistic observation, 14
Natural speech data, 71–91
– advantages and disadvantages of, 74–75
– analysis of, 91
– assessment of bilingualism with, 240
– and background information, 73–74
– characteristics of "good" and "poor," 79–84
– creating a corpus with, 73
– defined, 72–73
– elicited imitation data vs., 122–123
– eliciting specific linguistic phenomena with, 87–88
– experimental methods vs., 93
– preparation of, 187–194
– procedures for collection of, 78
– questioning in collection of, 85
– and requests for repetition, 85
– researcher's role in collection of, 75–77
– and storybooks, 85–86
– and storytelling/pretend play techniques, 86–87
– and topic selection, 84–85
– transcription of, 91, 170
– and triggered natural speech, 88–91
– and use of props, 87
Neuroscience, 256, 267–268. *See also* Brain research
Neville, H. J., 238
Nonrepeated measure variables, 97
Norm-reference tests, 240
Noun phrases, 27
NSF (National Science Foundation), 50

OAI (Open Archives Initiative), 54
Object permanence, 268
Observational method. *See also* Natural speech data
– data interpretation in, 214–215
– experimental method vs., 13–15, 93
– research combining experimental method and, 268
– steps in, 22–23
Oller, D. K., 233, 243
Omnidirectional microphones, 57
Open Archives Initiative (OAI), 54
Open Language Archives Community, 54
Order effect, 104
Original recordings, 65–67
Orthography, 173–174
Overgeneralization, 87–88

Park, A., 231
Peabody Picture Vocabulary Test, 240–241
Pearson, B. Z., 233, 243
Pease-Álvarez, L., 242
Peña, E. D., 243
Peng, R. D., 259
Penn Treebank Project, 71n2

Perception, 211
Phillips, C., 24
Phonemes, 27–28
Phonetic edits, 63
Phoneticians, 173, 174
Phonetics, 173–175
Phonology, 211
Phrases, 27
Piaget, Jean, 268–269
Picture description tasks, 136
Picture naming tasks, 244–245
Picture selection task, 154
Play techniques, 86–87
Poldrack, R. A., 262
Poline, J.-B., 262
Popper, Karl, 75, 215
Populations, research, 18–19
Post-raw data collection, 52
Praat (software), 175
Predictive hypothesis, 16
Preferential looking data, 224–225, 248, 254–255
Pre-raw data collection, 52
Preschool Language Scales, 241
Pretend play techniques, 86–87
Pretraining, 126, 128
Primary research, 73, 259, 261, 262
Priming, masked, 245
Props, 59–60
– in act-out toy-moving task, 137–138, 141–144
– in elicited production task, 134
– and natural speech data, 87
– and Preschool Language Scales, 241
– in truth-value judgment task, 152
Prosody, 121
Publication, 112, 262
Puppets
– in elicited imitation task, 125
– in elicited production task, 134
– in grammaticality judgment task, 162
Pye, C., 193

Qualitative research
– overview, 20
– quantitative research vs., 21
Quantitative research
– overview, 20–21
– qualitative research vs., 21
Quasi-independent variables, 96, 215–216
Quené, H., 110–111

Questioning, 85
Questionnaires, 238
Questions after stories task, 154

Raw data. *See* Linguistic data
Reaction time measures, 245
Recency effect, 129
Receptive bilinguals, 236
Reconstruction, language, 121–122
Recording devices
– and act-out toy-moving task, 142
– and elicited imitation task, 125
– overview, 57–59, 62
– and truth-value judgment task, 151
Recording sessions, 44–45
Reductionist theory, 24
Regulatory requirements, 29–36
Reinforcement, 146
Relative clauses, 94–96, 98–105, 107, 179, 207–209
Reliability, 101–102, 142
Reliability checks, 63, 177–178
Repeated measures analysis of variance (ANOVA), 109–111
Repeated measures variable, 98
Repetition, 85
Replicability
– components of, 49
– and data interpretation, 213–214
– overview, 261
– and research notes, 57
– and scoring, 196–197
Replication crisis, 261
Representative samples, 105
Research design
– development of experimental, 16–17
– populations selected in, 18–19
Researcher–child interaction, 47–48
Research folders, 50, 55–57
Research kits, 60
Research populations, 18–19
Research process, 29–48
– child safety and care in, 45–47
– contacting families and schools in, 36, 40–42
– ending of, 48
– establishing relationships in, 42–43
– getting to know participants in, 43–44
– and non-intrusive research, 42
– regulatory requirements in, 29–36
– and requirements for working with child subjects, 33, 36–40

– researcher–child interaction in, 47–48
– taking children to recording sessions in, 44–45
Research proposals, 275–276
Research questions, 94–95
Response bias, 159
Rich interpretation, 75, 215, 248
Ritchie, W. C., 231n2
Root clauses, 27
Rowland, C. F., 78, 132
Rumiche, R. L., 239, 241, 242

Safety, 45–47
Sample sizes, 19
Sánchez, L., 242–244
Santelmann, L., 218
Sapir, Edward, 158n1
Schools
– general principles for working with, 42
– making contact with, 36, 40–42
– making research visits to, 42–43, 61
– natural speech samples from, 77
Scientific inference, 213–214, 219. See also Data interpretation
Scientific method, 12–25
Scoring
– of act-out toy-moving task data, 199
– conceptual, 243
– of elicited imitation task data, 195–197
– of elicited production task data, 197–198
– sample criteria for, 207–209
– of truth–value judgment task data, 200–201
Secondary research, 19, 73, 259
Second language acquisition, 120–121, 229, 233. See also Bilingualism research; Language acquisition research
Self-rating instruments, 243
Sentences, 26. See also Stimulus sentences
Sentence structure, 191
Sequencing effect, 104
Sequential bilinguals, 231
Shared data, 262, 263
Simultaneous bilinguals, 231
Single-factor between-subjects design, 99
Single-factor design, 99
Single-factor within-subjects design, 99
Smith Cairns, H., 162
Software, 73, 175, 262–263
Somashekar, S., 218

Sound waves, 168
Spanish, 242
Speaking style, 26
Speech acts
– in natural speech data, 188–190
– overview, 25
Speech modes, 190
Speech transcription. See Transcription
Spelke, E. S., 254
Spelling, 173–174
Split-screen technique (intermodal preferential looking paradigm), 254
Spontaneous speech, 219–221. See also Natural speech data
Sprouse, J., 24
Stage II records, 67–68
Stager, C. L., 251
Stahl, D., 78
Statistical analyses
– in experimental research, 107–111
– selection of appropriate, 24
Statistical power, 105
Stimulus sentences
– in act-out toy-moving task, 142, 144, 145
– in elicited imitation task, 119, 121, 124–126
– in elicited production task, 135
Storage, data, 49–50, 64–68
Storybooks, 85–86, 134–135
Storytelling techniques, 86–87
Stuffed animals, 125
Subordinate clauses, 27, 209
Successive bilinguals, 231
Sundara, M., 225
Switch design, 251–252
Syntactic structure, 191

TE (treatment effect), 107, 108
Tees, R. C., 253
Theory, 11, 13, 24
Thornton, R., 132
TNS (triggered natural speech), 88–91
Tomasello, M., 78
Toy-moving task. See Act-out toy-moving task
Training courses, 30
Transcription, 167–180
– of act-out toy-moving task, 179, 198
– capturing data with, 168
– in data creation process, 62–63
– of elicited imitation task, 175–177, 195–196

– of elicited production task, 197
– of natural speech data, 91
– overview, 167–168
– and parts of transcript, 169–170
– principles of, 168–169, 173–175
– procedures for, 23, 171–172
– and reliability checks, 177–178
– symbols for, 271
– of truth–value judgment task, 180, 199–200
– and utterances, 169–171
Transformation, 168
Transversal studies, 18
Treatment effect (TE), 107, 108
Triggered natural speech (TNS), 88–91
Truth–value judgment (TVJ) task, 146–153
– assumptions with, 217
– data collection in, 153
– interpretation of data from, 222–224
– overview, 146–147
– preparation of data from, 199–201
– procedures of, 151–153
– properties of data from, 148–151
– selection of, 149
– transcription of data from, 180
– uses of, 149
TVJ. *See* Truth–value judgment task

Univariate design, 100n22
Utterances, 25, 169–171, 188. *See also* Mean length of utterance

Valdés, G., 243
Valian, V., 220
Validity, 102
Van den Bergh, H., 110–111
Variability, 106–107
Variable binding, 223
VCLA. *See* Virtual Center for Language Acquisition

Video recordings. *See also* Linguistic data
– of act-out toy-moving task, 142
– overview, 57–58
– transcription of, 168, 171. *See also* Transcription
– of truth–value judgment task, 151
Virtual Center for the Study of Language Acquisition (VCLA)
– and collaboration, 264
– data creation by, 60–61
– labeling and storage at, 67
– Multilingualism Questionnaire developed by, 238, 242
– resources from, 265
Virtual Linguistic Laboratory (VLL)
– and collaboration, 264
– Data Transcription and Analysis Tool of, 22, 51
– overview, 7
– resources from, 264–267
VLL. *See* Virtual Linguistic Laboratory

Wagers, M., 24
Weber-Fox, C. M., 238
Weisler, S., 26
Werker, J. F., 251, 253
Wexler, K., 150
Wh-questions, 17, 78, 89, 90
Wireless broadcast microphones, 57
Within-subjects factorial design, 99
Within-subjects variables, 97, 104
Word order, in experimental designs, 16
Words, 27
Working memory, 138
Working transcripts, 63

Yes/no questions, 17, 85, 218
Yes response bias, 159

Zamuner, T. S., 253

About the Authors

María Blume, PhD, is an associate professor in linguistics at the Pontificia Universidad Católica del Perú. She received her PhD in linguistics at Cornell University. Her research interests include first and second language acquisition, bilingualism, cognition, and the acquisition of morphology and syntax and their interaction with pragmatics. She was a member of the Cornell Language Acquisition Lab and founded and directed the University of Texas at El Paso Language Acquisition and Linguistics Research Lab. She is a founding member of the Virtual Center for the Study of Language Acquisition (VCLA) and through support of the National Science Foundation has collaborated with members of the VCLA in the creation of a series of materials related to research in language acquisition: the Virtual Linguistics Lab and the Data Transcription and Analysis Tool. She recently coauthored a book published by Cambridge University Press: *Bilingualism in the Spanish-Speaking World: Linguistic and Cognitive Perspectives* (Austin, Blume, & Sánchez, 2015).

Barbara C. Lust, PhD, is a professor of developmental psychology, linguistics, and cognitive science at Cornell University, where she has taught for over 30 years. There, she and her students and collaborators have built the Cornell University Language Acquisition Lab, which houses and supports ongoing research on language acquisition involving more than 20 languages. Together they have constructed a range of materials for the crosslinguistic interdisciplinary study of language acquisition. Her research interests focus on crosslinguistic analyses of language acquisition with a view to factoring out universal from language-specific factors in a comprehensive theory. In addition to numerous journal and book articles, she has authored *Child Language: Acquisition and Growth* (2006; new edition in preparation). With Claire Foley, she coedited *Language Acquisition: The Essential Readings* (2004). With María Blume, she codirected the development of an international cyberinfrastructure-based project to support research and teaching in an interdisciplinary framework, "Transforming the Primary Research Process Through Cybertool Dissemination: An Implementation of a Virtual Center for the Study of Language Acquisition" (NSF CI-0753415).